Architecture, Critique, Ideology

Axl Books
www.axlbooks.com
info@axlbooks.com

ISBN 978-91-86883-13-3

Architecture, Critique, Ideology
Writings on Architecture and Theory

SVEN-OLOV WALLENSTEIN

AXL BOOKS

Contents

Introduction: Architecture, Critique, Ideology

This book gathers together essays written over the course of the last decade, all of which in one way or another deal with the tradition of critical theory, and with the fate of such a theoretical enterprise within architectural discourse. For some, this tradition has increasingly come to seem problematic, although the criticisms are not all of a piece: on closer inspection, it is clear that they are comprised of several contradictory and incompatible strands, some of which involve the rejection of the idea of a critical theory altogether, others of which call for a redefinition and rethinking of some of its basic parameters and assumptions. This book situates itself among those strands of thought that defend the legacy of critical theory, although it also argues that such a defense must remain open to contemporary challenges, theoretical as well as practical.

The referent of the very term critical theory is by no means obvious. Historically, the term generally refers to the Frankfurt School, and the legacy of Adorno and Benjamin in particular; in a larger timeframe it also denotes the philosophical tradition that begins with Kant's Critical Philosophy and continues—more like a constantly broken and twisted line than a straight one—through Hegel, Marx, and beyond. My proposal here involves understanding the term as freely as possible, so that it also intersects with the work of thinkers who in many ways stand opposed to the philosophical tradition in which one would normally locate the Frankfurt School. The rejection by many of these thinkers, such as Deleuze and Foucault, of dialectics, as well as of certain models of subjectivity, the reluctance of such thinkers to accept the diagnosis of late capitalism as involving an "administered world," and, most fundamentally, the role of theory as such, are issues that render the unity of such a tradition difficult to uphold. When confronting these different claims and orientations, my proposal is not that we need to understand them better so as to make a more informed choice between them, but instead that we must explore the possibility of an interaction that will begin by rendering the differences more acute, and, in this, will also allow them to infiltrate and transform each other. This I take to be crucial for the development of that elusive entity called "theory," which sits uneasily between the practices and internal intellectual reflection of each of the arts (architecture being one of them—and they all have specific problems that indeed resonate with those of the others, but they cannot be simply mapped onto one another), and, on the other hand, that seemingly abstract and forbidding entity called "philosophy," which is often understood as an investigation of concepts and universals (truth, mind, language, even being as such) taken to be already presupposed in the other disciplines and practices, although without these concepts being reflected and thought through.

The relation between theory and practice—presuming that they even can be fundamentally distinguished, which is doubtful—is a highly contested one, as can be seen in the constantly recurring claims that theory (and, by implication, even more so philosophy, existing as it does on the distal side of theory) is useless or even harmful for practice, which in turn alternates with the opposing claim that only a grand theory can save practice from becoming blindly complicitous with social, economic, or other forces that transcend and condition it. This divide between the generality of concepts and the particularity of practices is obviously not of recent vintage, but it has acquired a particular intensity in the present, where singularity and difference are the battle cries of the moment, while all things on another level melt into air precisely because of their maximal interconnectedness. If all things are singular, local, and specific, and seem to resist the generality of theories, it is precisely because they form part of a network that in turn operates by continually differentiating itself, and in this exerts a systemic power that remains opaque to those who inhabit its singular points. These two sides must be thought together without reducing one to the other, which is why *there is no one answer* to the problem of the relation between theory and practice: they call upon each other in specific situations, and the movement neither proceeds from top to bottom, which is how one, rightly or wrongly, tends to understand the great idealist systems (with the possible, partial exception of Hegelianism), nor from the bottom up, as in the attempts to create a physiological aesthetic to succeed idealism in the second half of the eighteenth century, which today find an echo in many claims that aesthetic issues are fundamentally to be dealt with in cognitive science, evolutionary theory, or even empirical biology. Instead, this relation is brought to life *from both ends*, by works that question their own status as well as the categories we use to apprehend them, and by a thought that seeks other determinations than those offered by a seemingly self-enclosed sphere of concepts.

The subtitle of this book, "Writings on Architecture and Theory," seeks to point to this indeterminacy, or rather this quest for singular determinations—which perhaps was what Adorno, following Benjamin, once aspired to in the idea of *constellations*.[1] The "and" indicates the need for an articulation, or

1.   See Adorno, *Negative Dialektik, Gesammelte Schriften* (Frankfurt am Main; Suhrkamp, 1997), vol. 6, 164–169; *Negative Dialectics*, trans. E. B.

an articulating, in both cases, without specifying in advance, from an a priori position, what this must look like: the filling in of the blank left by the conjunction must be the result of a specific invention, in which the conjoining neither begins from the solidity of an a priori, nor ends with a fixity laying claim to have removed the unease associated with the position of theory.

Similarly, the relation that critical theory establishes with its other, *ideology*, should avoid freezing the terms in a syntagm that orders them hierarchically, so that one of them would be general and the other, or others, specific, as, for instance, in a "critique of architectural ideology," once proposed by Manfredo Tafuri, to which he returned ceaselessly, each time rendering the notion more and more opaque and self-reflexive.[2] Instead, the three terms, *architecture*, *critique*, *ideology*, must be allowed to co-exist at the same level, which renders their respective borders fluid, if not fuzzy, in a way that here calls for an at least somewhat more detailed, albeit tentative comment, however much their actual articulation, as always, remains to be seen in each case.

Architecture
In order for such a theory to become productive, it cannot refer exclusively to buildings, bricks, and mortar, nor, by simply

Ashton (London: Routledge, 1973), 162–166.

2. The outer limit of this trajectory was perhaps signaled by his "Per una critica dell'ideologia architettonica" (first published in *Contropiano* 1969; trans. Stephen Sartarelli in Hays, *Architecture Theory Since 1968* [Cambridge, Mass: MIT, 1998]), and the methodological preface to *La sfera e il labirinto*, "Il progetto storico" (1980), trans. Pellegrino d'Acierno and Robert Connolly in Tafuri, *The Sphere and the Labyrinth: Avant-Gardes and Architecture from Piranesi to the 1970s* (Cambridge, Mass.: MIT, 1990), where the self-reflexivity of the very language of critique strikes back almost with every step at the methodological assurance of the 1969 essay. If the first text wants to confront architectural discourse with the material contradictions of a reality to which it offers only imaginary solutions, the "real problem," Tafuri states in the second text, "is how to project a criticism capable of constantly putting itself into crisis by putting into crisis the real." (9)

zooming out and stepping up to another level, to environments and large-scale urban structures, but should, more generally, explore spatial signifying practices that also include texts, images, and various modes of representation, which, to be sure, all revolve around that kind of material instantiation that is commonly referred to as architecture, but also extend outwards into intellectual culture as a whole. This fluid status, which conjoins notions like presentation and representation, reality and its image, materiality and immateriality, is one of the reasons why theory and practice cannot be opposed as, for instance, the intelligible and the sensible might be. There is something sensible and material in all thought, be it architectural or not: thought has an embodiment that may take on all manner of guises, but that is never simply external clothing upon an inner sense. Conversely, there is nothing that is purely material and mute: nothing is simply *there*, in space or time, without extending into the imaginary and the sphere of concepts, and detaching itself, if ever so slightly, from the temporal present. Just as all theory is already a claim about our way of inhabiting the world and prefigures an embodiment, all ways of being in the world have their horizons and apertures toward the intelligible, if there is to be a world at all—a world that is not a closed set, as the image of administration tends to suggest, but exists by virtue of the gaps and porosities, the leakages and lines of flight that it produces inside itself.[3]

3. Bureaucracy and administration could instead be taken as *fields of immanence*, in the sense suggested by Deleuze and Guattari's reading of Kafka; see *Kafka, pour une littérature mineure* (Paris: Minut, 1975); *Kafka: Toward a Minor Literature*, trans. Dana Polan (Minneapolis: University of Minnesota Press, 1986). Particularly relevant would be the discussion (chap. 8) of the role of architectural and spatial models in Kafka's novels: that the court has no absolute outside means that it constantly produces multiple outsides on the inside, so that the initially disconnected rooms of the court prove to be adjacent in ways that defy the hierarchical structure, and all openings turn out to be impasses just as all impasses have their openings.

Architecture, as Hegel famously said, is the first of the arts (both in the sense that it precedes the others as their ground, and in the sense that it is the lowest in the hierarchy), because it deals with gravity, opacity, and that which is inextricably bound up with use and action, and in this sense it is also the art that most of all resists becoming aesthetic. The first truly *beautiful* art, Hegel suggests, is sculpture, which becomes itself by disengaging from architecture, thereby providing the latter with the function of surrounding and housing the image of the God in the temple.[4] This material resistance, which has often led to architecture being placed at the margins of aesthetics, should however rather incite the opposite move, so that aesthetics is transformed into a type of inquiry that disengages from beauty or other similar normative concepts, or, if they are to be retained, requires that we release this inherited vocabulary from its entrenchment in a normative canon. Beauty—a term that for a long time seemed useless, but that, today, some want to revive—could be taken as the name, but a name only, of that particular constellation of concepts and intuitions, thoughts and particulars, which gives us a maximum of things to think, without necessarily ordering them in a logical fashion, instead gesturing in the direction of a different and spontaneous ordering (which is the Kantian definition of the aesthetic idea). But as such, it cannot escape the historical mediations that situate it within a horizon of finitude and bind it to a particular time and place (which is the Hegelian understanding of the historicity of spirit). And finally, it cannot avoid, even though many

4.   See Hegel, *Vorlesungen über die Ästhetik*, *Werke*, eds. Eva Moldenhauer and Karl Markus Michel (Frankfurt am Main: Suhrkamp, 1986), vol. 14, 270; *Hegel's Aesthetics: Lectures on Fine Art*, trans T. M. Knox (Oxford: Clarendon Press, 1975), 633, and my discussion of this transition in "Hegel and the Grounding of Architecture," in Michael Asgaard and Henrik Oxvig (eds.), *The Paradoxes of Appearing: Essays on Art, Architecture, and Philosophy* (Baden: Lars Müller Publishers, 2009).

works actively resist this on the level of content, the promise of a different world, no matter how veiled and tenuous, simply by virtue of its stepping out of this world and mimetically extracting a double that transcends it (which is Adorno's idea of the artwork as the placeholder for utopia and reconciliation). Aesthetics, a term that has been discredited almost as much as beauty, should not thus be understood as severing works from the world—which in the particular case of architecture makes little sense—but as a way to understand their particular purchase on and inscription in the world: what they give to think, in concepts or otherwise, how they express a world of which they inevitably form a part without being reducible to it, and how they insert a wedge into the world, splitting it from itself without installing themselves in a different world.

From another, though related angle, architecture's implication in power seems equally to condemn an aesthetic reading to irrelevance or naiveté. For doesn't architecture, before it crosses over into the space of the imaginary and sets up a double of the world, belong to *real* space, to *this* world? This it would do not just in terms of its insistent materiality, but more profoundly because it orders and segments our lives, imposes divisions of inside and outside, up and down, which are just as much economical, political, and social as they are tangible and physical. But once more, in keeping with the sense of the aesthetic delineated above, it is just as true that all such divisions have a dimension that directly addresses the sensible, and not primarily in terms of taste, but as an element where higher-order structures of society are made palpable, where they are inextricably entangled with contradictory passions and affects. Thus, if power is actualized in architectures, it is in a way that immediately breeds resistance, so that actions and reactions, subjections and refusals, continually tap into and feed off each other, which is why architecture, to a much larger extent than the other arts, is a matter of contestation even at the level of affectivity. Architecture is power in action, never just a symbol of power, and the sphere of *aisthesis* as it is taken here, as the domain where the senses are joined with thought, is the space where this is played out.

Critique

The obvious relation of the term *critique* to a whole tradition running from Kant and Hegel through Marx up to Benjamin and Adorno has already been noted, as has the general sense in which the term is understood here, such that it comes to include positions that not only deviate from the legacy of dialectical critique, but also would appear to stand opposed to it. What is at stake is the sense of critique as reflection on our historical present that attempts to excavate conditions, possibilities, and limitations of aesthetic production, which on the one hand is inevitably inscribed in the structures of the current world, and on the other hand takes issue with it, attempts to go beyond it, or at least taps into its contradictions so as to set congealed structures in motion. In order to do this, critique cannot retreat to positions that have already been absorbed, which is why the broader understanding of critical theory corresponds to the necessity of rethinking the concepts that were at the basis of its earlier forms: subjectivity, experience, contradiction, negation, form, autonomy, nature—all of which have been subjected to fundamental transformations both in philosophy and the arts since the 1960s.

Such a rethinking of the basic tenets of critical theory has been underway for some time within the Frankfurt School itself, specifically in Habermas and his followers. In their line of reasoning, the concept of mimesis—which Adorno understands not as simple imitation and duplication of some given reality in artistic form, but as an archaic form of merging with the object that survives inside representation, as an inner subversion of identity thinking—must be rejected, since it allegedly sets itself up as an alternative to discursive rationality without being able to supply any normative criteria for its own application.

These criticisms, first of all, not only seem misguided in relation to Adorno, but, furthermore, also lead in a direction wholly opposed to what I am contending is a necessary step: to push Adorno's idea even further. Mimesis, Adorno often underlines, can just as little replace instrumental reason or identity thinking (to think, he states unequivocally at the outset of *Negative Dialectics*, means to identify) as it can be wholly be suppressed by it. Rather, it operates as an inner corrective, a reminder of what this thinking can never exhaust, since its conceptual domination is built upon the repression of the mimetic, which nevertheless leaves scars or traces in experience that art and philosophy register, each in their own way, without being simply mapped onto each other.

This criticism on the basis of a misguided understanding of Adorno's use of mimesis is then connected to the second and more far-reaching claim that Adorno would have failed to undertake the turn from a philosophy of consciousness to a philosophy of language, and thus would have remained trapped in "metaphysical thinking." This we see, for instance, in Albrecht Wellmer, who speaks of Adorno's failure to attain a "postmetaphysical aesthetics of modernity"[5] that would shift the focus to the communicative role of art instead of remaining entrenched in late modern strategies of refusal and negation, which in turn would be based in an outdated philosophy of consciousness. Two things must be noted here. It is clear that the idea of art as communication, which is what this argument takes to constitute the solution, is what *Aesthetic Theory* opposes from beginning to end, rather than being something Adorno would

5.   See Wellmer, "Adorno, die Moderne und das Erhabene", in Franz
      Koppe (ed.), *Perspektiven der Kunstphilosophie* (Frankfurt am Main:
      Suhrkamp, 1991), 190.

have overlooked or failed to grasp: communication is what is demanded of art not only by the culture industry, but also by those who opt for a culinary high-brow aesthetic, precisely because it defuses art and makes it into a specific sphere of experiences to be placed alongside the other spheres, eventually endowing it with a compensatory function. In addition, while Adorno does indeed in many contexts insist on the constitutive resemblance of art to language, its *Sprachähnlichkeit*, he adds that language becomes art precisely as "writing," i.e., through that moment of self-reflection, opacity, and refusal of meaning that makes it into an enigma and calls for a particular type of interpretation, which is also the basis for his (perhaps unjust) rejection of hermeneutics.

Third, and most generally, there is a presupposition that a philosophy of consciousness would be metaphysical, whereas a philosophy of language would somehow escape this condition, and constitute an unequivocal and assured progress, since it would once and for all solve the problems posed by its predecessor. Regardless of how one understands the term metaphysics, it seems obvious that none of this can be taken for granted. Finally, regardless of whether refusal and negation are sufficient concepts to grasp artistic work, other means are equally available that just as little give in to the idea of communication, which probably is, as Heidegger once said of the notion of *Erlebnis*, "the element in which art dies."[6]

Not unlike the proponents of communication, the advocates of the post-critical take leave of the idea of art as resistance and negativity, and instead claim that it ought to operate in complicity or collusion with the production of images, pleasures,

6.   *Der Ursprung des Kunstwerkes*, in *Holzwege*, *Gesamtausgabe* (Frankfurt am Main: Klostermann, 1977), vol. 5, 67. In a handwritten marginal note (b) Heidegger adds that the true task is to "attain a wholly different element for the 'becoming' of art" ("ein ganz anderes Element für das Werden der Kunst zu erlangen")

and affects in (post)modern capitalism, in order for it to be "instrumental," "projective," or "operative." At the same time, while such rejections are themselves based on unacknowledged theoretical assumptions, and some of them, at least in the form they are presented, are ideological in a rather simplistic sense, they can also be taken as pointing to deeper issues that also have bearings on our third concept, that of *ideology*.

Ideology

In the most far-reaching sense of the term, ideology would take us all the way back to the beginnings of philosophy, to Plato's theory of forms, which is a *logos* of the *idea* or *eidos*, and as such the first ideo-logy (which incidentally also holds for the more restricted sense of the term, as comes across in the necessity of "noble lies" in *The Republic*). Most contemporary uses of term however draw on the model proposed by Marx in *The German Ideology*, i.e., the *camera obscura* that gives us an inverted picture of the world, so that ideas and not material processes come to be seen as the determining factors. Against this, Marx suggests that it is only determined individuals who produce determined social relations, and what is decisive is not how they represent their life process to themselves, but how it actually occurs, in what way they are active and produce material objects. The production of ideas, law, metaphysics, religion, etc., is thus inextricably tied to the material production process, and with the interaction (*Verkehr*) that it involves, and consciousness (*Bewusstsein*) is finally never anything other than conscious being (*bewusstes Sein*), i.e., a kind of being-aware that arises directly out of the actual life process.[7] But this direct reflection is nevertheless an

7. "Das Bewusstsein kann nie etwas Andres sein als das bewusste Sein, und das Sein der Menschen ist ihr wirklicher Lebensprozess. Wenn in der ganzen Ideologie die Menschen und ihre Verhältnisse wie in einer Camera obscura auf den Kopf gestellt erscheinen, so geht dies Phänomen ebensosehr aus ihrem historischen Lebensprozess hervor, wie die

ARCHITECTURE, CRITIQUE, IDEOLOGY

inversion, Marx continues; it gives us an inverted image, like a *camera obscura*, in the same natural way that objects are reproduced in inverted form on the retina. In order to set the picture straight, we must ascend from the earth to the heavens, not the other way around, as in the philosophy of German Idealism: we must start from actual, active human beings, not from how they are imagined or represented. Thus, Marx concludes, the ideal forms of ideology will lose all semblance of autonomy, and they will no longer have a history and development of their own—which is the beginning of a true "positive science" that gets rid of "phrases" about consciousness, even though it provides no sure recipes, and the true difficulty begins with the "actual presentation" (*wirkliche Darstellung*).

As a general theory, this formula in many respects seems far too simplistic and it is surely not a mere coincidence that the rather crude gesture of a "never anything other" (*nie etwas Andres*) is established by way of what looks like a pun; any sustained attempt at proving this point would have shown the limitations of such reduction. First, in a curious trading on metaphors from technology and physiology (which Marx is far from the only one to use),[8] it appears to naturalize ideology (it arises "in the same way …"); second, it makes the dispelling of ideology's mirages into the fairly straightforward task of reversing a picture whose content would be correct in itself. Marx's idea of reversal should, however, be seen in the light of the "process of decomposition" that he sees existing in the aftermath of Hegelianism, where everything appears to be played out in the space of pure thought, and where the gradual putrefaction of

Umdrehung der Gegenstände auf der Netzhaut aus ihrem unmittelbar physischen." Marx, *Die deutsche Ideologie*, in Marx-Engels, *Werke* (Berlin: Dietz, 1969), vol. 3, 26.

8.   For a discussion of the camera obscura as model in Marx, Freud, and Nietzsche, see Sarah Kofmann, *Camera obscura: de l'idéologie* (Paris: Galilée, 1973).

spirit produces new substances both on the left and the right. Seen in context, these remarks are not so much general claims about ideology as a settling of accounts with Marx's own left-Hegelian past—which in turn raises the question to what extent he remains a Hegelian, whether there is a break between the young and the mature Marx, if the concept of alienation in the Paris manuscripts remains pertinent for the systemic analysis developed in *Capital*, and many other related questions. The central issue here, however, is that of the subject as the bearer of ideology: is there a way of overcoming ideology that would not simply discard the "phrases of consciousness" as belonging to the element of warped reflections, but rather inscribe subjectivity as a complex figure of openings and closures, both conditioned and conditioning?

It was precisely these problems that motivated Althusser's new take on ideology as a structure that does not belong to a subject's way of representing the world, but rather is constitutive of subjectivity as such.[9] While the general theoretical framework that underpins these claims has probably crumbled beyond repair—specifically the idea of pure theory or science that breaks with the empirical object just as much as with the subject, and installs itself in a "void"[10]—it may be useful to return to some of its details, since, surprisingly enough, they might have a productive relation to architecture in particular. For Althusser, ideology

9.   See "Idéologie et appareils idéologiques d'État. (Notes pour une recherche)" (1970), reprinted in Althusser, *Positions (1964–1975)* (Paris: Les Éditions sociales, 1976); trans. Ben Brewster, in Althusser, *Lenin and Philosophy and Other Essays* (New York: Monthly Review Press, 1971) as well as the more developed argument in *Sur la reproduction* (Paris: PUF, 1995).

10.   While such a void, as a particular experience of the limit of subjectivity, is not without interesting philosophical implications, it seems too difficult to claim that it could warrant the authority of theory over ideology. For a reading of the motif of the void, see François Matheron, "La récurrence de vide chez Louis Althusser," in Matheron (ed.), *Lire Althusser aujourd'hui* (Paris: L'Harmattan, 1997).

is not a flawed or inverted representation, but a material, bodily encoded practice that establishes normalcy by providing precepts for actions to be repeated without mental or intellectual considerations, as captured in his paraphrase of Pascal's instruction for becoming a Christian: *fall on your knees, move your lips, and you shall become a believer.* This normalcy is not limited to skills and various forms of unexamined know-how, but includes the very sense of being someone, of being a subject with a particular identity and features, so that the subject does not *have* an ideology, but *is* ideology through and through. Rather than originating from within, Althusser suggests, the subject is constituted by interpellation, i.e., by an address—whose historical forms may vary, from the divine voice addressing the sinner to the police officer in the street yelling "Hey, you there!"—to which the subject responds by turning around, assuming the identity of the address, and henceforth knowing who and what it is.

In this context it is crucial that this operation is fundamentally carried out by what Althusser calls "ideological state apparatuses" (the church and the school being the two most significant ones), which rely neither on coercion nor on the production of false images, but rather on organizing modes of conduct. While they are not architectural in any specific sense, they may be taken to involve the kind of spatial signifying practice that was proposed above as a general sense of architecture, in creating divisions, enclosures, and trajectories for the subject. They are "diagrams," as Foucault would say of the Panopticon prison,[11] i.e., abstract machines that distribute forces and points

11. Foucault introduces the term with reference to the military camp, as "the diagram of a power that acts by means of general visibility," and later, slightly more systematically, in relation to Bentham's Panopticon, which "must not be understood as a dream building: it is the diagram of a mechanism of power reduced to its ideal form; its functioning, abstracted from any obstacle, resistance or friction, must be represented as a pure architectural and optical system: it is in fact a figure of political technology that may and must be detached from any specific use." See

of application, and as such must be distinguished from the concrete physical forms that they might take (schools, hospitals,
prisons, military facilities, etc.).

This architectural connection is further indicated by the
way in which Althusser's theory recalls the actual origin of the
term at the end of the eighteenth century, in the writings of the
French *Idéologues*, who in fact had important connections to the
architects of the period, notably Ledoux. As Antoine Picon has
pointed out, Destutt de Tracy, the major proponent of the new
theory of ideology, published his *Eléments d'idéologie* in 1804, the
same year as Ledoux's magnum opus *L'Architecture considérée sous
le rapport de l'art, des mœurs et de la législation.*[12] Destutt de Tracy's
conception of ideology is not the one that would emerge in
Marx—false consciousness, systematic distortion of reality—but
rather a sequel to earlier sensualist epistemologies, from Locke's
Essay Concerning Human Understanding to Condillac's *Traité des
sensations.* For Destutt de Tracy, the analysis of the genesis of
our knowledge coincides with an analysis of the sign: the sign is
both something arbitrary, since it always results from singular
and contingent sensations, and something essential, since it is
that which allows us to form, discern, and hold onto ideas. For
our purpose here, the interesting aspect of Destutt de Tracy's
treatise is that man's primordial relation to and sensing of himself, as it emerges in and through such signs, comes from the
resistance offered by the outside world, and above all the resistance to movement. This is why architecture can be understood

Foucault, *Surveiller et punir: Naissance de la prison* (Paris: Gallimard, 1975),
202, 239; *Discipline and Punish: The Birth of the Prison*, trans. Alan Sheridan
(New York: Penguin, 1977), 171, 205. Foucault's use of the term might
have been incidental, but it was taken up and developed in a systematic
fashion by Deleuze in his *Foucault* (Paris: Minuit, 1986); *Foucault*, trans.
Séan Hand (Minneapolis: University of Minnesota Press, 1988).

12.   See Antoine Picon, "Pour une généalogie du statut du projet," in *Mesure
pour mesure: Architecture et Philosophie*, special issue of *Cahiers du Centre de
Création Industrielle* (1987)

as a prefiguring or projecting of future human sensations: the architect composes a pattern of possible movements, a possible trajectory of the body, and for Boullée and Ledoux this means that geometrical structures, before they are reflections of some immaterial and supratemporal order, first and foremost are tools that have an impact on our affectivity and give rise to a new type of sentient individual. This could be understood as an aesthetic turn, although not toward contemplation, but toward action and doing, which makes it possible for architecture to be understood as the production of a new sensorium (and here one may note that the current interest in architecture as something that bears upon affects and affectivity together with the vocabulary of a projective architecture, seems to resuscitate such theories). Ideology in this sense begins its operations already on a level that precedes reflexive consciousness, and if it works through images, it is not because they are false or inverted representations or pictures of a pre-existing real, but because they are *themselves real*, forces and powers that shape the subject.

The idea of critical theory

This shaping is however not exerted on some inert matter, but is itself a process that splits up into actions and reactions, subjection and resistance, which means the subject constituted is always more than itself, and it has a unity that is *lacking in a both negative and positive sense*; it has both a lack *of being* and a lack *to be*, as Lacan famously suggests, both a negativity emanating from the past that constitutes it, and one that it has to be as it is directed towards the future. This idea could be developed with reference to the Lacanian sources of Althusser's theory, on which he draws in a reductive way that, at least in the analysis of ideology, tends to obliterate the instability and openness of the subject—the interpellation "never misses its target," Althusser writes, to which Lacan might retort that there is a subject, as a structure of self-representation that spans a constitutive gap, precisely to the extent that the address in fact never exactly hits it, but opens a trajectory of identifications that inscribe the subject in ever-widening circles, from the Imaginary to the Symbolic. Or, what would be closer to my concerns here, it could be seen in relation to Foucault's claims that resistance comes first, since the diagram is only realized in a multiplicity that escapes it, and draws its organizing power from that which refuses to be organized: the law does not exist in order to eradicate crime, but to produce a set of proliferating illegalities that can be assessed and classified, and the visibility of the Panopticon, we might say, only exists because its luminosity is submerged in an element of chiaroscuro. If ideology works by constituting subjects, it also fractures them, produces them as shot through with lacunae and gaps whose suturing is always temporal, and thus temporary (from a Foucauldian point of view, there would however not be one predominant lack or absence, but rather a multiplicity of crevices, or, perhaps more accurately, a porosity); it works by always failing, always missing the mark.

So what, then, would be the implications of this for a critical theory, both in general, and in relation to architecture? In relation to architecture, there is an initial division to be made—even though it must remain porous and allow for numerous breaches—with respect to time, i.e., between theory as way of reading and interpreting architectures (once more, in the wide sense of the term) that already exist, either as past works that need to be opened up or present ones that call out for judgment, and theory as a constructing, projecting, and imagining of a critical capacity belonging to architectures that do not yet exist. The relation between past, present, and future is however not a linear one, as seems to be presupposed when critical theory is deemed useless for a practice to come. It seems more promising to understand the time of critique like a complex loop: it is present work that makes it possible to open up the monuments of the past beyond mere passive admiration and philology, just as it is such a reinterpreted past that in turn strikes back at the present, because both of them, in different ways, come toward us from the future. The activity of critique, in keeping with the Greek etymology of the term, would be a *splitting* that tears apart the three aspects of time in order to configure them differently; it is an unhinging of time from its axes, as was glimpsed (but no more than glimpsed) in Adorno's understanding of how contemporary works burst open past ones and let us discern in them that which did not add up, but was concealed underneath their seemingly unbroken surfaces, although Adorno too often seems to have settled for the linearity of the modern as the experience of the no longer possible. A more complex version of this idea can found in Deleuze's theory of the untimely and the virtual, in which each temporal segment is opened up to a larger dimension of pasts and futures that are not merely logical possibilities, but *real* without being *actual*, in the sense that they impact on the actual, not causally, but by infiltrating it, swarming behind the scene of representation like so many doubles (Deleuze's theory draws initially on Bergson and Proust, and later on Leibniz and cinema, but despite the attention it has attracted, including in architecture theory, it is in need of further development and clarification; the general direction in which it points is however clear).

As for the idea of critical theory in general, here it may suffice merely to delineate a few of the points that I think can be extracted from the following essays—even though they were not explicit or articulated at the time of writing; but such is the problem of any preface, written as it must be at the end, when writing ought to have begun again—and in which the legacy of critical theory needs to be confronted with other traditions, subsequent and parallel to it. Rather than conclusions, they are guidelines for future research, and if the vocabulary of Adorno here is used as a guiding thread, it is only one thread among many.

1. *Interpretation is a second work.* If the object embodies contradictions, and these can be read out of it by an interpretation, the latter nevertheless remains an invention of theory. While these contradictions do originate in society, which for us inevitably means the world of contemporary capitalism, and are reflected in the work, this reflection is not a simple mirroring that has a bearing on content or the "objective moment," as Adorno says, but occurs through an act of mimesis that in turn generates tensions and contradictions within the construction, form, or immanent structure of the work. Teasing out these contradictions from the object is itself a creation, neither superior nor inferior to the first work, and in this sense interpretation produces a second work alongside the first, which in turn cannot avoid embodying contradictions that it itself cannot master. Thus, neither work nor interpretation is the key to the other; instead, both have multiple points in common, though without being reducible to a third underlying matrix. This inevitably entails a crumbling of the hierarchy between the muteness and opacity of the work and the eloquence of interpretation that Adorno, notwithstanding his many precautions, often ends up reproducing.

2. *Autonomy is an effect of a frame.* Our concept of autonomy must be articulated differently from the articulation of the concept available to Adorno, since the idea of closure that guided him is no longer the same as ours. This does not mean that it would have simply evaporated, but rather that it has been transformed along with the development of technologies of both production and distribution. These shifts are indicated by, for instance, the inverted constellation of concepts and particulars in conceptual art and everything that would follow in its wake, by the open or processual artwork that Adorno indeed glimpsed but attempted to enclose within the negative concept

XXV

of the "informal,"[13] by the incessant interrogation (both theoretical and practical) of the status of the art object that understands it as more of a product of discursive conditions than a
perceptual given, and a host of other shifts, all of which belong
to a phase of aesthetic reflection that emerged in the sixties just
as Adorno's work was drawing to close. Autonomy—as in the
"knight's move" of the work, its "swerve" (ideas borrowed from
Shklovsky and Russian formalism), to which Tafuri referred toward the end of his analysis of modernism as that which prevents
the work from simply merging with reality[14]—must not be taken
as an objective property that some things may have while others
simply lack, but as a kind of limiting or framing condition that
determines what belongs to the inside of the work and what to
its outside. Autonomy is the effect, the *work*, of a *beside-the-work*,
a *parergon*, as Derrida noted already in Kant's aesthetics,[15] and
in this sense it cannot be eliminated without the work ceasing
to exist. The process underway since Adorno's time might be
analyzed as the gradual introjection of such framing conditions
into the work itself, so that they now can become its material
instead of its outer boundaries, as can be seen in many works "at
the limit" of architecture.

 3. *Contradiction must be rendered more fluid so as to incorporate dif-*

13.   See Adorno, "Vers une musique informelle" (1961), in *Quasi una fanta-
      sia, Gesammelte Schriften* 16; *Quasi una fantasia: Essays on Modern Music*,
      trans. Rodney Livingstone (London: Verso, 1992).
14.   See Tafuri, *The Sphere and the Labyrinth*, 16, and Shklovsky, *Knight's
      Move*, trans. Richard Sheldon (Normal. Ill.: Dalkey Archive Press,
      2005). The work's distance from reality is itself conditioned by reality,
      it is the way in which reality is taken up and deflected, which does not
      make the distance any less real; conversely, the work could be said to in-
      ject this distance into the real itself. If in Shklovsky's view the sideways
      move of the knight occurs because the direct road ahead is blocked, as
      Tafuri notes (ibid, 308 note 29), then this move is itself not somehow
      less real, but rather introduces a different spacing of the board itself.
15.   See Derrida, "Parergon," in *La vérité en peinture* (Paris: Flammarion,
      1974); *The Truth in Painting*, trans. Geoff Bennington and Ian McLeod
      (Chicago: University of Chicago Press, 1987).

ference. This need to rethink the idea of contradiction signals that negative dialectics, in its massive dependence on the Hegelian legacy, must be loosened from its fixtures (which obviously does not rule out that this could also be carried out through a more attentive reading of Hegel himself). It needs to confront other traditions that understand difference in another fashion—the task could be to cross-read Adorno's *Negative Dialectics* with, say, Deleuze's *Difference and Repetition*, both of which share the question of how to approach the singular or the "monadic," of difference as the limit of the non-identical and the sensible as a differential, of the limits of conceptual subsumption, although they reach results that at first may seem opposed to each other, or perhaps just simply unrelated (almost as if the articulations of Hegel's *Logic* would have been torn asunder and its severed parts had started to move away from each other at increasing speed). While a reconstruction of a space in which such different claims could communicate might seem like an excessively abstract and even abstruse proposal, it will have an impact on the very vocabulary of critical theory. For Adorno, it was necessary to retain traditional concepts like subject and object, self-consciousness, identity, etc., and he always insisted on their double nature: as sediments of a reified tradition, they also contained petrified meditations that could once more be set free; just like artworks, concepts have an inner historicity that does not seal them in the confines of the past, but rather makes it possible for them to take on new meanings in other contexts. It may be the case, however, that the unquestioned presuppositions that many of these terms carry with them today may block thought rather than open it; the passage from the language of critique to the critique of language— which, to stress this once more, is not the same as a linguistic turn towards communication—is however always a tenuous one. The antinomy between philosophy as a "creation of concepts" (Deleuze) and as a de-sedimentation of older ones is no doubt as such too simplified, and yet it cannot be simply dismissed.

4. *The critical and utopian work of the work must be pluralized.*
Because the work is not simply a reflection, but fundamentally a
movement of working over or working through, and in this akin
to Freud's *Durcharbeitung*, it liberates a singular transcendence
that allows us to perceive particulars in a way that releases them
from conceptual subsumption without simply becoming a nom-
inalism—*das Miteinander des Verschiedenen*, the being-together or
togetherness of the diverse,[16] which for Adorno was the moment
of utopia or reconciliation, albeit veiled, ungraspable, and only
accessible in a negative mode. While this moment cannot be
simply erased, as some would like to do,[17] if the entire edifice
of Adorno's aesthetic theory is not to mutate into a series of

16. See Adorno, *Negative Dialektik*, 153; *Negative Dialectics*, 150. Both Adorno
and Deleuze are in a sense the conflicting heirs to Hegel's logic of essence, in which the movement of difference (*Unterschied*) takes us from
diversity (*Verschiedenheit*) through opposition (*Gegensatz*) to contradiction (*Widerspruch*), and then to a "return to the ground" (*Rückgang in
den Grund*) that is also a foundering (*zu Grunde gehen*). For Adorno,
the possibility of a togetherness of the diverse that escapes its binding
together in oppositions and contradictions, would be the *utopian limit*
of negative dialectics where it ceases to be both negative and dialectical;
for Deleuze, this state of a free difference in the sensible need not rely
on a projection of the future, but determines the place to be reached
as a site constituted in a now-and-here that is also a *now/here*, or, if we
read this term backwards, as Samuel Butler once proposed (with a minor transposition of letters to reflect the backwards pronunciation), as
an *erewhon*. The ideas invented by philosophy—which here seems almost
indistinguishable from artworks—are, Deleuze suggests, "not universals
like the categories, nor are they the *hic et nunc* or *now here*, the diversity
to which categories apply in representation. They are complexes of
space and time, no doubt transportable but on the condition that they
impose their own scenery, that they set up camp there where they rest
momentarily: they are therefore the objects of an essential encounter rather than of recognition. The best word to designate these is
undoubtedly that forged by Samuel Butler: *erewhon*. They are *erewhons.*"
Deleuze, *Différence et répétition* (Paris: PUF, 1968), 364f; *Difference and
Repetition*, trans. Paul Patton (London: Continuum, 1994), 285.

17. For instance Wellmer, who suggests that Adorno's failure to recognize
that he already possesses all the elements of a postmetaphysical aesthetic
is due to the fact that he sees them in the "distorted" optic of reconciliation; see Wellmer, "Adorno, die Moderne und das Erhabene," 190.

formalist analyses of modern art, it needs to be broken up spectrally, in the sense of refraction as well as that of a haunting, that which cannot stop returning to us as a ghost, as Reinhold Martin suggests with particular reference to architecture.[18] From Adorno's point of view, the spectralization of reconciliation might suggest that its basis in an interpretation of natural history needs to look different in the age of modern technology: how can we think a philosophy of nature when the difference between nature and the artificial has, as Deleuze once proposed, disappeared?[19] In what sense would a non-coercive, non-violent relation between inner and outer nature be possible in a world that on one level seems to have erased the last vestiges of otherness, while on another level reproduces it as immanent risks that proliferate precisely because of the domination of nature?

Interpretation, autonomy, difference, and utopia—to these four concepts others could no doubt be added. To pursue the task of critical theory as bequeathed to us by Adorno means to think through them, with and against him, in order to come back to him from a vantage point that belongs to the future.

18.   See Martin, *Utopia's Ghost: Architecture and Postmodernism, Again* (Minneapolis: University of Minnesota Press, 2010). In Martin's analysis, the architecture of postmodernism appears as an integral part of the spatial or "territorial" ordering of capitalism itself, and rather than just a symptom or cipher for other forces, it is itself one of their crucial agents. Architecture produces a powerful tool for the implementation of capital, and it is precisely its immanence in power that blocks it from perceiving power other than in the distorted mirror of its own autonomy. Its various modes of acting and representing, its *thinking* in the widest sense, thus also amounts to an active *unthinking* of other possibilities, above all the idea of utopia, which then returns, spectrally, in the form of enclaves and divisions inside social space. For a further discussion of Martin's analysis, see chap 4 below.

19.   See the interview with Raymond Bellour and François Ewald, on the occasion of the publications of *Le Pli: Leibniz et le baroque*, "Sur la philosophie," *Pourparlers* (Paris: Minuit, 1990), 212: "On Philosophy," *Negotiations*, trans. Martin Joughin (New York: Columbia University Press, 1995), 155.

* * *

The first chapter, "Manfredo Tafuri and the End of Utopia," locates a starting point in the work of Manfredo Tafuri, and more generally, the Venice School, which during a period of intense activity and debate constituted the focal point of the debates on the legacy of Marxism and the possibility of a "critique of architectural ideology," as was the title of one of Tafuri's programmatic essays, published in 1969.

Tafuri has an enduring and even haunting presence in contemporary architectural discourse. To some, his type of Marxist analysis, deeply embedded in the conflicts of the Italian left in the 1970s, would today seem simply outdated—or at least this is what many would wish. The question of the ideological role of modern architecture—which Tafuri and his colleagues studied in great depth, drawing on analyses of architecture and urban planning in the Soviet Union, in the social-democratic state of the Weimar Republic, and in American capitalism—however remains just as pertinent today, and the impasse with which this analytical work has left us, in the guise of the divide between a critical and an operative reading of history, remains a crucial issue, no matter how much we would like to mitigate and even repress it. In fact, the idea of the Metropolis as the essential site of capital, developed by Tafuri and Massimo Cacciari, is still very much alive today, although approached from the opposite angle, most famously in the writings and projects of Rem Koolhaas, who can be understood as a rebellious disciple of Tafuri. The question remains to what extent this type of reworked avant-garde sensibility—to analyze the structures of the emergent as opposed to the residual, and then declare an unconditional support for the new—intends to simply identify with the aggressor, or to what extent it can be understood as a more fluid and flexible way to deal with the present. Tafuri's critical analysis of the restructuring of capitalism after the 1929 crash, and the emergence of the plan as an instrument that effectively transforms architecture into a tool and displaces its earlier utopian projections, undoubtedly provides an essential subtext for these current debates.

The second chapter, "1966: Thinking the City," develops the idea of the city as it emerged as a general problem in the writings of, on the one hand, Robert Venturi and Denise Scott Brown, and on the other hand, Aldo Rossi. While seemingly opposed on all levels—the relation to history, materiality, technology, aesthetic sensibility, the choice of architectural models— both sides drew on the idea of the city as a force that resists the capacity for control and planning claimed by a tradition that henceforth would appear as modern, and thus opposed to something like that which is known as postmodern, which soon came to appear as a blanket term for a whole set of rather divergent tendencies. As Tafuri had suggested, the problem of how to grasp and take charge of the city had already emerged as essential in the eighteenth century, but took a new turn with the invention of urbanism as a new discipline in the writings of Ildefonso Cerdá in the latter half of the nineteenth century. Rather than subjecting the city to a gridded and disciplinary structure imposed from above, must we not understand it as a living entity whose powers must tap into, create conduits for, its flows—in short, as a biopolitical entity? The problem of how to control the city would subsequently be at the center of the modern discourse of urbanism, particularly in the development of CIAM, and the task of reintroducing complexity was one of the key factors in its demise. For both Venturi-Scott Brown and Rossi, this layered and non-totalizable nature of the city is what renders it resistant to planning and control, although they see the problem from opposite ends: for Venturi-Scott Brown, it is the simulated history, the stylistic plurality, and the quality of images that make Las Vegas into a paradigm; for Rossi, it is the depth of actual history, the basis of all styles in underlying types, and the material presence that makes Rome into a model. In both cases there is, however, a crucial moment of fiction that draws on artistic models—for Venturi-Scott Brown, the photographically based work of early pop art, for Rossi, Renaissance painting, both of which moments signal a crisis for the inherited vocabularies of form, order, and structure, but also the necessary incursion of fantasy if these problems are to be thought through (the presence of cinematic imagery would later play the same role in Koolhaas).

The following chapter, "The Pyramid and the Labyrinth," approaches the question of control from another angle, in which the dissolution of architecture, or its reduction to the underlying, fluid and intensive element of space in general, was not so much a threat to its capacity for ordering social relations as a precondition for it. The idea of space as such emerged out of a long debate on the role of empathy in nineteenth-century aesthetics, and, through the works of August Schmarsow, it was relayed into early architectural modernism. In Sigfried Giedion this was understood in terms of a "stream of motion" that draws all elements into its dynamism, at once rendering the idea of architecture as the creation of stable forms problematic, and opening up a different avenue, where architecture could become a means of shaping space by tapping into an underlying informal element where all things exist in a state of "interpenetration." As one of the primary tools for the creation of conduits, architecture through this in fact attains an even greater power than before, precisely because of its capacity to striate a first, smooth space and make it into a secondary, legible, and controllable element. For some, this new power heralded a possibility of shaping life in terms of transparency—affirmative in the case of Walter Benjamin, more hesitant in some of the projects and writings of Sergey Eisenstein. This dialectic of control and its various others—freedom, latitude, the right to reversal and upheaval—continues in the planning discourse of the postwar period, but also in the situationist project to construct moments that would unleash the hidden force in a given situation, bring its congealed passions back to life, even though they too, as can be seen in the clash between Debord and Lefebvre, repeated the same conflict between the creation and imposition of a condition for freedom, and its actual exertion. Finally, in the work of Bernard Tschumi, this is brought out in terms of a tension between the "pyramid" and the "labyrinth" (terms themselves derived from Bataille), i.e., between the creation of higher-level orders that transcend the sensory, and the immersion into the labyrinthine and erotic space of the body that proposes to extract a sense of the event of architecture, a form of deregulation that however enters into a problematic proximity to the very spatial logic of capital itself, in which pyramid and labyrinth may be no more than the two sides of the same loop.

Chapter four, "The Recent Past of Postmodern Architecture," traces certain key themes in the debate on the postmodern as it emerges from the sixties onward, and passes through philosophy, social theory, the visual arts, and architecture. While postmodernism, or postmodernity, or the postmodern—terms that by no means had, and still do not have, any clear historical demarcation—may seem like last year's embarrassing outfit, and to this extent the vocabulary suffers the fate of most such recent pasts, its pastness is also a recentness that haunts the present, a ghostlike return in theory as well as in practice. The questions posed under this umbrella term—the philosophical legacy of the Enlightenment idea of progress and the continuation of a Kantian critique of reason that turns against the metaphysical foundations of the critique itself (Lyotard), the impact of late capitalism and globalization on the imaginary and the arts, and our capacity for a "cognitive mapping" that locates subjective experience in relation to a systemic order (Jameson), the dissolution of medium specificity of the arts and their entry into the general or "expanded field" of inscription (Rosalind Krauss) that opened up in conceptual art and its various successors—remain just as pertinent, though we are less inclined today to bring them together into one single narrative. In this debate, however, architecture held a particular place of importance, both because if was perhaps the first of the arts to turn the postmodern into a stylistic phenomenon, thus unwittingly bringing about its obsolescence, but also because it just as often became that out of which postmodernism was read as a general cultural condition, a paradigm with which other expressions were understood and measured. Two recent studies, by Jorge Otero-Pailos and Reinhold Martin, are here used as equally paradigmatic ways to discuss the presence of postmodernism's past in the present. In the first perspective, it appears as emerging out of an interior debate in architecture, where a new experientialist approach gradually displaced the technological and art-historical ones, making way for the emergence of a new type of theory that could draw first on phenomenology, but subsequently also on many other philosophies, and of a new type of theorist, the architect-historian, who could lay claim to a new and more profound access to history. In the second, it appears as an integral part of the spatial or territorial ordering of capitalism itself, for which architecture is not just a symptom or a cipher, but just as much a crucial agent: architecture produced a powerful tool for the implementation of Capital, and it was precisely its immanence in power that barred it from perceiving it other than in the distorted mirror of its own autonomy. Its various modes of acting and representing, its *thinking* in the widest sense, thus also amounts to an active *unthinking* of other possibilities, above all the idea of utopia.

The fifth chapter, "Looping Ideology," examines the work of a particular architect who for decades has been a key reference in the debate on architecture's capacity to intervene in society, and whose provocative claims have fueled almost infinite discussions: Rem Koolhaas. Tracing the themes of inside and outside, a split or division that relates and sets apart, through the projects of Koolhaas and the OMA, provides a framework for a reading of a particular work, the CCTV center in Beijing. Conceived both as a signature building and a technological marvel, and as a means of reflecting on the current relation between media and architecture, the CCTV center proposes a particularly acute version of architecture's critical purchase on the world and of its surrender to it. It is, OMA suggests, a "singe loop of interconnected activity"—this, in many senses: on the level of structure and program, in comprising two physical trajectories, one dedicated to broadcasting, the second to research and education, both of which merge at the management headquarters at the top of the building; on the level of psychological impact, in proposing a behavioral effect on the employees, so that the adjacency of different functions should foster a spirit of collaboration; and finally, in allowing for a path of public access that runs through the entire structure, and offering views not only of Beijing, but also of the production process itself in all of its details, therewith producing a sense of transparency, literally as well as metaphorically. In this sense, it projects the idea of transparency and openness while at the same time making legible and visible the current constraints on this idea, holding these two aspects together without erasing the difference between them. The building stages their inner contradiction, it promises something that it at same time cancels, materializing repressive mechanisms while simultaneously allowing us to see through them. Its critical operation in this sense has to do with the production of *divisions* and conflicts in the real itself, rather than with an adopting of an external stance outside the system in order to pass judgment on it.

Chapter six, "Thinking Otherwise," revisits the problem of resistance and intervention from a different angle, the problem of utopia and heterotopia. If utopia was actively unthought in postmodernism, as Reinhold Martin suggests, might we not approach its "no-," the no-place of the *ou-*, in terms of an other place, a *heteros topos* that does not locate itself in some other-worldly outside of our spatial system, but at its margins, twisting and skewing the world of the everyday so that it releases a virtual double of itself, an imaginary place that would also entail something like the placing or materializing of the imaginary? This may be taken as the proposal of Michel Foucault's 1967 lecture "Of Other Spaces," which has had a long and confusing reception in architectural discourse. In fact, the lecture belongs to a whole series of reflections on the various senses of utopia and heterotopia that engaged Foucault in the later part of the sixties (and in which one must note that he never rejects the concept of utopia but always sees it emerging from within a constellation of other concepts), and in hindsight it can be read as already pointing beyond the analysis of discourses and epistemic regularities, the archaeologies of knowledge and of the human sciences that ran the risk of ending up in a linguistic idealism. Connecting Foucault's reflections on the place as inhabited by an otherness that calls for a particular kind of invention also provides a perspective on the various new takes on the site that would emerge in the visual arts and architecture from the late sixties onward. Thus the work of Robert Smithson, beginning in the dialectic of institutional space and its outsides, "site" and "nonsite," soon developed into a mobile practice for which the site was just as much discursive as physical and institutional. Similarly, the projects that would follow Peter Eisenman's Houses, his "artificial excavations," explore the site as a layer of

different times and narratives, and bring together the heterotopias of space and language in an architectural poetic located at
the very limit of architecture.

The seventh and concluding chapter, "Noopolitics, Life,
Architecture," looks at the impact of the affective and corporeal in architectural discourse. Such an affective turn has had
extensive ramifications in the human and social sciences, but,
in architecture, was particularly bound up with the idea of the
post-critical. If architecture ultimately aspires to reach us at a
visceral level, what sense could there be in attempting to provide
it with a critical and reflexive function? In their demand for immediacy and presence, such claims are in many respects echoes
of the vitalist philosophies from the beginning of the twentieth
century, but they can also appear as allied with recent philosophies of life and desire, from Foucault's analyses of biopolitics to
Deleuze's reinterpretations of Nietzsche and Spinoza, as well as
Agamben's search for a potential of life that would lie at the limit of sovereign power. While each of these theories in their specific way attempts to discover a dimension other than that of the
reflexive subject, none of them simply proposes to take leave of
the critical, but rather to reinvent it by locating a level of agency
and resistance located beneath the subject, in its multiple, contradictory, and affective ways of being imbricated in the world.
As Maurizio Lazzarato proposes, drawing on both Foucault
and Deleuze, what is at stake here is a dimension of power that
reaches into the noetic, the possibility of a control that bypasses
our cognitive screens and aims at the most profound reality of
the mind, against which he suggests that we must tap into what
is the other side of such power, the "General Intelligence" that
these technologies also make possible, and whose capacities for
reversal and flight Capital must always strive to contain. In the
case of architecture, it is clear that, however much it not only
participates in such technologies, but also propels their develop-

ment and constitutes an essential testing ground, this does not necessitate any abandonment of critique or theory as such, only a critique and a theory that does not lag behind its object, which is why critical theory is in need of a constant reinvention.

I would like to thank my colleagues at the Department of Culture of Communication at Södertörn University, and my fellow editors at Site, all of whom have provided insightful commentaries on the following chapters during various stages of completion. Special thanks must go to the participants in the research project "Power, Space, and Ideology": Tor Lindstrand, Helena Mattsson, Håkan Nilsson, and Kim West.

The project and the generous funding provided by the Baltic Sea Foundation, together with the support from the Publications Committe eat Södertörn University, made the completion of this book possible.

Finally, thanks to Brian Manning Delaney, who provided crucial remarks on both style and content.

Some of following chapters have been published in earlier versions, but have all been substantially reworked: chapter 3 in the exhibition catalog *Fluid Street* (Helsinki: Kiasma, 2008); chapter 5 in Staffan Ericsson and Kristina Riegert (eds.), *Media Houses: Architecture, Media, and the Production of Centrality* (New York: Peter Lang, 2010); chapter 6 in Mats Leffler, Johan Linton, and Johan Stålberg (eds.), *In i kulturen: En vänbok till Per Magnus Johansson* (Gothenburg: Psykoanalytiska föreningen, 2010), and chapter 7 in Deborah Hauptmann and Warren Neidich (eds.), *Cognitive Architecture: From Bio-politics to Noo-politics: Architecture & Mind in the Age of Communication & Information* (Rotterdam: 010, 2010).

1. Tafuri and the end of utopia

The past and present of critique

"To dispel anxiety by understanding and internalizing its causes: this would seem to be one of the principal ethical imperatives of bourgeois art."[1] The opening lines of Manfredo Tafuri's *Progetto e utopia* (1973) provide a condensed view of his complex and tortuous relation to the modernity of architecture, and indicate his rather bleak view of the capacity of artistic practices under capitalism to transcend the structures that determine them. Understanding the ambivalence that marks architecture in particular, Tafuri suggests, may allow us to understand the reasons for the diremptions and anxieties that haunt the modern subject, not only as a psychological diagnosis,[2] but above all in terms of how they condition a whole discourse of form and design that in turn produces an illusion of mastery, leading us to affirm, even desire, the most troubling aspects of our existence as if they were

1.   Tafuri, *Progetto e utopia: Architettura e sviluppo capitalistico* (Bari: Laterza, 2007 [1973]), 5. Translated by Barba Luigi La Penta as *Architecture and Utopia: Design and Capitalist* Development (Cambridge, Mass.: MIT, 1976), 1. Henceforth cited as PU (Italian/English). The disputable quality of the English translations of some of Tafuri's early work has often been noted, and I have sometimes modified them. In the case of *Progetto e utopia*, Jean-Louis Cohen even speaks of a "massacre"; see Cohen "The Italophiles at Work," in K. Michael Hays (ed.), *Architecture Theory Since 1968* (Cambridge, Mass.: MIT, 1998), 514.

2.   "Anxiety" (*angoscia*) should here not be understood merely as psychological concept, but as an idea that amalgamates an existential ontology and a Freudian and Marxian vocabulary; see Anthony Vidler, *Histories of the Immediate Present: Inventing Architectural Modernism* (Cambridge, Mass.: MIT, 2008), 180ff.

1

an expression of our own will. For Tafuri, breaking this spell, one both theoretical and practical, means taking up a truly critical stance towards the present, an initial consequence of which is the seemingly sharp divide between the "operative" history that he saw in predecessors such as Sigfried Giedion, Bruno Zevi, and Reyner Banham—who remained under the spell of the utopian enchantment of the *project*—and a critical history that would reveal the present to be the result of contradictions located beyond the reach of architecture and urbanism.

But there is yet an additional move, in which the first is inscribed, beginning in the vast historical survey *L'architettura contemporanea* (1976), and leading up to the "historical project" announced in the introduction to *La sfera e il labirinto* (1980), which counters the utopian project by dismantling its unitary pretension, but in this also makes possible a different kind of relation between the operative and the critical. To some extent this may seem like a straightforward affirmation of philology, close reading, and the attention to minutiae that separate the historian's craft from the speculations of theory—and Tafuri's subsequent works on the Renaissance constitute monumental examples of such close reading—which is why it has sometimes been taken as an indication that there would be two sides of his work: the highly polemical readings of modernism that tend toward overarching theoretical claims, and the subsequent interpretations of the Renaissance that immerse themselves in historical details and micro-histories that would seem to burst asunder any possible global synthetic framework. This division seems even more firmly established by the attempt to locate different periods in Tafuri's oeuvre: after a first period in the 1960s, where he established his intellectual and institutional credentials with publications largely devoted to historical issues, he turns to polemical interpretations of modernism, roughly from *Teorie e storia dell'architettura* (1968) to the *Storia dell'architettura italiana, 1944–1985* (1982, 2. ed. 1986), after which he then turns back to historical work on the Renaissance, first in the monograph *L'armonia e i conflitti: La chiesa di San Francesco della Vigna nella Venezia del Cinquecento* (1983)— a book significantly dedicated to a single building read as a condensation of a whole period and its conflicts, and in this sense a paradigm for the micro-historical approach—and then in the two mighty tomes *Venezia e il rinascimento* (1985) and *Ricerca del rinascimento* (1992). This picture, which for a long time marked the Anglophone reception of Tafuri's work, was in fact largely due to the chronology of translations, and is ultimately misleading. Today there is rather a tendency towards a "*maximum integration*"[3] of its various facets. Tafuri publishes important works on the Renaissance throughout his career, and rather than speaking of different periods, we should perhaps speak of two tendencies or motifs that span his entire development, and often co-exist in the same work. In the following however, I will leave aside Tafuri's many studies of the Renaissance tradition, as well as the question as to whether his work is split into two parts, one dealing with the contradictions of the present, the other with historical accounts, or whether it displays a fundamental unity. This is because my aim here is not to produce an in-depth portrait of Tafuri's thought as a whole, but only to discuss some aspects of his contribution to a critical theory of modern architecture with bearings on the present.[4]

3.   Marco Biraghi, *Progetto di crisi: Manfredo Tafuri e l'architettura contemporanea* (Milan: Christian Marinotti, 2005), 6. As will become clear, my reading takes a different direction, and instead seeks to locate such a tension inside the unfolding of Tafuri's reading of modernism in its integrality, whereas Biraghi largely draws on Tafuri's later, or even final, position in *La sfera e il labirinto* (1980).

4.   When, in the 1980s, he begins to refocus on historical studies, it is however undeniable that his comments on the contemporary development become more distanced and estranged; see for instance the interview with Pietro Corsi, "For a Critical History," *Casabella* 619–620 (1995).

What will be in focus here is rather the tension between two other, albeit related claims made specifically in relation to modern architecture: on the one hand, that we must grasp the modern movement as the unfolding of a series of central contradictions, which always involves the movement of a dialectic that ends up producing a totality, no matter how negative; on the other hand, the desire not only to return all such overarching narratives to a more distant historical soil, but also to show that any such soil must be fractured from the outset. This tension permeates Tafuri's writings, and it engages all the senses of crisis, critique, and the critical: bifurcation, turning point, division, conflict, discord, judgment. What his heritage is—if it indeed is unitary, or deeply divided, or simply contradictory, and if so, what kind of logic organizes its contradictions—is in this sense already a question posed in the work itself, its own moment of crisis.

Following the initial quote above, Tafuri's work on modernism would seem to be about retrieving and even intensifying the anxiety constitutive of modernity, and allowing it to have its full impact on us—eventually, as we will see, letting it strike back at the very writing of history as a project in its own right, a project that must be subjected to the same fragmentation as the project of the avant-garde. From Tafuri's own point of view, the fatigue, even rejection, that his work occasions today among some contemporary theorists might then simply be understood as a repression or refusal of this anxiety, on all levels; similarly, the rejection of theory as unproductive often amounts to little more than a return to the most naïve aspects of theory. The fading of the dialectical models inherited from early twentieth-century avant-garde culture—which, it is often claimed, ought be abandoned, sometimes in favor of a transformed way of thinking difference and resistance, but increasingly often, and even more radically, in favor of an attitude that has for a while gone under the label "post-critical,"[5]—would thus simply appear as a regression, a return to an intentionally blind and self-sufficient version of ideology.

The question, however, is what such a Tafurian point of view might amount to, both in terms of a historical question of what was once at stake in a past that seems to move away from us at increasing speed, and in terms of a present that requires of us that we project this past towards a possible future; together these two aspects add up to something like a conflict between what Tafuri called the critical and projective, although this time in relation to our own recent past. To stubbornly uphold the ethos and conceptuality of a critique of ideology inherited from the 1960s and 1970s does not seem to live up to the phrase from Franco Fortini to which Tafuri sometimes refers: to be "cunning like doves" ("Astuti come colombi").[6] The mobility and intelligence of critique cannot lag behind the ruses of capital itself, lest the former condemn itself to fighting an arrière-garde battle that often becomes little more than a means to produce the false security provided by a moralizing and fundamentally empty rejection of the present; in short, it cannot simply eschew the operative dimension if it is to remain a source of creation and invention. Whether Tafuri's monumental work, incomparable in its erudition, depth, and complexity, might serve as the basis of such rethinking—whether, that is, it can engage us in a productive exchange of antiquarian, monumental and critical history in the Nietzschean sense—is an open question.

The shifts in cultural production that have marked the last decades, taking us through the debates about postmodernism,

5. For more on this, see chap. 7 below.
6. Franco Fortini (pseudonym for Franco Lattes, 1917–1994) was an Italian author and literary critic. For his connection to Tafuri, see Pier Vittorio Aureli, "Intellectual Work and Capitalist Development: Origins and Context of Manfredo Tafuri's Critique of Architectural Ideology," *Site* 26–27 (2009).

5

globalization, electronic capitalism, post-Fordism, and several other concepts created in order to grasp a fleeting and increasingly liquid present, can be read as a gradual abandonment of the Marxist conceptuality that once formed the matrix of the Venice School, but it can also be read as a continual displacement of a fundamental problem: how to connect the present mode of production to the artistic, architectural, and urban forms that surround us, in a way that doesn't simply render them legible as ciphers of power, even of regression,[7] but endows them with reflexive and critical agency that is nonetheless never simply present, but itself requires an act of invention.

In this perspective, the split between operative and critical history opened up by Tafuri belongs to the crisis of Marxist theory itself, which emerged at the moment when theory and practice no longer appeared capable of coming together. Many

7. "Ciphers of Authority, Figures of Regression," was the title of an essay by Benjamin H. D. Buchloh (first published in 1981 in *October*) that spawned a long debate on the significance of the return of traditional painterly styles in the late seventies and early eighties, and many of the arguments put forth echo those of the earlier debates on eclecticism in postmodern architecture. Considered as a judgment of taste—which runs counter to the essay's theoretical claims—few would today dispute Buchloh's verdict, and very little of the work that he attacks has withstood the test of time. On the theoretical level, however, the genealogy that the essay traces ought to be questioned. The epigraph as well as many of the critical remarks that Buchloh makes are drawn from Lukács's "Grösse und Verfall des Expressionismus" (1934), but he seems strangely oblivious to the rather problematic nature of the analogy he establishes between his own rejection of the neo-expressionism of the seventies and Lukács's attacks on modernism. Lukács's position is decidedly anti-modernist—expressionism is for him virtually synonymous with modernism in all of its forms—and as such in fact close to the various calls for a "return to order" that Buchloh associates with the expressionism of his own present moment. Virtually everything that Buchloh supports as progressive in the historical avant-garde would be deemed reactionary and proto-fascist by Lukács (as comes across particularly in the latter's remarks, as contemptuous as they are ignorant, on modern painting and music): his quarrel is not with the continued use of historical forms, whose relevance for the present he endorses, but with what he sees as the modernist dissolution of form as such.

other solutions imposed themselves at roughly the same time, some of which grappled with the status of theory as a stand-in for deferred action, endowing it with a tenuous and angst-ridden autonomy precisely because the moment to realize it was missed, as Adorno notes in the opening lines of *Negative Dialectics*; others turned the tables and transformed the divide into a positive starting point, as in the idea of pure theory in Althusser, in which the entire subjective dimension appeared as something caught up in the imaginary and unable to cross over into the space of thought. As a result of this disjunction, the critique of ideology began to point less to a set of clear-cut alternatives to the present state than to a kind of reflexive self-dismantling. In Tafuri's immediate vicinity, we find the "negative thought" envisaged by Massimo Cacciari as a negativity that breaks away from all ideas of reconciliation, and owes just as much to Nietzsche and Heidegger as to the critique of political economy.[8] The analysis of architecture and urbanism for Cacciari becomes one, although privileged, moment in the reading of modernity as an infinite crisis—infinite in the sense that there is no way of overcoming it, no movement that would take us "post" modernism or modernity, only an ever more profound descent into its formative contradictions.[9] The tonal-

8.   For the idea of negative thought, see Massimo Cacciari, *Architecture and Nihilism: On the Philosophy of Modern Architecture*, trans. Stephen Sartarelli with a preface by Patrizia Lombardo (New Haven: Yale University Press, 1993). For a discussion of the connection to Heidegger's analysis of nihilism and technology, see my *The Silences of Mies* (Stockholm: Axl Books, 2008), 22–40.

9.   The idea of a "beyond" of modernity is constantly rejected by Tafuri, who prefers to speak of a "hypermodernity," which for him seems like a wholly negative term; see chap. 14 in *Storia dell'architettura italiana* (Turin; Einaudi, 1986); trans. Jessica Levine, *History of Italian Architecture* (Cambridge, Mass.: MIT, 1989). The postmodern here appears as the dream of a "gay errancy" that thrives on the myth of a monolithic modern movement, to which it opposes an "end of prohibitionism." Vittorio Gregotti rightly notes that Tafuri's central theme in the writings on modernism is never overcoming, overturning, transgression, or

7

ity that permeates Tafuri's work is similarly that of a constant self-questioning, suffused with precisely the type of anxiety that modern art and architecture, as he interprets them, once set out to master; it is a discourse that increasingly comes to return to its conditions of possibility, not in order to rediscover a lost foundation or project a possible utopian future, but to undo the nexus between project and utopia characteristic of modernity. In this sense, the crisis is not a given situation that motivates the work, but its own aim and *telos*: the crisis is itself the project, as becomes increasingly evident in his writings from the end of the seventies.[10]

Tafuri draws on a wide array of often conflicting influences: Marx and Nietzsche, Adorno and Benjamin, Heidegger, Simmel, Weber, and the classic texts of German sociology from the first decades of the twentieth century, and all of these divergent traditions are brought together in a way that appears more as a violent enactment of tensions than as a synthesis. Thus, it would be utterly misleading to reduce his work to one figure or formula; it is rather a fusion of several motifs held in a precarious balance, sometimes entering into what seems like irresolvable conflicts. And furthermore, his work must be located in the context of the Venice School as a whole through its various phases, a history of crises, splits, and divisions that belong to the context of the Italian left of the sixties and seventies, all of which amounts to an extremely complex story that far exceeds the limits of our dis-

any other concept that would denote a going beyond, but rather *completion*; see Gregotti, "The Architecture of Completion," *Casabella*, op. cit. To this it must be added that while Tafuri never suggests that modernity could be overcome or left behind, there is still, and specifically in the work that emerged at the time of the book on Italian architecture, a kind of transgression and disruption of unity in the reading of the past, which lies at the basis of his idea of a "historical project" as presented in the introduction to *La sfera e il labirinto*.

10. For a sustained analysis of this idea, see the introduction in Biraghi, *Progetto di crisi*, 9–53.

cussion here.[11] This meandering quality notwithstanding, there is something like a basic intuition that recurs throughout most of Tafuri's various stories of modern architecture and his attacks on the illusions of operative history, and eventually folds back on his own writing: Architecture is structurally incapable of solving the contradictions that it addresses, which is just as much a theoretical presupposition as an empirical observation. The nature of this contradiction, however, will shift, from the fairly identifiable dialectic of city and nature, subjectivity and Plan, in the early work, to the multiple and shifting forces that in the later work finally make the very idea of contradiction tenuous, and instead necessitate a plurality of approaches that only with great difficulty can be brought into a dialectical matrix.

The earlier claim about a central contradiction underlies his analysis of how the modern masters were caught up in utopia—for the project is always also a utopia, as is stressed in the title *Progetto e utopia*, which is lost in the flattened English title, *Architecture and Utopia*—and thus also caught up in an ideology, which was further reinforced by generations of historians that attempted to show how these projects, if correctly understood, could contain the "hidden unity" and "secret synthesis" that will eventually heal our culture (Giedion),[12] or the "organic architecture" of the future (Zevi),[13] to cite two of the most influential

11. For discussions of the relevant political context, see Patrizia Lombardo, "Introduction: The Philosophy of the City," in Cacciari, *Architecture and Nihilism*. Pier Vittorio Aureli discusses the background in the Italian Autonomy movement, in *The Project of Autonomy: Politics and Architecture Within and Against Capitalism* (New York: Princeton Architectural Press, 2008). For surveys of Tafuri's intellectual background, see Andrew Leach, *Manfredo Tafuri: Choosing History* (Ghent: A & S, 2007), and Rixt Hoekstra, *Building vs. Bildung*, unpublished diss. (University of Groningen, 2005).

12. Giedion, *Space, Time and Architecture* (Cambridge, Mass.: Harvard University Press, 1941), vi.

13. Zevi proposes a large-scale revision of modern architecture just after the war in a trilogy of works, beginning with his *Verso un'architettura organica* (1945), followed by *Sapere vedere l'architettura* (1948), where

9

exegeses of modernism. Tafuri's critical take on his predecessors can in this sense be located within a third wave of modernist historians: the first (Giedion, Kaufmann, Pevsner) attempted to create a historical synthesis that would lend credibility to the modern movement as the true heir to the tradition; the second wanted to rethink modernism as a more complex phenomenon and retrieve aspects that had been lost or had remained underdeveloped (Zevi, Banham); those of the third wave devoted themselves to a reading of the critical limit of modernism, beyond which it could neither be simply continued nor begun anew, and which called for a step back that would take us out of architectural discourse and into a critique of modernity as such. Tafuri's work locates itself, uneasily and anxiously, on this critical line—sometimes retreating into the expertise of architectural culture, sometimes demanding a wholesale critique of society and a revolutionary action for which neither the architect nor the historian would be equipped; it lives off its own violent contradictions and its unfulfilled promises.

These contradictions are no longer directly translatable into the present, at least not in the specific form that they assumed in the landscape of Italian cultural politics of the sixties and seventies; the sharp division between operative and critical history seems difficult to uphold in the light of contemporary theoretical work on how history is written; the forms of power and subject production in the world of capitalism have become far more insidious and diversified than they were some forty years ago;

he launches a project to write a history of space, in the footsteps of Wölfflin, and finally by *Storia dell'architettura moderna* (1950, a revised edition of the 1945 book) The same year he also publishes *Architettura e storiografia*, where he constructs a monumental genealogy for organic architecture that takes us all the way back to the Stone Age, which makes him one of the most striking cases of an operative historian in Tafuri's sense. For a discussion of Zevi's historiography, see Panayotis Tournikiotis, *The Historiography of Modern Architecture* (Cambridge, Mass.: MIT, 1999).

and architecture, both as practice and theory, has moved into the digital and virtual, merging with the most sophisticated image technologies and post-Fordist forms of production, to the effect that ideas of resistance and critique might seem relics from the past, no longer capable of grasping what is in fact underway in the present.

And yet the task of critical theory remains as urgent as ever, precisely in the face of new power structures that demand a rethinking of the tools and procedures of critique. What, if any, would be the place of Tafuri and the critique of architectural ideology in this context? In the following, I will unearth some crucial aspects of Tafuri's legacy, which resonate with the question of what a critical theory—not only *of* architecture as a specific discipline, as an object *of* theory, but also in the widest possible sense, for which architecture however might hold crucial keys, so that such theoretical work might benefit from being translated *out of* architecture[14]—could mean today, and in this these issues are just as relevant to historical research as to an understanding of the present moment.

Towards a critique of architectural ideology

The work that established Tafuri as a central reference in architectural discourse, *Teorie e storia dell'architettura* (1968),[15] launches a fundamental attack on what he calls "operative criticism." By this he means an analysis that scans history in search

14. I borrow the expression "out of architecture" from Reinhold Martin, *Utopia's Ghost: Architecture and Postmodernism, Again* (Minneapolis: University of Minnesota Press, 2010). For more on this, see chap. 4, below.
15. Obviously, *Teorie e storia* does not appear *ex nihilo*, but came to be after a decade of work on both Renaissance and modern architecture. For this background work, see Giorgio Ciucci, "The Formative Years," *Casabella*, op. cit., the interview with Luisa Passerini, "History as Project," *Any* 25–26 (200), and Andrew Leach, *Manfredo Tafuri: Choosing History*. This period however remains peripheral to my question here.

of aesthetic norms, and which constructs its genealogies of the present in search of future action. Operative criticism "has as its objective the 'planning' ('*progettazione*') of a precise poetical tendency, anticipated in its structures and derived from historical analyses programmatically distorted and finalized," it is a "meeting point of history and planning" and "*plans (progetta)* past history by projecting it (*proiettandola*) towards the future."[16]

This attitude is reflected in, and underwritten by, its practical counterpart: a critical architecture that in its attempts to prefigure future social relations oscillates between utopia and playfulness, and forms an integral part of the effort to criticize architecture by architecture. The historical critique advocated by Tafuri lays claim to undo this equation, first by showing history to be a domain of problems that resists instrumental use, and then in the further claim—less an empirical observation and more a theoretical starting point, as we have noted—that it is simply illusory to believe that architecture would be capable of solving the social contradictions of the present (and, as seems to follow from this, solving any social contradiction).

What Tafuri calls for is not yet another analysis that would seek to uncover the essence of architecture, through various for-

16. *Teorie e storia dell'architettura* (Bari: Laterza, 4. ed. 1988), 161; *Theories and History of Architecture*, trans. Giorgio Verrecchia (London: Granada, 1980). 141. Henceforth cited as TS (Italian/English) *Progettazione* has here been translated as "planning," in other passages as "design." It would perhaps not be far-fetched to hear as well connotations of the idea of "project" (*Entwurf, projet*) in existential ontology from Heidegger to Sartre (and even more so in the case of *Progetto e utopia*, where the first term in the English translation is changed to "architecture"), which would imply that the project is a *projection of a nature* and aims for mastery and control. Tafuri's "project" merges several problems: apart from architectural design, we can also see traces of Heidegger's analysis of modernity and technology, Marx's theory of capital, the analysis of disenchantment in Weber, and of the dialectic of Enlightenment in Adorno and Horkheimer. Tafuri can in this sense be said to ground the modern architectural project in an encompassing analysis of all the dimensions of modernity, from metaphysics and aesthetics to technology, politics, and modes of production.

mal analyses or readings of history that retrieve unrealized possibilities, but a critique of architectural ideology, or as he puts in
the preface to the second edition of the book (1970): "just as it
is not possible to found a Political Economy based on class, so
one cannot 'anticipate' a class architecture (an architecture 'for
a liberated society'); what is possible is the introduction of class
criticism into architecture."[17] Any such prefiguring or anticipa-
tory architecture is for Tafuri locked into the illusion of a solution
through form or design, which is its primary ideological function.
And while it is true that he mobilizes a vast array of methods
and tools, in particular semiotic and structuralist, in order to account for the inherent dialectic of modern architecture, he never
undertakes any positive attempt to theorize what architecture
is, for instance in terms of linguistic or material structures, phenomenological experience, or something else, which in fact, given
his aims, would be counter-productive. Instead, as we will see,
what he wants to show is that the almost desperate attempts in
his own present, i.e., the late sixties, to grasp the language dimension of architecture, themselves result from the current crisis of
architectural language, from the very refusal of the architectural
sign to produce meaning anymore. In a certain way, one could
perhaps say that just as much as, on the one hand, Tafuri's radical historicizing seems to rest upon a conviction that architecture
indeed once was a language, he remains on the other hand just as
convinced that this is no longer the case, or that it at best is only
a dying or dysfunctional language that cannot be saved by any
attempted rescue rooted in semiology or communication theory;
in fact, the obsession with linguistic analogies that he sees in his
own present indicates that the "emergence, within architectural
criticism, of the *language problem*, is [...] a precise answer to the
language crisis of modern architecture." (TS 200/174)

17.   Cited from the English translation, xv (the 1988 Italian reprint excludes
      this preface).

13

The optimism and visionary power of the first generation of modernists has faded, and for Tafuri the postwar period heralds a false or incomplete self-critique that in turn generates a series of equally false returns, historicisms, humanisms, and empiricisms, all of which attempt to mitigate the thrust of the avant-garde by reconnecting to a past that cannot be anything but a mirage. The anti-historicism of the avant-garde was its moment of truth, Tafuri claims, in fact theirs was the only accurate response to history, and in a surprising move he traces the genealogy of the avant-gardist gesture all the way back to the Renaissance and Brunelleschi, whose intervention in Florence amounted to a radical critique of the medieval city and a new ethical imperative: "From the moment in which Brunelleschi institutionalized a linguistic code and a symbolic system based on a suprahistorical comparison with the great example of antiquity," an act that was "the first great attempt of modern history to *actualize* historical values as a translation of mythical time into present time," a "de-historicizing" began, since "the autonomous and absolute architectural objects of Brunelleschi were intended to intervene into the structures of the medieval city, upsetting and changing its significance. The symbolic and constructive self-sufficiency of the new three-dimensional spatiality radiated into the urban space a rational order that was nothing other than the absolute emblem of a strict ethical will." (TS 18f/14f)

The moment when Brunelleschi "broke the historical continuity of figurative experiences (*esperienze figurative*), claiming to be autonomously constructing a new history" (20/16), is also the remote origin of the guilt complex of modern historicists (as exemplified in Tafuri's text by Vittorio Gregotti and Louis Kahn) toward history, which thus is rooted in a more encompassing temporal structure that extends all the way back to the dawn of the early modern period. Repeating Brunelleschi's gesture, "the artistic avant-gardes of the twentieth century have pushed aside history in order to *construct* a new history," which is why this "neat cut with preceding traditions becomes, paradoxically, the symbol of an authentic historical continuity," and it constitutes "the only historically legitimate act of the time" (39/30). In the distance between us and Brunelleschi the problem of history unfolds, and it is set in motion by an inaugurating gesture that Tafuri described as an almost Nietzschean active forgetfulness; negation and not preservation is what sets temporality and historicity in motion, and the attempt to return to any of the intermediary phases is just as naïve as it is unhistorical.

This uncompromising attitude also sheds a certain light on the title of the book, the *theories* and *history* of architecture, which somewhat surprisingly amalgamates the singular and the plural. It is as if Tafuri would succumb to a rather naïve conception of a single and true *history* that would lie at the basis of all the different *theories* that attempt to capture it, making them all possible while also showing their radical insufficiency; yet it is difficult to see, on the other hand, how he could avoid acknowledging the existence of a multiplicity of *histories* or even *stories* that could be written, and that the idea of one singular history (that comes close to History in a Hegelian sense) to a great extent is the creation of the operative historians and their stylized versions of the past. In short: why not two plural forms? *Teorie e storia* is indeed as far removed as possible from conventional historiography, of which the book undertakes a ruthless methodological revision, and in its elliptic and erratic density it seems to resist all forms of instrumental use. While it is still "possible to badly misuse the book by using it for information purposes," as Tafuri says in an interview, "I wrote the book purely for my own ends [...]. It was a strange book, written without the public."[18] Conceived as a fundamental disruption or

18.   "The Culture Markets," interview with Françoise Véry, *Casabella*, op. cit., 39.

15

re-evaluation of previous historiography, its claim was nothing less that "all history had to be reassessed from the bottom up, in order to discover its theoretical foundations. We found—and personally speaking I was appalled—that even these foundations were rotten to the core [...]. This was true of the language of the avant-garde, the theoretical framework of architectural history and modern art history in general... we were locked in a castle under a spell, the keys were lost, in a linguistic maze—the more we looked for a direction, the more we entered magic halls full of tortured dreams."[19]

Regardless of the maze in which he admits to be trapped, Tafuri sometimes appears to claim that his version of historical critique is the only true science, which unlike the different versions of theory accepts that architecture cannot be grounded in itself, and in this it would be able to reach the true foundation, the ultimate bedrock of history.[20] This tension between a ruth-

19. Ibid, 37.
20. Aldor Asa Rosa, whose work during the seventies evolved in close parallel to the Venice School, defines the link between the critique of ideology and historical research such that it ends up almost as an argument for positivist objectivity, while still gesturing in the direction of a magical intuitionism. Referring to Tafuri's writings on the Renaissance, Rosa writes, "the 'critique of ideology' precedes and determines the discovery of 'philology,' and makes it both possible and necessary. Think about this: once no veil any longer exists, all that remains is to study, understand and represent the mechanisms of reality, for which one should refinedly use the instruments of *objective* inquiries (clearly, with some limits). Total disenchantment produces great historians. And Manfredo Tafuri was a great historian of this kind." (Rosa, "Critique of Ideology and Historical Practice", *Casabella*, op. cit., 35, Rosa's italics) To find true reality behind the veil seems not to be a far cry from the magical positivism that Adorno once detected in Benjamin's *Passagen-Werk*, and which is not wholly absent from Tafuri's historical work. And as Jean-Louis Cohen points out, "The notion of *critica operativa*, which Tafuri initially put out of doors, seems to have found its way back through the window," not because Tafuri at some particular moment would abandon his critical attitude and return to the propagandistic claims of classical modernist historians, but simply because what triggers the very writing of history is the perception of a current crisis, and not some disinterested stance toward past facts; see Cohen, "Ceci n'est pas

less questioning of History and the simultaneous continuation of a project to once and for all state the truth of history (*the* history of histories and theories) pervades these analyses, and it is no doubt a fundamental aspect of the crisis that lies at the origin of his writing, and which eventually will produce an anxiety on the level of his own discourse, akin to the one that was both acknowledged and repressed by the avant-garde.

Beyond the suggestion of a simple divide between theory and practice, the question must be asked as to what kind of non-relation they nevertheless in some way must entertain, a question to which Tafuri cannot be indifferent. Even if demystification only amounts to an intensified awareness of the insolvability of the constitutive contradictions, all ways of negotiating the situation cannot be equally valid. This seems to be why, on the one hand, architectural practice in Tafuri's discourse appears to be displaced by the task of the critical historian, and the choice he presents us with is a stark, even brutal one: either to develop a historical critique that unmasks ideology, or to engage in a practice subjected to the power of ideology, without the two being able to learn anything from each other. On the other hand, however, if "'[s]solutions' are not to be found in history," if "the only possible way is the exasperation of the antitheses, the frontal clash of the positions, and the accentuation of contradictions" (TS 270/237), and the "use we suggest for semiology and structural analysis should be to undertake a pitiless scrutiny of the meanings underlying 'innocent' forms and choices," then the ultimate aim is nevertheless to "confront the doer with his responsibilities" (256/214). To the question

une histoire," in *Casabella*, op. cit., 53. Some of Tafuri's own statements, where he totally rejects the idea of a "critique" that would mediate historical writing and practice seem exaggerated and philosophically naive, and to be contradicted by his own work, which is far more fluid; see the interview with Richard Ingersoll, "There is no Criticism, only History," in *Casabella*, op. cit.

of what such a responsibility entails, Tafuri seems to give an implicit answer in the reference to Max Weber's idea of value-free science that concludes the penultimate chapter: "We offer [...] those who act the possibility of measuring the unwanted consequences of their actions [...]. The translation of that measuring into decision is not the *responsibility* of science but of the man who *acts freely*" (257/216f, my italics). If the chasm between critique and practice first seems unbridgeable and appears simply to immobilize action to the extent that it would require a theoretical base, then we must also note the decisionist ring of expressions like "responsibility" and "freedom," which appear to have no strict theoretical signification within Tafuri's historical critique, but on the other hand, by appealing to an entirely subjective register, somehow binds or sutures (to use a Lacanian vocabulary) the imaginary self-understanding of the architect to the constitutive rifts of a symbolic order.[21]

This dualist scenario, where the Weberian *Wertfreiheit* escalates almost into a negation of the idea of value as such, is however contradicted by many of Tafuri's other writings. In his remarks on architects like Vittorio Gregotti and Aldo Rossi it is obvious that he perceives some attempts at responding to the crisis as more relevant than others. This appears to be based on aesthetic choices that nevertheless remain difficult to ground in his historical and theoretical analyses. A famous case of this is the often-cited words in his preface to the American translation

21.   The use of psychoanalytical vocabulary may seem out of place here, but I think it captures well how Tafuri's discourse functions on this point. The suture in Lacan is what creates a temporary link between the imaginary and the symbolic, and provides the subject with the place from which it may perceive itself and its actions as a unity. The suture cannot simply be taken as a false position in the sense that it would stand to be corrected by some improved perception of the self, and yet it obscures the dimension of truth in its fullest extent, because the latter cannot be accounted for within a theory of the subject as consciousness. For a discussion of Lacan's use of the term, see Stephen Heath, "On Suture," in Heath, *Questions of Cinema* (London: Macmillan, 1981).

of *Progetto e utopia*, where Tafuri sees the possibility of a return to "pure architecture, to form without utopia," to "sublime uselessness," as a strategy to counter the forces of the present, and claims that he "shall always prefer the sincerity of those who have the courage to speak of that silent and outdated 'purity'; even if this, too, still harbors an ideological inspiration, pathetic in its anachronism" (PU 1/39).[22] The rejection of operative critique notwithstanding, it seems reasonable to follow the suggestion of Panayotis Tournikiotis,[23] who reconstructs a Brechtian poetics of sorts between the lines in *Teorie e storia*. Such a position would in a sense be a substitute for the kind of critical architecture that is a priori impossible, and yet, a posteriori, one must be able to glimpse somewhere if critical thinking is not to end up in a pure *misérabilisme*—an architecture that in a planned estrangement dissolves myths without offering any reconciliation, places us before impossible contradictions and yet claims certain responses to be more adequate than others.

Project and utopia

In *Progetto e utopia* Tafuri provides us with his most concentrated and polemically acute version of modern architecture, understood as a process unified by its inherent contradictions.[24] The dense and

22. It is sometimes assumed that the reference here is to Peter Eisenman, although he is never named. The relation between Tafuri and Eisenman, and more generally between the New York avant-garde and the Venice School is a long-term—and indeed complex and contradictory— love affair that involves scholarly collaborations and many publications during the seventies, including the journal *Oppositions*, which played a key role in acquainting the anglophone world with Tafuri. For the institutional connections, see Joan Ockman, "Venice and New York," in *Casabella*, op. cit., and Diane Ghirardo, "Manfredo Tafuri and Architecture Theory in the U.S., 1970–2000," *Perspecta*, Vol. 33 (2002).
23. Tournikiotos, *The Historiography of Modern Architecture*, 214–19.
24. The first draft for the book, "Per una critica dell'ideologia architettonica", was published in *Contropiano* 1969; trans. Stephen Sartarelli in Hays, *Architecture Theory Since 1968*. Pier Vittorio Aureli notes that Tafuri's conception of a "critique of architectural ideology" and his

schematic form of the argument is no doubt problematic, and the perception of Tafuri as a totalizing theorist largely derives from this book; on the other hand it is the only text where he presents he something like a sustained analysis of the logic of modern architecture as a conflicted and internally broken unity, first on the level of the relation between architecture as a single artifact and the city and then, in turn, between the city and capital. This narrative, which remains a tacit presupposition, as it does—albeit in a more subdued form— in many of his other writings, fractures the synthetic unity of operative history while re-establishing this unity on another level beyond architecture, and it is admittedly what generates the dystopian mood of the text. The idea that Tafuri proclaims the death of architecture (made more emphatic by the drawing of Aldo Rossi, *L'architecture assassinée*, which became the cover of the US edition),[25] something that he himself always denied, is occasionally difficult to avoid, and even if it is not generated by a clash between theories—of architecture and (real and

rejection of operative criticism should be seen in the context of a new understanding of intellectual work, where intellectuals have become workers in a system that incorporates the forces that used to resist. Rationally planned and reformed capitalism, scientific management and modernization, became attractive options, and were identified as the new strategy of capital by the Operaista movement. The strategic invention of a "counter-plan" (*Contropiano*) implied an appropriation of the most advances parts of capitalist culture (all of which finds its echoes, Aureli notes, in current Italian political thought on cognitive work as "immaterial labor"). This required that the architect and planner were understood as intellectual workers, and not just as manipulators of formal design solutions. Seen from the perspective of the larger political context, Aureli argues, the reading of Tafuri's work as the promotion of a "death of architecture" proves to be misleading. See Aureli, "Intellectual Work and Capitalist Development."

25.   For Tafuri's shifting assessments of Rossi, from the positive claims in *Teorie e storia* about Rossi's *L'architettura della città* as delineating a genuine possibility for critical invention in the city to the negative judgment of the later work on the analogous city and its retreat into subjective fantasy, see Teresa Stoppani, "L'histoire assassinée: Manfredo Tafuri and the Present," in Soumyen Bandyopadhyay et al. (eds.), *The Humanities in Architectural Design: A Contemporary and Historical Perspective* (Milton Park: Routledge, 2010), and Biraghi, *Progetto di crisi*, 185–197.

effective) history—it is closely aligned with a certain theory *of* history that Tafuri's later work would submit to a severe scrutiny.

The already cited introductory definition of the task of bourgeois art, to "dispel anxiety by understanding and internalizing its causes," points to the unconscious entente between capital and the intellectual avant-garde, or a kind of malevolent ruse of reason, whose entanglement of sublimation and affirmation eventually reaches its point of culmination in the heroic phase of modernism. In this process, architecture, together with other arts, plays the role of trailblazer: in anesthetizing the subject it paves the way for another compliant subjectivity, it programs a new experience through a subterfuge that lets modernism appear as a protest against alienation and fragmentation while it in fact is one of the primary instruments for accelerating and rendering it not only acceptable, but also desirable.

This double move takes the form of a process of naturalizing, the initial steps of which Tafuri locates as far back as the first part of the eighteenth century. Here the mimetic exchange between art and nature enters into a phase organized around the city, which becomes the locus of a new type of architectural discourse that is made possible by a repression of its own conditions. When architecture assumes the task of shaping social relations required by the emerging capitalist order, it becomes caught up in a negative dialectic between urban form and the solitary object that will eventually dissolve the classical tradition. This opposition between object and milieu is spelled out by Abbé Laugier, when he reduces the city to nature by portraying it in terms of painting and the newly emerging theory of the picturesque, i.e., understands the city as an image. "Whoever knows how to design a park well will have no difficulty in tracing the plan for the building of a city," Laugier writes, for in both there must be "regularity and fantasy, relationship and oppositions, and casual, unexpected elements that vary the scene;

great order in the details, confusion, uproar, and tumult in the whole."[26] Laugier's anti-perspectival and anti-Cartesian gesture places nature and reason, landscape and townscape, on the same level, and just as the metaphorical grasp of the city as a piece of nature dehistoricizes it, it will also turn the process of industrialization into a natural phenomenon. Urban naturalism covers over the rift between the emerging city and a pre-capitalist rural order, and the task of architecture, or rather a certain *discourse* (the *theories*) of architecture, is to allow the Enlightenment to avoid a confrontation with its own premises. In this way, Tafuri's narrative of modern architecture combines the logic of Capital with the dialectic of Enlightenment: to hide the contradictions by formal manipulations, and to make it possible for us to enjoy them as an aesthetic-picturesque complexity, is for the Tafuri of *Progetto e utopia* the properly ideological role of architecture, which extends throughout the whole cycle of modernity up to the postwar attempts to recast architecture in terms of pop culture imagery and theories of complexity and contradiction, as in Venturi, or as a return to the typologies and the analogous city that lie dormant in history, and symptomatically may be accessed through a painterly imaginary, as in Rossi.[27]

This compensatory role of architecture, to cover over those contradictions that it itself is unable to solve, produces an inner unease that comes across in the eighteenth-century fascination with the exotic, with Indian and Chinese architecture, pavilions and false ruins—all of which are different ways of finding an "authentication from outside architecture," but that in fact initiated a "systematic and fatal autopsy of architecture and all its conventions" (PU 14/11). For Tafuri, this anxiety bears the name Piranesi, to whom he would return in many later publica-

26. Abbé Laugier, *Observations sur l'Architecture* [1765; reprint Westmead, Farnborough Hants: Gregg Press, 1996, 312f.], cited in PU 7f/4.
27. For more on Venturi and Rossi, see chap 2, below.

tions. Piranesi stages a violent fragmentation of the tradition, where a plethora of historical references whirl by in the desperate attempt of architecture to provide form to a reason whose newfound wakefulness seems to breed ever more monsters. In this, his work forebodes the danger of a complete loss of organic form, Tafuri suggests, which leads to a situation when rationality and irrationality can no longer be separated. In the visions of Piranesi's *Campo Marzio dell'antica Roma* (1761–62) we see the struggle between architecture and city, and how the ensuing crisis takes on "epic" dimensions, where the excesses of architecture, turning back to face its own aporias, disclose the truth of the dialectic of enlightenment: "In the attempt to absorb all of its own contradictions, architectural 'reasoning' applies the technique of shock to its very foundations" (18/15), and the city, whose overall unity was intended to provide a meaningful milieu for the single edifice, becomes a "gigantic 'useless machine'" (ibid). Similarly, and perhaps even more threateningly, the infinite interiors of the *Carceri* (1760) become co-extensive with reality, showing "the new existential condition of human collectivity, liberated and condemned at the same time by its own reason" (21/18), a condition of anonymity that reflects the "silence of things" (21/19).[28]

But in the wake of this loss of language there is also an opposite movement, where architecture discovers a scientific vocation that makes possible the construction of a rationalist typology, as in Durand and the "geometric silence" (PU 16/13) that his works declare in relation to the tradition, as well as, on the other hand, a new analysis of sensations, as in Ledoux and Le Camus

28.   Drawing on José Lopez-Rey's comparative analysis of Piranesi and Goya, Tafuri notes that the characters in Piranes's *Carceri* are present "more to allow the instrument of torture to function than to communicate the horrors of torture" (PU 21/19, note 10), a phrase that could have come straight out of Adorno and Horkheimer's *Dialectic of Enlightenment.*

de Mézières— although these two are finally only two sides of the same coin, i.e., the loss of a stable order of architectural language. Rational typology and the *architecture parlante* addressing sensations are the two answers to the language crisis produced by the Enlightenment. The seemingly fantastic and unrealizable quality of the projects of Boullée and Ledoux, which is what normally lends them the epithet "utopian," is thus not what is essential, rather we should see them as experiments aiming for a new design method where architecture seeks to "redimension itself, dissolving into the uniformity ensured by the preconstituted typologies" (16/13), even though the technical means for this were obviously lacking at the time.

On the level of the city, we see two analogous reactions: on the one hand a fascination with the picturesque and the complex, as in Laugier, of which Piranesi will draw the most threatening conclusions, and on the other hand a new relation to the tradition, exemplified by Giovanni Antolini's criticism of the plan for Milan. The radical architect here appears to discard all references to the historical city in favor of an integral structure that would bring all its parts together in a new way. In this bifurcation, Tafuri suggests, we can already discern how the two main currents in modern art and architecture begin to take shape via two types of response, the responses of "those who search into the very bowels of reality in order to know and assimilate its values and wretchedness," and "those who desire to go beyond reality, who want to construct *ex novo* new realities, new values, and new public symbols." (25/24)

Both of these options indicate a pervasive crisis of the idea of form as a mediating instance between architecture and urbanism. On the level of the city, the single object finds itself under the pressure of locating itself within a larger order, at the limit dissolving into the "absurd machine" envisaged by Piranesi. This is why, for Tafuri, early utopian urban theorists like Fourier, Owen, and Cabet contribute only tangentially to the experience of modernity: to the extent that they attempt to arrest the development at some earlier stage and prevent all that is solid from melting into air, they are doomed to fail, and in this, they already prefigure the corresponding failure of the moderate modern movements in the first part of the twentieth century.

Architecture was in fact the first art form that was compelled to accept reification, and it was faced with the task of integrating design into a single overarching project to organize production, distribution, and consumption within the space of the city. This it did, however, in the guise of a "Utopia of form" that made it march backwards into the future. Tafuri divides this process into three steps: 1. *The creation of an urban ideology* that overcomes the romantic critique of modernity, which still resonates in the urban utopias of the nineteenth century. 2. *The artistic avant-gardes*, which prepare the synthetic proposals of architecture in the form of seemingly contradictory and even destructive moves, which however coalesce through a kind of cunning of reason. 3. *The development of the Plan as ideology*, which Tafuri reads as the final stage of architectural modernism, before the advent of the Wall Street crash and the fundamental restructuring of capitalism, a restructuring that transferred the agency of planning from architecture to government bureaucracies and international capital.

The most provocative steps in this analysis are the second and third, which form the nucleus of Tafuri's negative dialectics of modern architecture. In the second, we encounter the disruptive gestures of the historical avant-garde, whose logic however leads it to re-create the shock of the Metropolis as an inner experience that we eventually end up affirming, as if it were the highest expression of our freedom. Baudelaire (Tafuri's interpretation here largely follows Benjamin) registers this in his reflections on the collision of mass and individual, even though the poet has yet to internalize the Metropolis as his own nature, and he remains torn between the attempt to save his individuality and a desire to throw himself into the anonymous flux of the city. He is driven by the urge to re-create the plentitude of the work, drawing on mythical correspondences between signs and ideas, while he is just as much conditioned by the prostitution of the commodity world and a leveling of the symbolical dimension that enters into the innermost core of his work.

For the ideology of consumption to be developed fully, Tafuri suggests that it must be understood as the only authentic use of the city. This means that the blasé attitude of the *flâneur* has to be transformed into active participation, and the process of liquefaction of values must appear to the emerging metropolitan subject as flowing from its own spontaneity. This will be the complex task of the historical avant-garde, which involves a whole set of nested operations: to liberate the experience of shock from automatism; to develop visual codes expressive of speed, transformation, simultaneity, and eclecticism; to reduce artistic experience to a pure object, which in turn can function as a cipher for the commodity; to involve the audience in anti-bourgeois ideology that transcends class distinctions. Across the artistic spectrum Tafuri discerns such moves being prepared and tried out, in cubism, futurism, Dadaism, and constructivism, which, even though they deploy these strategies with different aims, converge in the technique of collage or assemblage, where "the picture becomes a neutral field on which to project the *experience of the shock* suffered in the city"—the next task being that "one is not to 'suffer' that shock, but to absorb it, introject it as an inevitable condition of existence." (PU 80/86)

Tafuri here draws on Simmel's analysis of the new personality produced by monetary economy. This would be a subject who is able to deal with an intensified "nervous life" and the overwhelming assault of impressions in the Metropolis, by perceiving all singular values as devoid of substance. "All things float," Simmel writes, "with equal specific gravity in the constantly moving stream of money. All things lie on the same level and differ from one another only in the size of the area which they cover."[29] Does not such a description, Tafuri asks, where objects are transformed into interchangeable signs located on the same plane, already apply to Schwitters's *Merzbild*—and even more so if we see "-merz" as a truncated part of *Commerz*? The avant-garde taps into the new energies released by the downfall of inherited values and symbolical forms, and does so in order to transform shock and anguish into a productive force—it moves "from the anguished discovery of the nullification of values, to the *use* of a language of pure signs, perceptible by a mass that had completely introjected the universe without quality of the money economy" (PU 82/ 89). This also means that the old question of the unpopularity of the avant-garde, of its inability to reach the masses, regardless of whether this allegation is voiced by the right or the left, misses the point: the task of the avant-garde is to prepare, program, and project the future, to create new models for action that only later are to become familiar and be put to use in everyday life.

For Tafuri, cubism, in all of its seeming inwardness and focus on interiors and domestic utensils, is precisely such a project to organize human behavior within a machine universe, but also a strategy in which the will to master form strikes back at the artists. Form becomes the subjective response of the artist within an

29. Simmel, "Metropolis and Mental Life" (1903), cited in PU 81/87f. Tafuri's reading of Simmel here draws on Massimo Cacciari, who, rather idiosyncratically, takes Simmel's analysis to be pointing to an eradication of subjectivity, instead of to the specific and new forms of subjectivity and "mental life" (or better: "spiritual life," *Geistesleben*) that develops in the Metropolis because of the predominance of "objective spirit," which Simmel understands in a Hegelian sense.

27

objective universe of production, at the same time that cubism as a movement rejects subjectivism in order to discover the collage as a momentarily resolved tension between freedom and necessity, a dynamic contradiction that provides an "absolute form to the discursive universe of the *civilisation machiniste*" (84/91). And when Mondrian finally shows that it is the city itself that is the proper object of art, then painting must either die or be sublated in an almost Hegelian fashion, as if to underscore the transitory quality of the works of the avant-garde, their hidden intention to become part of a productive logic that annuls their status as art.

Here it can be noted that Tafuri's interpretation is at once close to and opposed to the one that would be suggested by Peter Bürger a year later, in his *Theorie der Avantgarde* (1974). For Bürger, the historical avant-garde fails to break down the barrier between art and life that had been set up by late nineteenth-century aestheticism, and what its project to rebuild everyday life on an artistic basis in fact achieves is a limitless expansion of the institution art, which makes it possible for the subsequent postwar neo-avant-garde to repeat the tragedy inherent in the first gesture in the form of a farce. Tafuri's perspective is more complex, however, since he includes architecture (which Bürger leaves out of the picture) as the organization of an entire cycle of production, within which the attempts of the other avant-gardes in literature and the visual arts to rebuild life are passing moments that in themselves tend toward a synthesis in architecture and design, whose utopias, as we will see, in turn were predetermined to be dissolved in Capital. Thus, for Tafuri just as for Bürger, the failure of the avant-garde lies in its success, although in Tafuri's case not in the creation of a henceforth fully autonomous art, but in the remodeling of the subject as the active participant in a universe of commodities, in which the autonomy of the institution art may be taken as a specific but limited consequence.

28

Before this process is completed, its penultimate stage appears in the form of a dialectic between form and chaos, where on the one hand movements like De Stijl aspire to control production and absorb chaos, and Dadaism, on the other hand, claims to show the absurdity of the world. But, Tafuri suggests, the nihilism of the latter is only propaedeutic, and finally ends up under the control of the former: Dadaism demonstrates the necessity of the Plan without being able to name it, which is shown by the convergence of these movements in the beginning of the twenties.[30] Dissolution of form and leveling of content give rise to a new constructive program that takes its point of departure in the limitless availability of materials and signs produced as an involuntary result of the preceding avant-garde.

In this way the various and diverging avant-garde movements are eventually absorbed in an expanded concept of architecture, which also throws them into crisis by presenting them with a systematic answer to their questions. This can be seen in the case of the Bauhaus, Tafuri claims, which operated as the "decantation chamber of the avant-garde" (PU 90/ 98), by systematically testing all the previous strategies with a view to their efficiency in reality and to the demands of production, and dissolved the utopian moment into an ideology operative as a moment immanent in activity itself.

In creating such an immanent ideology, architecture found itself suspended between two positions: it affirmed the plan as a way to organize the whole of production and consumption, but at the same time wanted to retain its autonomy as architecture,

30.   A singular and interesting example of this analysis would be the fate of the Dada poet Paul Dermée, who was replaced as editor-in-chief of *L'Esprit Nouveau* after the subtitle of the journal was changed from *esthétique contemporaine* to *activité contemporaine*, which indicates the shift from an intra-artistic program to one that aspires to take on the environment in its integrality; see the comments on this shift in Beatriz Colomina, *Privacy and Publicity: Modern Architecture as Mass Medium* (Cambridge, Mass.: MT, 1994), 361 note 1.

i.e., as a unique producer of aesthetic form, as can be seen for instance in Le Corbusier's claim to having revived a classical canon of beauty, or, as Reyner Banham suggests, in the continued presence of the Beaux-Arts tradition in modernist architectural composition.[31]

It is on the basis of these contradictions that Tafuri analyzes the attempts of the New Objectivity ("die Neue Sachlichkeit")[32] to adjust to the model of the assembly line, and all the compromises that characterize the struggle between Objectivity and expressionism. In its profound fascination for Taylorism in all of its forms, Tafuri sees an attempt—after the disappearance of the aura, i.e., the entry of the architectural work into the age of mechanical reproducibility as analyzed by Benjamin— to seize control over the entire process from the singular element to the city-totality, within which the individual object is dissolved in a cycle that also mobilizes the user and lays claims to displace

31. See Banham's introductory discussion in *Theory and Design in the First Machine Age* (London: Architectural Press, 1960), 14–23.

32. *Die neue Sachlichkeit* was an artistic movement that went far beyond architecture. Its roots were in literature, painting, photography, and cinema (the term was first used by Felix Hartlaub in 1923 with reference to a planned exhibition of post-expressionist art in Mannheim that eventually took place in 1925), and its general significance cannot be reduced to Tafuri's rather cursory reading. It is true that *Sachlichkeit* was generally perceived as opposed to the subjectivism of expressionism, but we must also bear in mind that the adjective "sachlich" may be translated more precisely as "relevant to the matter," "pertinent," etc., and that it also contains a reference to the *Sache*, the "matter" or "thing." In this sense *Sachlichkeit* means to pay heed to the things themselves, without prejudices, and it contains a stroke of pragmatism—a term, it should be recalled, derived from the Greek *pragma*, "thing". For a general survey of *Sachlichkeit* in literature, with a rich collection of source documents, see Sabina Becker, *Neue Sachlichkeit*, 2 vol. (Cologne: Böhlau, 2000); for the application of the term to painting and photography, see Hans Gotthard Vierhuff, *Die Neue Sachlichkeit: Malerei und Fotografie* (Cologne: DuMont, 1980). The most imprecise use of term is in fact in the field of architecture, where the term (sometimes used as a synonym for "Neues Bauen") often seems equivalent to the Bauhaus or even modern architecture in general, and its roots lie in the conflict in the Werkbund over industrial "typification" vs. traditional crafts.

older forms of aesthetic experience.[33] The open spaces of Mies and Gropius aspire to include the user in the organization of a collective life where, as Tafuri sarcastically notes, "Morris's romantic socialist dream—an art made by all for all—takes ideological form within the iron-clad laws of profit." (PU 94/101f) Tafuri's main example is Ludwig Hilberseimer's visionary manifesto *Großstadtarchitektur* (1927), which proposes the most radical model for the dissolution of the traditional architectural language.[34] Hilberseimer constructs an unbroken conti-

33.   In relation to a traditional humanist culture this may be perceived as a loss of substance, akin to the Nietzschean "devaluation of the highest values." This could be seen as situation where man errs into nothingness and becomes a "sleepwalker," as the novelist Hermann Broch portrays this transformation in his monumental trilogy *Sleepwalkers* (1931–32), whose respective parts each signal a crucial historical moment, taking us from the end of romanticism, through anarchy, to objectivity: *The Romantic*, *The Anarchist*, and *The Realist* (the original German titles also contain references to the respective main protagonists as well precise chronological markers: *1888: Pasenow, oder, Die Romantik*; *1903: Esch, oder, Die Anarchie*; *1918: Huguenau, oder, Die Sachlichkeit*). In the last part, in a series of essays called "Excursus on the Disintegration of Values" (in the novel presented as the works of "Bertrand Müller, doctor of philosophy"), Broch elaborates a vision of modernity in terms of a fragmentation of the different spheres of value—war for war's sake, art for art's sake, profit for profit's sake, etc.—and in the end, the main character Huguenau seems to embody an idea of "Sachlichkeit" as sheer opportunism, so that he in opting for personal gain in fact returns us to an empty and directionless subjectivism. Others understood *Sachlichkeit* as a possibility of extracting a different from of experience, endowed with a particular truth of its own, from the mechanization and serialization of the metropolis. For a analysis of *Sachlichkeit* along these lines, which also draws on the writings of Kracauer, Benjamin, and others proponents of the avant-garde, see K. Michael Hays, *Modernism and the Posthumanist Subject: The Architecture of Hannes Meyer and Ludwig Hilberseimer* (Cambridge, Mass: MIT, 1992).

34.   Ludwig Hilberseimer, *Grossstadtarchitektur* (Stuttgart: Julius Hoffman, 1927). Tafuri limits himself to Hilberseimer's radical proposals from the late twenties, and disregards his later work on the decentralization of cities, which leads up to a complete integration of landscape and urban space. Hilberseimer developed these ideas in his work in the US (*The New City*, 1944), at the IIT, where he worked closely with Mies van der Rohe. For a comprehensive analysis of Hilberseimer's successive theories of city planning, see Markus Kilian, *Grossstadtarchitektur: Eine planungsmetodische Untersuchung der Stadtplanung Ludwig Hilberseimers* (unpublished PhD dissertation, University of Karlsruhe, 2002).

nuity from the basic cell to the city in its totality, so that they in the end appear as the two endpoints of a single chain. The Metropolis is one big machine, where the basic unity lies on this side of traditional form, and the unity to be created lies beyond it, which means that the single edifice no longer constitutes a privileged or even interesting object, only a relative and mobile cut in a more encompassing structure. Place and space, nuances and exceptions must disappear in the Metropolis, Hilberseimer argues, and with them all of architecture's traditional dimensions. The strict reduction to cubic and geometric shapes, which in a sense are scale-less because of the erasure of all natural models, takes us away from the experiencing subject, or, more precisely, takes us in the direction of a transformed experience in which exchangeability and uniformity can be affirmed as such.

Hilberseimer thus states with cold precision, more clearly than any of his contemporaries— Taut, Gropius, or Mies—what modern capitalism needs. The architect as a producer of objects belongs to the past, and the real task is to organize the city as a cycle of production and to invent organizational models. In this *Großstadtarchitektur*, there is simply no more crisis of the object, Tafuri notes, since the object has already disappeared. Consequently, Hilberseimer no longer understands architecture as an instrument of knowledge, and the conflict between Objectivity and the expressionism of architects like Poelzig and Häring signals in a precise manner this divide between the cognitive and the technological, with no possibility of an exchange between them. The expressionist arrière-garde could in one sense have been able to play a critical role in relation to the reductive program of Objectivity, Tafuri suggests, but they were unable to propose true alternatives on the same level of technological objectivity, precisely because they depended on a model that belonged to the residual and not the emergent.

These two sides eventually clash in what constitutes the dramatic turning point in *Progetto e utopia*, when the reformist compromise that believes it possible to restore a natural equilibrium enters into a final crisis in the Siemensstadt project (1929–31). For Tafuri, this is the place where "one of the most serious ruptures within the 'modern movement' became evident," and he sees it as "incredible that contemporary historical study has not yet recognized this" (PU 107/116). The affirmation of a uniform design method that can be applied on different scales is derived directly from the utopian aspect, but the resulting dissolution of the architectural object only exacerbated the inner contradictions. For Tafuri this is the emergence of the unsolvable conflict between those architects whose aim was to save the aura, subjectivity, and expression (Scharoun and Häring) and those who adopted the assembly line as their model (Gropius and Bartning).

Siemensstadt is only one example out of many of the crises that the idea of the city traversed, although for Tafuri it takes on a paradigmatic value. He applies a similar argument to Ernst May and the large-scale undertaking "Das neue Frankfurt," which begins in 1925 and is the most systematic attempt at a concrete politicizing of architecture on the basis of a social-democratic model. Other cases are the plans of Martin Wagner (for Berlin), Fritz Schumacher (for Hamburg), and Cor van Eesteren (for Hamburg), each of which met with varying degrees of success (the most successful for Tafuri being Amsterdam), although they ultimately were caught up in a negative dialectic between the restoration of traditional values and the ineluctable logic of the Metropolis. Everywhere we find the same aspirations for a close alliance between leftist intellectuals, advanced parts of capital, and political administrations, but only a limited application in practice. For Tafuri this is due to the rootedness of the *Siedlung* structure in an anti-urban ideology, in an idea of *Gemeinschaft* that has already been devoured by the urban logic.

33

The *Siedlung* "was to be an oasis of order, an example of how it is possible for working-class organizations to propose an alternative model of urban development, a realized utopia. But the settlement itself openly set the model of the 'town' against that of the large city. This was Tönnies against Simmel and Weber" (PU 109/119); it was unavoidable that it end up being swallowed by the all-consuming development of capital. For Tafuri, any reformist attempts at restoring a lost balance are doomed in advance, and in the Siemensstadt project he locates the decisive internal crisis of the modern movement, already before the totalitarian repression would set in. The tension between those who wanted to save the aura of architecture, and those who opted for seriality and standardization, could no longer be mitigated, and from this moment on everything that followed was self-deception.

In the story presented in *Progetto e utopia*, where the postwar period only appears as a negative echo of a history already having traversed a full cycle, there is another hero, whose work by no means escapes the contradictions of the Siemensstadt moment, but somehow manages to transform them into a personal poetic: Le Corbusier, whose attempt to combine the "maximum level of programming of productivity" with the "maximum level of the 'productivity of spirit'" was carried out "with a lucidity that has no comparison in progressive European culture" (PU 115/125). In Corbusier we find a strict and yet flexible form of organization, in which capital, planners, and users were to collaborate in the most efficient way, and technology was to appear authentic and natural (whereas in someone like Hilberseimer it still appears as something rigid, external, and imposed from above, and thus as something that would simply *overtake* subjective experience instead of being its self-expression). Tafuri traces Corbusier's successive elaborations throughout the twenties of a series of concepts and analytical models, with a focus on his urban visions, in which the landscape as whole must become an integral part, and the natural site is absorbed into the project, as if in a final reversal of the Enlightenment analogy of city and landscape. The main case here is the Plan Obus for Algiers (1930), which summarizes this phase in a supreme gesture that understands the landscape elements as so many "true and properly *ready-made objects*" (117/127), and that takes possession of space in its entirety, and reduces it to a field of transformational possibility: "The technological universe ignores the *here* and the *there*," and the space of its operations is a "pure topological field" (118/128).

This system requires that we create a systematic articulation between production and consumption. Later, when Corbusier would say in *Poème de l'angle droit* (1955) that he wants the entire landscape to form a single image, a "dance of contradictions," then it is because only such an image allows the freedom of individual response and the necessity of the plan to come together. The techniques of shock, embodied in the various *objets à réaction poétique* proposed by Corbusier, are intended to involve the users at every level, to make them feel like active planners when they indulge in their own eccentric behavior, or in Tafuri's more cynical formula: to allow the public to "express its own bad taste" (PU 121/132). Similarly, on the level of technology there is a demand for flexibility and modulation in details, and with the Plan Obus we are confronted with the highest form of a *civilisation machiniste* —which is why we here, too, can detect the decisive crisis of the modernist Plan around 1930.

The question why none of Corbusier's large-scale projects were ever realized for Tafuri becomes synonymous with the question why the modern movement as such suffered a shipwreck against the rock of reality, or more precisely, of capital. To be sure, Corbusier can be taken as a paradigm for a pure intellectual who works without assignment, and his projects become visions without a basis in political and industrial processes. But more than just a personal shortcoming, this is also, above all, a symptom of a more profound inner contradiction in modern architecture as such, and it is this level that the reasons for Corbusier's failure must be sought.

Many historians have accounted for the crisis of modernism through references to the emergence of Stalinism and Nazism, but for Tafuri this obscures the question of architecture's own, internal relation to capital. This relation undergoes a profound mutation after 1929, which can be seen in the global restructurings within the New Deal as well as in the first five-year plans in the Soviet Union. The model we find in Keynes's *General Theory of Employment, Interest and Money* (1936) is the same as the one underlying the poetics of modern art, Tafuri suggests: to absorb and control the future in the present, and this is the moment when the plan as ideology (of architecture) passes over into reality (of political economy). The crisis of architecture sets in at the precise junction in history when capital and government bureaucracies make the objectives of the plan their own, which severs the link between architecture's project and its utopia, or rather renders its project obsolete and possible to uphold only on the level of personal fantasies, as in the case of Corbusier.

Later, in the postwar development that Tafuri only sketches as a kind of postscript, the response of architects was to develop a critique of technological civilization, or a new focus on the immanent problems of design itself. This is also the period of humanist revivals and various kinds of empiricisms, as well as of attempts to overcome the contradictions by providing them with aesthetic representations in a new image culture or theories of complexity. In a couple of strokes, as bold as they are reductive, Tafuri surveys the theoretical discussions of late modern architecture: the city as image (Lynch), the discussion with pop art (Venturi), architecture as situation (Constant), anti-design, attempts to control technology through a new appreciation of fantasy,[35] as so many attempts to evade the real problem, which is the degradation of architecture to a mere tool. And even though Tafuri never speaks of the death of architecture, one must nevertheless acknowledge that *Progetto e utopia* ends on a somber and pessimistic note; if architecture's death is not imminent, this does not imply that it lives on as before, but instead that it no longer constitutes the place where the true stakes are located, which is why it can mobilize all the resources of the imaginary, precisely as dissociated from the real.

It would be tempting to relate this diagnosis to the many similar endgames proposed at the same time, none of which, to be sure, entail any kind of simple cessation, but rather variations on a closure that calls for acts of anamnesis and working-through:[36] painting, the novel, even art as such, variation on the end which in hindsight all seem like reactions to the loss not only of the great organic forms of the nineteenth century, but, more profoundly, also of the category of the work as such. For a moment, admittedly brief, the epithet "postmodern" offered itself as an affirmative—or perhaps operative in Tafuri's sense—concept for this shift, and his work no doubt inadvertently contributed to this perception. What he offers can however in fact be seen as a highly critical analysis of the conditions of emergence of such a concept, which for him would be doomed to repeat the gestures of the historical avant-garde, although of-

35. Tafuri stresses the role played by Pierre Restany, whose role as a critic was crucial for the development of a French version of Pop Art, Le Nouveau Réalisme, and he notes that while many of its proposals were similar to those of the first avant-garde, in Restany's case they acquire a wholly different sense. For him, alienation must be overcome by a synthesis of technology and imagination, a "prospective aesthetic" that joins high-tech and Marcuse as a way of realizing Utopia here and now without any transformation of the relations of production.

36. For the connection between "endgame" and the Freudian "working-through" (*Durcharbeiten*), see Yve-Alan Bois, "Painting: The Task of Mourning," in Bois, *Painting as Model* (Cambridge, Mass.: MIT, 1990).

fering us neither project nor utopia, only the simulacrum of a transgression since long sunk into obsolescence and destined to become part of a culture of image consumption.

In this perspective, the obsession of the sixties with models derived from linguistics and communication theory appears like a repetition of the strategies of the avant-garde, "the first—still utopian—attempt at capital's complete domination over the universe of development" (PU 140/151), now remodeled into a project for achieving global cybernetic control. In this these models are the heirs of formalist theory, one of the decisive legacies of the early twentieth century, which reduced the symbolically dense forms of the tradition to pure signs, but was fundamentally unable to create anything but a technological utopia that in the end was apolitical,[37] and thereby easily could be adapted to modern marketing, so that the permanent destruction of values that was once the strategy of the avant-garde so seamlessly could pass over into the logic of consumption: "it is not by pure chance," Tafuri writes, "that historically the end of formalism is always to end by the *work on form* being used for 'advertising'" (153/163). In the case of architecture, this loss of

37. "This is completely clear in the case of such figures as Moholy-Nagy, Hannes Meyer, Schwitters, or Walter Benjamin," Tafuri writes (PU 142/153). Tafuri here bases his claim on Moholy-Nagy's brief 1922 essay "Constructivism and the Proletariat" (see Richard Kostalenetz [ed.], *Moholy-Nagy* [New York: Praeger, 1970], 185–86), which might seem far too meager a basis for his claims, both with respect to Benjamin and Russian constructivism, none of which proposed the idea of a pure, non-political technology. As Christina Kiaer points out, Tafuri's interpretation converges with the one proposed by Jean Baudrillard in *Pour une critique de l'économie politique du signe* (1972), against which she oppose an analysis that does justice to the dimension of fantasy and bodily experience in constructivism: see Kiaer, "Rodchenko in Paris," *October* 75 (Winter 1996). Furthermore, that Benjamin's understanding of technology would have been non-political seems like a curiously misguided proposal, and Tafuri on many other occasions argues the opposite. Regardless of such particular debatable cases, the question however remains whether, in the end, this affects Tafuri's general thesis about the avant-garde and technology.

authority finally leads to an ironic reversal: since it no longer is capable of taking control of the environment, architecture turns inwards, perhaps as the last and distorted echo of the "fatal autopsy" undertaken by Piranesi, and discovers the historical heritage that it was itself instrumental in breaking down, revealing it to be so many aestheticized illusions.

The plural ends of modernism

Tafuri's argument in *Progetto e utopia* rests on an unmistakable determinism, which in classic Marxist fashion, and in the name of a faith—never explicitly acknowledged as such, and yet surely one of its *operative* tools—in the linear development of history, a priori rejects all reformism as ideology, and as a refusal to acknowledge the true problem. As Hilde Heynen remarks,[38] Tafuri analyzes all the theories that could be seen as attempts to redirect the development—the garden city in all its varieties, the American Regional Planning Association, Frank Lloyd Wright's Broadacre City, Bruno Taut's *Auflösung der Stadt*—in terms of a nostalgia for Tönnies's *Gemeinschaft*, and their anti-capitalism is scorned as a "rejection of the highest level of capitalist organization, the desire to regress to the infancy of humanity" (PU 112/122).

If *Progetto e utopia* leaves us with rather gloomy prospects, this is already inscribed into the very force of its argument, which often becomes just as much a weakness. The desire for systematic closure generates a problem that seems like an inversion of the problem of operative criticism diagnosed five years earlier in *Teorie e storia*, this time however as a conflict between the demands of a singular *theory*, and the empirical vicissitudes of

38. See Heynen's discussion of "Das neue Frankfurt" in *Architecture and Modernity* (Cambridge, Mass.: MIT, 1999), 44–71, and of Tafuri, ibid., 130–137; cf. also Michael Müller, *Funktionalität und Moderne: Das neue Frankfurt und seine Bauten 1925–1933* (Cologne: Rudolf Müller, 1984).

39

the many histories whose multiplicity is reduced on the level
of conceptual organization, already from the initial analysis of
the Enlightenment dialectic between city and nature onward.
As Fredric Jameson notes, the monolithic picture of history in
Progetto e utopia is closely connected to the rejection of operative
criticism, and together they risk producing a paralyzing image.
Regardless of the non-synchronicities that Tafuri discerns in singular architects and individual works, and in all those moments
where the course of history seems undecided, they are nevertheless realigned with the general narrative, within which the end
seems prescribed by the beginning. Jameson reads Tafuri here
in parallel with Adorno's idea of a negative dialectic, which is
of course quite justified, as long as one bears in mind that, for
Adorno, this dialectic has as its aim to unravel the capacity of
the work to preserve something of the non-identical, and that
the monadic quality of the work cannot be thought without
some trace of an imageless utopia, no matter how feeble, being retained, whereas Tafuri, at least as portrayed by Jameson,
seems to end up as an account of the final stage of an administered world without exit.[39]

39.   See Jameson, "Architecture and the Criticism of Ideology" (1985),
       in *The Ideologies of Theory: Essays 1971–1986. Vol. 2, The Syntax of History*
       (Minneapolis: University of Minnesota Press, 1988). Jameson compares
       Progetto e utopia to Roland Barthes's *Le dégre zéro de l'écriture*, and above
       all to Adorno's *Philosophie der neuen Musik*, to which it has many striking
       affinities. Adorno proposes a reading of the development of modern
       music since Beethoven and the demise of classical forms up to the
       dialectical conclusion in Schönberg, where a subjectivity externalized in
       the technical system of dodecaphonic composition procedures strikes
       back at the mimetic impulse, and eventually leads to a stasis: *the dialecti-
       cal composer brings the dialectic to a halt*, in Adorno's dense formula. This
       is close to Tafuri's analysis of how the singular objects are dissolved in
       the assembly line conceptions of *Sachlichkeit*, in which the architect, just
       as the composer in dodecaphony, encounters his own subjectivity in the
       form of an external and estranged system, which in turn had been creat-
       ed in order to safeguard the artist's own rationality, control, and capac-
       ity to plan and project—the artist has been reduced, as Adorno suggests
       with an intricate paradox, to simply carrying out his own intentions.

These hard and seemingly uncompromising statements in *Progetto e utopia* are mitigated considerably in Tafuri's subsequent work on modernism (leaving aside here the formidable scholarship on the Renaissance that would follow, and the publication of *Storia dell'architettura italiana*, which is the last book-length study devoted to the present). It is as if the unswerving negativity of *Progetto e utopia* somehow was a necessary step, a way of getting rid of modernism's utopias and linear histories, by presenting them with grimmest possible counter-version of their own claims, in order to free a different sense of history as multiple and undecided.

Three years after *Progetto e utopia* Tafuri returns to the same moment in the monumental historical survey *L'architettura contemporanea* (co-written with Francesco Dal Co), where the dystopian tone of the earlier book has been subdued, no doubt first of all because of the very character of the historical survey, which demands attention to details and the inclusion of material refractory to the dialectical dramatization of the former book, whose intent was fundamentally polemical, or a "critique of architectural ideology," as was the title of a draft from 1969. But while many details remain the same, including some, though not all, of the crucial points of articulation, the overall approach has undergone important shifts, and rather than attempting to

As Hilde Heynen remarks (*Architecture and Modernity*, 248, note 185), Jameson pays little attention however to the specific philosophical context of Tafuri's claims, i.e., the theory of a non-dialectical, non-Hegelian negativity in Cacciari, which draws more on Benjamin than Adorno. As far as *Progetto e utopia* is concerned, it is true that Benjamin's analyses of Baudelaire and Paris in Tafuri are integrated as descriptive moments, but the question is whether anything remains of the idea of a dialectic "standing still", and of the dialectical image as the irruption of utopian forces from prehistory; the negative remarks on Benjamin's allegedly non-political understanding of technology suggest that this is not the case, or at least that these more positive Benjaminian concepts are left in a mere juxtaposition to a narrative that seems to preclude them. Tafuri's later writings in this respect indicate a more complex reading of Benjamin.

survey the almost 450 pages of dense analyses as a whole, in the following some of these displacements will constitute the guiding thread: first the introductory part that suggests a new methodological caution, and then the analysis of the postwar crisis of modernism, which, as we will see, proposes a reading of *multiple endings* instead of a movement leading up to a decisive contradiction that secretly had been guiding the dialectic throughout its entire course.

In the first paragraph of the introduction, Tafuri and Dal Co begin by pointing out the Janus-faced nature of modern architecture, but also its divergent, rather than simply dual nature: born out of a loss of identity inherited from humanism, it consists of a series of subjective efforts to retrieve this identity, which, however, all point in different directions; indeed, the very idea of a modern movement as a "collective and teleological doctrine" is "itself the product of a reassuring, but entirely inoperative fable, one whose origin we must seek out, whose function we must analyze."[40] They stress the complexity of their task, and that the history of architecture comprises many levels and intersections, from the control over the environment to intellectual labor in all of its aspects: "Obviously," they now write, "the intersection of all those manifold stories will never end up in a unity." (MA 7) Instead of the unidirectionality that gave *Progetto e utopia* its monolithic quality, what must now be made visible in this history is "whatever cracks and gaps [that] break up its compactness" (ibid.), which, as we will see, is also what provides the future with a different sense of openness.

Rather than in the dialectic of nature and city in the eigh-

40.   *L'architettura contemporanea* (Milan: Electa, 1976); trans. Robert Erich Wolff, *Modern Architecture* (London: Faber and Faber, 1986), 7. Henceforth cited as MA with page number. That this "fable," once the stock in trade of operative criticism, is now deemed "inoperative," may be a coincidental remark, yet it signals a different use of these terms than before.

teenth century, in Laugier and Piranesi—who earlier formed the outer limit of an entire cycle ending somewhere in the postwar period—the narrative now takes a new and chronologically less distant departure in the nineteenth century and Art Nouveau (which had disappeared from sight altogether in *Progetto e utopia*), thus bringing us closer to traditional modernist historiography, but also signaling the desire to avoid the sense of an encompassing dialectic. As a "*negative* prologue" (MA 12), Art Nouveau was an attempt to save a lost totality, "more the exhaustion of a world than the advent of new horizons" (13), after which the narrative moves to urbanism in nineteenth-century America, the birth of modern town planning, the architecture of American cities from 1870 to 1900, Catalan Modernism and Northern Romanticism, until it reaches the drama around the Werkbund, the Bauhaus, and the "Role of the Masters." In *Progetto e utopia* the analysis of the early modern masters formed the nucleus of the argument, the moment of *peripeteia* in modernism, after which it could only continue as self-deception or as a series of retreats, gradually delinking project from utopia in various aestheticizing moves; something of this indeed remains here, although the overall framing has been substantially displaced.

The analysis of the Siemensstadt case, whose crucial role on *Progetto e utopia* we have noted, at first sight remains the same, and it is once again staged as a conflict between the model of the assembly line and the lingering idea of expression: here there was a "head-on clash between the two dominant trends of central European avant-garde architecture: the 'formal void'— homage to the ascetic rigorism of the new objectivity—was challenged by the return to an architecture of images justified by appealing to an 'organic' myth." (MA 161). But rather than a dramatic shift, taking us from one sense of ideology to another—from the affirmative link between project and utopia that undergirded the fantasy of Architecture, to the repressed insight into its impossibility, subsequently generating a series of distorted compromise formations and defense mechanism, in an almost Freudian sense—it is now a moment in a dialectic that has many more stages and possibilities. This does not mean that modernism simply continues with its business as usual, only that the trauma is as it were built into what is to come as a generative possibility, and must be accounted for in much greater detail. Modernism now ends in many ways: tragically, by fading away, in stale repetitions, in weak compromises and loss of creative power—all of which are options worked out in detail in the chapter "The Activity of the Masters After World War II," which will be in focus in the following.

Generally, what the postwar period brought about was a dissolution of the "common language" that still remained on the horizon before the war, and a "multi-faceted debate which has now arrived at a final accounting" (MA 306), i.e., an account that surveys the various dissolutions of modernisms, all of which followed individual and highly sinuous trajectories, but can still be sorted into a few basic categories.

In the first group we find Auguste Perret, Walter Gropius, and Erich Mendelsohn, all of whom attempted to retain their prewar styles, but were unable to come to grips with the reality of the postwar landscape other than as surrender or a flight into the merely personal; in this sense, they are examples of an increasing irrelevance, and receive rather scant attention. Perret's persistent *esprit de géométrie*, only apparently rooted in technology, Tafuri and Dal Co suggest, on one level made it possible for him to extend his private language to the city, while he was continually aware that he was defending an anachronistic tradition, and his attempts at welding together the Beux-Arts language with new urban contexts was not, in the end, a way forward. Gropius and Mendelsohn, on the other hand, were marked by a rupture with Weimar and more generally European culture, and if Gropius remained faithful to rationalism, in the US he succumbed to an impersonal teamwork in which he was reduced to the role of a methodologist, leading his personality to disappear into the anonymity of American professional life. Mendelsohn for his part wanted to remain a master, and his expressionist prewar work was overtaken by personal lay mysticism, which only amounted to weary variations on older themes, Tafuri and Dal Co conclude.

If this first group is treated rather cursorily, the core of the chapter, at least the section that has provoked the most responses, deals with Mies (who had remained in the background in *Progetto e utopia*, where the position of radical reductionism and objectivity was ascribed to Hilberseimer). Instead of the kind of waning of creative power or mere repetition that characterize the first three protagonists in the postwar drama, Mies's American trajectory takes him toward a negation, alternately described as silence, withdrawal, and resistance to the kind of modernity that his work nevertheless inhabits to the fullest extent—a negation that can only become effective by pushing the present to its utmost limit.[41] Entering into the zeitgeist is for Mies a "categorical imperative" that, paradoxically, breeds a "supreme indifference" (MA 309) which marks both his pre- and postwar work, a nihilism closely related to the famous "almost nothing" (*beinahe nichts*, later transformed by Philip Johnson into the more catchy and no doubt misleading "less is more") that also, equally paradoxically, means to take on the transformed postwar cityscape.

Beginning with Mies's first major work in the US, the campus at Illinois Institute of Technology, Tafuri and Dal Co suggest that the isolation of the work from its context, a feature already present in early Mies, is the key issue. At the IIT, Crown

41. For a more detailed overview of various interpretations of this idea of silence and withdrawal, see my *The Silences of Mies*.

Hall constitutes a geometric prism lifted up from the ground, further emphasizing the caesura from the surroundings that had characterized Farnsworth House two years earlier. But rather than a purism, Tafuri and Dal Co perceive this as a reduction to minimal signs that create a kind of collusion of fact and value, which they summarize with Karl Krauss's laconic statement: "Since the facts have the floor, let anyone who has anything to say come forward and keep his mouth shut." (MA 311) These signs no longer signify, no longer speak of anything except the imperative to obey what is necessary: it is a "renunciation that makes it possible to dominate the destiny imposed by the zeitgeist by interjecting it as a 'duty'" (312), and the Miesian spaces "assume in themselves the ineluctability of absence that the contemporary word imposes on the language of form." (ibid.) His architecture takes control over chaos by distancing itself, but in this also renounces anything like an *architecture parlante*; it sets up an interior distance that does not produce the fullness of self-possession, but a fundamental absence and void, recalling the "formal void" that was earlier placed at the limits of modernism as project and utopia in Siemensstadt. Now, the void is endowed with a high level of consciousness, and it is not the passive outcome of a doomed compromise, but an *act of thought*, a particular form of architectural thought that must be deciphered rather than explained as a mere symptom.

These figures are condensed in the analysis of the Seagram building (1954–58), where the conflict between structure and subjectivity reaches its climactic point. This takes place through a series of reversals that all hinge on the idea of the void, or rather a series of absences that replicate and begin to resonate with one another. First, the building is set back from the street, creating a gap in the otherwise dense fabric of Park Avenue, to which it itself responds by turning into an absolute object, displaying a "maximum of formal structurality" coupled with a "maximum absence of images." (MA 312). Then, in a further move, this absence is projected back onto the void generated by the building's separation from the street, the plaza in front, which constitutes a "planimetric inversion of the significance of the skyscraper: two voids answering each other and speaking the language of the nil, of the silence which—by a paradox worthy of Kafka—assaults the noise of the metropolis." (ibid.)[42] The Seagram building exposes itself to the city in renouncing it, and the void that it creates becomes, through the resonances it produces, a "phantom of itself" (ibid.). The absence that it creates is not the stand-in for a supersensible truth, no longer the "language of the soul" that still animated early abstract art, but "contradiction interjected," in a formula that draws the analysis close to Adorno.[43]

42. The "paradox worthy of Kafka" no doubt refers to the short story "Das Schweigen der Sirene," where Kafka presents us with a series of interpretations of the encounter of Ulysses and the sirens. In Homer, Ulysses ties himself to the mast and blocks the ears of his oarsmen with wax in order for them to escape the deadly seduction of the song and keep working, while he is able to enjoy it without fear of being lured into acting. This is a division that Adorno and Horkheimer famously understand in *Dialectic of Enlightenment* as an archaic model for the genealogy of aesthetic disinterest, both in terms of a division of labor and as the origin of the traces of a first nature that subsists in art, to the effect that all singing henceforth has remained internally broken. Kafka inverts the story, and suggests that what is truly deadly is rather the silence of the sirens, and that while some may have escaped their song, no one has escaped their silence, which in the case of Ulysses was prompted by the look of happiness on his face upon seeing them. In Kafka, it is thus Ulysses who blocks his ears with wax, which prevents him from noticing their silence. At the end Kafka proposes another possibility, that Ulysses in fact knew that the sirens were silent, but faked not to notice this ("in a certain way held this appearance as a shield against the sirens and the gods," Kafka writes) in order not to receive divine punishment because of his victory. Finally, he suggests that this mystery is beyond human comprehension.

43. For a reading that follows Adorno, which also picks up the motif of the siren song, although in the version of *Dialektik der Aufklärung,* and leaves out the reference to Kafka's inversion of the story, see K. Michael Hays, "Odysseus and the Oarsmen, or, Mies' Abstraction once again," in *The Presence of Mies,* ed. Detlef Mertins (New York: Princeton Architectural Press, 1994).

As a singular end point, Seagram building is however already inscribed in a structure of doubling, repetition, and haunting (which is perhaps already a further implication of its being a "phantom of itself"). The ending that it proclaimed was in fact nothing but a beginning, as in the Chase Manhattan Building, the Union Carbide Building, and a proliferating series of further corporate high-rises. For Tafuri and Dal Co, this repetition follows the logic of tragic and farce proposes by Marx in *The Eighteenth Brumaire of Louis Bonaparte*: "What is tragic in the Seagram building is repeated as a norm in these in the form of farce." (MA 312) The ubiquity of the curtain wall, little plazas adorned with fountains, all proved to be the stock in trade of corporate architecture—which it would be "wrong to consider contrary to the intentions of Mies," just as it would be "wrong to reduce his intentions to just that." (ibid.) If Mies draws a kind of critical line, it nevertheless proves impossible to respect, and the farcical betrayal is already inscribed in the tragedy; the distinction between them proves unstable, as if the repetition would insinuate itself into the tragic division itself, multiplying it in a series of echoes, producing precisely the kind of flowing *modulation* and image profusion that was already part of the initial *modularity* with its "formal structurality" and "absence of images."[44] Just as the iconoclastic gesture is already teeming with images, the silence proclaimed by the return to facts reflects the noises of the Metropolis, as if to raise the sensory overload into an object of thought.

The idea of reflection is further developed with reference to the project for a federal court building in Chicago. Here, the homogenous glass surface becomes a mirror, transforming the "almost nothing" into a "large glass," as an echo of Duchamp. But rather than pursuing the Duchampian legacy, with its intricate visual and linguistic play, joining space and time in the famous

44.   For this reading, see Reinhold Martin, *The Organizational Complex: Architecture, Media, and Corporate Space* (Cambridge, Mass.: MIT, 2004).

"delay in glass," in which the gaze must enter and eventually even lose itself, Mies's surface is a reflective emptiness, without interior depth, throwing everything back onto the spectator and finally onto the world itself. Instead of Duchamp, it is ultimately Schwitters's *Merz* pictures that are cited as models, although in a slightly different sense than was the case in *Progetto e utopia*, where they signaled the transformation of everything into interchangeable signs, a process that preceded and prepared their integration in the architectural project. Here too the glassy expanse welcomes all phenomena, it "absorbs them, restores them to themselves in a perverse multi-duplication, like a Pop Art sculpture that obliges the American metropolis to look at itself reflected." (MA 314) But the result—the operation being as it were carried out from the opposite end of Schwitters's—is instead that "architecture arrives at the ultimate limits of its own possibilities," so that "alienation, having become absolute, testifies uniquely to its own presence, separating itself from the world to declare the world's incurable malady." (ibid.) Rather than gesturing toward an integration of sign and experience, Mies declares their difference and division, in a gesture that marks an end and a series of beginnings, in which the divide between tragedy and farce remains unstable, undecidable, and perhaps even irrelevant, as the trajectory of Pop abundantly shows.

If the Miesian ending is tragic, although shot through with farcical and no doubt other possibilities too, the place reserved for Le Corbusier is somewhat different. In *Progetto e utopia* he was portrayed as the most versatile and multi-faceted of the modern masters, with a "lucidity that has no comparison in progressive European culture," even though the "dance of contradictions" that his work staged on every level finally ended up being absorbed in the dialectic of the plan. After the war, Corbusier's path would lead him in other directions, although perhaps in the end, towards the same contradiction.

49

This is visible in the Unité d'habitations (Marseilles, 1947–52), which was conceived as a self-sufficient universe with all possible amenities and a high-level flexibility, and yet was unable to deliver what it promised: its self-sufficiency is in fact a withdrawal due to practical necessities that prevent it from giving form to the entire landscape, as was once the claim of the Plan Obus; the interior streets that were to connect the mobile homes through real mechanical vehicles in the end became little more that broader corridors; the surreal forms on the roof do not speak of the unity of space, but rather of discontinuity and indomitability. The *Unité* is in the end "a hypothesis not brought to conclusion, a gigantic fragment of a global conception of the city destined to remain pure ideology." (MA 317)

This period of Corbusier's oeuvre was also particularly rich in paintings and sculptures, and in this line of work Tafuri and Dal Co detect a turn to the oneiric and unconscious as a way to a spiritual transcendence that stands opposed to the unconditional demand for factuality in Mies: if the latter rejected such spirituality "in homage to a Kantian imperative," then Le Corbusier "welcomed it in homage to an effort to transcend the finiteness of subjective individuality." (MA 319) This was a way of bringing the contradictions that his prewar work had managed to contain out into the open, and Tafuri and Dal Co locate this in the church Notre-Dame-du-Haut at Ronchamp. Conceived as a "landscapal acoustic" (*acoustique paysagiste*) that would give rise to "inexpressible spaces" (*espaces indicibles*), this was a work made up of interruptions, "rendering absolute the programmatic loss of center" (ibid.); rather than a synthesis of signs, it is a "dialectical labyrinth" that underscores the division of illusion and reality while trying to surmount it.

The Chandigarh project, while not originally conceived by Corbusier—who was only brought in at a fairly late stage and limited himself to corrections of the original plan—has for its part been the object of much criticism, specifically for the rigid application of the Athens Charter, and it constitutes one of the few actual tests of the feasibility of his urbanist vision. What Tafuri and Dal Co see, is buildings that "call to each other across the distances" in an "unattainable colloquy" (MA 323), remaining alone and isolated, and an emphasis on the intervening space that no longer connects but disconnects. In many of these late projects, Tafuri and Dal Co conclude, hermetic symbols become the residential model, withdrawn from productive reality, and the "present becomes manifest as space that ruptures all relations between processes of economic valorization and autonomy of the word," to the effect that "'Speaking' is possible only by taking onto oneself the burden of such trauma." If architectural language here finds itself in a checkmate, it realizes that it can only speak by taking refuge in mystic spaces, "withdrawing from the metropolitan reality that it had mistakenly believed could be reconciled with itself." (ibid.)

As a kind of coda to the more grandiose battles with the impossible staged by Mies and Corbusier, Frank Lloyd Wright, the final of the masters, pursued the quest for his imaginary Usonia, and gradually came to identify with his own myth. Rooted in eighteenth-century anarchism with its visions of universal harmony, Wright's vision of a "great peace" coinciding with maximum mobility became increasingly remote from the existing city, and the mythical spiral that pervades many of his later works operated as a symbol of the interpenetration of nature and artifice, as a spiritual principle that would establish a "link between the contingent and the infinite" (MA 328). Yet rather than a purist asceticism, Wright's geometry, like technology, is only "an obstacle to be overcome," in the end "indicating the possibility of transcending the civilization of labor"—a gesture of romantic anti-capitalism that however remained powerless in the face of reality, and had to have recourse to elements whose "aggregation no longer shows the slightest necessity" (ibid.). Similarly, the fantasies of flying saucers that populate Wright's drawings and projects from the period may seem like graphic jokes, and while they, with their desire to take leave of the world, are rooted in the visions of the early avant-garde, from the *Letatlin* to Malevich's *Planits*, when these ideas come together in the spiraling structure of the Guggenheim Museum—the one building where "his flying saucers do truly soar in the city, even though anchored on the ground for a temporary landing" (329)—this was in a certain way his final attack on avant-garde art, aiming to create a "global experience" that involves both the space of existence and that of memory, but in this also obscuring the artworks on display. This "Pantheon," as Wright famously called it— displaying "the atmosphere of the quiet unbroken wave: no meeting of the eye with abrupt changes of form"[45]—was a synthesis of his desire to find hidden roots and an "ever more hermetical handwriting," which, eventually, returning to the city as the place where frontier ideology could communicate with post-technological future, "coincided with the sublimation of the immense American suburb", or quite simply "Disneyland" (ibid.).

What, then, can be learned from these various endings? "Autobiographies, returns to origins, ruthless and perverse subjective testimonies—these are last messages of the masters of the modern movement." (MA 330) To the succeeding generation, Tafuri and Dal Co note, these messages could only appear as "hermetic, if not simply useless" (ibid.), and the final outcome of utopia was a split between an architecture that became preoccupied with its own "being" (for which one can no doubt substitute the "sublime uselessness" of the preface to the English translation of *Progetto e utopia*), and one that pursued the initial

45.   Wright, *A Testament* (New York: Horizon Press, 1957), 169, cited in
       Tafuri and Dal Co, MA 329, without reference.

goals of the avant-garde, i.e., to achieve an overall control of the urban reality—which is the "dramatic dichotomy" facing the generation succeeding the modern masters.

The repercussions of this division extend throughout the following chapters, but rather than leading up to the kind of stark choice between delusion and uselessness that was the outcome of *Progetto e utopia*, in 1976 they usher in a state of transformation, uncertainty, and loss of direction. The concluding chapter, "The Experience of the Seventies," brings us into the present, and begins, perhaps somewhat surprisingly, with a series of references to Heidegger's reading of Stefan George in *Unterwegs zur Sprache*. Slightly misquoting a line from George's poem "Das Wort": "Kein Ding wo das Wort gebricht,"[46] which for Heidegger leads to the question of how poetry and thought inhabit language in ways that are parallel yet profoundly different, and that finally signals a positive poetic, the disappearance or lacking of the word here seems to point to an absence or least precariousness of the architectural thing once the unity of its language was shattered. Tafuri and Dal Co suggest that the parallel lines that can sometimes be detected in modern architecture just as much indicate a diversity and pluralism: we should not too quickly weld them into a unity, but rather, and here too following Heidegger (at least as Tafuri an Dal Co read him),[47]

46. The full citation from George's poem reads: "kein ding sei wo das wort gebricht." Tafuri and Dal Co overlook George's idiosyncratic spelling, which avoids capitalizing German nouns, but above all the optative form *sei*, which is missing in the citation above. The optative is crucial for Heidegger's reading, since it shows the positive dimension of the lacking of the word: the confidence in the power of traditional poetic language to name the thing must be shattered for a different relation between word and thing to appear, and the poem describes a process of renunciation (*Entsagung*) necessary for this relation to emerge. See Heidegger, "Das Wort," in *Unterwegs zur Sprache* (Pfullingen: Neske, 1959).

47. The reading of Heidegger here seems close to the one proposed by Cacciari, as also comes across in the latter's review of the book, " Eupalinos, or Architecture," trans. Stephen Sartarelli, in Hays *Architecture Theory since 1968*.

perceive the difference between world and thing, i.e., how architecture refuses to be subsumed under the social and historical universe of which it is nonetheless a part. There is an irreducible "estrangement" or "distancing" (MA 364) that governs contemporary work, Tafuri and Dal Co suggest, which opens "new lines of conduct" that must be acknowledged and made into a poetic based on difference and renunciation—obviously echoing the claims earlier made on behalf of Mies—that would dispel the myth of unitary origins and unidirectional historical genealogies.

Surveying a wide spectrum of responses to the demise of the modern movement, from the flight to technological objectivism (Piano and Rogers), returns to nature (van Eyck), formal experimentations that draw on architectural history (Stirling), nostalgic claims for an architecture that aspires to retrieve classical monumentality (Kahn) or the commercial flow of Las Vegas (Venturi), Tafuri and Dal Co detect a surrender of all hope of seizing control over the city, of which the isolated super-sky-scraper is the most telling indication. As "isolated monsters" whose own "inflexible organization acts as surrogate for the order lacking in the city itself" (MA 372), they constitute new forms of publicity, or as in the case of works by Roche and Dinkeloo, "a screen on which the images of surrounding life are projected, but without the 'renunciation' of Mies." (ibid.)[48] The resulting divide has cut off the avant-garde from the real, spawning an infinite series of attempts at recapturing what has been lost. And yet, Tafuri and Dal Co conclude, this is by no means an end: "If this book aims to demonstrate anything, it is precisely the impossibility of writing the word *finis* at any point in history." (392) The figure of the end remains operative, al-

48.   In chap. 4 below we will return to different readings of this game of reflections, which complicate the divide between renunciation and mere reflection, in Fredric Jameson and Reinhold Martin.

most like a gravitational pull impossible to resist, but as endings multiply, echoes intermingle, and repetitions begin to cut across and blur lines of division, as if the end of utopia was also the end of the utopia of the end.

The labyrinth of history

In the last of Tafuri's major works that deal with modern architecture as a whole, *La sfera e il labirinto*, which gathers essays written during the seventies, he once more speaks of the necessary plurality of languages that the historian must acknowledge, rejecting yet again, to be sure, any direct and simple operative relation to practice, but now for the additional reason of trying to undermine the claims of the Historian that seemed to underlie at least some of his earlier writings. The opposition between sphere and labyrinth seems to signal the conflict between two desires: first to step out of the flux of history, even in the guise of a self-confident writing *of* history that ultimately dominates and subsumes the event—as it were internalizing and mastering anxiety by producing the *account* of its causes, no matter how inevitable and irreversible these might be—and then the desire to enter the maze, to lose oneself in the labyrinth, with the risk of giving in to an aestheticizing infinity of interpretation that leaves everything as it is. The task of critical work is to acknowledge both these demands, to create a maximum tension between them without letting any one of them subsume the other.[49]

The essays develop themes ranging from Piranesi to the present, and in many respects they trace the same historical trajectory as *Progetto e utopia*. The larger theoretical claims that will be in focus here are however laid out in the introductory section, "The Historical Project," which presents a set of new methodological perspectives. While continuing his attempts to devel-

49. Later, in chap. 3 below, we will look at a similar opposition, that between the pyramid and the labyrinth, in the work of Bernard Tschumi.

op an account of architecture rooted in historical materialism, Tafuri also introduces a whole spectrum of other materialisms— of the body, the signifier, of language and discourse—that give rise to many unresolved tensions relating 1) to the very sense of *architecture* itself as both heteronomous and fragmented, yet endowed with a particular distance toward the world that conditions it, 2) to the role of *critique* as a form of writing that continually must question its own status and tendency toward closure, and 3) to the status accorded to *ideology* as something that cannot be dispelled as mere false consciousness, but in fact permeates the whole of intellectual labor, while at the same maintaining the ability of the analysis to be able somehow to situate and pierce through its veils so as to point towards its material conditions. Confusing, sometimes even contradictory, and more like the record of an inner struggle than a systematic exposition, his reflections stage the tension between pyramid and labyrinth in all its aspects, often to the point that a particular paragraph seems to be canceled by the following. History, Tafuri writes, citing Carlo Ginzburg, is akin to a jigsaw-puzzle that can never brought to a conclusion, a labor of Sisyphus that not only results from the complexity and wealth of materials to be treated, but also must take upon itself the task of questioning the nature of the object, even the very nature of reality as such. "The real problem," Tafuri states, "is how to project a criticism capable of constantly putting itself into crisis by putting into crisis the real."[50]

The reference to Carlo Ginzburg and the project of a micro-historical writing sets the tone for a work that was explicitly begun three years later in *L'armonia e i conflitti*, but was already prefigured in an earlier book, the little noticed collective work

50. *The Sphere and the Labyrinth: Avant-Gardes and Architecture from Piranesi to the 1970s*, trans. Pellegrino d'Acierno and Robert Connolly (Cambridge, Mass.: MIT, 1990), 9. Henceforth cited as SL with page number.

Via Giulia (1975, with Luigi Salerno and Luigi Spezzaferro),[51] whose thick description of a particular street in Rome reveals it to be a condensation of larger urban and political processes that must be approached from multiple perspectives. On the one hand, this approach focuses on a highly specific object that ultimately must be taken as a contingent part of the urban web, on the other hand it opens the object to an infinity of readings; the critical act cuts out something from a larger whole while at the same time showing how the part, as a monad of sorts,[52] reflects the whole. The crisis of the object, long since underway in the kind of modernism that Tafuri had already analyzed in *Progetto e utopia* via the case of Hilberseimer, where the logic of the assembly line dethrones the object as well as the subject if experience, here, and in a more general fashion, opens onto a critical act that itself must begin by dismantling and decomposing the object (the edifice, the street, the city, or any other entity assumed to be given in and through itself), and then proceed to a recomposing that understands it as a crystallization of more distant structures. But rather than just creating an effect of a temporary intersection, the object also produces something of its own that makes it possible for analysis to decipher the real as itself split and contradictory, which is what provides it with a certain distance that Tafuri, as we will see, eventually analyzes in terms that draw on Russian formalism as well as, albeit with more reserve, Adorno. This, I think, is the sense of the crisis of the real, its *krisis* in the Greek sense of division and splitting, which does not imply any rejection of the claim that there would

51. *Via Giulia: Un' utopia urbanistica del '500* (Rome: Staderini, 1975).
52. The term "monad" is not used by Tafuri, but the logic of the argument draws him close to Adorno's understanding of the term: the monad concentrates the world within itself, and in this it lets us understand the contradictions of the world in a condensed form. For Adorno on the monadic structure of the work, see *Aesthetic Theory*, trans. Robert Hullot-Kentor (London: Continuum, 1997), 237–239.

be a real as such. Even though Tafuri occasionally seems to enter into the vicinity of the various theories of simulation and of reality as merely an effect of discourse that were emerging at the time, he ultimately rejects them, although not without first letting them infiltrate his own writings, which is one of the reasons for their meandering and hesitant quality, attributes that that go so far as to make the texts cry out to be deciphered rather than read, more so than any of his previous texts.

Ultimately, Tafuri suggests, for historical writing this is a problem of *language*, and the language problem that earlier was diagnosed in architecture now invades critical discourse itself. This discourse cannot avoid speaking a multiplicity of languages, and it must draw on a vast array of vocabularies borrowed from disciplines whose reduction to a common structure remains fundamentally tenuous. Architecture, as shorthand for many overlapping fields, cannot be reduced to a language that would be its own, but can only be grasped as a dispersal—which, Tafuri notes, while still distancing himself from such a conclusion, seems like the final outcome of a "Lacanian left" (SL 2).[53]

But is it at all possible to write a history that respects such multiplicity? Does not the act of writing necessarily produce

---

53. The meaning of terms like "left" and "right" is far from obvious. Tafuri's formulation might be taken in the sense that the "left" would understand the symbolic order as historical through and through, whereas the "right" would uphold a more emphatically structural view that sees historical transformations of language as mere fluctuations, ripples that can never shake the great Law of the Father and the Signifier. A bit further on, Tafuri cautions us that the "privilege attributed by Lacan to the pure materiality of the signifier" should not be identified with any "infantile attempts at reconstructing a lost fullness for disenchanted words" (SL 6), but he leaves the positive meaning of this materiality unexplained. K. Michael Hays has attempted to formulate a systematic theory of architecture on the basis of the Lacanian symbolic, but only with a general reference to Tafuri's negative view of the resurgence of the "language problem" in the sixties; see Hays, *Architecture's Desire: Reading the Late Avant-Garde* (Cambridge, Mass.; MIT, 2010), 1–21, on Tafuri 3–4.

a particular reduction, and more specifically, does the Marxist framework to which Tafuri—although with increasing distance—still adheres not require a concept of totality and determination in the last instance that must always override fragmentation, as merely a surface effect in consciousness, i.e., as *ideology*? The writing of history, Tafuri suggests, is, to be sure, always a production, an analytical construction just as much as a "deconstruction of ascertainable realities" (SL 3); but that writing is itself implicated in the objects that it treats means that the historical project must always be a project of a crisis. Still, in order for discourse to not just turn around itself, it must also point to that which resists its appropriating force, fracturing and implicating it while yet providing it with an object that still, no matter how distantly, promises a *truth*—a truth that cannot, even though there is no way to simply release it from the veils that cover it, be understood as just one more move in the space of ideology. Writing is a movement that loses itself in the object, decomposes and recomposes it, guiding a truth that remains just as elusive as indispensable.

As a preliminary name for that which resists the historical project as a fantasy of externally dominating and subsuming the object, Tafuri suggests, somewhat surprisingly, the *body*, which he here understands through the optic of Nietzsche's genealogy of morals. This would be the material origin of values that proves to be fundamentally multiple, as Foucault had already suggested in his reading of Nietzsche, and in opposition to many other such claims to locate an originary dimension in the physical and elemental, it shows that the knowledge brought to bear on the body, but also implicated in it, no longer provides any recognition or consolation, but that it in fact will take us away from ourselves.[54]

54. The reference to the body, here filtered through the writings of Franco Rella, obviously contains deep problems, not simply because it seems

But in this, Tafuri notes (as if he felt the need to immediately undo his own claim, in line with the hesitation that permeates the text in its integrality), there lies the risk of performing a dissemination for its own sake that he here indiscriminately ascribes to both Derrida and Foucault, and which he sees as eventually ending up in the production of new units, fragments of meaning that somehow would be significant in themselves. If we must inject "the profound fragmentation of the real itself" (SL 5) into the analysis, so that it becomes visible as made up of several levels, this does not yield mere differences; if architecture does not form a unitary ideological block, and the critique of architectural ideology has still only identified its most immediate and visible aspects, this implies that there is need for an analysis that probes even further into its constitution.

Form, Tafuri suggests following Simmel, should rather be understood as a boundary of the object that at the same time is a limit of language, imposed as a historical crisis that prevents any fullness of form, subjective or objective, from ever being established. There will be no unique name or term for this crisis, as Nietzsche, as well as Marx, has taught us, and "words that are petrified and hard as stones"[55] must be taken apart so as not

to introduce a level that only with great difficulties, if indeed at all, can be integrated into a Marxist analysis. Furthermore, it can be asked what body is implied here: the phenomenological, affective, desiring, fantasmatic, constructed? The reference to Foucault's 1971 "Nietzsche, Genealogy, History" might seem to indicate that Tafuri would be following the path toward an analytic of knowledge and power, but in fact he only preserves the negative moment in Foucault's essay, i.e., the moment of dispersal in relation to a philosophy of the subject. Generally, Tafuri's comments on Foucault are, as we will see, confusing to say the least, moving between praise and scorn without ever settling down to provide a clear argument. This comes across above in the collective volume *Il dispositivo Foucault* (1977), which documents the only systematic confrontation with Foucault undertaken by the Venice School, and which is fraught with confusions and misleading interpretations; for more on this, see chap. 6, below.

55. Nietzsche, *Morgenröte*, No. 47, cited in SL 7. Today, Nietzsche writes, we must, unlike the ancients who thought that they had made a dis-

to turn into the impenetrable monuments that are particularly erected by architectural history. The stones pile up, but it is neither sufficient just to tear them down again, nor to probe the interstices between the rocks where new crevices can always be found, new subterfuges invented, and new games played; what is needed is an analysis of the battle that is constitutive of space as a contradictory layering. This battle, however, can not as such be dated to any specific point or event in time, as if there first would have been a harmonious order that subsequently was lost, which to some extent was the underlying hypothesis of *Progetto e utopia*—a kind of negative foil that Tafuri would no doubt have rejected, but which his narrative cannot help reproducing—where the moment signaled by the name Laugier was the turning point. The "historic space" that must be uncovered is now understood as inherently complex, made up of words, stones, technologies, and practices, none of which can be given exclusive priority.

But what, then, would be the direction in which this spectral analysis is moving? The unavoidable conclusion of the foregoing, which, however, Tafuri must attempt to avoid, seems to be that analysis simply has no end: no level, neither base nor superstructure, neither consciousness or discourse nor the spaces of practices and actions, is absolute, and the infinite analysis that Freud perceived as a constant threat to the success of psychoanalysis appears as the inevitable result. The reference to modes

covery when they forged a word, stumble over rock-hard, immortalized words, and rather break a leg than a word ("Jetzt muss man bei jeder Erkenntnis über steinharte verewigte Worte stolpern, und wird dabei eher ein Bein brechen, als ein Wort.") The image of stone and petrification plays a similar role in Marx, where the role of critique is to set hardened relations in movement, force them to dance, by singing back to them their own melody: "man muss diese versteinerten Verhältnisse dadurch zum Tanzen zwingen, dass man ihnen ihre eigne Melodie vorsingt!" *Zur Kritik der Hegelschen Rechtsphilosophie*, Karl Marx/Friedrich Engels Werke (Berlin: Dietz, 1976), vol.1, 381.

of production cannot be an ultimate reference, since they are themselves traversed by ideologies that help to produce them; "isolated in themselves, [they] *neither explain nor determine*," Tafuri writes (SL 10).

But how should we then understand the term "ideology", if it no longer can be understood as mere superstructure? First of all, it acts in groups (*per fasci*; the Italian term is certainly not fortuitous here), as can be seen in the case of the poetics of the avant-garde, which displays the full political spectrum, from left to right. This polymorphous quality, and the way in which ideology is capable of performing all kinds of functions, indicates that it cannot simply be eliminated by analysis, as if it were only a mirage to be dispelled by the clarity of consciousness. The distance that this sets up in relation to the earlier work is marked out when Tafuri claims that it would be useless to "tear into the methods of 'operative criticism'" (SL 11), at least to the extent that this would pave the way toward a restructuring of the disciplines. Operative criticism is no doubt ideology too, but as the analysis of project and utopia gradually folds back into the idea of a historical project that, itself, although without being utopian, must question and perhaps even negate (*ou-*) its own place (*topos*), the distinction between the operative and the critical turns out to be far from clear. If analysis and project at present are divided, Tafuri writes, this is no longer just in the sense that had been suggested earlier, i.e., that the first would be unable to give precepts to the latter, but also, and more fundamentally, because the very project of history finds itself challenged, and any claim to the opposite means that it would be "obliged to betray itself consciously" (11). The final page of a historical account must be taken only as a suspension, a "pause that implies ellipsis marks" (12), and in this it further intensifies the "unease" confessed at the final page in *L'architettura contemporanea* (MA 392).

A history that in this way reconstructs itself as a perennial transformation must become a criticism and a doubt capable of continually turning back on themselves; it is not a series of philological proofs,[56] or the establishing of links between different fields, but rather "probes what appears to be a *void*" (SL 13); it seeks the interstices between technologies and languages without suturing them into a signifying whole, and "*projects the crisis of techniques already given*" (ibid.), by which we should no doubt also understand the techniques of historical interpretation. But—and Tafuri immediately turns the tables once more—if there is no solution to the project of history as crisis, we must just as little simply stop in the face of the multiple, "in astonishment at the edge at the enchanted forest of languages" (ibid.). If historical analysis is incapable of demystifying per se, it is nevertheless part of a social struggle, and must risk a temporary "inactuality," which seems to detach it both from the past as a set of given facts and documents, as well as from the present as a circumscribed contemporaneity. While its immediate relation to practice remains blocked, it upholds a place in the battle of space, and its instruments, we might say with and against Tafuri, while lacking any definitive instrumentality, cannot avoid being made to operate, become operative, precisely because they cannot, *must* not, form a self-enclosed whole that could be presented in a discourse on method.

But even though the battle of space as such cannot be dated, there is nonetheless a specific fragmentation of architecture since the Enlightenment, Tafuri notes, the seemingly disjointed

56.   All of which is of course a profoundly Nietzschean distrust, and can be understood as the attempt to wrest another sense from the term "philology." The task of history, as Nietzsche suggests, is not the reestablishing of a first unity, but an explosion of terms into divergent signifying chains, which affects the reading of both ancients and moderns. See the notes from 1875 for a planned work on the theme "Wir Philologen," *Kritische Studienausgabe*, eds. Colli-Montinari (Berlin and New York: de Gruyter, 1988), vol. 8.

nature of which may be taken as a positive point of departure, instead of the established "texts" of finished works; this fragmentation signals a constant "beyond" against which analysis must measure itself, and which produces the constant ruptures in modern architecture that the "monumental constructions of the Modern Movement" (SL 14) and its official historiographers attempt to cover over. To trace this process of fragmentation—and here Tafuri strikes a more recognizable Marxist note—means to follow the dialectic of concrete and abstract labor, intellectual labor and modes of production, and the history of architecture must relate both to concrete projects and their implications for a general history. This amounts to an "explosion" of the work and dissemination of its unities, all of which must become the object of separate analysis, and in this sense there can be no single methodology that takes account of the totality of the work; the critical act is rather a "recomposition" or "remontage" that breaks the magic circle of language by showing its foundations, but also indicates the mode of functioning of this language, which is not merely that of a distorted reflection that analysis could correct.

Here, the alternative that permeates these methodological reflections recurs: either we may simply immerse ourselves in the free play of valences, following Barthes and the *plaisir du texte*, or we must return to external factors. Both are to some extent legitimate: the former is the operation performed by operative history, which notwithstanding its claims to historical analysis floats outside of time and space, and forms a "mass of weightless metaphors" (SL 15); the second, with which Tafuri no doubt aligns himself, measures language against its outside, which, he underlines, need not be taken as vulgar Marxism that erases the specificity of architecture. The model here is Benjamin's "The Author as Producer," which suggests that neither form nor content should be taken as essential in themselves, since what must be analyzed is the position of the work within the relations of production.[57]

At every step, this Benjaminian idea of production calls into question the capitalist division of labor, as well as signals the need for an analysis of "structural cycles," i.e., the way in which architecture is integrated into larger historical processes. This is indicated by the historical role of ideology, and the historicizing of its concrete intervention opens up a new field of inquiry: we must, Tafuri writes, "enter into the magic castle of ideologies" in a way that prevents us from being caught up in a "hypnosis" and an "engrossing game of mirrors" (SL 16) This means to "unravel the intricate and labyrinthine paths traveled by Utopia" (ibid.), which was already the proposal of *Progetto e utopia*. Here, however, there is also a different move that just as much must be accounted for, the "knight's move," as this idea was formulated by Viktor Shklovsky,[58] which is an idea significantly missing from *Progetto e utopia*. There is a "swerve" that gives the work a particular autonomy by taking a step aside from the real, producing an estrangement,[59] in terms that were also picked up by Brecht, or

57.   Here it must be noted that Tafuri shifts the perspective of Benjamin, which in "The Author as Producer" is not that of the historian, but precisely the one that Tafuri wants to avoid, i.e. that of a partisan critic supporting particular forms of contemporary work. The context of Benjamin's essay is the debate of the period on the political efficacy of literature, and on whether a formalist or the content-oriented criticism is the most relevant, to which Benjamin responds by declaring the distinction invalid.

58.   See Shklovsky, *Knight's Move*, trans. Richard Sheldon (Normal. Ill.: Dalkey Archive Press, 2005).

59.   The notion of art as a device or technique of estrangement (*priem ostranenija*), and Shklovsky's demand that the artist must "make the stone stony" by removing the "algebraization" of knowledge, in fact have a strong resemblance to the phenomenological quest for originary intuitions and the "things themselves," and they draw on a long series of influences leading back through Bergson to Novalis and German Romanticism. On Husserl and Russian formalism, see Victor Erlich, *Russian Formalism* (The Hague: Mouton, 1980). For the connection to Bergson, see James M. Curtis, "Bergson and Russian Formalism," *Comparative Literature*, vol. 28, No. 2 (Spring 1976): 109–121. Tzvetan

a kind of "surreality."[60] It is useless to define ideology simply as false consciousness, Tafuri writes, since no work simply reflects a preexisting ideology, which does not mean that the swerve itself is not charged with ideology; there is always a margin of ambiguity, as well as compromises that must be made for the distance to the real to become effective.

As a reaction to this, the avant-garde attempted to reduce the swerve in order to take control of the world; the decantation chamber of the Bauhaus, analyzed in *Progetto e utopia*, would be a perfect case of this, in its implicit claims to test various earlier strategies with a view to the efficiency and capacity to become functional within a universal design strategy. In the earlier analysis, this strategy was understood as a temporary link in a larger chain, beyond which the Plan as a comprehensive instrument was gradually transferred from architecture to the level of State and Capital, with the 1929 crash as the decisive turning point. Now, the claim seems inverted: the unity must be fractured from the outset, and progressive and regressive tendencies, anti-urban nostalgia, communalist and anarchist elements intermingle, cross and fuse, to the point of making many of these projects impossible to locate in terms of political claims. This complexity in turn necessitates methodological eclecticism, on the part of the historian, so that finally the very

Todorov points to the connection to Novalis and Romanticism in *Critique de la critique: Un roman d'apprentissage* (Paris: Seuil, 1984). For a discussion of the relation between theories of estrangement from Shklovsky to Brecht, and the architecture of the early avant-garde, see Alexandra Vougia, *Estranging Devices: Architectural Modernism and Strategies of De-alienation*, diss. (London: Architectural Association, 2016).

60.   Tafuri here draws on Max Bense's *Aesthetica: Einführung in die neue Aesthetik* (Baden-Baden: Agis 1965). For Bense, aesthetics must draw on mathematical form, which he found in dimensions like metrics and rhythm in literature, just as he, conversely, wanted to discern an idea of style in mathematics. Both are based in universal operations carried out on simple elements or signs that ultimately lead to a general theory of informatics, which remains far from Tafuri's proposals.

term architecture, Tafuri writes, must be used in the broadest
sense: there are no common denominators that would allow for
a clear-cut classification of all its uses and ramifications. But if
this means to destroy the work, Tafuri cautions us that it is not
done in order to reach something like the "Word," which he
here associates to Foucault's archeology, i.e., a set of rules that
would organize things solely through the schemata of discourse.
Instead, the avant-garde hypotheses must be seen in relation the
history of urban planning, which follows a different trajectory
described by the medicalization of the city that was intrinsic to
physiocratic thought, a process that must not be taken as simply
equivalent to the industrial revolution.[61]

And yet the problem of relative autonomy, as in the images
of the swerve and the knight's move, remains, and Tafuri points
to the analysis proposed by Robert Klein of the gradual disappearance of the referent and the emergence of abstractionism in
modern art as a model. There is, Klein suggests, an unfolding crisis of the "nonfigurative norm" against which the image could be
measured, a norm that eventually ends up being absorbed inside
the work itself, and renders obsolete the twofold figure of impres-
sionism and psychologism.[62] But how can this shift be connected
to architecture? It must be understood in terms of a pervasive

61. The appeal to a "Word" here rejected by Tafuri applies in fact only to
    some of slightly apocalyptical concluding sections of *Les mots et les choses*,
    and has little or no relevance in relation to Foucault's work on power/
    knowledge from the seventies, which would have been the obvious
    reference here. Ironically, the "medicalization of the city" is precisely
    one of the central themes of Foucault's work from the mid-seventies
    onward, as is visible not only in his lectures (which Tafuri could not
    have known), but also in several interviews and writings that were
    published at the time, notably the collaborative volume *Les machines à
    guérir* (Brussels: Mardaga, 1977). I discuss some of these texts and the
    relevance to architecture in my *Essays, Lectures* (Stockholm: Axl Books,
    2007), chap. 8, and *Biopolitics and the Emergence of Modern Architecture*
    (New York: Princeton Architectural Press, 2009).
62. See Klein, *La forme et l'intelligible: Écrits sur la Renaissance et l'art moderne*
    (Paris: Gallimard, 1970).

dialectical opposition to classicism, Tafuri proposes, which constitutes the basic problem of modern art, but also must be able to inform our reading of the pre-modern forms, and in this sense—which echoes the claims about Brunelleschi's avant-garde gesture in *Teorie e storia*—"Tuscan humanism can function as a rearview mirror" in which "are reflected the ghosts of the contemporary bad conscience." (SL 19) Against the too facile rejections of autonomy, Tafuri also points to Adorno's warning in *Aesthetic Theory*: the dissolution of the art character, "de-artification" (*Entkunstung*) should not be made into a slogan, and the theory of the aura and its disappearing in the age of mechanical reproducibility must be handled dialectically. In Tafuri's reading, Adorno's caution however bespeaks a certain nostalgia, which also is supposed to transpire in his treatment of the notion of fragment as belonging to the totality as that part which resists it.[63] There can be no nostalgia, no pre-existing totality, only a *subsequently constructed whole* in analysis that can be broken at any point.

What is needed on a more specific level, Tafuri proposes, is a new history of intellectual labor, as it has been anticipated by

63.   Tafuri here engages in a strange misreading of the exchange between Benjamin and Adorno. When Adorno says that the "exhibition value" (*Ausstellungswert*) suggested by Benjamin as the progressive and emancipatory quality of post-auratic art is merely an afterimage of the process of exchange, it is difficult to see that this is something that "does not in reality greatly modify Benjamin's original thesis, which could quite readily admit that that the 'exhibition value' is the 'imago' of the exchange process, but only in works that have not completely incorporated that process within themselves" (SL 20). What is stake, and more patently so in the correspondence in 1936 around the Artwork essay (whereas Adorno's critique is more subdued in *Aesthetic Theory*), is in fact the idea of autonomy, which Adorno defends against Benjamin's avant-garde and "anarchist" (so Adorno) desire to "liquidate" (so Benjamin) high art in the name of immediate political efficiency; see the commented translations of the letters in *Aesthetics and Politics* (London: Verso, 1979). Tafuri's position in fact seems much closer to Adorno than to Benjamin, at least in this context. His claim that Adorno's understanding of the fragment would be nostalgic is equally misleading, and follows from the same skewed reading of this debate.

Rodchenko, Corbusier, and others: a history of planning that goes beyond the architect, and shows how the avant-gardes have been transformed into techniques. This means to undo the traditional role of the architect, and, seen in this light, the proposals of *Progetto e utopia* were less a series of statements of end and closure, and more an invitation to pursue the task of linking architecture (understood in a broad sense that includes technologies, models of organization and planning), critique (as the project of a history that would be able to decompose and recompose the elements of the trajectory of modernism in a way that cuts across disciplinary borders), and ideology (as the element of thinking and acting that includes illusions and well as partial truths, and does not allow for a thought that would simply see reality at is, since this reality its itself made up of subject and object positions that include the historians own). What this analysis can offer, Tafuri writes, is "an intermittent journey through a maze of tangled paths, one of the many 'provisional constructions' obtainable by starting with these chosen materials. The cards can be reshuffled and to them added many that were intentionally left out: the game is destined to continue." (SL 21)

2. 1966:
Thinking the City

"We seek the crowd. Events, choices, changes, contrasts. The Metropolis is more than just work, school, career. It is freedom, anonymity, choice, chance, adventure, play. The whole complex. The resistance of distances and queues. The similarity of moments in the press, in radio, and television. The movement of individuals and groups, cars and buses. Participation is a condition of life."[1] The opening statement by the curators of the exhibition "Hej stad" ("Hello City") at Moderna Museet in Stockholm in 1966 seems to capture the particular energy of the debate around the urban form that exploded during the 1960s. To some extent a rare event in Sweden, where the discussions on architecture and urbanism were still largely conditioned by the planning discourses of functionalism and social engineering, this exhibition, both defiant and open in its attitude, inserted itself into a wider context. Drawing on what at the time were the most advanced forms of artistic expression available, it attempted to rethink the city as a zone of conflict and intensity, to open it up towards a future that was in fact unknown, but it also looked back to a debate on the city that is as old as modernism itself, and that had haunted the architectural avant-garde since at least the 1920s. Revisiting the terms of this debate, and per-

1.   *Hej Stad*, catalog (Stockholm: Arkitekturmuseet, 1966), 5. The exhibition was curated by Sture Balgård, Eva Björklund, and Jörgen Lindvall, at the time students at the School of Architecture at the Royal Institute of Technology in Stockholm, as well as Mårten Larsson, from the Arkitekturmuseum. The exhibition was the opening exhibition of the recently relocated museum, and in this sense a highly symbolic event.

ceiving that which earlier had been seen as a problem as rather a possibility, "Hej stad" assumed the task of projecting the past toward some unknown future, and it did so in the mode of a greeting ("Hello"), as if to underscore the suddenness of a disruptive encounter, but also of an event that must be seen as a promise.

"Hej stad" was the sequel to a previous exhibition, "Alarm," organized the year before at Teknorama and curated by the same team, which likewise had posed the question of urban renewal. Reviewers of "Hej stad" describe a feeling of confusion and sensory overload, which was already present in the former exhibition, but here seems to have escalated even further: "A chaos of light and sound sensations. One attempts to find a common thread. Was it right to retain the exhibition format from 'Alarm'? To add even more images? And even more wailing sinus notes? And even more ambitious intentions?"[2] The combination of electro-acoustic music (by Ralph Lundsten and Leo Nilsson), texts, images, and statistic information of various kinds, seems to have aspired to the creation of a total work of art, somewhat uneasily straddling the divide between the attempt to produce an immersion in the present and a pedagogic ambition that calls for an intellectual distance.

This ambition echoes the program launched previously in the earliest manifesto of Swedish modern architecture, *Acceptera* (1931, a the year after the Stockholm Exhibition), which was cited on the first page of the catalog for "Hej stad" (reprinted above a cartoon that speaks of the need for a better understanding between cultures, adding a non-nationalist flavor that marks an important shift with respect to much of the rhetoric in 1931): "Accept the reality at hand—only then do we have the prospect of mastering it, of getting the better of it in order to change it,

2.   Bo Grönlund, "OOOOOOH AAAAAAH hej stad," review *in Göteborgs Handels- och Sjöfartstidning*, April 13, 1966.

and of creating a culture that would be a flexible tool for life. We have no need for the out-grown forms of an old culture in order to uphold our self-esteem. We cannot sneak out of our own time from the rear. Neither can we jump over that which is troublesome and unclear into a utopian future. We can do nothing other than look reality in the eyes and accept it in order to master it."[3]

We should note that the use of the verb form "accept"—in Swedish, as well as English, at once an infinitive and an imperative form—does not simply signify, in 1931 or in 1966, a simple and uncritical surrender to the forces that be, but rather the necessity of entering into the contemporary moment in order to channel and steer its processes: acceptance is not obedience, but rather the means to acknowledge the present in order to asses its possibilities, predict the outcome of actions, and plan for the future. On the other hand, a profound *fascination* with the present is manifest, along with a desire to identify with that which is emerging, for better or worse, even with the logic of the spectacle, which to some extent seems an integral part of most avant-garde architectural discourse. If the idea of future urban forms always appears to release a vast array of both utopian and dystopic energies, the most interesting cases of this are perhaps those that manage to include both of these positions, play them off against each other and generate a profound insecurity that allows us to enter into a "beyond good and evil" experience— not necessarily in order to remain there, but to use this leveling,

3.   *Acceptera* (Stockholm: Tiden, 1931), 198. The book was published the year after the Stockholm Exhibition, and was co-written by six of the most prestigious architects and intellectuals of the time: Gunnar Asplund, Wolter Gahn, Sven Markelius, Gregor Paulsson, Eskil Sundahl, and Uno Åhrén. For a reading of this text and the way it constructs a highly strategic version of Swedish history and architectural modernism, see the introduction to Helena Mattsson and Sven-Olov Wallenstein (eds.), *Swedish Modernism: Architecture, Consumption and the Welfare State* (London: Black Dog, 2010).

or willing suspension of previous aesthetic and socio-cultural hierarchies, as a means to grasp what is emergent instead of residual in our present.

The exhibition was organized in a series of stations that dealt with themes ranging from "Change, event" to "Contrasts and combinations in the structure of the city," "Individuals and groups," Old and new pleasures and playgrounds," "Scales of various traffic machines," "Human scale and attitudes toward traffic," and a host of other thematic juxtapositions that reflected the urban debate of the time in what one must assume was a dialectical, even pedagogical way. The structure of the catalog on the other hand emphasized the sense of immersion: consisting almost entirely of citations, from the Bible to current journalism and political debates, it demanded a response from the visitors, but at the same time also deprived them of their sense of orientation. Some of the texts expressed an anxiety over urbanization and the loss of earlier forms of life; others reveled in the marvels of technology; some deplored the alienation of modern Metropolitan life; others cherished it as the possibility of freedom and movement. It was more like a manual for thinking further than an imperative to affirm or reject. In this it reflected a sense of openness, also encapsulated in the quote drawn from one of the key texts of the historical avant-garde, Bruno Taut's *Stadtbaukunst alter und neuer Zeit*, which prophetically concluded the catalog with a praise of "eternal building," not in the sense of a noun, but of a verb: eternity belongs to the process, to the activity of *bauen* and not to the resulting edifice. "Hej stad" was a rare moment in attempts to capture and channel that openness and energy, which, subsequently, for many reasons, largely disappeared from Swedish architectural culture; it was an attempt to tap into an energy that seemed to be in the air.

Metropolis and the limits of modernism

During the 1960s, the city began to emerge as the essential co-
nundrum of modern architecture, perhaps even as that which
would eventually force it to become something other than modern, although the prefix "post-" would soon be appropriated by
those who advocated a revival of historical styles. Modernism,
both as a concept and as an effective historical reality, had already been questioned from a number of perspectives in the
work of historians emerging after the Second World War, all
the way from the attempts to retrieve lost organic possibilities
in Bruno Zevi, to Reyner Banham's vision of renewed modernism that would finally cut the ties to the Beaux-Arts tradition
and become truly modern.[4] In these and other successive re-
readings of the past, the possibility of retrieval however came to
appear increasingly remote, and it was overlaid with new concepts and experiences derived from a transformed technological
landscape. Urban space suddenly became the object of reading,
it appeared as a text or a historical palimpsest, or a collage; or
it became an organism based in processes of metabolism, or a
system or assemblage of flows and conduits.[5] Sometimes this

4. For discussions of the successive generations of postwar historians, see
    Panayotis Tournikiotis, *The Historiography of Modern Architecture* (Cam-
    bridge, Mass.: MIT Press. 1999), and Anthony Vidler, *Historians of the
    Immediate Present: Inventing Architectural Modernism* (Cambridge, Mass.:
    MIT, 2008).
5. A particularly interesting case of this transformation, although less
    known and situated at the margins of the architectural discourse of
    the late sixties and early seventies, is the work of the French research
    collective Cerfi (Centre de recherche et de formation institutionnelles).
    Drawing on Foucault, Deleuze, and Guattari, they began to theorize the
    city as an assemblage of "collective facilities" that channel, block, and
    incite desire. In the end, they suggest, this implies that the city cannot
    be taken as an ultimate category, but emerges as a higher level of col-
    lective facilities that in turn is inscribed in a larger territorial organiza-
    tion that again is part of an even larger system, and so on, without any
    defined limits. The city becomes a fixating and stabilizing machine, or
    a kind of relay or switch that on a certain level overcodes and connects
    flows that originate on a lower level and continue on a higher one. See

transformed perception was intended to lay the foundation for a new urban science, but first and foremost it was perceived as heralding a time of experimentation, a hedonist affirmation of the imaginary, chance, and openness, in the face of which many (though not all) of the earlier modernist utopias simply seemed far too bereft of pleasure to sustain interest.[6]

To some extent, the city had always remained on the horizon as the key problem ever since the final break-up of the classical paradigm in the beginning of the nineteenth century, or even earlier. Manfredo Tafuri, in his influential *Progetto e utopia*

Cerfi, *Recherches* No. 13 (1973), *Généalogie du capital: 1. Les équipements du pouvoir*, and my "Genealogy of Capital and the City: Cerfi, Deleuze, and Guattari", in Hélène Frichot, Catharina Gabrielsson, and Jonatan Metzger (eds.), *Deleuze and the City* (Edinburgh: Edinburgh University Press, 2016).

6.   "Urbanism," writes Jonathan Crary in a study of the urban imaginary of J. G. Ballard, "collided with that moment in capitalism when the rationalization of built space became secondary to problems of speed and the maximization of circulation. Urbanism continued to operate in an increasingly bereft domain: it sought to impose spatial intelligibility onto a locale that was being transformed by the antiterritoriality of capital." See Crary, "J. G. Ballard and the Promiscuity of Forms," *Zone* 1/2 (1986), 159. The reactions to such deterritorializing forces were of course highly variable, from attempts to regain control, to more celebratory modes, as in the case of Archigram and others who perceived these forces as heralding a culture of individual desire and fantasy. This development finds an interesting parallel in the trajectory of Roland Barthes, leading from the early critique of ideology (*Mythologies*, 1957) through a scientistic structuralism (*Éléments de sémiologie*, 1963) to a hedonism of reading understood an act of writing, as in his famous distinction in *Le plaisir du texte* (1973) between texts that are "lisible" and those that are "scriptible." A crucial turning is the remarkable self-destructing analysis of Balzac in *S/Z* (1970), where the sheer "scientificity" of the categorical system leads to an almost total dispersal of the object of study. What is important, Barthes often underlines in the later work, is not so much to dispel the illusions of ideology, but rather to dismantle the very idea of *truth*. Interestingly enough, these statements can be read in conjunction with his understanding of the city as a text, which Barthes first formulates in terms of the possibility of an urban semiology ("Sémiologie et urbanisme", 1967), but then gradually transforms into a new type of *jouissance* in the drift of signs and in the temptation of the late modern flâneur to lose himself in a forest of symbols, as in *L'empire des signes* (1970).

(1973), goes so far as to locate the beginning of this crisis in the mid-eighteenth century and the paradigmatic attempts of Abbé Laugier, in his *Observations sur l'architecture* (1756), to cover over the gap opened up between the nascent urban form and nature by representing the former in terms of landscape painting. This crisis—which in Tafuri's chronology antedates the invention of proto-modernist architectural languages, and the unhinging of style from the classical orders in the 1820s—could, he suggests, be kept at bay throughout the nineteenth century by the various projects for urban reform and renewal, but became rampant once more at the time of the early modern masters. If the activities of the avant-garde aspired towards a synthesis based on architecture and design, these disciplines were soon faced with problems emanating from the level beyond their own technical competence, from the city as a big machine, and finally, they were shipwrecked on the rocks of capital itself, the ultimate machine, whose concrete effects on the spatial ordering of social relations could not be theorized within a discourse of architectural form.

During a transitional stage, the idea of the *plan* seemed like the instrument that would finally allow architecture to exert its own competence over the whole urban territory, although this illusion, Tafuri suggests, was soon dispelled by the global economic restructuring that occurred in the wake of the Wall Street crash. Within the policies of an expanding and active state, architecture became a mediating link between utopian projection and political realism, and the avant-garde urban visions of the 1920s were in fact only failed attempts to provide formal solutions to problems whose answers could not be found at the level of design.

One of the most telling of these visions was the attempt within the *Neue Sachlichkeit* to adjust to the model of the assembly line. This was an attempt to recast the task of architecture on the basis of a generalized Taylorism, and to seize control over

77

the entire process that leads from the singular element to the city-totality, within which the individual object is dissolved in a cycle that also mobilizes the user and lays claims to displace older forms of aesthetic experience. This is displayed in Ludwig Hilberseimer's manifesto *Großstadtarchitektur* (1927), which proposes a reading of the city as a continuous chain where no link has priority, and where eventually the moment of *groß* takes precedence over *Stadt*. The issue is no longer the Metropolis as a bounded place with a specific identity, the "mother city"—thus severing the "metro-" from its Greek root *meter*, mother—but the Metropolis-machine, whose basic habitat unity is the singular cell, while the edifice, and eventually the city, ceases to be a basic form. Just as place and space, nuances and exceptions must disappear for this Metropolitan logic to unfold, and with them all of architecture's traditional dimensions, so too the new scaleless architecture takes us away from the experiencing subject and its identification with an affective environment, or more precisely, opens up the possibility of a subjective perception whose anonymity constitutes a moment of inescapable *truth* condensed in the image of the assembly line.

Significantly enough, this loss of place, which extends from the disruption of the image of the city, to use Kevin Lynch's expression, to the violent displacement of the phenomenological space-time coordinates of the perceiving subject, could also be reinterpreted as a kind of emancipatory nihilism, as was the case in the writings of Massimo Cacciari, whose early work developed in close connection to Tafuri's. Cacciari takes his cues partly from Heidegger, and somewhat surprisingly argues that if modernity does not allow for dwelling as that which Heidegger, in most traditional readings, would appear to mourn,[7] then the lesson to be drawn from his work is that this condition is not

7.   For more on this, see chap. 4 below.

just de facto irreversible, but must be affirmed. In the essay "Eupaulinos, or Architecture," written in the form of a review essay of Tafuri and Francesco Dal Co's *Modern Architecture*,[8] Cacciari emphatically denies that Heidegger's writings on technology and dwelling advocate a return to an authentic world, or any nostalgia for a pre-modern unity of man and world. Their task, Cacciari suggests, is rather to create the conceptual underpinning of an *authentic housing for inauthenticity*, and for an architecture that testifies to the absence and impossibility of dwelling in the modern Metropolis. Heidegger thus points to the double nature of modern architecture, its misunderstanding of itself: he renders "impossible or inconceivable the Values and Purposes on which this architecture nourishes itself,"[9] but he also shows what it in fact performs. Modern architecture, Cacciari later claims, in fact undertakes a radical "uprooting from the place (as a place of dwelling)," which is the "exact opposite of Heidegger's *Holzwege*." The architecture "'without qualities' of the Metropolis—a conscious image of fulfilled nihilism—excludes the characteristics of the place."[10]

This uprooting, of which Cacciari finds the clearest expression even as early as in Adolf Loos, is not just simply nothingness or a negative nihilism, but rather is an understanding of dwelling itself as an act of resistance. The nostalgia that per-

8. "Eupalinos, or Architecture," trans. Stephen Sartarelli, in K M. Hays (ed.): *Architecture Theory since 1968* (Cambridge, Mass: MIT, 1998); Manfredo Tafuri and Francesco Dal Co, *Modern Architecture*, trans. Erich Robert Wolf (New York: Rizzoli, 1980), 2 vols. Another important aspect of the background to Cacciari's discussion can be found in Dal Co's introductory essay "Dwelling and the Places of Modernity," in *Figures of Architecture and Thought: German Architectural Culture 1890–1920*, trans. S. Sartarelli (New York: Rizzoli, 1990). For a discussion of Cacciari's relation to Heidegger, see my *The Silences of Mies* (Stockholm: Axl Books, 2008), 22–40.
9. Cacciari, "Eupaulinos," 394.
10. *Architecture and Nihilism: On the Philosophy of Modern Architecture*, trans. Stephen Sartarelli (New Haven: Yale University Press, 1993), 199f.

meates both the Werkbund and expressionism (specifically in the latter's resistance to the *Sachlichkeit* of someone like Hilberseimer, to which it opposes a synthetic and mediated return to the symbolic and humanist features of the tradition) has, in Loos, already been transformed into a project that radically accepts its own finite condition, but in this it also opens up another time, or rather "the multiplicity of times that must be recognized, analyzed, and composed," so that "no absolute may resound in this space-time."[11] Throughout Cacciari's various re-readings of Loos, he stresses the need for a complete acceptance of the disruptions of modernity, but also the demand that this condition be accounted for again and again, in continuous acts of displacement and transformation. In this, it can paradoxically enough become the basis of a positive and productive nihilism, which is the other side of that which first appears as a purely "negative thought," and that "registers the leaps, the ruptures, the innovations that occur in history, never the flow, the transition, the historic continuum."[12] The Metropolis becomes the limit of the project of modern architecture, its moment of crisis, but also an opening and a possibility, in the sense that there can be something like a "project *of* crisis,"[13] a way to understand the loss of unity as a moment of freedom.

Controlling space

The problem of how architecture and urban planning could seize control over the forces and dynamisms of the Metropolis had been closely connected to the emerging social sciences at the turn of the century, as can be seen in the writings of German sociologists such as Weber, Simmel, and Sombart, and in

11.   Ibid., 203.
12.   Ibid., 13.
13.   For this reading, see Marco Biraghi, *Progetto di crisi; Manfredo Tafuri e l'architettura contemporanea* (Milan: Christian Marinotti Edizioni, 2005).

the theories developed by their French colleagues, most notably Tarde and Durkheim. If the city was sick, it needed to be cured, and only a joint effort of the sciences and the discourse of urbanism could set it back on the right track.

But at the time when urban sociology was emerging as a systematic field of inquiry, urbanism as a discursive tradition had in fact already been inaugurated in Ildefonso Cerdá's *Teoría general de la urbanización* (1867), a massive unfinished work that attracted few readers, and whose influence on posterity was largely indirect.[14] Published the same year as the first volume of Marx's *Capital*, Cerdá's *Teoría general* proposed an analysis of modern society that in some respects was just as encompassing as its German counterpart. While it was conceived as a theoretical reflection on, and ideological support for, his 1859 extension plan for Barcelona, Cerdá presents his treatise with great self-confidence as an entire new science that requires a new vocabulary—"the study of a new subject, a completely new, intact, virgin one, in which everything being new, even the words, which I had to seek and invent, had to be new"[15]—covering both the object (urbanization as a physical process) and the discourse (urbanism, city planning), and that should give us access to the

14. *Teoría general de la urbanización* (Madrid: Imprenta Española, 1867); partial English translation as *The Five Bases of the General Theory of Urbanization*, ed. Arturo Soria y Puig, trans. Bernard Miller and Mary Fons i Fleming (Madrid: Electa España, 1999); partial French translation by Antonio Lopez de Aberasturi, with an introduction by Françoise Choay, *La théorie générale de l'urbanisation* (Paris: Europan, 2005). The absence of immediate posterity can to some extent be explained by the accusations of socialist leanings that Cerdá soon faced, but the most likely reasons is the unfinished state of the book, as well as its size (the first part, the only part published, comprises two volumes, 800 pages each). Among his immediate successors, only Arturo Soria y Mata mentions him explicitly, in his 1894 treatise *Ciudad Lineal*. For general studies of Cerdá's work and his influence, see Fabian Estape, *Vida y obra de Ildefonso Cerdá* (Barcelona: Ediciones Península, 2001), and Ernst Christian Hengstenberg, *Ildefonso Cerdá und sein Einfluss auf Theorie und Praxis des Städtebaus*, diss. (Munich: Technische Universität, 1986).
15. Cerdá, *The Five Bases*, 80.

general principles that govern the connections of human beings and their objects.

Urbanism is the object of a treatise that must be able to comprehend the entirety of social life, and it deals not only with technical issues in a restricted sense, as can be seen in the overall plan of the book. The two volumes published were in fact only the first of four parts: the first part deals with urbanism as a concrete phenomenon, and provides us with a "dissection" (consisting of a general exposé followed by statistical material relating to the city of Barcelona), the second part would have established the theory, the third would have laid out its technical applications, and the fourth, finally, would have returned us to a concrete application in the case of Barcelona.

In the first part, where he outlines his universal theory, Cerdá emphasizes that nothing of importance has been written on the topic before his own book, but that such a theory is required by a new civilization based on movement and communication, on speed, the steam engine, electricity, and various systems of transport and telecommunications.[16] This also demands that it go beyond traditional forms of how to think the city—thus the necessity of forging a new vocabulary, and Cerdá stresses that *urbs* and its various derivations captures this better than city, *ciudad* (the term still used in his earlier treatise *Teoría de la construcción de ciudades*, 1859–61) with its roots in *civitas*, and whose associations to citizenship and legal and political issues tends to obscure the material dimension that he wants to highlight. Materiality does however exceed the idea of stability and permanence of physical structure derived from the Vitruvian lexicon: urbanism must comprehend the link between rest and movement, housing and circulation, in the widest possible sense, with movement as the

16. As comes across in his earlier *Teoría del enlace del movimiento de las vías marítimas y terrestres* (1863), written as a companion to project for an intermodal freight transportation system for the port of Barcelona.

key issue: "a vast swirling ocean of persons, of things, of inter-
ests of every sort, of a thousand diverse elements."[17] The history
of the urban, Cerdá suggests, is in fact nothing but the history
of man based on technical mutations that above all become visible in forms of locomotion and transport. The theory that Cerdá
proposes significantly eschews traditional symbolisms and centrality, and instead advocates a lateral grid structure that is in
principle extended infinitely, so that the difference between the
rural and the urban eventually would be dissolved. The task is to
create a continuous and optimally governable system,[18] including on the level of social inequities. When read alongside Marx,
Cerdá may at first sight appear as one more reformist theoreti-
cian, for whom the balancing out of class differences was the essential task, as comes across in the plan for an even distribution
of parks, churches, social services, etc. throughout the urban grid,
in order to avoid unrest and conflict. But the reforms that he proposes are not simply additions to existing structures or piecemeal
engineering intervention, but more like a re-forming from the
bottom up, a way of reordering the logistics of the life process
itself, in which the particular spatial and architectural structures
deployed are tools that as such can be exchanged for others within
the larger project.

This new science needs to combine a quantitative as well as
a structural approach, the first based in statistics, whereas the
structural models as well as the tools of historical analysis are
derived from anatomy and biology, with Cuvier and Saint-
Hilaire as primary sources. *Dissection* is the key word for the
urban anatomist, and the body provides the structural model,
which on one level is a traditional motif derived straight from
Alberti, but, here, also relates to a developing discourse of the

17.   Cerdá, *The Five Bases*, 79.
18.   For this reading, see Pier Vittorio Aureli, *The Possibility of an Absolute
Architecture* (Cambridge, Mass.: MIT, 2011), 9ff.

83

life sciences, which gives it a particularly modern inflection. Cerdá's work can in this respect be located at a crucial position within what Adrian Forty calls the formation of a modern architectural vocabulary, in which we find a set of new alliances with the sciences.[19] The body is no longer a model for architecture in the symbolic sense—an idea that had already begun to be phased out at the beginning of the century, from Durand onward—and instead emerges as a living entity, on which urbanism in turn acts as an organic structure on a superior level.

In her study of the interplay between "rule" (the formation of a systematic language of architecture) and "model" (utopian projection), Françoise Choay proposes that we should understand the nascent discourse of urbanism in the second part of the nineteenth century as a mode of instauration that performs a gesture similar to Alberti's in his *De re aedeficatoria*. This instauration has five fundamental aspects, Choay suggests, all of which she locates already in Alberti: it should form an *organic totality*; it should be signed by an author that presents himself in the *first person singular*; it should be *autonomous*, i.e., not subjected to any other tradition or discipline; it should propose *universal principles* and *generative rules* that allow for the creation of new things, and not just transmit a body of practical precepts; and finally, its rules must apply to *architecture as a whole*, from the singular edifice to the city in its totality.[20] As an instauration, the treatise is scientific (it is body of *rules*), it opposes a negative and

19.   See Forty, *Words and Buildings: A Vocabulary of Modern Architecture* (London: Thames & Hudson, 2000), for instance the discussion of the concept of "circulation" and its connection to the life sciences, 87–101. The section that deals with urbanism (103–117) however contains no reference to Cerdá or to the specific history of the term "urbanism."

20.   See Choay, *La règle et le modèle* (Paris: Seuil, 1980), 30. For Choay, this instauration is what constitutes Alberti's modernity, and sets him apart from Vitruvius, in whom we find merely a survey of empirical observations not organized into a systematic structure; se *La règle*, chap. 2, esp. 146–155.

a positive image of the city, in order to propose a remedy (it is a *model*); and finally projects the idea of the constructor as a hero, a master Architect who is the *subject* of the instauration.

While it is true that all these features are abundantly present in *Teoría general*, Choay's analysis may also downplay something of the newness of Cerdá's theory, precisely by portraying it as an almost Cartesian set of rules for the direction of the mind, a move that may also have lead her to inscribe Alberti's modernity in an epistemic order that would have to wait for Cartesianism to emerge.[21] Cerdá's *Teoría* could perhaps more fruitfully be read as a biopolitical treatise in the sense of the term proposed by Foucault,[22] i.e., not so much as a body of universal rules as a way of monitoring and surveying the physical, material, and spatial conditions of the *population*, which now displaces the old body politic, or more precisely comprehends it as living multiplicity

21. The characteristics ascribed to the inaugurating treatise come close to the idea of the philosophical system that we find delineated in Descartes and the tradition of rationalism, and is only consolidated in a full-blown form in German Idealism, in Fichte, Schelling, and Hegel. The emphasis on the system as the projection from a subject is foreign to Renaissance thought as it is most often understood, as still largely dependent on Neo-Platonism, and for which the world still appears an infinitely interpretable text, a web of analogies and correspondences that cannot be fully grasped within a first-person perspective; see, for instance, the analysis of the "prose of the world" in Michel Foucault, *Les mots et les choses* (Paris: Gallimard, 1966), 32–59, and, from a different perspective, Hans Blumenberg, *Die Lesbarkeit der Welt* (Frankfurt am Main: Suhrkamp, 1986), 69–85. These interpretations, however, tend to focus on the sciences, and downplay the new claims made for art in the Renaissance, which is the focus of Choay. The question remains as to what extent we can project later philosophical claims back in time, or inversely, see these later claims as already prefigured in earlier artistic practices.
22. For this reading, see Andrea Cavaletti, *La città biopolitica: Mitologie della sicurezza* (Milan: Mondadori, 2005). Françoise Choay also reads Cerdá in a Foucauldian perspective, although largely drawing on the theory of discipline and Foucault's collaborative research on the hospital and the medicalization of urban space; see *La Règle et le Modèle*, 280–84. From the vantage point of the present it seems that Foucault's later work on biopolitics, especially the 1977–78 lectures on *Security, Territory, Population* (still unpublished when Choay's book was written), would be more relevant to Cerdá.

that can no longer be simply controlled and disciplined through the imposition of a geometric segmenting of space, but must be seen as a political *nature*. Politics is a physics, as the physiocrats had already said, which is why it requires particular forms of governing capable of drawing on, channeling, and extracting a surplus value from the population's life. What is at stake, at least if we look at what would develop on the basis of Cerdá, is not a defined set of precepts, but a fluid and impure concept of theory that requires conceptual tools borrowed from a host of other disciplines; the attempt is not to unearth something like an essence of architecture or of the city, but to understand them as living and evolving entities.

Perhaps it would not be wholly misleading to say that the discourse of modern architecture has two main roots: one the one hand it launches the idea of an architectonic form that at a certain point could claim to break away from the eclecticism and stylistic profusion of the nineteenth century and to discover a new coherence, a universal (or later, "international") style— i.e., a style that in fact no longer aspires to be a style, but the expression of the *truth* of the epoch, gathering its industrial and technological advances into an optimal solution to a problem. Le Corbusier's early writings, from his 1923 *Vers une architecture* onward, is a paradigmatic case of this, and for a long time this narration tended to inform a certain type of architectural history, which could draw selectively on the statements of the early modern masters themselves. This is a narrative that purports to take us from confusion to clarity, simplicity, honesty, and truth, and it is predicated upon certain visual and morphological characteristics that locate the trajectory of architecture as closely parallel to that of painting and sculpture, for instance as a common path toward abstraction. On the other hand, architecture may be understood as *a way of spatializing power relations*, as a way of implementing diagrams and providing materiality to the abstract machine of Capital,[23] and here urbanism, with its focus on larger processes, flows, and networks, becomes essential. In this second story, the debates on style, ornaments, monochromatic surfaces, etc., appear as effects of a more profound development, which can be understood as the spatial regimentation concomitant with the production of the modern subject—a theme which on closer inspection in fact can be seen to permeate the writings of the early modernist architects themselves, in which the assumed emotional and affective responses of the subjects inhabiting modern architecture are always present. Corbusier's *machine à habiter* is in this perspective not at all the epitome of a machine aesthetic that looks to formal models, but *precisely, literally*, a machine that on the basis of a given input produces life, enhances the living body, and steers its vital flows, whose achievement of an optimal solution to the problem of the habitat is closely aligned with an analysis of family, sexual reproduction, and a whole biopolitical discourse.

Any straightforward alternative between these two stories can of course only result from an idealization. In reality they are intertwined at each historical moment and can only be artificially separated; and yet the tension between them can be taken to organize many of the debates of the twentieth century, ranging from differing claims made in the name of modernism about which one of them is truly modern, to the later claims that one of them must be discarded in order for modernism to be overcome. One such problem with repercussions across the whole field of culture and politics emerged in the postwar attempts,

23. "Diagram" and "abstract machine" are here used with reference to Deleuze and Guattari; cf. Deleuze, *Foucault*, trans. Seán Hand (London: Athlone, 1988), and Deleuze and Guattari, *Thousand Plateaus*, trans. Brian Massumi (Minneapolis: University of Minnesota Press, 1987). These terms are obviously highly fluid; for a discussion of various uses and applications to architecture, which however have tended towards largely formalist interpretations that are distant from the emphasis on relations of power in Foucault and Deleuze, see *Any* 24 (1998), "Diagram Work."

inside and outside the CIAM,[24] to rethink the idea of control that seemed to have obsessed early modernists, and it sparked the question how to achieve complexity and unpredictability without surrendering to chaos. How to find techniques for planning the unplanned and even unplannable, how to approach the event in its sheer contingency as that which architecture must not only tolerate, but also support, was a question that directly engaged the biopolitical dimension, but also that of form: were there particular forms, structures, assemblages, etc., that would allow and even incite a free behavior, that would engage the user's capacity for reinterpreting the environment and making dwelling and inhabiting into active modes of being rather than adjustment to given parameters?

At the historical juncture that is our theme here, the experience of the city as something beyond control, as something that not only *de facto* was out of control, but perhaps *ought* to be allowed to unfold in a way that defied rational planning, resulted from the tremendous shifts that occurred in the postwar period and reached its first climactic point in the sixties. The models of urbanism that would emerge from the break-up of the modernist city could however at first sight not have seemed further apart. Some turned towards futurist visions of technology, as in the case of collective projects like the British group Archigram or the Italian Archizoom, or to a heretic reading of the history of architecture in the light of pop art, as in Robert Venturi's *Complexity and Contradiction in Architecture* (1966), later transformed into a new appraisal of the semiotic flows of capitalism itself, which demand of us a certain "learning from Las Vegas," as Venturi and Denise Scott Brown would famously claim in their 1972 book. Others took a turn towards various versions of history as the reservoir of depth, as in the case of

24.   For more on CIAM and the problem of planning vs. contingency, see chap. 3 below.

Aldo Rossi, who in *L'architettura della città* (1966) proposed that the architectural process as the preservation of sense must be re-grounded in an inescapable historical contingency. The urban fabric, Rossi claimed, was organized around a set of artifacts and monuments that constituted a memory, a more profound permanence that makes both repetition and difference possible. Consciously or not, "Hej stad" at Moderna Museet partakes of all these tendencies, and coincidental as it may be, the year 1966 seems to form something of a crucial juncture.

Grasping this moment in all its inner contradictions is no doubt a momentous task, and in the following, I will merely attempt to delimit its outer perimeters, as they appear in urban models of Venturi and his colleagues, and in Rossi. Many other versions were proposed, but it makes sense to say that most other proposals could be located somewhere between these two extremes. On many levels they are diametrically opposed, in the sense that the answers they provide diverge completely; on closer inspection, the difference begin to resonate, as if they were revolving around some absent center.

Style and image

Venturi's revolt is part of modern architecture's extended and complex exchange with mass culture, which for a long time led a clandestine life in architectural discourse, at least in its official historiography. The focus has however shifted, and the recent emergence of this connection as an object of research corresponds to a step back from some of the most visible claims of early modernism, or at least those claims that for a long time guided modernist historians. For most architects—no matter how much they may have understood their work as a break with the past, undertaken in the name of formal purity, abstraction, or some other concept that today is little more than an object of suspicion or even disdain—it was patent that any modernity in search of its own style must also include and project a new lifestyle, that it must be able to influence everyday behavior, generate a distinctive look, and fashion desirable objects, if it is to seize hold of the general public and become *desirable*. The utopian moment in modernism is in this way an integral part of a new visual culture and the system of media and image distribution that had already begun to emerge in the middle of the nineteenth century—the age of mechanical reproducibility, as Benjamin said with reference to photography and cinema, although he, too, though more obliquely, references architecture—and it has as one of its main objectives the production of a desiring subject that itself exists as an agent of consumption, first and foremost precisely of the *image* of modernity.

This is why it can arguably be deemed superficial simply to reject the problem of style as superficial; instead it must be thought as an element belonging to the very substance of architecture, if the latter is understood as a means of persuasion and identification through form and image, which it can and must be. This issue had been raised sharply by Schinkel, as a question of what could be accepted as the organic expression of the contemporary moment, which in his case meant to oppose the imminent threat of fashion as a severing of form and content. In 1826, returning to Berlin from his journey to England, where he had encountered the technological marvels of industrialism, he notes "the modern age makes everything easy, it no longer believes in permanence, and has lost all sense of monumentality." This is an epoch, he continues, "in which everything becomes mobile, even that which was supposed to be most durable, namely the art of building, in which the word fashion becomes widespread in architecture, where forms, materials, and every tool can be understood as a plaything to be treated as one wants, where one is prone to try everything since nothing is in its place (*weil nichts an seinem Orte steht*), and nothing seems required."²⁵ These questions were then pursued in what would become known as the German style debate, opened by Heinrich Hübsch in 1828 with his simple question: "In what style should we build?" ²⁶ This idea of a style that would not be a superficial appendix, but express the inner constructive logic, also informs the later discourse of tectonics, where the truth of architecture was dependent on whether a new "juncture" between inside and outside could be established, an organic bond between *Stilhülse* and *Kern*, *Kunstform* and *Kernform*.²⁷ The title of Corbusier's first book shows his aspirations to attain such a reunification: *Vers une architecture*, "towards an architecture," i.e., a situation where architecture would begin to *exist at all* in the emphatic sense, which was lost in the first English translation in 1927, *Towards A New Architecture*, which emphasizes mere novelty. Just as for Schinkel, *newness* as such is not essential, but it is rather *truth*, in the sense of a formal language consonant with the current standard of technology and social development; if the answer seems new, it is only because the question remains the same— for Corbusier even explicitly the same as in ancient Greece. As he famously states, the modern racecar is just as much as the Parthenon the solution to a well-posed problem, and as such, it is dependent on a long process of type formation that eventually

25. Schinkel, cited in Fritz Neumeyer, "Tektonik: Das Schauspiel der Objektivität und die Wahrheit des Architekturschauspiels," in Hans Kollhoff (ed.), *Über Tektonik in der Baukunst* (Braunschweig: Vieweg & Sohn, 1993), 59. This *threatening* idea of fashion would, just like the idea of technology, become transformed into an instrumental one in the beginning of the twentieth century, where the question no longer bears on *whether* architecture resembles fashion, but on *what type* of fashion it should choose as its model, as can be seen in the writings of Adolf Loos and Le Corbusier. For further discussion, see Mark Wigley, *White Walls, Designer Dresses* (Cambridge. Mass.: MIT, 1995).

26. For this discussion, see Wolfgang Herrman (ed.), *In What Style Should We Build? The German Debate on Architectural Style* (Santa Monica: Getty Center, 1992).

27. See Werner Oechslin, *Stilhülse und Kern: Otto Wagner, Adolf Loos und der evolutionäre Weg zur modernen Architektur* (Berlin: Ernst & Sohn, 1994).

reaches perfection.

Corbusier's understanding of modern architecture as a mass medium that must utilize the most sophisticated techniques of publicity, which has been analyzed in detail by Beatriz Colomina,[28] does not contradict the search for classical perfection; it is precisely its modern condition of possibility. His editorial work with *Esprit nouveau* as well as his own publications show his command of marketing and visual techniques, and how eternal values can only be realized through a strategic intelligence that employs all the tricks of a new trade. The one and unique style, embodying not taste but universal necessity— and which thus may present itself as non-style—can then, on the level of affective impact, be understood as yet another image, just as functionalism in order to impose itself as a desirable look need not function better than anything that preceded it, only project the image of modernity and progress in a convincing way.[29]

When early modernism is viewed in this perspective, the idea of an overcoming of a "great divide" between avant-garde and mass culture as the basis of the shift between the postmodern and the modern becomes tenuous.[30] The image of such a divide was perhaps for the first time visible in the debate between Benjamin and Adorno in the thirties, where we in Benjamin would find an affirmation of new reproduction technologies, the decay of the aura, and the entry of the artwork into the

28. See Beatriz Colomina, *Privacy and Publicity: Modern Architecture as Mass Media* (Cambridge, Mass.: MIT, 1994).

29. See, for instance, Jean Baudrillard, *Pour une critique de l'économie politique du signe* (Paris: Gallimard, 1972), 229–255, and the concluding discussion in Reyner Banham, *Theory and Design in the first Machine Age* (London: Architectural Press, 1960), 320–25.

30. I borrow this expression from Andreas Huyssen, *After the Great Divide: Modernism, Mass Culture, Postmodernism* (Bloomington: Indiana University Press, 1987). Many other similar discussions could be cited, although Huyssen seems to me to formulate it in the most concise and systematic fashion.

sphere of social circulation ("exhibition value," as Benjamin somewhat curiously calls it), in Adorno the consistent attempt to uphold a Kantian claim for aesthetic autonomy and to save the negative transcendence of the work from being submerged into the world of the commodity—a claim that eventually, in the postmodern era, would finally have become antiquated.[31] But against a dualist reading of this discussion, it may be argued that purity and transcendence were always values resulting from a particular twist within the logic of the commodity rather than a break with it, and that the various forms of exchange between the work and commodification in fact are what have defined the dialectic of autonomy from the outset. This does obviously not mean that autonomy would be an illusion or a simple mirage, only that it is always conditioned by its other, and that the resistance that the work puts up to the world, the distance that it produces to the world, always needs to borrow its resources from this same world, and that these resources will always return inside the work, although not necessarily, perhaps even not at all, as an objective moment, as a depiction of representation of an empirical outside—all of which is already there in Adorno's early argument against Benjamin, and will subsequently become an integral part in his theory of autonomy.

Learning from Pop

Coming back to Venturi, it is undeniable that we find here a new sensibility, and a highly effective rhetoric that sets up a whole series of oppositions between new and old, but rather than seeing this as a break with the past, it may be more productive to see it as a re-activation of elements that were already there, and are simply reconfigured in a new way. While his two manifesto-like works, *Complexity and Contradiction in Architecture*

31.   The letters of Benjamin and Adorno are translated in *Aesthetics and Politics* (London: New Left Books, 1977), 100–141.

(1966) and *Learning from Las Vegas* (1972, co-authored with Denise Scott Brown and Steven Izenour), are replete with negative
judgments about the past, they can also, and more positively,
be seen as the beginning of an American tradition of cultural
studies[32] that emerges from a dialog with pop art, attempting to
map the experience of the commercial landscape as a different
type of order: "Some of the vivid lessons of pop art, involving
scale and context," Venturi writes in the conclusion to the first
book, "should have awakened architects from prim dreams of
pure order," and henceforth it is "perhaps from the everyday
landscape, vulgar and disdained, that we can draw the complex
and contradictory order that is valid and vital for our architecture as an urbanistic whole."[33]

Not without irony, Venturi presents *Complexity and
Contradiction* as a "gentle manifesto," and, in the introductory
sections, he manipulates his historical references with subtle
displacements, reinterpreting rather than simply rejecting the
modernist legacy. His examples are drawn from the whole of
architectural history from the Renaissance to Le Corbusier,
Aalto, and Kahn, in order to delineate a different take on tradition than the one championed by predecessors like Pevsner and
Giedion. The examples are widely separated in space and time,
not in order to point to eternal principles, but rather to provide
a kind of counter-historical thrust to the linear narratives of
progress.[34] Just as the images in *Complexity and Contradiction* still

32. See Fredric Jameson, *The Seeds of Time* (New York: Columbia University
Press, 1994), 141. In this sense there is a straight line leading from Ven-
turi to Koolhaas; see the comments on Venturi in *The Harvard Guide to
Shopping* (Cologne: Taschen, 2001).

33. Robert Venturi, *Complexity and Contradiction in Architecture* (New York:
The Museum of Modern Art, 1966), 104. Henceforth cited in the text
as CCA.

34. On one level there is no fundamental methodological difference
between Giedion and Venturi: both of them mobilize different elements from the past to justify current production, and from Tafuri's
perspective they are equally operative. What Venturi opposes is rather

94

obey—gently, one might say—the codes of architectural photography, the argument of the book, even though it proposes new criteria, largely remains within the confines of architectural-historical analysis with its connoisseurship and erudite references. *Learning from Las Vegas* on the other hand draws on a descriptive phenomenological technique, and the order on the Strip paradigmatically appears as an image seen through a windscreen.[35] In its flattened and serial quality, the imagery shares some of the features of certain groundbreaking art works from the period, most patently Ed Ruscha's laconic *Twentysix Gasoline Stations* (1963) and *Every Building on the Sunset Strip* (1966),[36] but also, perhaps more obliquely, Dan Graham's *Homes for America* (1966). Both employ seriality to dismantle the autonomy of high modernism, although with different intentions and results: Ruscha aims for a deadpan pop matter-of-factness and an emptying out of signification, whereas Graham draws on the genre of photojournalism to produce a conceptual work that explores the hidden social connotations of minimalist reductionism.[37] In

a normative trajectory leading from past to present, which is why he eventually embraces the posthistorical model in *Learning from Las Vegas*, where all styles and forms exist in a total availability.

35. Which perhaps makes the method *phenomenalist* rather than *phenomenological*, the point being that the gaze through the windscreen, together with the sense of movement, tends to suspend the worldly anchoring of both subject and object in favor of a series of disincarnate images. Such distinctions may seem out of place here, but given the importance that phenomenology would have somewhat later in discussions of embodiment, anchoring, grounding, etc., it makes sense to read Venturi et al as deploying a kind of phenomenalist counter-strategy.

36. Ruscha's work even appears in a mock version, as an "'Edward Ruscha' elevation of the strip," *Learning from Las Vegas* (Cambridge, Mass.: MIT, 1977 [1972], 32–33. Henceforth cited as LLV.

37. For a discussion of these different pictorial strategies, see Jeff Wall, "Marks of Indifference: Aspects of Photography in, or as, Conceptual Art," in Ann Goldstein and Anne Rorimer (eds.), *Reconsidering the Object of Art: 1965–1975* (Los Angeles: Museum of Contemporary Art, 1996). The seeming emptiness in Ruscha is of course teeming with possible narratives; for an imaginative reading that establishes a connection to the cinema of the period, see Walead Beshty, "The City Without Quali-

the case of *Learning from Las Vegas*, the aim is that we should suspend our value judgment, at least temporarily, in order to transform the very ideas of value and judgment, thus making possible a mode of perception that thrives on precisely those values that had been eradicated from the canon of modern architecture. Irony, ambiguity, and polysemy are the weapons wielded against the imperatives of modernist utopianism, and if architecture is a mode of communication on all levels, it should not insulate itself as a utopian counter-image against the messiness of the historical city, or as a semiotic surplus in relation to its contemporary, commercial, and low descendant: in short, learning from Las Vegas means to learn how to take a new look at, and take on the look of, everyday life.[38]

Complexity and contradiction in architecture for Venturi result from its necessary participation in an equally complex and contradictory social and communicative urban form; its language is inevitably that of a multiplicity of styles and layers that need not be reformed on the basis of some radical new grammar.[39] If we are to reinstall the social function of archi-

ties: Photograph, Cinema, and the Post-Apocalyptic Ruin," *Site* 7–8 (2004).

38.   In the most systematic interpretation of Venturi and Scott Brown's work so far, Aron Vinegar stresses that we should not reduce the book to a precursor to the subsequent debate on postmodernism, or to a mere apotheosis of consumer culture, as is often the case, but rather understand it as a new take on everyday life. Drawing on Stanley Cavell's distinction between skepticism and the ordinary, Vinegar proposes that the proposal is that we should strive to attain a different mood, open to the ambiguities of perception and sensibility, rather than to settle for a choice between the modern and the postmodern. See Vinegar, *I Am a Monument: On Learning from Las Vegas* (Cambridge, Mass.: MIT, 2008), and Aron Vinegar and Michael J. Golec (eds.), *Relearning from Las Vegas* (Minneapolis: University of Minnesota Press, 2009).

39.   As we will see in chap. 4, other readings are possible. As Reinhold Martin suggests, Venturi and Scott Brown's ideas may be understood less in terms of a plea for populism and the dissolution of the high–low distinction than as a normalization, i.e., an adjustment of architecture's language through the methods of social science, drawing through the models of Levittown and Las Vegas.

tecture, we must speak the vernacular, and not escape to the inventions of ideal languages cleansed from the polysemic drift of actual history. Robert Stern has summarized these claims in three theses: *ornamentalism*, the detachment of the exterior from the interior, which is the basis of the famous thesis on the "decorated shed"; *contextualism*, the reinsertion of the building into the texture of the city; *allusionism*, the transformation of historical memory into a reservoir of available forms that no longer require an overarching formal unity.[40]

Current experience, Venturi suggests, has freed us from the weight of Puritanism, and we are able to affirm a richness of sense instead of a misguided clarity, which does not mean that we must jettison unity and truth, only that this now refers to the "difficult unity of inclusion rather than the easy unity of exclusion" (CCA 16). Such an inclusion opposes the idealized versions of the primitive and elemental, and it shows that Mies's "less is more" only makes sense as long as we pose strictly limited problems, whereas in the case of Philip Johnson's version of the Miesian glass boxes it shows its true face, in Venturi's famously laconic quip: "less is a bore" (17). This need not contradict the "desire for simplicity" (ibid.) in someone like Kahn, but simplicity must come from an inner complexity, just as the simple image offered by the Doric temple results from complex displacements and distorted geometries. Positive cases of this in the modern period include Le Corbusier (to the extent that he does not follow his own precepts) and Aalto, whose "complexity is part of the program and structure of the whole rather than a device justified only by the desire for expression" (18f).

We need to begin in the ambiguity belonging to perception

40. Robert Stern, "New Directions in Modern American Architecture: Postscript at the Edge of Modernism" (1977), reprinted in Kate Nesbitt, *Theorizing a New Agenda for Architecture: An Anthology of Architectural Theory, 1965–1995* (New York: Princeton Architectural Press, 1996).

itself, Venturi suggests, in what he, following the gestalt theory of Josef Albers, understands as the unavoidable discrepancy
between physical fact and psychological effect—a theory that is
just as applicable to abstract expressionism as it is to pop, although Venturi's preferred models are the recent pop painters.
Apart from Gestalt psychology, Venturi also, and more surprisingly, draws heavily on literary New Criticism, normally type-
cast as the epitome of high modernist autonomy. In parallel to
their discovery of the metaphysical poets, Venturi reassesses
mannerism, less in terms of a historical investigation than as
a search for elements for a new poetics that at the same time
finds support in a venerate classical and humanist tradition. He
cites the works of T. S. Eliot, Cleanth Brooks, Kenneth Burke,
and William Empson, and their exploration of the ambiguity of
poetical language (the most important source being Empson's
Seven Types of Ambiguity, 1957). Architecture, Venturi states, is
always "form *and* substance—abstract *and* concrete—and its
meaning derives from inner characteristics and its particular
context" (CCA 20). The *and* indicates an oscillation, which is
the source of the "ambiguity and tension characteristic to the
medium of architecture" (ibid.). Venturi's aim is however different from that of New Criticism, in the end even opposed to
it: instead of using ambiguity to undermine referentiality in the
name of aesthetic autonomy and the aloofness of the work, he
perceives it as a condition for participation in the messiness of
the world. An analogous displacement occurs in his use of T. S.
Eliot's technique for using citations: if these in Eliot become
signs of modernity as a wasteland, of a history that can only be
retrieved in fragments, and fundamentally display a tragic sensibility, in Venturi they become the material for an affirmation
of the present as plenitude and richness of sense.

   It is instructive to compare this semantic analogy between
architecture and language with the syntactic analysis launched

at the same time by someone like Eisenman. Both of them aspire to ground architecture in language, and both perform a
kind of decontextualization, in the sense that historical material
is detached from its organic dependence on particular moments
in time, although this leads in different directions: for Venturi,
the language dimension is *semantic*, that which transmits historical meaning and tradition, and the faith in this continuity of
meaning is what allows him proclaim a distance from a type a
modernism perceived as destructive of meaning; for Eisenman,
language is a generative *syntactic* structure that permits new and
unexpected statements to be produced, and makes it possible
for architecture to finally become a modernist, self-referential
art by neutralizing its inherited humanist desire to signify.[41]
At the end of the essay "A Significance for A&P Parking Lots,
or Learning from Las Vegas," two years after *Complexity and
Contradiction*, Venturi and Scott Brown reference both Joyce
and Eliot, and speak of a recycling of fragments and citations
as a "decreative" impulse in literature, connecting it to a pop
sensibility that would be able to extract new values from old
clichés by integrating them in a new context; for Eisenman the
issue is rather to call upon a new avant-garde and an abstract
generative capacity that breaks with the very idea of meaning
in architecture.[42]

41.   Once more, readings that align them rather than oppose them are
      equally possible, as in the case of Reinhold Martin, who suggests that
      both options depend on the insertion of architecture in an ecology of
      signs, in which the tension between semantics (Venturi) and syntax
      (Eisenman) is merely an inner fluctuation; see chap. 4, below.
42.   Significantly, Eisenman's work during this early phase makes virtually
      no reference to the city and urbanism, but remains within the orbit
      of the singular object, as in his series of Houses, or even the single
      architectural element that must be freed from its traditional semantic
      dimension. In this sense his work during this phase is a constant quest
      for autonomy, or for architecture to simply, once and for all, become
      modernist, as he understands the term. On the level of the city, a pure
      syntax would seem like a much more difficult proposal. Later, when
      Eisenman in the seventies begins his project "Cities of Artificial Excava-

The new complexity is a "both-and," an open additive process that is intended to generate a semantic surplus, unlike modern architecture, which for Venturi appears as an "either-or" where every element is required to be precisely itself and nothing else. Citing Louis Kahn's statement, that "Architecture must have bad spaces as well as good spaces" (CC 25), he advocates a multiplicity of signifying levels, which also may involve errors and distortions—details detached from the whole, scalar incongruities, contradictions between parts—that nevertheless contribute to the whole. Further on, with ironic reference to Giedion, he also determines this as "another dimension of 'space, time and architecture' which involves the multiple focus" (32). Complexity emerges when singular elements or whole assemblages have double or multiple roles, which for Venturi constitutes a more adequate response to the demand for flexibility than the separation between materials and functions in modernism. As always, the examples are garnered from sources far apart—Sant'Elia's futurist Città Nuova with its continually shifting functions, Corbusier's Plan Obus for Algiers, where the residential building at the same time constitutes the support for a highway, and Rauschenberg's Combines, where the pattern on the painting's surface are transferred to contiguous physical objects in order to produce an oscillating perception of the medium—with the purpose of showing that the modernist version of the tradition is in fact highly selective, and that it, when seen in a broader perspective, in fact displays a constant interest in complexity. The latter is not opposed to order, for it is only a strong order that may contain transformations and draw its energy from them: "Our buildings must survive the cigarette machine." (42)

The order that he advocates is a "difficult whole," which su-

tion," the new reference to the city also entails a return to semantics (without the term being used), even though of very different nature; see chap 6, below.

persedes the organic and expressive model of form that radiates from the center outward: the outside must be able to disconnect from the inside, a claim that eventually would lead to the thesis of the decorated shed. In these initial formulations the task is rather to show that the modern tradition too often makes use of gradual transitions and residual spaces, and Venturi suggests that we "break away from the contemporary concept (call it sickness) of spatial continuity and the tendency to erase every articulation between spaces, i.e., between outside and inside, between one space and another (between one reality and another)" (CC 82). This rejection of the inside-outside model, with its claim for expressive continuity, turns it back on a long legacy extending back at least to Louis Sullivan's famous form-function equation, itself based in a romantic philosophy of nature,[43] and instead opts for what we could call an allegorical method that emphasizes the separation of outward signs from inner core, and the need to understand the unity as the effect of interacting fragments, but also a contextualism acknowledging that the limit between inside and outside is the place where architecture begins to exist. "Since the inside is different from the outside," Venturi writes, "the wall—the point of change—becomes an architectural event," and architecture "occurs at the meeting of interior and exterior forces of use and space," so that the wall becomes "the spatial record of this resolution and its drama." (86)

The emphasis on fragments as the source of the whole also implies an idea of a series of inflections that mediate between the two: a maximal inflection generates complete continuity, a minimal one the autonomy of parts, which opens for a set of different possibilities rather than a normative ideal. This becomes particularly relevant on the urban scale: "An architecture that can simul-

43. For a discussion of Sullivan's indebtedness to a romantic philosophy of nature, see Forty, *Words and Buildings*, 177–79.

taneously recognize contradictory levels should be able to admit the paradox of the whole fragment: the building which is a whole at one level and a fragment of a greater whole on another level." (CC 103) Thus, it is on the level of urbanism that complexity and contradiction may be played out to the fullest extent, and where the inflected part-whole relationship attains maximal efficacy; it is here that the fragmentation of the urban landscape shows itself not as lack of order, and but as different and more difficult one that requires a multi-focus vision.

Learning from Las Vegas

Two years after *Contradiction and Complexity*, Venturi and Denise Scott Brown publish the article "A Significance for A&P Parking Lots, or Learning from Las Vegas,"[44] which would then reappear with slight alterations as the opening chapter of *Learning from Las Vegas*. Here we enter directly into the present, and we move beyond the tone of the gentle manifesto with its erudite historical references. To be sure, at the end of the article they underline that their only claim is to analyze Las Vegas as architectural communication, and not to pass a value judgment—but they also add that there is no reason to believe that "the methods of commercial persuasion and the skyline of signs analyzed here should not serve the purpose of civic and cultural enhancement" (LLV 6), and the reluctance to judge seems largely like a rhetorical move made in order to overcome the resistance of the modernist reader by inciting a willing suspension of disbelief. What we must strive for, they claim, can no longer be a radical reform, but to learn from the existing urban landscape, and this is why we must suspend a

44.   The initial article was published in *Architectural Forum* (March 1968), and reprinted in Nesbitt, *Theorizing a New Agenda*. The text cited here is the later version in *Learning from Las Vegas*. There are also important differences in terms of layout and the use of images from the first edition 1972 and the second 1977; see Vinegar, *I Am a Monument*. The texts cited in the following however remain the same.

judgment whose roots have become invisible to us. This suspension is a precondition for an immersion in a new visual experience, and once more pop shows the way.

Here, too, the argument commences with an attack on the modern obsession with space, which has made us "bewitched by a single element of the Italian landscape: the Piazza" (LLV 6) and eclipsed the experience of Los Angeles and Route 66. For the authors of *Learning from Las Vegas*, the key problem is instead the *sign*—or, more precisely, if we think of this as a transformation wrought upon Giedion's modernist space-time: space thought on the basis of information given through a sign, a *sign-space*, and time as understood through the sequential perception of signs, a *sign-time*. This space-time must include advertising, billboards, neon signs, and a whole spectrum of details that only existed as external and unessential additions to buildings as they were conceived in modernism, but now form the elements of the language of the street, within which the building is only one part of a complex message that eschews the unambiguous, an instead thrives on its multi-level address.

Modernism's fixation on the specificity of the medium and the demand that we should not mix media, genres, and styles have in fact, Venturi and Scott Brown suggest, produced an aversion to the iconological and the pictorial—a sign intended for orientation is only used under protest, since it indicates a weakness in spatial organization, assumed to present itself as immediately legible without external aids. But while the pervasive ideal of abstraction was intended as a reduction taking us back to the essence of architecture, the pictorial moments still asserted itself—as in the machine, the airplane, the silo, and all the other models constantly called upon to support the look of modernity—and we might as well acknowledge and make use of this insistence of the image, Venturi and Scott Brown propose, since it allows us to link up with the iconography of commercial culture and the visual ecology that unfolds around the highway. If the architecture of signs first seems anti-spatial and communicative, it is to a great extent because it is oriented towards the landscape scale of the car and the highway.[45] Three decades ago (approximately the year of publication of Giedion's massive work) a psychological sense of space was enough, they note, but now, one must turn left to turn to the right, and put one's trust in "enormous signs in vast spaces at high speed" (LLV 9). These new messages are of the same order as the signs placed perpendicular to the street so as to communicate the price of products: the graphic sign in space is the building block of the new landscape.

The historical significance of the A&P parking lots is ultimately that they signal a "current phase in the evolution of vast space since Versailles" (LLV 13). They are an integral part of a landscape now determined as "megatexture," where space is organized by symbols in such a pervasive fashion that the building itself can become a sign: the restaurant itself can look like a hamburger. Fake facades are a typical case of the architectural symbolisms that pervades the nature of the commercial Main Street, as indicated by the morphology of the desert city, visible precisely as signs placed at right angle to the highway. If they are removed, the city itself vanishes, and in this sense, Las Vegas can be taken as the apotheosis of the desert city.

Venturi and Scott Brown predict that Las Vegas will be possible to cite in the same way that Rome was once marshaled as

45. Venturi's claims have an obvious background in the construction of the interstate highway system in the mid fifties, which produces a qualitative leap in a spatial modernization. As Jorge-Otero Pailos shows, the (unacknowledged) influence behind this thesis seems to have come from Venturi's teacher, Jean Labatut, who in turn drew on his work on camouflage techniques during the First World War, as well as cubist painting and the philosophy of Bergson; see Otero-Pailos Otero-Pailos, *Architecture's Historical Turn: Phenomenology and the Rise of the Postmodern* (Minneapolis: University of Minnesota Press, 2010). For more on this connection, see chap. 4, below.

a contrast to the anti-urban American landscape: "Las Vegas is to The Strip what Rom is to the Piazza" (LLV 18). The reference to Rome may seen far-fetched, but in fact remains decisive for their claim, just as the link between the A&P parking lot and Versailles, and not only as the substitution of one historical-aesthetic paradigm for another: in both cases a higher and more abstract spatial grid (shopping-religious capital-entertainment capital) is projected onto the local configuration (mall-church-casino), resulting in "violent juxtapositions of use and scale" (ibid). On the Nolli map of eighteenth-century Rome, the relation between private and public formed the underlying matrix; in Las Vegas, Fremont Street is oriented toward the railway station and The Strip toward the airport, and in this, they signal the symbolic opposites of our time.

The important thing is to realize that commercial space is not some visual chaos, but that *system* and *order* rule on The Strip. To the innocent eye—or rather, to the eye unconsciously modeling its gaze on modernist architectural purism—the image may seem simply disorderly, but through an active unlearning of such prejudices, they suggest, we will see an underlying logic based in the highway, resulting in an easy visual order on the street, and a difficult order of buildings and signs. The highway system constitutes the common order, the roadside the individual counterpart, and together they produce a sequential unity of opposites organized by the car, and not the pedestrian, as in the European model, thus also indicating the central mediating role of the parking lot. This new logic, while reorganizing space so as to become a non-continuous and parceled order, also resists the visual capacity of the pedestrian with his camera: it is difficult to photograph, since it must be seen as a moving image.[46] In ar-

46.   As Denise Scott Brown suggests, "New analytic techniques must use film and videotape to convey the dynamism of sign architecture and the sequential experience of vast landscapes; and computers are needed to

chitectural terms, this translates into the increased importance of the side elevation, which becomes as important as the façade, since it is the surface that is exposed to the traffic for the longest period of time. A new typology of signs is what is needed, rather than a formalist analysis of architecture.

Stylistically, architecture can have no restraints; forms are universally available, and their point of convergence is the gambling room, where we, in contrast to the brightly lit and shimmering outside, find ourselves in a constant semi-darkness that dissolves limits and contours, in a space-time that is disconnecting, disorienting, and aspires to create a world of its own. The casino is a big, low space, partly for technical and economic reasons, but more fundamentally because the contemporary perception of monumentality has been transformed. Maybe our cathedrals are chapels without a nave, Venturi and Scott Brown propose, public spaces adjusted to "anonymous individuals without explicit connection with each other," which is the truth of our time: "You are no longer in the bounded piazza but in the twinkling lights of the city at night." (LLV 50)

Depth and memory
In Aldo Rossi's *L'architettura della città* we encounter what at first sight appears as the complete opposite of Venturi's fascination with the sign, the open expanse of the highway, and the availability of a historical language that has severed all substantial ties

---

aggregate mass repeated data into comprehensible patterns." See Scott Brown, "Learning from Pop" [1971], reprinted in Hays, *Architecture Theory since 1968*, 64. The reference to repeated data, computer aggregation, and patterns should be noted just as much as the introduction of film and video; as Reinhold Martin stresses, the form of the feedback loop together with the theory of pattern recognition, originating in György Kepes's work at MIT during the war (first publicized in his *Languages of Vision*, 1944), was crucial for the formation of postmodern as an immanence that could be analyzed and surveyed by systems theory; see chap 4, below.

to the past. "By architecture," Rossi states in the introduction, "I meat not only the visible image of the city and the sum of its different architectures, but architecture as construction, the construction of the city over time," which is "the ultimate and definitive fact (*dato*) in the life of the collective."[47] Architecture gives concrete shape to the rhythms of collective life, it adds layer upon layer, temporally as well as spatially, and it can be compared to a memory or a consciousness. It brings together the particular and the general, individual and collective, in the building of a city that is both a rational process and the production of the value of place, a locus that is always individual, a *locus solus*.

Architecture produces urban "facts" (*fatti urbani*), which is one of Rossi's basic categories. The fact is something made, and by human hand (*manufatto*), which finally applies to the city in its entirety; on the other hand, over time these facts become detached from their initial meaning and form a permanence, something that remains through the flow of history and can be overlaid with new meanings.

The paradigm for such facts or "primary elements" are *monuments*—"signs of the collective will as expressed through the principles of architecture, [which] offer themselves as primary elements, fixed points in the urban dynamic." (AC 12/22)[48] These

47. *L'architettura della città* (Milano: CittaStudiEdizioni, 1995 [1966]), 9; *The Architecture of the City*, trans. Diane Ghirardo and Joan Ockman (New York: Opposition Books, 1982), 21. Henceforth cited as AC (Italian/English). Rossi's prefaces to later editions are cited from the English translation.

48. Rossi's theory of the monument can be contrasted with other attempts at reviving monumentality, most obviously the ideas of Giedion, Léger, and Sert in their co-authored manifesto "Nine Points of Monumentality" (1943), which starts from atomized entities and then proceeds to construct complexity, in response to a need for "powerful accents" in the "vaster urban schemes," as their fifth thesis claims; see the reprinted text in Giedion, *Architecture, You, and Me: The Diary of A Development* (Cambridge, Mass.: Harvard University Press, 1958). For Rossi, as we shall see, the complexity of the city is always prior to its singular elements. For a discussion of the "Nine Points" and the context in

permanences are in turn the foundation for an "urban science" (*scienza urbana*) that on the one hand aspires to autonomy, since its basic datum is the architecture of the city, which has no other foundation than its own existence. On the other hand, Rossi borrows concepts and tools from a host of other disciplines and theorists, often anthropology and the study of myth. "For if ritual is the permanent and conserving element of myth," Rossi, writes, "then so too is the monument, since, in the very moment that it testifies to myth, it renders ritual forms possible." (16/24) This idea of myth and ritual is borrowed from Fustel de Coulanges (above all his *La Cité antique*, 1864) who emphasizes their role in the construction of institutions: by being continually re-narrated, myths take on new meanings, while the ritual aspect provides a fixed form. Rossi's sources are however many and variegated: Adolf Loos, Maurice Halbwachs, Friedrich Engels, Ferdinand de Saussure, Lewis Mumford, Claude Lévi-Strauss, and Quatremère de Quincy, to cite but a few, and he synthesizes many different and conflicting perspectives.[49]

It has been noted that the wide array of references, the many themes addressed, and the absence of a clear method, produce a particular disorder; the book, in Françoise Choay's harsh judgment, is a "florilegium of absurdities."[50] But at the same time, might we not say that the experience accumulated—above all that

1943, see Eric Mumford, *The CIAM Discourse on Urbanism* ((Cambridge, Mass.: MIT, 2000), 150–52.

49.   The spatial conditions of memory and the work of Halbwachs have recently been suggested as a key influence, in Mattias Ekman, *Edifices: Architecture and Spatial Frameworks of Memory*, diss. (Oslo: Oslo School of Architecture and Design, 2013). Others have pointed to Loos and Lévi-Strauss as the decisive sources, both theoretically and for the essayistic techniques; see the Italian architecture collective Baukuh, "Le promesse non mantenute di *L'architettura della città*," in *Due saggi sull'architettura* (Genua: Sagep, 2012), 77ff.

50.   Choay, "Conclusion," in Choay, Pierre Merlin and Ernesto D'Alfonso (eds.), *Morphologie urbaine et parcellaire* (St. Denis: Presses Universitaires de Vincennes, 1988), 156.

relating to the vicissitudes of the European city during the phase of postwar reconstruction, which Rossi observed closely as an editor of *Casabella*—necessitated a particular form, a construction from parts no longer linked by any order than that given by the flow of time and history? The erratic, at once fragmented and repetitive quality of the book, where themes seem to disappear and return haphazardly, and key concepts are given varying definitions, as if the idea were to gradually enrich them by approaching from many angles, one after the other without synthesis, can be taken as a conscious strategy. The disjointed composition of text, its lack of theoretical closure and direction, would then reflect its object of study, and in this Rossi's work has also been deemed a supremely *"urban* book"[51]—and, might we not say, that the science imagined by Rossi is not just *of* the urban, but integrates essential features of its objects, so as to itself become urban, even urbane?

The common thread that he extracts from all of these seemingly confusing sources is, however, a critique of progress and a sense of cultural continuity: the question is not to add new things, but to appreciate and perceive in a new way what already exists. Creation is not individual, but a collective and largely unconscious process, whose irrational associations, predominant in Loos, Rossi corrects through his reading of Lévi-Strauss. On a methodic level, this divide translates into a tension between a scientistic dimension that lays claim to universal models and rational principles, based on quantitative methods (one of the preliminary titles for the book was in fact *Manual of Urbanism*), and an acknowledgment of the finitude of all understanding, due to the

51. Baukuh, "Le promesse non mantenute," 64. For the genesis of the book on the basis of Rossi's many preceding articles, see Hendrik Tieben, *Aldo Rossis Auseinandersetzung mit Geschichte, Erinnerung und Identität am Beispiel des Projekts des Deutschen Historischen Museums*, diss. (Zurich: ETH, 2005), and Elisabetta Vasumi Roveri, *Aldo Rossi e L'architettura della città: Genesi e fortuna di un testo* (Turin: Allemandi, 2010). Rossi's essays have been collected in *Scritti scelti sull'architettura e la città, 1956–1972* (Milan: Clup, 1975).

irreducibly qualitative and singular of each locus: "In fact, while each urban intervention seems fated to rely on general criteria of planning, each part of the city seems to be a singular place, a *locus solus*." (AC 10/21) In the end this might even lead to a tragic insight, as when he in the end of the book notes: "Perhaps the laws of the city are exactly like those that regulate the life and destiny of individual men," like a "biography" with "its own interest, even though it is circumscribed by birth and death." (229/163)

If the tension between universal principles and finitude generates an oscillation between the urban structure as a whole, and the particular urban facts with their individual form and history, this implies that the "architecture of the city" can be read in two ways, as a subjective or an objective genitive, but at least in some passages Rossi seems unequivocally clear: "architecture presupposes the city" (AC 151/113, mod.). It proceeds from complexity to unity, from the city to its parts, and the individual entities exist by virtue of their differential relation, as he proposes with reference to Saussure (13/23). The priority of the city means that it is like a universe of its own; it cannot be viewed from the outside or be provided with an origin external to itself. Rossi's world is already replete with objects and significations that do not form any natural hierarchy or order, and in this sense architecture need not be provided with complexity by given additional features, instead it exists in a field of an originary complexity that it then proceeds to simplify and reduce, also on the level of functions, which is why no particular function can be assumed as its basis. This clam about the city's autochthonous nature also means that references to nature tend to disappear, which opposes Rossi's analysis to Tafuri's, where architecture, at least in its *theory*, was called upon since the mid-eighteenth century to cover over the rift with nature by projecting the image of the city as a spatial continuity with "artifacts of a homogenous nature" (69/63). But because of this primordial complexity, the city's immanent origin can, paradoxically, only be thought in the plural, which is why Rossi's structural science, while drawing on Saussure and Levi-Strauss, must end in the monographic analysis and the close description of individual urban facts. There can be no general rules or principles, and the basic category remains that of the urban fact, that which is done (*fatto*), and, by being preserved, instigates a temporal horizon of future overlays and modifications.

In order to introduce us into the problem, Rossi cites edifices whose function has shifted completely (the first example is the Palazzo della Ragione in Padua, and he returns to it in varying perspectives throughout the book), and which in this sense seem independent of their form, at the same time as it is precisely this unique form that we immediately perceive and experience. The individuality of the edifice thus resides both in the form, and in its existence in space and time, which overlays it with significations dependent on contingent events and unpredictable uses (of which our subjective memories and psychological associations form a part). These accumulated differences, together with a presupposed underlying substratum, is what constitutes an urban fact. It is only by way of a rigorous and multi-faceted description of such complex facts, which are once is material and psychological, quantitative and qualitative, that we can claim to grasp something like the "soul" of a city, a concept that on some occasions may seem close to a concept like Norberg-Schulz's *genius loci*, but in fact is something essentially different in stressing the non-natural, man-made, and artificial dimension of the city, whereas the theory of *genius loci* draws on a phenomenological grounding of architectural forms in the passage from nature to culture that preserves, intensifies, and gives a conscious design to what was already there in nature.[52]

52.   For more on Norberg-Schulz and the phenomenology of place, see chap. 4, below.

111

Permanences have a dual quality: they provide productivity with a necessary substratum, but they can also turn pathological when severed from the system of the city (Rossi's example is the Alhambra in Granada); they can connect the layers of the city by bringing the past into the present, but also cut us off from both past and present by violently arresting time. Productive permanence, or the "monument" as Rossi often simply says, supports development rather than checking it, since it always remains open to the future. The paradigm of monumentality is Roman through and through: the Forum Romanum "constitutes one of the most illustrative urban artifacts that we can know; bound up as it is with the origins of the city; extremely, almost unbelievably transformed over time but always growing upon itself; parallel to the history of Rome as it is documented in every historical stone and legend," ultimately "reaching us today through its strikingly clear and splendid signs" and pointing forward by its "extraordinary modernity" in an almost utopian fashion: "in it was everything that is inexpressible in the modern city." (AC 163f/120)

Alongside the monumental permanences, urban facts can also be grasped in more fluid concepts like "area" (*area*), which can be marked off by natural limits, but in the end must be understood as the "projection of the city's form on a horizontal plane" (AC 70/63). The area is the minimal context required for the analysis of an urban fact, and in this respect it is an analytical abstraction that makes it possible to discern the relation between the city as totality and the various parts with their respective character. It can be concretized as "neighborhood" or "district" (*quartiere*),[53] which have a relative autonomy and distinctive features that can be described typologically, socio-

53. Rossi emphasizes the varying senses of the term: it can mean a block, a neighborhood, a residential district (the English translation uses *district* and *residential district*), but it can also be used as a translation, "as imprecise as it is useful" (AC 97/81), of the German *Siedlung*.

logically (working class district, upper class district, etc.), and in a number of other ways, and in their differential interplay they constitute a social ecology. Unlike the primary elements they do not preserve their singular parts, only a basic structure that gradually shifts its contents, and in this they display a different set of space-time functions; their unity, Rossi claims, however always requires the primary elements, which are what ultimately makes up the unity of the city: The primary elements "possess a value 'in themselves,' but also a value dependent on their place in the city. In this sense a historical building can be understood as a primary urban artifact; it may be disconnected from its originary function, or over time take on functions different from those for which it was designed, but its quality as an urban artifact, as a generator of a form of the city, remains constant." (106/87) Such facts have the capacity to act as catalysts and enhance the process of urbanization, which is why they must be understood in such a wide sense that they in the end may seem to dissolve the materiality of the fact, or a least the idea of a stable support: "Frequently they are not even physical, constructed, measurable facts; for, sometimes the importance of an event itself gives place to the spatial transformations of the site." (107/ibid., mod.)[54]

Typology and fantasy

A key concept in Rossi's theory is *place*, which he defines as both singular and universal, and as constitutive of the individuality of urban facts. His conception draws on a long tradition from the sacred sites of antiquity, echoes of which he finds in Palladio and Milizia, as well as in the places of Christian pilgrimages,

54. In some passages Rossi comes close to the expanded idea of monument launched by Alois Riegl. For a discussion of Riegl on monuments, see Thordis Arrhenius, *The Fragile Monument: On Conservation and Modernity* (London: Artifice, 2012), 92–107.

outer spatial markers of an inner invisible grace that make up the miraculous geography of Catholicism. Building, monument, and city are fundamentally linked to a "first sign" (*primo segno*, AC 141/106); and who, Rossi continues, "can distinguish anymore between an event and the sign that marks it?" (142/ibid).

But if the singularity of the urban fact is thus grounded in the indiscernibility of event and sign, then the act or gesture of marking that inscribes the event and generates the fact or work opens onto myth and fiction, where the exchange between the city as work and the work as city unfolds: "I often think," Rossi writes, "of the piazzas depicted by the Renaissance painters, where the place of architecture, the human construction, takes on a general value of place and of memory because it is so strongly fixed in a single moment. This moment becomes the primary and most profound idea of the piazzas of Italy, and is therefore linked with our spatial idea of the Italian cities themselves." (AC 141/106) The architecture of the city is for Rossi essentially, and not just metaphorically, akin to an artwork: it is the ultimate "human thing" (*cosa umana*", 33/26), and urban facts are expressions of an "aesthetic intentionality" (107/87).[55]

But through what kind of conceptuality can we approach such a work? The tension between singular and universal returns, in that here, too, the experience of place, a street, a building, etc., is always individual, while we on the other hand cannot avoid describing these singular facts in categories with a general

55. Rossi's *cosa umana* draws on Lévi-Strauss's famous proposal that the city is "la chose humaine par excellence"; see *Tristes tropiques* (Paris: Plon, 1955), 122. The analogy between a city and a poem or a symphony is relevant, Lévi-Strauss says, because they are all located "in the encounter between nature and artificiality" (121), which for Rossi means: in the encounter between collective, i.e., non-conscious, and conscious processes. Rossi's persistent use of "aesthetic intentionality" can however be confusing, since what he in fact shows is that the urban fact in its very facticity is independent of its origin, and that the initial intention in no way guides later overlays of new uses and senses.

value, in *typologies*, if we are to understand the city as a collective work. All manifestations of social life, Rossi claims, have in common with the artwork that they are born in the unconscious, and, ultimately, the difference between individual and collective must be reduced.

The concept of typology has a long and stratified history that takes us back at least as far as to Quatremère de Quincy who, at the time when Vitruvian discourse, understood in the most general sense, as a system of mimetic figures that reference an ideal conception of Greek and Roman sources, was beginning to loosen its grip on architecture, formulated it in an attempt to forge a new sense of tradition. First, the type is not the image of a thing that is to be imitated or copied, as in the case of the model, but situated at one further remove, or in Quatremère's terms, an "element that itself must serve as a rule for the model," which is why it, unlike the model, can produce works that do not in any way look like each other: "Everything is exact and given in the model; everything is more or less vague in the type." Secondly, since "nothing comes from nothing," any creation of something new involves a reference to type, as it were a "kernel around which the development and variation of forms is gathered and ordered."[56] The type is a "logical principle that is prior to form and constitutes it." (AC 32/40), Rossi says, and this is why it must be separated from the model, which is a material copy located at a lower level of abstraction. In acting as a generative rule, the type preserves a potential to breed new forms, while it from the opposite end may be used as an analytical instrument to order and classify a given multiplicity of concrete models or architectures. "No type can be identified with only one form," Rossi notes, "even if all architectural forms are reducible to types." (34/41) For instance, the type of the domicile has not

56.   Quatremère de Quincy, *Dictionnaire historique*, vol. 2, entry "Type," cited in AC 32f /40.

115

changed from antiquity to today, even though our ways of living have been radically transformed, and new ways are possible. In this sense, the type can be understood as "the very idea of architecture, that which is closest to its essence." (ibid./ibid.)

Rossi intervenes in a discussion current at the time, where his most important recent predecessor in the Italian context was Giulio Carlo Argan. Citing Quatremère, Argan understands the type as an abstraction from a set of given models, leading to a "root form" that contains the possibility of future variations and is independent of particular functions. In the relation between type and model, abstraction and tradition, Argan sees a dialectic of creation: "Through this reduction of earlier artworks to a 'type,' the artist is emancipated from the dependence on determined historical forms, and he neutralizes the past. He assumes that the past is absolute and no longer capable of progression." This, Argan continues, separates the type from the model, which implies a value judgment (something is assumed to be perfect and worthy of imitation): "The acceptance of a 'type' implies the suspension of historical judgment, it something negative," but in this the abstraction of the type prepares something new, to "handle the demands of the present situation by criticizing and overcoming past solutions that have been deposited and synthesized schematically in the type."[57]

After Rossi's invention, the debate was continued by Alan Colquhoun, who sees the rediscovery of typology as a critique of the alleged scientific basis of modernist design methods, within which the "biotechnical determinism" that in the end imagines a synthesis of biology and technology (Buckminster Fuller is his example) always needs to refer to an element of intuition and genius, or "expressionism," if it is to arrive at a definite result, all of which means to evoke two irreconcilable bases for design.

57.   Argan, "Sul concetto di tipologia architettonica" (1962), reprinted in Argan, *Progetto e destino* (Milan: Il Saggiatore, 1965), 79, 81.

For typology becomes an acknowledgment of the necessary role of the past, above all on the level of providing a language for which expressionism appears primitive and consisting of "single-word exclamations."[58]

The final step in the discussion was taken by Anthony Vidler, who locates a decisive historical displacement in the concept of typology itself. In the first phase (from Laugier to Quatremère), nature is at the center, and all the tectonic elements and geometries of architecture are prefigured in the rational order of nature. In the second phase, the machine and industrial production take center stage, but in both cases, architecture is grounded in an order outside of itself. In the third phase, with Rossi as the main case, the city itself becomes a source of types; it is "emptied of specific social context from any particular time and allowed to speak simply of its own *formal* condition,"[59] Vidler suggests, which seems somewhat misleading, at least in relation to *L'architettura della città*. Vidler's "third typology" is not based on earlier forms or types, but "de-composes" them to fragments that may be "re-composed" in new contexts; it is a radical "ontology of the city" that breaks with the form–function equation in a way that is also claimed to be radically political in a somewhat obscure way. The example given is Rossi's project for a city hall in Trieste, whose form refers back to the eighteenth-century prison, which, today, Vidler suggests, indicates the "ambiguous condition of civic government." Rather than merging the type city hall and prison, Rossi makes then contradict each other, resulting in a dialectic "as clear as a fable: the society that understands the reference to prison will still have need of the reminder, while at the very point that the image finally loses all

58.   Alan Colquhoun, "Typology and Design Method" (1967) reprinted in *Essays in Architectural Criticism: Modern Architecture and Historical Change* (Cambridge, Mass.: MIT, 1985), 49.

59.   Vidler, "The Third Typology" (1976), reprinted in Nesbitt, *Theorizing A New Agenda*, 261, Vidler's italics.

meaning, the society will either have become entirely prison, or perhaps, its opposite."[60] This concept of a third typology seems torn between options that appear irreconcilable, or at least in need of meditation: a de-composing of older forms into fragments, and a humanist rejection of the "fragmentation, de-centralization, and formal disintegration introduced into contemporary urban life by the zoning techniques and techno-logical advances of the twenties";[61] an affirmation of the formal autonomy of architecture, and a claim for its pervasively politi-cal nature. These tensions are, to be sure, already there in Rossi, but here they have come to the fore in a much more explosive fashion.

Generally, what gradually unfolds in this series of displace-ments of the concept seems to be the consequences of the ten-sion between the idea of the city as founded on contingency and singular gestures crystallized into urban facts, and the theory of types as a set of universal principles. Rossi for his part un-derstands the concept of type as radically opposed to a func-tionalist analysis, first and foremost since he perceives the latter as caught in an organicist analogy that deprives the fact of its autonomy by automatically explaining it through the particular purpose that it serves, and thus transforms the type into a spe-cific model whose role would be to organize a given function. Functions (in the plural) are obviously always part of the game, but only have a partial explanatory force; as we noted in the case of Palazzo della Ragione, they may come and go, and are more like accidences on the surface of the urban fact's substance than its *telos*, and as such they cannot on their own account for its complexity, which lies in the interplay of permanence and transitory features. But the question is whether Rossi, with the idea of typology, doesn't give in to his rationalist tendencies, in

60.   Ibid., 262
61.   Ibid., 263.

a way that in fact brings him close to the "disingenuous functionalism" that he otherwise rejects.[62] The emphasis on the
groundlessness of the city, or rather its constitutive multiplicity
of grounds and origins, seems here to succumb to a rationalism
that a priori organizes all future developments, as a condition
of possibility of empirical form—one must note that the idea of
type is originally and irrevocably Platonic, and when, in Rossi, it
eventually becomes transposed to the psychology of the creator-
architect, this changes little of its founding structure.[63]

The idea of typology is extended further in the later concept
of analogous cities, where the dissolution of the fact–fiction divide is taken one step further. Rossi starts off with a painting
by Canaletto, showing an imaginary Venice where buildings
by Palladio (in reality located in different places) are brought
together in a single space, and proceeds to construct an analogy of a possible Venice that belongs to no particular time and
place. In the preface to the second edition of *L'architettura della
città* he speaks of this as the answer to a need to formulate "a
more complex *rationalism* than the schematic one offered by
the historiography of modern architecture," in the sense that
the "geographical transposition of the monuments within the
painting constitutes a city that we recognize, even though it is
a place of purely architectural references."[64] The analogous city

62.   As is argued in Baukuh, "Le promesse," 104ff (thus the title of essay:
      this is one of the "promises not kept" by Rossi).
63.   The *typos* plays in important role in Plato, where it often designates
      the "imprinting" activity whereby a form is inscribed in matter. This
      has been read in different ways, either as a violent imposition, or as
      mediation between the form and the receptacle, which still echoes in
      the much later architectural application of the concept. For a discussion
      of the term in Plato, see Serge Margel, *Le tombeau du dieu artisan* (Paris:
      Minuit, 1995), 132ff. Rossi's transference of the type to the mind of the
      architect takes place just after *L'architettura della città*, in the preface to
      the Italian translation of Boullées *L'architecture*. See Rossi, "Introduzi-
      one a Boullée", *in Scritti scelti*.
64.   *Architecture of the City*, 166 (this preface is not included in the Italian
      reprint). The concept of the analogous city is subsequently developed

119

is a fiction, and yet it lays claim to a truth, a pure architectural language that fuses the universality of typology with the generativity of analogy.

Inventing the city

In the preface that accompanies the English translation of the *L'architettura della città*, Peter Eisenman highlights the complex relation that Rossi establishes to the modernist as well as humanist tradition, in which the reduction of urban facts brought about by analogy is the key issue. If the urban facts of various kinds that Rossi analyzes can be taken as a skeleton, a system of real anchoring points in history, then the movement of analogy will rather distance us from any such material structures: "the analogue is detached from specific place and specific time, and becomes instead an abstract locus existing in what is a purely typological or *architectural* time-space," which for Eisenman is a symptom, in the end of a failed and finally impossible attempt, "through the erasure of history and transcendence of real places to reconcile the contradictions of modernist utopia—literally 'no place'—and humanist reality—built 'some place.'"[65] When real history is transposed to a collective memory, and the

more systematically in a study of the Veneto region; see "Caratteri urbani delle città venete," in Aymonino et al, *La città di Padova* (Rome: Officina, 1970), which is the only text where Rossi engages in the monographic writing that he earlier deemed the only possible way forward. In the preface to the Portuguese translation (1971) of *L'architettura della città* we can see how typology eventually fuses with analogy: "Ultimately, *the history of architecture is the* material *of architecture*," Rossi suggests, and if typology in *L'architettura della città* had a "major though not primary importance," it now constitutes "the essential basis of design" (*Architecture of the City*, 170). The thesis of the autonomy of form in relation to functional organization has become crucial, and it does not just point to a multiplicity of functions that precludes any particular one of them from being decisive: "Form is absolutely indifferent to organization precisely when it exists as typological form." (174)

65.   Peter Eisenman, "The Houses of Memory: The Texts Analogy," preface in *Architecture of the City*, 8.

original function to a reservoir of abstracted typologies, we find ourselves in a nowhere whose relation to actual history is basically rhetorical. Place and scale are dislocated, while Rossi still aspires to anchor his claims in a humanist tradition from Alberti onward, which for Eisenman is an impossible task. "For Aldo Rossi," Eisenman writes, "the European city has become the house of the dead," like a "giant or collective house of memory, it has a psychological reality which arises from its being a place of phantasy and illusion, an analogue of both life and death as transitional states."[66] Rossi's book itself becomes a project for an analogous city, a model of historical analysis that lays claim to truth and science, but which also wants to become a generative instrument that only half-heartedly and as it were against itself acknowledge its fictional status.

Regardless of whether Eisenman projects his own themes onto Rossi (which he undoubtedly does, above all the concepts developed in his own "Artificial Excavations" during the same period),[67] in a certain way, his reading makes it possible to see how the models proposed in *Learning from Las Vegas* and *L'architettura della città*, precisely as two extremes, also end up touching each other, almost like the two sides of a membrane or sheet of paper that are in contact at every point and yet stay infinitely separated. We might say, somewhat twisting Saussure's famous image, that none of them is simply a signifier or a signified of the other, but both are signifier-signifieds that encircle a common absent center, a master signified that would be the City-Architecture, forever lost yet continually promised anew. This is why they both, their differences notwithstanding, move within a space of history as simulation, to be sure acknowledging this in various degrees, oscillating between re-creation and invention, and in the end become indistinguishable from a particular type of fiction.

66. Ibid, 10.
67. For more on this, see chap. 6, below.

Perhaps we might venture the following equation: as Las Vegas relates to Rome, Rome will relate to Las Vegas—two images, generated through a similar process of analogy, fiction, and simulation, neither of which can lay claim to a more substantial truth than the other, and which appear to exchange their defining characteristics the longer and more closely we look at them. To be sure, Rossi's Rome is, his emphasis on close description notwithstanding, not the factual Rome, but as it were its idea, which becomes even more pronounced in the case of Venice and the analogous city; similarly, *Learning from Las Vegas*, in spite of its many accounts of the experiential dimension of the city and its particular moods, is in the end only about a fictional Las Vegas. In both cases, the empirical and the rational intersect, in Rossi's types and in the movement of "learning from," even though the examples chosen are never mere examples, but as it were *exemplary* examples, paradigms that orient architectural thought.

For Rossi, the material is the sedimented historical depth of the European city, and his problem is how this tradition can be continued without giving in to those permanences he calls pathological. This problem is foreign to Venturi and Scott Brown, for whom the opposite to modernist abstraction and its erasure of history is commercial mass culture and the new megatexture of the recently invented cityscape with its surrounding highway system, for which the term "sprawl," they underline, merely signals the absence of an adequate analytical vocabulary. Arguably, both of them remain caught in their specific traditions—which is in fact what they each in their own way might claim as an antidote to a false universalism—and any exchange between them might seem pointless; and yet, reading them together produces a new optic, since they see the same crisis from opposite perspectives. Both of them want to counter a loss of sense and rethink architecture as symbolic communication, but whereas

Rossi scans the depth of time vertically in search of a dialectic of permanence and change, Venturi and Scott Brown perceive it as a surface, upon which signs and symbols detached from historical depth have become freely available for new uses.

When Rossi conceives the city as a language and a history, it is on the basis of the highly stratified cultural material offered by the traditional European city, with Rome as the paradigm; in Venturi, the material is given by the flow of sign and commodities in late capitalism, which has become a kind of second nature—behind Las Vegas there is nothing else apart from the empty desert, as if to indicate the meaninglessness of nature.[68] In both of these models, everything is already culture, although in different ways: in Rossi every sign points downward through the layers of time toward the permanences that safeguard the continuity of urban facts, in Venturi and Scott Brown signs are scattered along the Strip, and in the intertextuality (a concept not yet in use at the time, but which in many respects seems more suited than the late-modern formalist vocabulary of New Criticism) of the commercial megatexture images refer to nothing else than to simulacra of history. In Las Vegas, the semiotic field has no outside, and every new image of history, preferably seen through the windscreen at high speed, is just another image soon to be replaced by yet another; in Rome, the external sign is anchored in the depth of time, even though this too involves fantasy and fiction, and eventually a theory of analogy that brackets historical references in favor of a virtual space of combinatorics that projects Rome back onto Las Vegas.

68.   In a passage Venturi describes the limit of the city as a total break, which the absolute indifference to the nature: "Beyond the town, the only transition between The Strip and the Mojave Desert is a zone of rusting beer cans. Within the town, the transition is as ruthlessly sudden. Casinos, whose fronts relate so sensitively to the highway turn their ill-kempt backsides toward the local environment, exposing their residual forms and spaces of mechanical equipment and service areas." (LLV 35)

Depth and surface, historical memory and the transitory quality of the present, Rome and Las Vegas would be like two extreme models, both of which also understand the city through the lens of artworks, Rossi drawing above all on Renaissance painting, Venturi on the photographically based work of early pop art. They seem at first, as we noted earlier, like the outer markers of a debate that marked the period, and between which many other alternatives were suggested, but as they begin to trade places and exchange their attributes, they also move into the very center of the debate, ceaselessly revolving around a gap left by what in one sense may be taken as the effect of the absence of Architecture, but on the other hand, and inversely, just as much as en effect of the presence of the *City* as a stucturing-destructuring force for which the inherited languages of form, order, and structure no longer provided sufficient analytical vocabularies.

3. The Pyramid and the Labyrinth

Space and interpenetration

In a book that posterity has come to rediscover as one of the most decisive texts of early modernist architectural theory, albeit one that received little attention in its own time, Sigfried Giedion's *Bauen in Frankreich* (1928),[1] it is proposed that the division between subject and object, and between the organic and the technological, is undergoing a fundamental change. In the modern world, Giedion prophesizes, individual things will be dissolved into a single, intense, and malleable space, where mind and machine are absorbed into a new kind of spatial unity that he terms "interpenetration" (*Durchdringung*).[2] This space of interpenetration, however, does not depend exclusively on a series of technological achievements, it also signals, through the changes that it effects in consciousness, a political shift toward a space of communality, a being-together of subjects and objects as well as of classes and social groups; it is an emancipation that heralds a collective order, while at the same time providing architecture with a decisive yet diffuse role in the creation of this order.

1. Sigfried Giedion, *Bauen in Frankreich, Bauen in Eisen, Bauen in Eiesenbeton* (Leipzig: Klinkhardt & Biermann Verlag, 1928); *Building in France, Building in Iron, Building in Ferroconcrete*, trans. J. Duncan Berry (Santa Monica: Getty Center, 1995).
2. For a discussion of Giedion's various uses of "interpenetration," see Hilde Heynen, *Architecture and Modernity: A Critique* (Cambridge, Mass.: MIT, 1999), 30ff, and my *Essays, Lectures* (Stockholm: Axl Books, 2007), chap. 5.

The examples cited are drawn to a great degree from modern engineering, the Eiffel Tower and the Pont Transbordeur in the harbor of Marseille,[3] and from the architecture of Le Corbusier and Gropius. The concept of interpenetration used to bind all these cases together first involves a set of architectural parameters: spatial volumes that intrude upon each other, levels that are made to intersect by the partial removal of floors, osmotic relations between interior and exterior, buildings composed of several intersecting volumes that create a fluid whole. But beyond the architectural domain in a more specific sense, Giedion also discerns general implications for social space as a whole. The leveling of compositional and tectonic hierarchies, as it extends along a continuum from the single building to the city—eventually depriving these two poles of the their absolute status, if not rendering them obsolete—corresponds to a leveling of social divisions between forms of labor and social classes. A common task begins to emerge, Giedion suggests, although it requires that we discard traditional ideas of architecture as a bearer of merely aesthetic and formal values if we are to perceive the true stakes. This incipient space is indissolubly at once architectural, perceptual, and social, and in drawing together the subjective and the objective, the social and the aesthetic, it prepares and promises a new form of life. Space no longer appears as an empty, neutral container for things or as a set of abstract coordinates, but rather as a field of transformation, traversed by forces—it is, we might say, using a term forged much later, a smooth space made up of virtual relations, rather than an already striated geometric space into which entities would be inserted—and architecture faces a new task: no longer to produce self-sufficient forms that symbolize, represent, or even express

3.   The bridge was one of the technological icons of the time and the subject of photographs by Germaine Krull as well as a film by Moholo-Nagy, *Marseille, Vieux Port*, from 1929.

something that would precede them, but rather to create specific conduits for a stream of life that flows through them and
to enhance its potential; to *striate* the *smooth*, so as to extract a
surplus value for form out of what otherwise would remain a
threatening formlessness.

Giedion here synthesizes a long historical development that
he edits and transforms into a story of his own. In relation to
recent architectural history, he emphasizes the role of construction, which finally, after having been pushed down into the un-
or subconscious throughout a long and confusing nineteenth
century, in the twentieth century is raised up to the conscious
level: "Construction in the nineteenth century plays the role
of the subconscious (*des Unterbewusstseins*). Outwardly, construction still boasts the old pathos; underneath, concealed behind
facades, the basis of our present existence is taking shape."[4]
The new conception of space would then be both the result of
construction and the element in which it unfolds, a product
and a precondition, an invention and a discovery. Here Giedion
seems oblivious to a long legacy of predecessors, and with this
question of space as a foundational category we enter into one of
the most decisive prehistories of modernist architectural theory,
which still reverberates in many discourses that would claim to
either disown or pursue the modernist legacy, both with and
against the later and more general use that Giedion would make
of the term from *Space, Time and Architecture* (1941) onward.[5]

The discourse of space as an explicit category in aesthetic
theory has a short but dense history, and it can be traced back

4. *Building in France*, 87.
5. Giedion's later work, notably the massively influential *Space, Time and
    Architecture* (1941, with many subsequent expanded editions), in fact
    constitutes a step back from the radicalism of the positions in 1928. The
    radical transformative, social as well as technical, potential of interpen-
    etration has faded, and the concept of architecture in a fairly traditional
    sense is reinstalled.

to the turn towards new psycho-physic theories that emerged in the mid-nineteenth century, and then to the discussions of "empathy" (*Einfühlung*) from the 1870s, as they developed from the pioneering work of Robert Vischer, through Adolf Hildebrand and Heinrich Wölfflin, up to the first explicit claims for space as the founding idea of architecture made by August Schmarsow in the 1890s.[6] Drawing on the legacy of Kant's transcendental turn—in which space and time were reinterpreted as forms of intuition and thus as conditions of possibility for knowledge rather than as features of the things themselves—but filtering it through a new experimental science that aspired to displace traditional philosophy, categories and forms of intuition were here understood on the basis of scientific data. Superficially, this may be seen simply as a curious and easily refutable misunderstanding of Kant's project, but more productively it can be interpreted as part of a gradual transformation of the very idea of the a priori into what, following Foucault's analysis of the epistemic formation of this period, could be called objective transcendentals, in which the contents of knowledge are made to function as transcendental reflection: they are both empirical givens and the conditions for any empirical givenness as such.[7] These data were mostly drawn from psychology, although history and the emerging social sciences also made their respective contributions, resulting in the emergence of the kind of psychologism or historicism against which the two major new movements at the turn of the century would subsequently react, analytic philosophy with Frege and phenomenology with Husserl. While the anti-psychologistic gesture of Husserl was instrumental in bringing about the renewal of transcendental

6.   For a collection of source documents, with a detailed historical introduction, see Harry Francis Mallgrave and Eleftherios Ikonomou (eds.), *Empathy, Form, and Space: Problems in German Aesthetics, 1873–1893* (Santa Monica: Getty Center, 1994).

7.   See Foucault, *Les mots et les choses* (Paris: Minuit, 1966), 329–333.

philosophy (whereas Frege's analysis of thoughts as entities separate from the mind eventually gave rise to the linguistic turn), the sharp divide it at first seemed to set up against its own immediate past was misleading, and the dynamic and genetic dimension of the subject soon returned in phenomenology, which indicates the extent to which it was never a question of simply returning to Kantian a priori structures. Husserl's true problem was rather that of a dynamic transformation of the transcendental for which the preceding investigations into the psychological genesis of knowledge could neither be ignored nor simply assumed as factual answers to the problem of epistemology, but instead called for a different type of founding. In aesthetics, the attempt to reground the discipline through a rapprochement with the new forms of psychology and psychophysiology had already been particularly fertile, and it is this line of thought that can be followed up in relation to the statements of Giedion, who unwittingly synthesized a whole gamut of theories and discourses.

The historically decisive formulations of this new field of inquiry can be found in Gustav Fechner, who advocates the shift in the most general terms: aesthetics, in order to finally become a science, must be developed from below (*von unten*), starting in empirical observations, and not from above (*von oben*), as in the idealist tradition from Schelling and Hegel.[8] We should not analyze abstract ideas of art and beauty, Fechner suggests, but investigate our actual experiences, and aesthetics in this version becomes an experimental psychology that seeks the laws governing psychological processes, which in turn are ultimately grounded in physiological states.

8. See the introduction in Gustav Theodor Fechner, *Vorschule der Ästhetik* (Leipzig: Breitkopf & Härtel, 1876), 1–7. The book, which contains the most cited formulas, is Fechner's last, but the ideas of an "experimental aesthetics" had appeared in many of his earlier writings, and he can be said to have initiated the new turn.

The theory of empathy was an attempt to account for this lawfulness, and if we bracket the earlier discussions of the term in Schleiermacher, whose main interest was the hermeneutics of historically distant texts, we encounter its first relevant use in the young Robert Vischer's dissertation, *Über das optische Formgefühl: Ein Beitrag zur Ästhetik* (1873). Vischer distinguishes between everyday seeing (*Sehen*) and the specific and focused look (*Schauen*) that we direct towards artworks, and his question is why, in the latter case, we have a tendency to appreciate certain forms. The answer lies in a transference that occurs spontaneously between the mind and objects, on the basis of our physical interaction with them: in empathy we become part of what we see. For Vischer this ultimately depends on a process of natural identification, an empathic transference that occurs in relation to all things, but attains a higher level in art and the optical sense of form, through which we get access to "a higher physics of nature,"[9] with a formula that might have been garnered directly from Schelling. Consequently, empathy is present just as much in the production as in the reception of artworks, and the process of which these two moments are part goes beyond the subject-object divide towards an integral philosophy of nature: empathy works in two ways, and the *Ein-fühlung* is a "feeling-in" of the subject in the object as well as of the object in the subject.[10] Ironically, the demand for empirical science made

9. *Über das optische Formgefühl: Ein Beitrag zur Ästhetik* (Leipzig: H. Credner, 1873), 40.
10. In Husserl and other early phenomenologists, notably Edith Stein (*Zum Problem der Einfühlung*, 1917), the problem of empathy is mostly seen as an epistemological issue, and aesthetics plays no role; conversely, as phenomenological aesthetics begun to develop in the circle around Husserl, empathy received little attention, and when Werner Ziegenfuss summarized the early discussions in his dissertation *Die phänomenologische Ästhetik* (Berlin: Arthur Collignon, 1928), the concept does nor appear. Later scholars have attempted to retrace these connections, although they are still relatively obscure; see Gabriele Scaramuzza's pioneering *Le origini dell'estetica fenomenologica* (Padua: Antenore, 1976),

by Fechner almost immediately reverts to its speculative opposite, although not necessarily as a misunderstanding, but rather
as a working out of an inner tension that is constitutive of the
new physiological aesthetic as such. When art is brought back
into and grounded in the sensorium—a process that had been
underway since the initial stages of aesthetics, in Baumgarten's
writings from the first half of the eighteenth century—the sensible, the sphere of *aisthesis*, does not remain the same, i.e., it is
no longer a lower domain subordinated to our higher faculty
of reason, to which it merely would deliver material in a raw
and unprocessed state, but begins to acquire a relative autonomy that also demands a new and expanded understanding of
thought itself.[11] The hierarchy between the sensible and the
intelligible is transformed into a fluid exchange, continuing
through the ambivalent position of aesthetics in Kant (on the
one hand a transcendental aesthetic, with space and time as the
sensible elements of pure reason, on the other hand a new dimension of the faculty of judgment that requires a critique of its
own), the rapidly shifting theories of philosophy's grounding in
intellectual and aesthetic intuition in Schelling, the fluctuating
evaluations of art in Nietzsche, and beyond Nietzsche to a long
legacy of twentieth-century thinking on art. Nietzsche's own
treatment is in fact exemplary of these ambivalences, from the
early claims in *The Birth of Tragedy*, where art is determined as
the "highest task and the proper metaphysical activity of life,"
through his middle period, where he turns to a positivist critique of speculative aesthetics—which echoes in some of his last
writings, where aesthetics is mockingly portrayed as "nothing
but applied physiology"—to his final period, where art is under-

chap. 1. To my knowledge the relations between early modernist architectural theory and phenomenology remain uncharted.

11.　I discuss the new determination of sensibility in Baumgarten in more
detail in my "Baumgarten and the Invention of Aesthetics," *Site* 33
(2013).

ARCHITECTURE, CRITIQUE, IDEOLOGY

stood in terms a perspectivism that calls for an entire reevaluation of the sensible, outside of the Platonic hierarchy.[12] As these examples show, the trajectory of the aesthetic is anything but a straight and linear development; it sidetracks, backtracks, and follows a sinuous line that nonetheless eventually ushers in an important strand of twentieth-century art theory, where another feature becomes decisive, which was also there from the beginning, albeit relegated to the margins, i.e., that the sensorium is itself something that is produced by technological means.[13]

Within the nascent theory of empathy, Vischer's initial intuitions were developed further in Heinrich Wölfflin's "Prolegomena to a Psychology of Architecture" (1886), which asks the question how pure tectonic forms can be understood as expressive. Here too the human body is taken as the ground, and the physiological aspect is even more pronounced, whereas Vischer largely remained within a more limited optical dimension. It is because of our body that we can understand weight,

12.   For the idea of a highest metaphysical activity, see the final sentence in the "Preface to Wagner" in *Der Geburt der Tragödie, Kritische Studienausgabe*, eds. Colli-Montinari (Berlin: de Gruyter, 1999), vol. 1, 24. The later remark on aesthetics as "applied physiology" is made in the context of an attack on Wagner, and we should not immediately see this as exhausting the possible meanings of aesthetics for Nietzsche: "My objections to Wagner's music are physiological objections: and why still dress them up in aesthetic formulas? Aesthetics is, to be sure, nothing but applied physiology." ("Meine Einwände gegen die Musik Wagners sind physiologische Einwände: wozu dieselben erst noch unter ästhetische Formeln verkleiden? Ästhetik ist ja nichts als eine angewandte Physiologie.") *Nietzsche contra Wagner, Kritische Studienausgabe*, vol. 6, 418. On perspectivism and the overthrowing of Platonism as a "new interpretation of sensibility," see Martin Heidegger, *Nietzsche I* (Pfullingen: Neske, 1961), 231–254.

13.   In order to correctly use the "weapons of the senses," Baumgarten suggests, we need to immerse ourselves in "aesthetic empirics" (*ästhetische Empirik*), which involves all aspects of the situation, from the purely physiological responses of the body to technical instruments like microscopes and telescopes, barometers and thermometers, all of which have in common prolonging and expanding our senses. See the second of his "Letters to Aletheiophilus," in Baumgarten, *Texte zur Grundlegung der Ästhetik*, ed. Hans Rudolf Schweizer (Hamburg: Felix Meiner, 1983).

contraction, pressure, the bearing of loads, etc., which for Wölfflin ultimately stems from of a dynamic inherent in nature itself. Matter strives to descend and to attain a state of formlessness, while the "formative force" pushes towards gathering, elevation, and a higher unity. Forms can thus be taken to develop organically out of matter because of an "immanent will" that wants to "break free," and while Wölfflin perceives himself as Aristotelian, he seems to be more of a Baroque thinker, and there is an unmistakable Leibnizian inspiration in this idea of "plastic forces."[14] In Wölfflin the concept of space as such, however, tends to recede into the background in favor of the biomorphic drive, and it comes to be understood more in the sense of an environment or an "Umwelt" of an organism that itself remains the center.

Seven years later the theme is brought to a new level in the works of Adolf Hildebrand and August Schmarsow. Hildebrand's "The Problem of Form in the Fine Arts" analyses the perception of sculpture, and for him space is a continuum, like a basin of water where individual bodies form separate volumes. In architecture our relation to space is expressed directly, it becomes present in terms of a "total spatial image" within which all tectonic relations acquire their significance. This conceptual development culminates in Schmarsow's "The Essence of Architectural Creation" (1893), where the autonomy of the single architectonic elements is even further reduced in favor of a total experience. We cannot understand the work of architecture if it we see it as stones and vaults, Schmarsow claims; instead it relates to a total sense of space originating from our body as a zero-point where the spatial coordinates intersect. Architecture produces a "feeling of space (*Raumgefühl*), it is a

14.   For the connection between Leibniz's conception of *vis plastica* and Wölfflins's analysis of Baroque art, see Gilles Deleuze, *Le Pli: Leibniz et la baroque* (Paris: Minuit, 1988), 6.

"creatress of space" (*Raumgestalterin*), and only on this basis can its parts and tectonic details be expressive and have a specific meaning.

The radical conclusion that could be drawn from this is that the body is not simply—primordially speaking *not at all* even—*in* space, as if in a container: the objectivity of space is fundamentally a projection, arising from or woven out of the subjectivity of the subject. While these ideas are only germinating in Schmarsow, he anticipates many of the themes that will become central in the phenomenological tradition from Husserl to Heidegger: the reduction of objective Cartesian extension, the analysis of the kinesthetic sphere through which the ego organizes a system of motility and tactility, the difference between the objective-physiological *Körper* and the living *Leib*, even the idea of the earth as an ontological ground of the tectonic categories.[15] But he also lays the ground for something that would only enter phenomenology in Husserl's late work, and then in Heidegger, i.e., a *historicizing* of the ground, in which this foundational space is itself pried open and turned into a techno-corporeal assemblage. The history of architecture, Schmarsow proposes, should be written as the history of the "senses of space," which also means to write a history of the *body*, and of the changing character of intimacy and self-relation. Architecture is rooted in an experience of space, which in turn is founded upon the body, but this body is itself subjected to change; it is inscribed in all those technological assemblages that

15. As Husserl deepens the analysis of intentionality and its embodiment, he eventually hits upon the earth as the unmovable background of all theoretical acts, an "originary ark" that grounds all of our categories. Husserl's fragment, "The Earth as Originary Ark Does not Move," was written in 1934, the year before Heidegger's "The Origin of the Work of Art," with which it shares many motifs. For an attempt to cross-read some of these issues, see my "Husserl and the Earth," in Tora Lane and Marcia Sá Cavalcante Schuback (eds.), *Disorientations: Philosophy, Literature and the Lost Grounds of Modernity* (London: Rowman & Littlefield, 2014).

condition our experience of space, so that it becomes a subject-object compound, able to orient itself in the world because it is itself a product of this world.

The project of the avant-garde as we find it in *Bauen in Frankreich* and many other similar texts from the period is one possible outcome of this,[16] even though it in the end probably takes Schmarsow's own ideas far beyond their original meaning: the task becomes to actively produce a new space, to break down the barriers between subjects and objects, people and things, in order to allow for a new structuring of everyday life from the bottom up, based on interpenetration. In claiming that architecture is not first and foremost a set of forms and structures placed in a neutral and pre-given spatial container, but a technique for generating space and the experience of the subjects that inhabit it, Giedion is thus drawing a conclusion that was already prefigured in at least half a decade of intense research in aesthetic psychology.

This conclusion will in the last instance strike back at the traditional concept of architecture, something Giedion does not fail to notice. If we must abandon the idea of architecture as an art form that produces autonomous and free-standing objects to be judged according to inherited aesthetic and morphological criteria, this means that it must be understood as part of a larger process, a "stream of movement" (*Bewegungsstrom*) that will require different analytical tools and concepts. "It seems doubtful," Giedion notes in the beginning of his book, "wheth-

16. Other important texts from the period include Theo van Doesburg, *Grundbegriffe der neuen gestaltenden Kunst* (1925), and Moholy-Nagy, *von material zu architektur* (1929). The latter concludes with a celebration of Gropius's Bauhaus building in Dessau and Brinkmann and van der Flugt's Van Nelle factory in Rotterdam, both of which evince an "illusion of spatial interpenetration of a kind that only the subsequent generation will be able to experience in real life—in the form of glass architecture." Moholy-Nagy, *von material zu architektur* (Berlin: Gebr. Mann, 2001), 236.

er the limited concept of 'architecture' will indeed endure. We can hardly answer the question: What belongs to architecture? Where does it begin, where does it end? Fields overlap: walls no longer rigidly define streets. The street has been transformed into a stream of movement. Rail lines and trains, together with the railroad station, form a single whole."[17]

The idea of a stream, flow, or flux (*Strom*) might here seem merely metaphorical, but it shows the profound link not only to the tradition of empathy, but also to contemporary philosophical thought, above all Husserl and Bergson, both of which seemed equally oblivious to their recent past. Rather than a container or a Cartesian substance undergoing modifications, for Husserl phenomenological consciousness is a "stream of experiences" (*Erlebnisstrom*) held together by its inherent temporal structure of retentions and protentions, just as Bergson's vitalism speaks of an *élan vital* held together by the power of memory. Giedion's stream belongs to the same philosophical conjuncture, the difference however being that it does not take place in the immanence of a consciousness, but in a movement pertaining to an exterior of which consciousness is itself part; rather than a mere objectivity, this exterior now assumes itself some of the characteristics of subjectivity, or more precisely becomes a kind of subject-object, an intensive field out of which entities emerge.[18] Whether this is closer to Husserl or to Bergson is perhaps a moot question (the element of exteriority is probably closer to Bergson, at least if we follow Deleuze's interpretation); it is a possibility inherent in both of them.

17.   *Building in France*, 90.
18.   Elsewhere I have tried to show how the same thing can be applied to Malevich's "non-objective world" (*gegenstandslose Welt*, literally "without objects," *bespredmetnost*). It is not world that would be simply lacking objects, but a field that art must attain through a process akin to the phenomenological reduction, and out of which objects emerge. See my *Essays, Lectures*, 186ff.

At the same time, this stream of motion into which architecture is as it were submerged, is also what is *produced* by architecture, no longer taken in the "limited sense," but as generalized constructive activity; it is not simply dissolved, but retains a capacity to give shape to a stream that otherwise would be simply formless. And what its techniques for spatial interpenetration produce is a particular kind of *transparency* that allows subject and object to remain on the same plane, open to each other, but also an instance of control and regimentation; the openness of interpenetrative space is a function of a constructive power that produces transparence.

Dialectics of transparency

Giedion's proposals might be understood as utopian, and his interpretations of the past were never mere records of facts, but always were oriented toward the opening up of possible futures—they are indeed operative, as Tafuri suggested, but self-consciously so—which is one of the reasons why his idea of a constructive subconscious had such a massive influence on Benjamin's work on the Parisian arcades, most directly in the case of the sections on architecture, but also as a general theoretical model for the way in which technology impacts on structures of consciousness and perception, in tearing open a gap in the fabric of time that heralds a coming transformation.[19]

19. Upon receiving the book, Benjamin writes to Giedion: "When I received your book, the few passages that I read electrified me in such a way that I decided not to continue with my reading until I could get more in touch with my own related investigations." (Benjamin, letter to Giedion February 15, 1929, cited in Sokratis Georgiadis's preface in Giedion, *Building in France*, 53). For the relation between Benjamin and Giedion, see Detlef Mertins, "Walter Benjamin's Tectonic Unconscious," *Any* 14 (1996), and "The Enticing and Threatening Face of Prehistory: Walter Benjamin and the Utopia of Glass," *Assemblage* 29 (1996). Tafuri, notwithstanding his constant references to Benjamin, seems to have overlooked this connection, which places both Benjamin and Giedion on the operative side.

Benjamin's suggestions that modern architecture heralds a culture characterized by a positive "poverty,"[20] where the use of transparent materials like glass would reduce the space of bourgeois interiority and its psychological depth, are largely derived from Giedion. In this world of poverty, the organic synthesis promised by late nineteenth-century culture would be displaced by the rationalism of the engineer that releases us from a false culture, and makes possible a life that can be lead without "leaving traces."[21] The traces that bourgeois life secretes and accumulates in its shielded interiors sever us from the collective in becoming reified markers of an equally reified individuality, whereas for Benjamin the true task is to forge a mode of life that opens us up to the communal, for which the transparency of new materials, and eventually the new sense of space, is a precondition. "Things made of glass have no 'aura,'" Benjamin suggests, and "generally speaking, glass is the enemy of the secret. It is also the enemy of possessions."[22]

Like Giedion, Benjamin imagines that the new technology will fundamentally change our capacity for perception, even remodel the very categories of space and time, as when in the essay on the work of art in the age of mechanical reproducibil-

20. See Benjamin, "Erfahrung und Armut" (1933), *Gesammelte Schriften* (Frankfurt am Main: Suhrkamp, 1997), vol. 2/1, 213–19. Cf. *Das Passagen-Werk*: "It belongs to the technical forms of Gestaltung that their progress and success are proportional to the transparency of their social content (glass architecture comes from this)" (GS V, 581).

21. "This was something to which Scheerbart with glass and Bauhaus with steel had opened a path: they have created rooms where it is difficult to leave traces." ("Erfahrung und Armut," 217) To "erase the traces" is the theme for Benjamin's commentary to a poem by Brecht from *Lesebuch für Stadtbewohner*; see Benjamin, *Versuche über Brecht* (GS II/2).

22. "Erfahrung und Armut," 217. The idea of a world without possessions, or rather one that would make possible a different relation to the object than the one organized along the lines of use and exchange value (with their concomitant tendency to fetishism), was a crucial theme among some constructivist theoreticians, notably Boris Arvatov. See Christina Kiaer, *Imagine no Possessions: The Socialist Objects of Russian Constructivism* (Cambridge, Mass.: MIT, 2005).

ity, he argues that cinema functions as a kind of psychoanalysis of the "optical unconscious" that will allow us to see and take possession of space in a different way. Similarly, Giedion and Benjamin both understand the Pont Transbordeur as a condensation of the same kind of technological sensibility that we encounter in the microscope, the telescope, the X-ray image, and the aerial photograph, which eventually would usher in a transformed concept of nature. Benjamin tends however more to stress the role of photographs in allowing us to decipher the city and the relations of labor in a changed perspective, and that technology as such is insufficient, even though he too is ambivalent on this point, as comes across particularly pointedly in the Reproduction essay. For both of them what is ultimately at stake is the possibility of a fusion of nature and technology, or, as Benjamin suggests in a note in the *Passagen-Werk*: "One could formulate the problem of the new art in the following way: when and how will the worlds of mechanical forms, in cinema, in the construction of machines, in the new physics, etc., appear without our help and overwhelm us, *make us conscious of what is natural in them?*"[23]

This opening up, or de-auratization, of the architectural object was intended as a way to create a new social mobility and an openness between groups and classes, and Giedion's and Benjamin's proposals can in this respect be taken as paradigmatic for a whole generation of avant-garde thinkers and artists. In hindsight, it is clear that this among many of them (though by no means all) this was based on a fantasy of control and exertion of power: transparency erases the division between inside and outside, private and public, and in this it produces a new subjectivity that is attuned to new social demands and programs, for which the architect or artist becomes a Demiurge.

23. *Das Passagen-Werk*, *GS* V, 500 (my italics).

The idea of transparency forms an integral part of early modernist architecture, although its underlying motifs are multiple and entangled. The glassy surface may be read as an instrument for an openness and candor that are imposed from the outside rather than emerging from the inner spontaneity of the subject, but can also be read as a means of producing opacity or a variable light in order to enhance a sense of pleasure and enjoyment;[24] it may fuse interior and exterior in a sweeping movement, or render the passage impossibly difficult by multiplying reflections and doubles. There is a whole history of modern architecture to be written, which would investigate how this phantasm has been negotiated, the contradictions that it harbors, and the way in which it continues to inform the architectural imaginary far beyond the projects of the early modern masters.[25]

24. Benjamin's direct reference when it comes to the use of glass is the poet Paul Scheerbart, whose visions in *Glasarchitektur* (1914) of a world based on transparency acted as a catalyst for many in the early avant-garde. Scheerbart's book was aiming at a moral change of man, but it was also a poetic sketch that resists any unambiguous and programmatic readings. Scheerbart imagines how glass architecture would evolve from a singular building until it covered the whole face of the earth, providing a complete enlightenment, an infinite luminosity. While there is a austerity and poverty in Benjamin's fascination with transparency, Scheerbart stresses the sensuous and voluptuous aspects of glass—what attracts him is not so much transparency, and definitely not any kind of austerity (and on this point he seems to have been fatally misread by many avant-gardists) as the possibility of modulating light and shade, heat and cold, and the achievement of a state of maximum comfort and luxury, where interior and exterior blend together in a delightful continuity and our homes become "cathedrals" for the fulfillment of desires. We have to get rid of our nostalgia for the heavenly paradise, Scheerbart suggests, so that we may realize it here and now in terms of a hedonist culture based on luminosity.

25. A crucial reference would here be Colin Rowe and Robert Slutzky's 1964 essay "Transparency: Literal and Phenomenal," which attempt to spiritualize technology by defending the autonomy of architecture as art from the attacks mounted by the historical avant-garde. Rowe and Slutzky weld together the themes of transparency, interpenetration, and space-time in a formalist conception that makes it possible to think the trajectory of modern architecture as a way to an autonomy, self-referentiality, and aloofness from the world that preserve the depth

As a slight sidetrack from our theme here, we can note there is a strikingly parallel take on this debate to be found in Sergei Eisenstein's unrealized film project *Glass House*, and the notes and sketches that accompanied it, which cast a particular light on many of the architectural aspirations of the period. First conceived in 1926, during a stay in Berlin where he was to oversee the premier of *The Battleship Potemkin*, Eisenstein takes issue with the fantasy of glass architecture as social utopia. He imagines a completely transparent skyscraper replete with paradoxical interpersonal situations, as if to display the impossibility in a capitalist society of achieving any reconciliation between its centrifugal forces, propelling people into solitude, and the demands of mass society for participation and communal life.

One the one hand, Eisenstein's reading of glass architecture and its social claims is negative and ironic: Western architects, in spite of their formal skills in manipulating concrete, glass, and steel, forget about the "real man," who becomes only an image and not a "tenant" with his "luggage in his hand, his wife and kids." But on the other hand, for Eisenstein transparency is also a crucial formal discovery, an architectural device for breaking out of cinema's architectural confines, even to make it "step out if itself." The *Glass House* project allows Eisenstein to elaborate on the possibility of a non-naturalist cinema, an art of multiple points of view and entries (which he connects to Joyce, whose *Ulysses* he discovered at the same time), and in this sense the project remains on the horizon as a theoretical resource, long after the shooting of the actual film had been finally abandoned after the disappointments in Hollywood in the early thirties—in fact, until the very end of his life. On May 22, 1946, Eisenstein

and values of a humanist culture, and for which the analogy with painting will be essential. For a discussion of this, see my *The Silences of Mies* (Stockholm: Axl Books, 2008), 59-63.

writes in his diary: "Everyone, once in a his life, writes his 'mystery play'; mine was the Glass House."[26]

In many respects the *Glass House* notes are close to Eisenstein's working notes toward the film version of Marx's *Capital*, in radically exceeding the strictures of cinematic language and even the domain of the visual as such: it was "an impossible film," François Albera says, "a project destined to remain virtual."[27] But this virtuality was indeed a highly productive one, and it continued to inform much of Eisenstein's subsequent work. The transparency of the glass house condenses the formal and the political into one charged image, with multiple intersecting points of view, and where the interpenetration not just of subjects and objects, but also of actions, generates a dialectical drama that shows the promised transparency to be ridden with fears and tensions; it harbors a mystery: that transparency and interpenetration on another level produces opacity, confusion, and division. The question of how to negotiate the relation between political agency and formal complexity, how to transform the dislocation of perception into a model for social critique, traverses the avant-garde in all of its guises, and whether the quest for transparency, material as well as social, will help bring about this model for social critique, constitutes one of its founding problems.

Producing complexity, or the planning of chance

When Giedion notes that "walls no longer rigidly define streets," and that "the street has been transformed into a stream of movement," his vocabulary is derived from a first machine age discourse on energy, movement, and velocity, claiming to dissolve all firm objects that pose obstacles to a new type of free-

26. Cited in François Albera, "Introduction," in Eisenstein, *Glass House* (Paris: Les Presses du Réel, 2009), 11.
27. Ibid, 9.

dom, which however itself needs to be organized along the lines of rational construction. From the point of view of the postwar developments, it would be possible to see this as already pointing ahead to the need for a more stratified analysis that describes the conduits of such forces, how they are channeled and rerouted—in short, we could say that the futuristic energetics of the first wave of the avant-garde already calls upon the cybernetic reconstruction that was to be undertaken in the second wave. If architecture in Giedion's vision ceased being the paradigm for order and stability to the point that its limited concept would be dissolved, then this transformation, which we could perhaps understand as its general concept, indicates a new role within the emergent network space: architecture provides a spatial form to the flows themselves, and must henceforth be seen as part of a more encompassing organizational technology.[28]

The erasure of the boundary between street and building, and in the next step between inside and outside in a more general sense, can then be taken as one of the fundamental modes in which modern architecture attempts to exert a generalized spatial control. On the other hand, this just as much implies an increasing capacity for free movement, the creation of a space that allows for variegated subject trajectories and modes of perceiving, of which Corbusier's idea of the *plan libre* is probably the most famous case. The machine of architecture is not just a machine for living, but also a viewing machine, a movement machine, and perhaps at the most general level a war machine in the twofold sense proposed by Deleuze and Guattari: it points to the idea of a smooth and non-segmented space, it breaks down an earlier segmented space, and yet it always re-creates, as a kind of counter-effect, various new forms of striated and segmented imperial spaces that function like apparatuses of cap-

28.   For this reading, see Reinhold Martin, *The Organizational Complex: Architecture, Media, and Corporate Space* (Cambridge, Mass.: MIT, 2004).

ture.[29] This double-edged quality of the machine may account for the conflicted reactions that it produces, but also for the fact that these reactions themselves reproduce the same ambiguity: the revolt undertaken in the name of freedom and the right to movement always carries within itself, as a shadow impossible to cast off, new regimentations—all of which implies that, as Foucault noted, there is nothing that could *guarantee* freedom, no legal or physical institutions, or any other types of structures, that could once and for all define a space of liberty.[30]

When modernist architecture after the Second World War increasingly came under fire, it was thus perhaps not only because of its failure to fulfill its promises, but also because it in fact began to realize them, in a process that, as Tafuri notes (even though he dates this back to the shift between the twenties and thirties and the reactions to the Wall Street crash), deprived architecture of one of its most cherished self-images, i.e., that it could remain the sovereign subject of this process. The most obvious case of this is the program for a "functional city" based on zoning, first proposed in the 1933 Athens Charter, but published by Corbusier nine years later, and which began to exert a profound influence on postwar urbanism and decision-making at the same time that its theoretical foundations were questioned by a new generation of architects, to some extent also by Corbusier himself. The rejec-

29.   For the war machine and the apparatus of capture, see Gilles Deleuze and Félix Guattari, *Thousand Plateaus*, trans. Brian Massumi (Minneapolis: University of Minnesota Press, 1987), chap. 9 and 10.

30.   The analysis of this predicament proposed by Foucault, responding to a question in an interview by Paul Rabinow on whether architecture has a possible emancipatory power, remains pertinent: "I do not think that there is anything that is functionally—by its very nature—absolutely liberating. Liberty is a *practice*. So there may, in fact, always be a certain number of projects whose aim is to modify some constraint, to loosen, or even to break them, but none of these projects can, simply by its nature, assure that people will have liberty automatically, that it will be established by the project itself." Foucault, "Space, Knowledge, and Power," *Essential Works*, eds. Paul Rabinow and James D. Faubion (London: Penguin, 2001), vol. 3, 354.

tion of modernist architecture and planning discourse as authoritarian, ignorant of the specificities of place and space, and based on an abstract universalism that erases the local and regional in favor of a flattened corporate architecture, was in fact voiced most clearly by the architects themselves, and the gradual breakdown of the CIAM (*Congrès Internationaux d'Architecture Moderne*) can be seen as the most visible symptom of this process. Founded in 1928 with Giedion as one of its initiators and the first secretary-general, the trajectory of CIAM until its final demise in 1959—when Corbusier had already left, and a series of dissidents, above all Alison and Peter Smithson and then the Team X, had come to radically challenge its founding principles—constitutes like a seismic curve reflecting this process.[31]

On the level of formal solutions, we find a critique that claims that the apparent rationalism of modernism is simply another style, a mere rhetoric that in fact is just as much (or little) functional as any other style, as for instance in the readings proposed by Reyner Banham of the machine aesthetic of early functionalism. The modernists, too, came under the influence of this critique, in particular Le Corbusier himself, who during this period began to look for a more informal strategy, "un art autre" as he named it after the survey published by Michel Tapié in 1952.[32] This rejection was to a large extent based on a recovery of certain humanist values that were assumed to have been eradicated from prewar urbanist discourse, as in the case of the neighborhood and its possibilities for social interaction that was opposed to the rarefaction of the *Ville Radieuse* of early

31. For the history of CIAM, see Eric Mumford, *The CIAM Discourse on Urbanism, 1928–1960* (Cambridge, Mass.: MIT, 2000). On the activities of Team X, cf. Max Risselada and Dirk van den Heuvel (eds.), *Team 10, 1953–1981: In Search of a Utopia of the Present* (Rotterdam: NAi, 2005). Important source documents can be found in Alison Smithson (ed.), *Team 10 Primer* (Boston: MIT, 1968).
32. Miche Tapié, *Un art autre, ou il s'agit de nouveaux dévidages du réel* (Paris: Gabriel-Giraud et fils, 1952).

Corbusier. The question of form as style was however a limited one, and when the idea of the street as a place of encounter was re-introduced, it was as a tool to articulate—or, more precisely, to *plan*, which already begins to indicate the dialectics of this process—a spontaneous complexity emerging out of unpredictable encounters. Rather than a wholesale rejection of earlier solutions, this implied a continued emphasis on the emancipatory aspects of urbanism, and together with the task of carrying on a tempered and moderated rationality whose disenchantment of aesthetic hierarchies were to form the basis of a democratic and egalitarian social order. But that the complexity was to be planned and produced testified to the inherent contradictions of these proposals: the discourse of planning somehow had to undo itself, or produce its own counter-discourse in order to retain its legitimacy, and a complexity that defeated prediction must be engendered on the basis of a few a priori principles. It would no doubt be possible to write a history of postwar architectural theory on the basis of the question of how to create this type of complexity: from the Team X and the splinters groups in CIAM, through Robert Venturi's *Complexity and Contradiction in Architecture*, Aldo Rossi's *Architecture of the City*, and Colin Rowe and Fred Koetter's theory of collage, and up to Rem Koolhaas's *dynamique d'enfer*, the question of how to affirm chance and contingency without simply destroying the profession of the planner imposes itself as a question of great theoretical as well as political urgency. In all of them the same dialectical problem surfaces, with varying degrees of lucidity and self-consciousness: how can the unpredictable be organized, at once unleashed and contained, and what is the role of architecture, traditionally the very model of stability in the arts, in setting up the conditions for something like a programmatic instability?[33]

33.   For Venturi and Rossi, see chap. 2, above; for Rowe and Koetter, see *Collage City* (Cambridge, Mass.: MIT, 1978); for Koolhaas, see chap. 5, below.

In this context it is not irrelevant to note the very term function has a decisive background in biology, not just as in the machine aesthetic and its mimesis of particular technological forms, or the tyranny (or poem, as in Corbusier) of the straight angle, but in the sense of a process of adaptive process where living being interacts with its surrounding world and forms a dynamic whole, which is the true source of Sullivan's famous formula "Form follows function." The biological background highlights the extent to which modern architecture from very the start was a program to administer and control life, to render it productive and useful, all of which could be subsumed under the Foucauldian concept of biopolitics, which is why the surface qualities of style and aesthetics should be reintegrated into an analysis that accounts for a deeper underlying logic that goes all the way back to the latter half of the eighteenth century.[34] As the Swedish modernist manifesto *Acceptera* (1931) says, using a phrase from first Bauhaus manifesto, the task of modernist architecture is not to engage in any "non-sensical talk of aesthetics," but to provide a "*Gestaltung von Lebensvorgängen*," a "shaping of life processes."[35] The idea of regimentation of space

34. I discuss this extended genealogy of modern architecture, which breaks with idea of modernism as predicated upon particular aesthetic, morphological, and tectonic features and instead locates it within a complex of knowledge and power in which the modern subject emerges as an entity that is both disciplined and free, in my *Biopolitics and the Emergence of Modern Architecture* (New York: Princeton Architectural Press, 2008).

35. The claim is that utilitarian art has a beauty of its own, an evident and transparent form, an "intuitive *Gestaltung*" of the form-function complex rather than a "mechanical romanticism". The Germans, the authors of *Acceptera* say, speak of this in terms of *Gestaltung von Lebensvorgängen*, the "shaping of life processes," in order to withdraw from "aesthetic debates with their endless nonsensical talk"—but, they add, there is, indeed, just as much nonsensical talk with respect to the practical sphere. Opposing both of these nonsensical discourses, they propose that "art is order," i.e., "an object displaying a perfect order and an unbroken continuity between form and function." This is, of course, the ideological operation par excellence: a naturalization that also involves the "process of life" in its integrity and postulates a continuity

that could be taken as the secret aim of Giedion's "interpenetration" is an integral part of this: if architecture ceases to refer to some eternal canonical reservoir of beautiful forms (although in many cases it preserves, intensifies, and even claims to be the only valid contemporary meaning of the classical reference, as in the case of Corbusier), this is because it undertakes a different task, i.e., to provide a spatial and territorial machinery for the production of the modern subject.

Constructing the moment

One highly significant countermove to this understanding of architectural and urban order—and which, as if at the same time extending and inverting Giedion's claim by placing an emphasis on the role of the street and the kind of unpredictability that is produced by movement, as well as on Benjamin's belief on the strategic use of modern image culture—can be found in the situationist movement.[36] In fact, many of those who criticized the early modern movement argued that if architecture should re-connect to the fabric of urban life, it must also accept the new consumer society with its concomitant technologies and mass cultural forms. This was the basic outlook of the British Inde-

---

among object, function, and user that allows for no further questions because it is intuitive, evident, and transparent. See *Acceptera* (Stockholm: Tiden, 1931), 139f. "Germans" in the above quoted no doubt refers to Walter Gropius and his introductory remarks to the 21 theses on "Systematische Vorarbeit für rationellen Wohnungsbau," in *bauhaus* 1, no. 2 (1927): "Bauen bedeutet Gestaltung von Lebensvorgängen. Die Mehrzahl der Individuen hat gleichartige Lebensbedürfnisse. Es ist daher logisch und im Sinne eines wirtschaftlichen Vorgehens, diesen gleichgearteten Massenbedürfnisse einheitlich und gleichartig zu befriedigen." ("Building means shaping of life processes. The majority of individuals have similar vital needs. Thus it is logical, and in the spirit of an economical undertaking, to satisfy these mass needs in a uniform and similar way.")

36. For an overview of how situationist theory engages with the legacy of modernist architecture and city planning, see Simon Sadler, The *Situationist City* (Cambridge, Mass.: MIT, 1999).

pendent Group with its proto-pop strategies, for instance in the use of collage techniques, which were at once formally close to and yet ideologically wholly opposed to the *détournement* of the situationists, and later of the French and American versions of pop art. The reuse of commercial images in situationism instead aimed for a total revolution: to overthrow consumer society from within by appropriating and perverting its images, to attain the revolutionary moment in a given society be exacerbating and intensifying its contradictions at strategically located points, and not to indulge in the kind of permissive and liberal attitudes toward desire and fantasy that permeated other influential theories of images and consumption, like Banham's "aesthetic of expendability." From 1963 and onward, the opposition to pop art and its alleged political indifference even became an officially professed aim of situationism.

In bringing together art, politics, and revolutionary activities in terms of an analysis of the spatial ordering and regimentation of everyday life, situationism can to some extent be understood as a retrieval of motifs from the historical avant-garde,[37] and it was undoubtedly beset by the same contradictions, on the level both of group psychology and of its theoretical premises. The project to produce freedom, to create a "situation" that would liberate the subject not only from social constraints, but also from a self that is the result of an introjection of a social imaginary (the society of the spectacle) is a highly tenuous operation that might easily slip into authoritarianism and repression.

In spite of its short life-span and more or less imaginary

37. It has often been pointed out that their critique of modern architecture, together with the discovery of a kind on urban unconscious, retrieves motifs that can be found already in surrealism and perhaps even in Baudelaire (the *dérive* can of course be understood as a postmodern version of the *flaneur*). As Benjamin prophetically noted, "To comprehend Breton and Corbusier would mean to bend the spirit of contemporary France like a bow, so that knowledge hits the moment straight in the heart." (*Das Passagen-Werk, Gesammelte Werke* V, 573)

existence, a feature shared by many situationist projects, the "Imaginist Bauhaus" created by Asger Jorn after breaking away from the Hochschule für Gestaltung in Ulm (which under the direction of Max Bill at the time was the epitome of a certain type of rationalist modernism) can be taken as one of the formative events of the situationist analysis of modernism, although, as we have seen, it also resonates with many other similar revolts against modern town planning in the first two postwar decades. For the situationists, the fate of modern architecture and its instrumentalization under the aegis of the CIAM appears as wholly inscribed in a process of rationalization and bureaucratization that permeates both capitalism and socialism, in relation to which the suggestions of situationism may on the one hand simply appear as a willfully anarchistic counter-rhetoric doomed to be remain at the margins, and on the other as an almost uncanny intensification of certain features of modernism itself. We have already noted the extent to which this perpetual oscillation between freedom and subjection is already at work in the initial modernist program, and what these revolts in fact imply should perhaps not be seen as an outright rejection—although this is undoubtedly how situationism understood itself—but could perhaps more productively be understood in terms of a re-working or a working-through in an almost Freudian sense. Against the tyranny of the grid and the straight angle situationism may propose a radical individual freedom that significantly enough must endorse the intentionally *useless*, as in Günther Feuerstein's 1960 projects in the German section SPUR for radically impractical apartments, which included sensations of physical pain and discomfort produced by destroying air-conditioning, walls, and windows,[38] or

38. "By declining labor-saving devices, devising tortuous routes through his apartment, and fitting it with noisy doors and useless locks, Feuerstein refused to allow his own home to become another cog in the mecha-

in more complex way, in their refusal to accept renovations that lead to higher housing standards, since this would solidify the idea of the two-room apartment unit as a monadic satellite disconnected from the social world, where media and communication systems intensify alienation and render political action impossible.[39]

But on the other hand, situationist architectural projects on a more grand scale, such as Constant's *New Babylon*, can just as much be understood as another and even more radical way to first dislodge, and then *reprogram* subjective experience, and in their emphasis on unpredictability and on strategies for blocking out the repetitive aspect of experience and short-circuiting possibilities for spatial identification, they radically circumscribe individual freedom: whoever enters the maze of the New Babylon is supposed to never return to the same place, and must be subjected to a very strict regimentation of movement, and the openness ascribed to the trajectory is in fact, on the level of architectural strategy, a result of the most precise and refined techniques.[40] Feuerstein wants to allow the body to break free from

nized world. It would no longer protect him from the environment nor the sensations of his own body: ripping out his air conditioning and throwing open his windows, he could swelter, shiver, and struggle to hear himself think above the roar of the city; later he might bump and hurt himself against one of the myriad sharp corners in his flat, and sit at his wobbly table and on his uncomfortable sofa. Or he might unwind by throwing paint against the walls and drilling holes through them, filling out his flat with traces of his own ideas and history" (Sadler, *The Situationist City*, 7–8).

39. For a discussion of this theme in relation the new French suburbs, which fueled the imagination of artists and thinkers from Godard (*Deux ou trois choses que je sais d'elle*, 1966) to Debord and Lefebvre, and the emergence of a French consumer society in the 1950s and '60s, see Sylvère Lotringer, "Consumed by Myths," in Bernard Blistène et al., *Premises: Invested Spaces in Visual Arts, Architecture & Design From France, 1958–1998* (New York: Guggenheim, 1998).

40. For this reading of Constant, see Hilde Heynen, *Architecture and Modernity* (Cambridge, Mass.: MIT, 1999), 151–173. See also Mark Wigley, *Constant's New Babylon: The Hyper-Architecture of Desire* (Rotterdam, Witte de With, 1998), and the contributions in Catherine de Zegher and Mark

the cage of reason by subjecting it to random events that become possible through erratic acts of destruction of an existing architecture (smashing the window, tearing holes in walls and floors); Constant wants to *ensure*, on the level of an architectonic structure that itself is wholly controlled, that randomness will always prevail over the repetition and identification of singular places and locations, and thus his environment must in some respects become infinitely more coercive and constraining than any modernist *plan libre*. The belief that there is authentic life beyond the spectacle, a beach buried somewhere deep below the pavement, not only is a romantic fantasy, but also entails the idea of how this authentic life could be (re)produced and as it were suggested to the subject as an offer that it simply cannot refuse.

Most of the concepts proposed in situationist theory—the *dérive*, psycho-geography, unitary urbanism, and most fundamentally the very idea of *situation* itself—contain this ambiguity. On the one hand, they are meant to make possible a reflexive use of the materials in a given culture by enabling the construction of a situation or a moment—a tactics for re-mapping the spatial structures of a city whose secrets can be unearthed by, for instance, performing semi-distracted strolls that establish previously unseen connections, or for refunctioning images and artifacts that contain within themselves the potential for a revolutionary momentum if combined in the right way, a tactics that must be seen in terms of more encompassing *strategy* for the subversion of society in its totality.[41]

This is also the source of the conflict that led to the rift be-

Wigley (eds.): *The Activist Drawing: Retracing Situationist Architectures from Constant's New Babylon to Beyond* (New York: Drawing Center, 2001).

41.   The question of tactics vs. strategy in avant-garde movements would require a separate analysis; for a study of situationist architectural discourse that takes its cues from Debord's retrieval of Clausewitz and his construction of a model for a "war game," see McKenzie Wark, *50 Years of Recuperation of the Situationist International* (New York: Princeton Architectural Press, 2008).

tween Debord and Henri Lefebvre. For the latter, whose analysis of the structures of everyday life forms the backdrop of many situationist concepts, it is decisive that fantasy and historical moments (with the Paris commune constituting the paradigm for both of them) can be integrated in a systematic theory capable of accounting for the subjective dimension of history without reducing it. But rather than the systemic analysis that at the time claimed to move away from subjectivity and experience toward the construction of a pure Theory (most obviously in the case of Althusser and his followers), for which individual experience would be caught up in the order of the imaginary, Lefebvre insists on the power of the subject and imagination to engage in the concrete dialectic of everyday practice, even to the point that he would insist on being a "romantic revolutionary" and on the need for resuscitating the dimension of feast and carnival, against the kind of critical analysis whose obsession with structures for him merely reflected and reinforced the technocratic world that it aspired to overthrow. In this there is also a moment of pleasure or enjoyment (*jouissance*) that is essential for theory to be meaningful, but also belongs particularly to architecture,[42] a bodily encounter with the built environment that cannot be reduced to the particular ways in which it spatializes the social order, but that also transgresses this order in a form dispersal and expenditure that still belongs to the *capacity* of the subject, not to its *undoing*.

This idea of a theory that begins in and returns to the complexity of the concrete was crucial throughout Lefebvre's work, and it emerges in the aftermath of the Second World War[43] in

42. As comes across in the recently rediscovered text, *Towards an Architecture of Enjoyment*, ed. Lukasz Stanek, trans. Robert Bononno (Minneapolis: University of Minnesota Press, 2014).

43. Sylvère Lotringer notes that Lefebvre initiates his program for a critique just after the Second World War, and the first volume is contemporary with the emergence of new housing programs and suburbia.

the guise of a "Critique of Everyday Life" (*Critique de la vie quoti-dienne*, 1947), a title that would recur in two later works, *Critique de la vie quotidienne II: Fondements d'une sociologie de la quotidien-neté* (1962), and *Critique de la vie quotidienne III: De la modernité au modernisme* (1981), and may be taken as a guide through his labyrinthine oeuvre. Lefebvre's re-anchoring of the analysis of capital in the realm of the everyday calls for a mediation of in-dividuality and history; and *experience*, as the place where alien-ation and reification appears, to a large extent replaces work as the founding analytical category—which also entails the need to account for the irruption of pleasure as a particular and ineradi-cable phenomenon. In this his work is obviously part of a more encompassing process of revision in Marxist theory, shifting the accent from the economic sphere to socio-cultural processes, and in many ways it runs parallel to the Frankfurt School, of which he however never seemed to have taken any notice. More generally, this displacement translates the postwar integration of economy in the production of a symbolic order, which in turns weakens, or as some would argue, obliterates the socio-logical distinction between avant-garde and cultural industry that a previous generation of critical theory could rely on.

In the case of Lefebvre, this emphasis on concrete experience comes across in a thoroughgoing critique of the idea of planning (in many ways parallel to that of Tafuri), as the way in which a state-controlled capitalism colonizes the lifeworld.[44] This critique

This is also the moment when a new society of consumption begins to take form, which Lefebvre would ceaselessly criticize throughout his subsequent work. This is however also what lends a retroactive and nostalgic tone to his writings—everyday life is that which has been lost, and the possibility of reinventing it must draw on older models. See Lotringer "Consumed by Myths", and Lefebvre's own comments in the introduction to the third volume of *Critique de la vie quotidienne*.

44.   In the second volume of *Critique de la vie quotidienne* Lefebvre develops the idea that this colonization constitutes a projection back onto the French territory of the techniques of domination that earlier had been applied to the colonies; see the discussion in Kristin Ross, *Fast Cars,*

however perhaps retains a Kantian inspiration in not merely being negative, but in proposing something like a complex entanglement of possible experience, limits, and negative illusions, of an Analytic and a Dialectic. Everyday life is on the one hand regimented by the state and capital as the twin faces of the same systemic power, on the other hand it always harbors a potential for reversal and transgression. It is via an analysis of the street, the café, the store—and, perhaps more surprisingly, the holiday resort—that we may understand how structures are produced and reproduced as a spatial ordering (which in this sense can be accounted for exclusively neither in terms of base nor superstructure), but also as the permanent possibility of upheaval.

Both Lefebvre and situationism—the first immediately because of personal experience, the second through a historical mediation that passes through the lettrist movement and a literary avant-garde that remains to be charted—are the heirs of surrealism, and they both echo a critique of early functionalism and modernism that was already present in Bréton. Precisely because of the historical distance, this heritage and its fascination with immediacy is more pervasive in situationism, whereas it is tempered and held up to scrutiny in Lefebvre. For him it is necessary that imagination and historical moments be integrated into a coherent theory that inscribes subjectivity and immediacy, although without betraying it. The situationist situation is close to Lefebvre's moment, but also comprises the claim that this situation should be *constructed*, which unwittingly reproduces the paradox in most Marxist theories of revolution, and no doubt goes back to Hegel or even Rousseau: one must determine the situation of freedom, while any substantial definition of it does an unacceptable violence to it. For Lefebvre this points to a theoretical as well as moral shortcoming: to construct the situation

Clean Bodies: Decolonization and the Reordering of French Culture (Cambridge, Mass.: MIT, 1995).

means to underestimate the objective dimension of history in the name of voluntarism, but also to reduce the subjective contingency of the moment that is the condition of the emergence of freedom. In spite of the considerable intelligence and often mischievous ruses dedicated to bringing about such situationist situations, the concept of situation still remains problematically empty as to its ulterior purpose, which is why it must be given to us from the outside, in an act that cannot avoid becoming repressive. Using a Kantian vocabulary that is to be sure not the one used by Lefebvre here, but yet constitutes a background for his idea of critique, we might say that the situationist situation is both blind and empty: blind because its intuitive immediacy lacks the dialectical categories that would mediate it with the totality, empty because its categories must be imposed from the outside by an act of will that does not emerge out of the sensible and intuitive material. In this way, the split between Lefebvre and Debord is not just a personal one, but might by taken as translating a constitutive rift in the avant-garde and the dialectic inherent in its promise of an emancipatory architecture: to plan the unplannable, losing control by immersing itself in the formless while extracting another level of mastery from it.

Constructing the event

Using a conceptual pair devised by Bataille, we could perhaps say that situationism, along with all the various political and/or artistic movements that would follow in its wake, pits, against the "pyramid" of modern architecture with its fantasies of control, the "labyrinth" of the street with a corresponding fantasy of a controlled *loss of control*.[45] If the pyramid is a thought of altitude

45. Bataille develops the opposition between the labyrinth and the pyramid in several of his writings, above all *L'expérience intérieure*. For a discussion, see Denis Hollier, *Against Architecture: The Writings of Georges Bataille* (Cambridge, Mass.: MIT, 1989), 57–73. The English title chosen for Hollier's book—whose French title is *La prise de la Concorde*—some-

and omnivisibility, the labyrinth opens up a space of eroticism and *jouissance*, it is a transgression that turns not only against an alleged Puritanism of modern architecture, but also "against architecture" as such, as the very paradigm of the attempt to subsume events under their concept; and yet the labyrinth is an architecture too, equally if not even more meticulously constructed in order to produce a particular spatiality.

At a later moment in the unfolding in this chain of concepts, Bernard Tschumi, whose early work picks up important themes from situationist theory, would propose that architecture must always be both pyramid and labyrinth at the same time: it must transcend the sensuous and concrete in the direction of an authoritative form from which the world can be surveyed, *and* descend into a multiplicity of events that upsets all perspectives; in Tschumi's own terms, which once more revisits the clams of Giedion, it must be both space as concept and spacing as event, without dreaming of finally becoming the one or the other.[46]

From early on, Tschumi's question deals with architecture as event and social process, as in *Do-it-yourself-city* (1968),[47] where the idea of participation in planning shows an aspiration to create an architecture of involvement, as well as a proximity to Archigram and the idea of an ephemeral and in the end imaginary architecture. He however opposes the idea that we should attempt to extract new forms from early modernism, since modernism in his view has implied a continual idealization and dematerialization, for which the forging of a concept like space around the turn of the century was a decisive step, followed by

what exacerbates the claim, even though it has an obvious base in Bataille's own writings.

46.   See Tschumi, "The Architectural Paradox," in Tschumi, *Architecture and Disjunction* (Cambridge, Mass.: MIT, 1994). This volume cited in the following as AD with page number.

47.   See Ferrando Montes and Bernard Tschumi, "Do-It-Yourself-City," in *L'Architecture d'aujourd'hui* no. 148 (Feb-March 1970): 98–105.

159

the insistence that architecture be understood as a language. The concept of space is not itself space, he emphasizes, and instead of giving in to an abstract and scientific-sounding vocabulary, we must attempt to develop practices based on corporeal experience, and approach the dimension of the sensible as a non-totalizable and disjunctive field. At first, this may seem like a rather straightforward Kantian turn: space is not a concept, and it cannot be constructed, but refers us to an irreducible sensibility. But as we have seen, Tschumi's proposal is in fact in line with the formative development of modernist space, or rather picks out one aspect, and in no way is simply opposed to it; his claim is not that space is simply there, as a pre-given form, but that it itself results from actions and events, and constitutes a flow that fuses subject and object. He does, however, sometimes tend to see the sensible dimension as an underlying level, as if it were a question of a dualism in a sense reminiscent of the young Nietzsche, so that order would be only a mask for an underlying stream: "Behind all masks lie 'dark' and unconscious streams that cannot be dissociated from the pleasures of architecture. The mask may exalt appearances. Yet by its very presence, it says that, in the background, there is 'something else.'"[48]

This something else is what provides architecture with its autonomy: its uselessness is its necessity, a surplus in relation

48. Tschumi, "The Pleasure of Architecture," AD 91. K. Michael Hays reads the early work of Tschumi through Lacan, casting it as a desire confronted with an impossible Real, "both the hard, impenetrable core that resists discursive appropriation (it is prior to symbolization) and at the same time the exorbitant emptiness that remains after symbolization is complete (even as it is produced by symbolization itself [...] it can never be translated or rendered knowable as a positivity, this architectural Real, but only experienced through an unassimilable, negative Other—spaced out and projected backward, as it were, out of its own structural effects." See Hays, *Architecture's Desire: Reading the Late Avant-Garde* (Cambridge, Mass.: MIT, 2010), 135. My interpretation here crosses Hays's at several points, although my focus on the dialectic of control and openness as a generative problem places the accents slightly differently.

to function as use value, even though this paradoxically seems to appear only as a *lack*: "*I would therefore suggest that there has never been any reason to doubt the necessity of architecture, for the necessity of architecture is its non-necessity. It is useless but radically so.* [...] Defined by its questioning, architecture is the expression of a lack, a shortcoming, a non-completion."[49] The other side of this negativity of non-completion is however the *event*, an affirmative gesture that draws on experienced space as a becoming. Rather than something subjective and interior, or an objective outside given over to conceptual schemata, this is an undoing of the subject-object divide that implicitly and explicitly draws on the series of more or less distant historical models that we have been tracing here, from Giedion's stream of movement and the interpenetration of inner and outer, to Lefebvre, situationism, and Bataille.[50] But if Giedion's idea of architecture ultimately

49.   "Questions of space," AD 47, 49, Tschumi's italics. As Hays notes (*Architecture's Desire*, 138), this can be read as a rejoinder to Tafuri's remarks in the preface to *Progetto e utopia* on the "sublime uselessness" that he prefers to the "deceptive attempts to give architecture an ideological dress (for further discussion of Tafuri's claim, see chap. 1 above). While the "sublime" in this *sublime inutilità* is probably intended only in the sense of something extreme, would it not also be possible, only slightly overinterpreting the term, to hear an echo of the Kantian sublime as the mode of appearing of a concept that cannot be exhibited in intuition, that defies the productive imagination's capacity to present a case, precisely because it is infinite? Kant's example in the third Critique is freedom, which in Tafuri's case could be taken as the freedom of architecture from use value and ideology, even though this too, he quickly adds, "harbors an ideological aspiration, pathetic in its anachronism."

50.   In the introduction to *La production de l'espace* (Paris: Anthropos, 1974), 48ff, Lefebvre famously distinguishes three senses of space: space as perceived (*l'espace perçu*) or as the object of spatial practices (*pratiques spatiales*), space as represented conceptually or as a representation of space (*représentation de l'espace*), and space as lived or experienced (*l'espace vécu*), the space of representation (*l'espace de représentation*), even though he later in the book seems to largely disregard it. Tschumi's "experienced space" is aligned with Lefebvre's third space (or "thirdspace," *espace tiers*), which seems to come last, as a surplus added to the preceding two terms or resulting from their interaction, but in fact must be understood as the primordial one, a kind of existential-ontological space from which other two are abstracted, and in this sense it comes

was that of a discipline capable of organizing and rationalizing this dynamic stream, giving form to that which always threatens to overflow it, then Tschumi's event-space signals an understanding of form that proceeds inversely and thinks form on the basis of its continual undoing and displacement, as in the idea of a cross-programming that overlays normally incompatible activities.

In the three-part essay "Architecture and Limits" (originally published in *Artforum* 1980–81, where it had an impact far beyond a specialized audience of architects), Tschumi surveys the field of contemporary architecture as it appeared in the beginning of the eighties, and points to certain works, located at the limit of architecture, which are nevertheless indispensible in resisting "the narrowing of architecture as a form of knowledge as mere knowledge of form" (AD 105), while he at the same time rejects the solution of a simple affirmation of autonomy that would simply turn architecture into art: architecture cannot avoid programs and functions, even though it must always also be something more. If the twentieth century has irrevocably fractured the Vitruvian conceptual triad, this poses new problems. Beauty (*venustas*) disappears or is absorbed in the discourse of linguistics or semiotics, which no longer supplies rules for beauty, but instead interrogates the limits of the "'prison-house' of architectural language" (110), which for Tschumi necessitates that we once more pose the question of subjectivity in architecture. Structural stability (*stabilitas*, or *firmitas*, to use Vitruvius's term)[51] too is a faint memory, and the idea of an integrity or

close to many of Heidegger's proposals. For an attempt to systematize Lefebvre's terminology on this point, se Edward Soja, *Thirdspace: Journeys to Los Angeles and Other Real-and-Imagined Places* (Cambridge, Mass.: Blackwell, 1996), 53–82.

51.   In fact, *De architectura* presents us with a chain of loosely related concepts, and it is above all the tradition emanating from Alberti's *De re aedificatoria* that has seen the triad *firmitas, utilitas, venustas* as the organizing figure. This triad however only appears once in *De architec-*

natural expressivity of materials can only be maintained as an ideology.[52] It is only in relation to the third Vitruvian term, utility (*utilitas*) that Tschumi perceives a potential for development, particularly to the extent that architecture would be able to take body, desire, and movement as its guiding threads. "Movements," he writes, "are the intrusion of events into architectural spaces" (111), and in order to both account for and generate such events, we must look to the complexity pertaining to the program, which he suggests has been downplayed both in modern functionalism and the postmodern manipulations of style. It is in relation to the programmatic in a wide sense, and not the aesthetic or technological aspect, that inventions can be made, even though this requires that we rethink what it means to pro-gram as an act that opens towards something aleatory rather than subjects itself to a set of already given requirements.

In the collage work *Manhattan Transcripts* (1976–81), completed at same time as the *Artforum* essay, Tschumi attempts to articulate what such a space, an "event space," would be. This takes him in the direction of new notation methods drawing on cinema as well as music and the visual arts. These transcripts consist of series of tripartite diagrams: fragments of photographs that show a murder in Central Park and the perpetrator's escape toward 42nd Street, drawings of architectural fragments, and finally a choreographic script of sorts, with arrows indicating the paths taken. The three systems of notation provide a series of shifting and incomplete perspectives, while architec-

tura, at 1.3.3, and *venustas* comes back parenthetically at 6.8.10, but in a different combination, together with convenience (*usus*) and propriety (*decorum*). Thus, several other conceptual structures may be taken as equally important, and bringing them all together into a unified system seems impossible.

52.   Or, which Tschumi does not say, as an *aesthetic*. The strength of a position like the one of Kenneth Frampton's critical regionalism, is that assumes this aesthetic dimension and tries to articulate its relation to both politics and technology. For more on Frampton, see chap 4, below.

ture, to the extent that we conceive of it as a bounded object, only appears on the horizon, both as something that ultimately might envelop the whole flow of frames and cut-up vistas (the Pyramid as the Idea that can only be partially glimpsed), and as a fluid and indeterminate whole that results from the events themselves, and whose quality changes as we move through the series (the order arising from the choices made in the labyrinth), as it takes us from Central Park to 42nd Street.

Beyond the visual and notional complexity of the Transcripts, the crucial idea here, too, is the idea of an expanded sense of program: rather than a return to the dialectic of function and form, the prying open of these parameters so that they enter into new and unforeseen constellations—not necessarily contradicting or negating each other, not pitting the autonomy of form against the heteronomy of function, but inventing or uncovering a multiplicity inside the congealed notion of *utilitas*—means that the program should not just welcome the event, but itself be constituted by it, just as the sequence of frames in the Transcripts lets us glimpse something like a continually displaced architecture. Paradoxically, the program becomes a term for that which cannot be regulated in advance, while it still, as architecture, and not just etymologically, cannot avoid being a *writing in advance*, a script that precedes the events and provides them with an enabling as well as limiting frame. Tschumi emphatically opposes this movement of "de-," dis-," and "ex-,"[53] of decentering and splitting, to the historicism of the "post-" and the "neo-," but at the end, and equally significantly, he also connects it to a movement that transfers power and agency away from the subject, towards another Pyramid that remains or is re-created on the horizon as a vague threat: "Today we have entered the age of deregulation, where control takes place *outside* of society, as in this computer

53.   Se "De-, dis-, ex-," AD 215–225.

programs that feed on another endlessly in a form of autonomy recalling the autonomy of language described by Michel Foucault. We witness the separation of people and language, the decentering of the subject. Or, we might say, the complete *decentering of society*." (AD 225) Apart from the rather misleading remark on Foucault, what these, admittedly brief, remarks seem to signal is the ambivalence, or rather the *undecidability*, of the pyramid-labyrinth opposition: the labyrinth always refers to some distant, obscure, and yet insistent pyramidal logic, just as the pyramid itself can be considered as a emerging from a multiplicity of labyrinths. Thus, rather than a dualism, we should see their relation as mutually implicative; they are two vectors that traverse the same force field. Similarly, the decentering or deregulation (a term that it is difficult not to associate with neoliberal market policies) of society is recalibrated through the loop,[54] programs that recursively feed on one another, re-creating an order that no longer seems to have a localizable subject or agent.

Dislocation and mapping

More than thirty years ago, Fredric Jameson proposed that a certain spatial dislocation was one of the basic features of postmodernism and the cultural logic of late capitalism.[55] Generally, in Jameson's take on postmodernism, the inherited model of depth that undergirded such conceptual pairs as essence-appearance, interiority-exteriority, and signifier-signified, was presumed to have been flattened out and turned into a mere effect of the folding of surfaces, producing a hallucinatory pres-

54.   In the following chapter, we will see how Reinhold Martin's interpretation of postmodernism makes extensive use of the idea of the feedback loop, in a way that seems consistent with Tschumi's proposal.

55.   See "Postmodernism, or, The Cultural Logic of Late Capitalism" (1984), reprinted in expanded form in *Postmodernism, or, The Cultural Logic of Late Capitalism* (Durham: Duke University Press, 1991. See also chap. 4, below.

ence in the face of which the subject, incapable of withstanding the influx of affects, would be reduced to state of fragmentation, just as the chain of signifiers that hold language together would be broken into a state of schizophrenia. Fusing together radically different and even opposed concepts from Derrida, Deleuze, Lyotard, and Baudrillard (without mentioning any one of them, or considering the very different contexts from which they had emerged) Jameson produced a theoretical amalgamation that in hindsight appears in need of a careful reconsideration and dismantling, but which at the time was crucial in establishing the unity of something like the postmodern.

For Jameson, these momentous shifts, whose effects extend throughout culture, are most vividly displayed in the kind of spatial dislocation occurring in architecture, represented, in his postmodernism essay, by John Portman's Westin Bonaventure Hotel (Los Angeles, 1974–76). Portman's architecture constantly confuses the perceptions of the spectator, its mirror facade replicates twisted images of the exterior as if it were itself nothing but a screen, and its interior does not provide the sense of a spatial whole, but rather that of a labyrinth or a set of disjointed parts. In Jameson's reading this maze-like quality does not, however, produce the sensuous and erotic *jouissance* that Tschumi in the wake of situationism ascribes to his "event-space," instead (and Jameson here draws on a somewhat skewed Lacanian vocabulary, whereas the problem he locates would be much more readily grasped in Lefebvre's terms) it exacerbates the split between the subjective level of an Imaginary too close to be made into an object, and a systemic Real too far away to be able even to provide a horizon, leaving the Symbolic emptied out, as it were, and without a signifying order that would convey orientation.[56] Or more precisely, this Real can only be

56. For Jameson, the Lacanian Real can in the end be understood as "History," and in this respect he is followed by Hays. While this interpreta-

grasped on the level of theory, but never understood within subjective space, since the latter is, in turn, condemned to remain
within a state of fragmentation, which is how the world system
appears when it is reflected in individual consciousness. Thus,
Jameson says, there is a need for a Symbolic dimension that
would be able to overcome this divide, a "cognitive mapping"
that sutures together these two seemingly irreconcilable dimensions. The waning of affect experienced on the subjective level
would then be the outcome of a situation where such cognitive
mapping is lacking: waning and overload are two sides of the
same coin, and the task of art would be to produce an affect that
would be theoretical, or inversely, the task of theory would be
to connect to affectivity without letting go of systemic thought.
Pyramid and labyrinth must be understood as intertwined if a
dialectical totality is to emerge, and sacrificing one for the other
means to sacrifice experience as it must unfold as a whole.

Perhaps it is starting from this divide between the subjective
and the systemic that will allow us to understand the continued
relevance of concepts developed in and around situationism for
current thinking. Echoes of these ideas can be heard in political movements that celebrated passion, dancing in the streets
with a highly symbolic and often nostalgic violence—the highly
theatrical skirmishes with the police and opponents as a way
to ensure that power is still *there* in a defined spatial sense, that
it can be confronted *head on* through the use of physical force.
At the opposite end we find Rem Koolhaas's remark that the
dispersal within the generic city, which for him constitutes the
likely future of our urban forms (apart from their resuscitation

tion is attractive to the extent that it provides a *general* link between
subjectivity and social structures, it also risks doing a disservice to both
Lacan and social theory: it empties out the ontological thrust of the
Lacanian Real, and at least implicitly construes it as something to be
grasped in a pure theory, just as it inversely pushes actual history into
the dim and unspecific beyond of History with a capital H.

as museums over various phases of modernity, as in the case of Paris or New York) has led to a street that is altogether dead, yet replete with public art and bristling with motion—as if "two deaths" could come together and produce a new life.[57] In this perspective, reclaiming the street would be a useless fantasy, or perhaps more diabolically: a highly *useful* fantasy that diverts attention from the merely compensatory character of the street as the locus of true public life, which re-emerges a second time, at the precise moment when life has moved into electronic space, turning the street into a kind of appendix, at best indifferent, at worst the source of confusion.

Should this simply be construed as an opposition between a youthful naiveté and revolutionary fervor, and the slightly cynical posturing of the blasé and/or historically (or in Koolhaas's case, perhaps posthistorically) conscious architect? Even though this construal might well be true, perhaps something more can be said, in relation both to the historical roots of this aporia as well as to our present condition.

"The street is once and for all what characterizes modern politics. Whoever can conquer the street, can also conquer the masses; and whoever can conquer the masses, thereby conquers the state," wrote Joseph Goebbels in his 1934 pamphlet *Kampf um Berlin*.[58] From the far left to the far right, the street—indeed no longer "rigidly defined" by walls, but more like a stream of movement that must be channeled and tapped for its energy—was understood as the violent nucleus of modern politics, and from this labyrinthine order radiates those lines of force that finally

57.   "The street is dead. That discovery has coincided with frantic attempts at its resuscitation. Public art is everywhere—as if two deaths make a life. Pedestrianization—intended to preserve—merely channels the flow of those doomed to destroy the object of their intended reverence with their feet." "Generic City," in Rem Koolhaas, *S, M, L, XL* (Rotterdam: 010, 1995), 1253.

58.   Joseph Goebbels, *Kampf um Berlin; Der Anfang* (Munich: Eher, 1934), cited in Paul Virilio, *Vitessse et politique* (Paris: Galilée, 1977), 14.

come together in the pyramid of the state apparatus. When Paul Virilio cites Goebbels's phrase at the outset of his "dromological" treatise *Speed and Politics* (1977), the questions he seems to be asking is to what extent this claim for the street can still be valid, and, consequently, how we should conceive of the order that transcends it. In a society dominated by telematics and informatics, could such a physical locus, where forces are pitted up against each other and deadly blows are exchanged, still exist as the source of politics? Have we moved into another spatial order, although it significantly enough seems possible to name it only by using concepts from the former: the site, the city of bits, the information highway, etc., as if virtual and electronic space could only exist by mimicking the set-up of the first-order space and life? What does this exchange of concepts mean? Does it speak of the incapacity of contemporary culture to properly name its own space, a loss of the sensible that may call for either a violent restoration of the old gods, or a detached observation of how all that was once solid now has vaporized into air?

The historical lesson that can be learned from a re-reading of the texts and works of early modernism, through the proposals of situationism up to their legacy in later architectural discourse, is that such an anxiety, or euphoria, perhaps was there from the start. Instead of proposing alternatives between which there would be a simple choice, it is more worthwhile to meditate on those new imbrications that are in fact produced at the intersection of electronic and physical space. It is true that we for a long time have lived off the energies unleashed by the fantasies of dematerialization that began somewhere in 1960s, in the theories of conceptual art or of the step into the information society, and whose most recent echo is the theory of immaterial labor—all of which, on different levels of theoretical sophistication and empirical precision, are marked by a certain desire to leave the body, that tiresome image of facticity and mortality, and to move in the direction of some new and glorious body that will open ever new avenues of pleasure and desire and relieve us of the specter of the Real. But it is undoubtedly true that matter and materiality do not go away or become in any way less important, only that they *change* their status and mode of being in relation to new forces and relations of production, without ever becoming more or less real. If the Real withdraws from experience, or rather fragments, leaving us with the alternative of *jouissance*, or of schizophrenia, as Tschumi and Jameson respectively suggest, where does that leave architecture?

If one is willing to abide by an inherent vocabulary, the question would be what kind of tectonics will emerge in our present type of space, once it succeeds in formulating its own vocabulary—which indeed presupposes that there is or once was some vocabulary of first-order space that could be taken as somehow directly referential, true and transparent, although that this is so is of course by no means obvious. On the level of urbanism, it would mean neither to turn the street and its concomitant spatial order, as the site of corporeal passions and affects, into an object of nostalgic affirmation, nor to declare it dead and a thing of the past (both strategies will eventually, within a slightly different time frame, transform it into a museum), but to investigate what it may become, with full awareness there is no natural state, that there is no point at which there would be a natural balance between the labyrinth of sensible experience and the pyramid of systemic theory. This type of dispassionate reading of the street, and/or of urban space in general, would then perhaps not so much imply a waning of affect, as Fredric Jameson proposes, so much as an invention of other possible affects and passions—which also harbor their resistant counter-affects and counter-passions that reinvent the street by connecting the physical concreteness of the site with the systemic horizon.

4. The Recent Past of Postmodern Architecture

Recentness and the present moment

To every present there belongs something like a historicizing of the recent past. This past is that from which we set ourselves apart, that which we have just ceased to be, and must discard in order to seize the *momentum* of our own *moment*, two words that at least since Hegel have shared a semantic field. Sometimes such a rejection may simply obey the logic of fashion (nothing is more degraded and embarrassing than last season's outfits), sometimes it may aspire to a retrieval of the true tradition, as in many important strands of early modernism: yesterday was a moment of confusion, eclecticism, even moral deprivation, whereas the present allows for a grasp of the true tradition that will resuscitate the sense of a profound task to be carried on into the future.[1]

But how should we then relate to our own moment? Undoubtedly there is a curious twist to be detected in a present whose most recent past would be the characterized by the insis-

---

1.   The alternative between fashion and moral claims is obviously not just insufficient, so that there would be many nuances in between that should be respected, but in fact part *of* the problem: the moral discourse of early modernism was itself an intellectual haute couture that aspired to render all other discourses embarrassingly outmoded, which is lost when one assumes the distinction as such as somehow already unproblematically given.

tence of the prefix "post-," i.e., a postmodernity that claimed to have superseded the historicist one-upmanship of modernity (which in turn made it possible to unmask the postmodern as yet another version of the modern) and to have made the past accessible in a kind of posthistorical montage culture beyond which there can be only more of the same. To move beyond this canceling out of historical differences and this flattening of depth, does it simply mean to reinstall a modernist ethos, or does it call for some other type of historical reflection?

The terms "postmodern," "postmodernity," and "postmodernism" have had a strange destiny, and their different trajectories through the arts, the humanities, and the social sciences are difficult to piece together into a single narrative; it is nonetheless true that architecture in many of them served as the point of departure, either as a symptom to be decoded or as a paradigm for a positive theory. During the early and mid 1980s, it however seemed both possible and productive to use the term as an overarching concept to denote a wide set of tendencies in philosophy, aesthetics, sociology, and political theory. This was a possible point of convergence that we today mostly perceive as an illusion, and from which things could only diverge, which is probably why the term sank into oblivion or at least came to be seen as part of the problem rather than of the solution—and particularly so in the case of architecture, where the term quickly often came to denote a new style rather than a set of problems, and so was destined to become irrelevant almost from the outset.

Or, perhaps we simply became postmodern in the sense that the questions and types of research that emerged under its blanket became normal sciences in Kuhn's sense, and thus there was no longer any need to use the term as a polemical marker in order to delimit a Then from a Now. The challenging task thus rather became to find new connections to the past, to reevaluate earlier phases of modernism in order to see how they were re-actualized in the present, as well as how current problems allowed for a kind of spectral analysis (a term that not only has optical connotations, but also harbors a ghostlike presence) of the past. This is undoubtedly one of the salient and most positive outcomes of these debates: an irreversible distance (which need not imply rejection) from modernism that made possible a series of new takes on the past, liberated historical research from preconceived ideas, and in the end showed modernism to be an inherently multiple and polymorphous entity made up of innumerable regional inflections and versions, so that all single and massive divisions between before and after proved to be only local effects.

While the term postmodern has come to seem increasingly misleading as a productive characteristic of contemporary thought, there is today a kind reverse movement that has gained currency in many popular descriptions of what is perceived to be wrong with the contemporary world: cultural relativism, skepticism against objective knowledge, leveling of qualitative distinctions, and the postmodern appears once more as a nebulous concept that must be fought in the name of values, tradition, humanism, culture, etc. This use is mostly (though far from exclusively) found in neo-conservative discourses, and it has little chance of proposing anything meaningful about the past, let alone the present. Even though such a tendency should be resisted, this cannot be done by simply reclaiming the term, whose former imaginary unity is precisely what is being once more retrieved in these wholesale rejections, even though in an infinitely more shallow and vacuous form than previously.

The problem, then, would rather be: what *was* the postmodern moment, why did it appear possible to gather together a series of questions, each with their own history, rhythm, and horizons, into a unified complex; and, in the present context, what was the role played by architecture in all of this? Such a question does obviously not mean to invalidate the respective problems posed in an earlier phase, but rather that we should allow present and past to question each other, without any spurious claim that we today would know better. The terms proposed to grasp the present will undoubtedly not fare any better than "postmodernism," and if we from the vantage point of the present can discern the illusions of past grand syntheses, this does not mean that we are not caught up in our own illusions.

Furthermore, the very semantic profusion that characterizes the term would no doubt make any survey of the various versions that have been proposed a momentous task, and the outcome would probably be the same confusion. Rather than aiming for generalities that just as quickly produce their counter-examples, I will here instead briefly look a three spheres, each with a particular complex of questions, and each with a decisive input into the amalgam known as the postmodern.

Postmodernism as an interrogation of the legacy of the Enlightenment

This was the version closely associated with Lyotard and the debates initiated by Habermas, and it engendered a vast amount of the misunderstandings that have circulated in the discussion for such a long time that they have become almost unquestionable truths. One of the reasons for this confusion is the crucial shift that occurs in Lyotard's own work between an epochal and a modal version of the postmodern. The modal version, which is the one that he would continue to defend throughout most of his later writings, is launched in a programmatic essay from 1982, "Answering the Question: What is the Postmodern?" Here he proposes a curious temporal twist, when he says that the postmodern *precedes* the modern as a *futur antérieur*, a future that is seen from the point of view of the past:

It [the postmodern] is undoubtedly part of the modern [...]. The "generations" flash by at an astonishing rate. A work can become modern only if it is first postmodern. Thus understood, postmodernism is not modernism at its end, but in a nascent state, and this state is recurrent. [...] The postmodern artist or writer is in the position of a philosopher: the text he writes or the work he creates is not in principle governed by pre-established rules and cannot be judged according to a determinant judgment, by the application of given categories to this text or work. Such rules and categories are what the work or text is investigating. The artist and the writer therefore work without rules, and in order to establish the rules for what *will have been made*. This is why the work and the text can take on the properties of an event; it is also why they would arrive too late for their author or, in what amounts to the same thing, why their creation would always begin too soon. *Postmodern* would be understanding according to the paradox of the future (*post*) anterior (*modo*).[2]

In this sense, the question posed here about the recent past of the postmodern can itself be taken as a continuation of the modal version of the postmodern in its relation to the modern, in a way that also puts the present at stake. The recent past of the postmodern would then pose the question of what kind of event it constituted, an event that still finds echoes in the present, and whose conceptualization by no means needs to have been accessible at the time, but rather reaches us in the form

2. Lyotard, "Answering the Question: What is the Postmodern?" in *The Postmodern Explained to Children* (Sydney: Power Publications, 1992), 22–24. The question in Lyotard's title has sometimes been rendered as "What is Postmodernism," which is a grave distortion, since the interpretation of the postmodern as a particular "ism" is precisely what Lyotard opposes.

177

of a deferred action in the Freudian sense that was also crucial for Lyotard. Furthermore, in its resistance to a cumulative and linear time, the postmodern is for Lyotard also, which may seem paradoxical, a continuation of the avant-garde. This transpires in his many essays that attempt to locate the postmodern in the wake of the Kantian sublime, and in his emphatic rejection of any interpretation of the term that aligns it with an afterness characterized by a posthistorical consumer culture, populism, and the frictionless availability of old style and forms divested of their explosive charge—all of which for him would rather be fea-tures of a satiated and complacent modernity. His version of the postmodern is instead an imperative to experiment that stands opposed to any *rappel à l'ordre*, which is why it often appears, his own distinction notwithstanding, simply like a radicalized modernism.

The temporal twist or loop of the future anterior decisively modifies the more conventional hypothesis of the earlier book, *The Postmodern Condition* (1979), where Lyotard had launched an influential diagnosis of the dissolution of the "grand narratives," i.e., those universal syntheses that had been promised in the name of History and/or Science, and instead proposed a sketch for a cri-tique of reason that drew on both Kant and Wittgenstein. Today, he claimed, we live in a plurality of language games that neither need nor can be gathered into a unity called Language. Later on, above all in *The Differend* (1983) and adjacent texts, where the modal version takes precedence, this dispersal of language games would become an ethical demand instead of a statement of a purported historical fact: in consonance with his fidelity to the avant-garde, and against a discourse of Capital as infinite prog-ress, power, and control, where language becomes information and performance the main criteria of intellectual work, he op-posed an idea of an artistic, philosophical, and political experi-mentation that both uncovers and actively produces incommen-

178

surabilities and gaps in our experience. That experience does not form a whole is no longer a historical truth to which we would have to adjust, but the normative basis for a philosophical project, in many ways reminiscent of Adorno's negative dialectics, although pushed further so that it eschews Adorno's founding idea of a utopian reconciliation.[3]

The key reference in the work that turns towards a modal rather than an epochal understanding of the postmodern, is however Kant. The title of the 1982 essay cited above, "Answering the Question: What is the Postmodern," is an unmistakable reference to Kant's 1784 text "Beantwortung der Frage: Was ist Aufklärung" and to the task of continuing critical philosophy in a new setting, even though the connection of Kant in this particular text is mainly brought to the fore in relation to the sublime. In the many essays on Kant, eventually leading up to the systematic readings in *L'enthousiasme: La critique kantienne de l'histoire* (1986) and *Leçons sur l'analytique du sublime* (1991), Kant's critical division of reason into autonomous yet subtly in-

3. The idea of a systematic aesthetic theory is something that haunt's Lyotard's work from beginning to end, and at least since the beginning of the seventies the idea of a critical function of art unfolds in a constant debate with Adorno. For Lyotard, this takes place through an emphasis on the visual arts, and a resistance to theories of textuality, reading and interpretation, against which he proposes a long and meandering reflection on the figural, the libidinal, the affective, passibility, resistance, touch, presence, and a host of other terms that translate the necessity for philosophy to always refer to a dimension of the sensible that overflows it. Lyotard's work on the visual arts also comes across in his work as a curator: with "Les Immatériaux" (Centre Pompidou, 1985) he created one of the first major thematic exhibitions on the theme of the postmodern. For details on the exhibition, see Antonia Wunderlich, *Der Philosoph im Museum: Die Ausstellung "Les Immatériaux" von Jean François Lyotard* (Bielefeld: Transcript, 2008), Francesca Gallo, *Les Immatériaux: Un percorso di Jean-François Lyotard nell'arte contemporanea* (Rome: Aracne, 2008), and Yuk Hui and Andreas Brockmann (eds.), *Thirty Years after Les Immatériaux* (Lüneburg: Meson Press, 2015). For a discussion of the exhibition in relation to Lyotard's development, see Daniel Birnbaum and Sven-Olov Wallenstein, *Spacing Philosophy: Jean-François Lyotard and the Philosophy of the Exhibition* (forthcoming).

terwoven spheres is what inaugurates a postmodern critique of reason, whereas Hegel's speculative philosophy of history, where gradually emerging totalities integrate ever widening circuits of experience, would be an eminently modern figure of thought.

Compared to the later work, it is obvious that *The Postmodern Condition* in spite of its own claims presents us with a histori- cal narrative, or a "meta-narrative," in Lyotard's vocabulary, which takes us from a (naïve?) faith in narratives to a new (and more sophisticated?) distrust, and in this sense the book itself is a self-defeating story of the progress of consciousness, as many of his critics pointed out. The modal shift towards the idea of the postmodern as the future of the past, a temporal duplication that recurs at every moment, can be takes as a response to these objections, but it also dilutes the former hypothesis if consid- ered as a diagnosis of our specific historical present.

At the same time, this rejection of the idea of break located at some point in time, and the turn towards a theory of the co- existence of modern and postmodern figures that returns to a reading of Kant and his idealist aftermath, indicates the complex- ity of the relation to the Enlightenment, and also why Lyotard's version under no circumstances can be understood as a simple rejection of reason. Rather it must be understood as continuation of a self-reflexive and self-critical tendency that begins in Kant, which today, Lyotard suggests, should take leave of those par- ticular metaphysical presuppositions that once grounded Kant's critical philosophy (the teleological unity of subject's faculties, the underlying idea of an order of creation, the unitary idea of experience grounded in Newtonian science, and no doubt many other as well), which in fact may be understood as a fidelity to the Kantian project, as Lyotard suggests that it must look today.

The idea of a wholesale rejection of Enlightenment and rea- son was however the basis of the criticism that Habermas voiced against postmodernism. Curiously enough he rarely discussed any of Lyotard's claims, instead, in his most sustained and thorough discussion he shifted the terrain and addressed what he took to be an irrationalist strand in the whole of post-Hegelian philosophy, running through Nietzsche, Heidegger, Adorno, and up to contemporary French philosophy.[4] The contemporary targets for his attack were Derrida and Foucault, for whom the term postmodernism was in fact irrelevant. Neither Derrida nor Foucault made any claims about decisive breaks in or with modernity, and both of them were indifferent to all talk of the postmodern as a countermove to the Enlightenment. Derrida's deconstruction began a reflection on a much longer process, the unity of metaphysics as it as unfolded from Greek philosophy to the present, which he analyzed in the wake of Heidegger, eventually rejecting the entire idea of *one* metaphysical tradition in the singular as a far too totalizing idea; for Foucault the question was how we should understand the deep and complex genealogy of the modern subject, which eventually led him back from the eighteenth and seventeenth centuries to early Christianity and Greek thought, and not at all to a question whether there had occurred a major shift in the twentieth century that would have made it necessary or desirable for us to abandon the legacy of the Enlightenment—a term that only begins to appear in Foucault's later work, and when he was asked whether was for or against it, he responded that such an alternative was a case of blackmail.[5]

For Habermas, these highly different and at times radically opposed trajectories could nevertheless be brought together as a rejection of modernity and/or the Enlightenment. To this he op-

4. See Habermas, *The Philosophical Discourse of Modernity*, trans. Frederick G. Lawrence (Cambridge, Mass.: MIT, 1987).
5. See, for instance, "What is Enlightenment?" in *Ethics, Subjectivity and Truth: Essential Works of Foucault*, vol. 1, ed. Paul Rabinow (London: Penguin, 2000), or the interview with Gérard Raulet, "Structuralism and Post-Structuralism," in *Aesthetics, Method, and Epistemology: Essential Works*, vol. 2, ed. James Faubion (London: Penguin, 2000).

posed the idea of the Enlightenment as an "unfinished project,"[6] to be sure with many negative and repressive consequences, for instance the colonization of the lifeworld brought about by the expansion of technological and instrumental reason, to which he opposed a communicative reason that cannot be subjected to an undifferentiated and totalizing critique otherwise than at the price of self-contradiction. Regardless of the merits of Habermas's work on communicative reason and modernity, it however remains true that his analyses of many of the alleged postmodern philosophers are one-sided and unproductive as points of departure for discussing their more precise claims.

Postmodernism and late capitalism

An affirmative and historicizing version of postmodernity, based on the kind of narrative that Lyotard had rejected, was however developed at roughly the same time by Fredric Jameson, in his 1984 essay on the "cultural logic of late capitalism."[7] Jameson takes his cues from Ernest Mandel's analysis of late capitalism,[8] and interprets postmodern culture as a series of specific responses to the transition to the third stage of capitalism occurring sometime in the 1960s.[9] These responses make up the various postmodern styles, characterized by features such as the dismantling of expressivity, subjectivity, and other depth

6. Se Habermas, "Modernity: An Unfinished Project," trans. Nicholas Walker, in Maurizio Passerin d'Entrèves and Seyla Benhabib (eds.), *Habermas and the Unfinished Project of Modernity: Critical Essays on The Philosophical Discourse of Modernity* (London: Polity Press, 1996).

7. See Jameson, "Postmodernism, or The Cultural Logic of Late Capitalism," *New Left Review* 146 (1984). This highly influential essay was subsequently expanded in *Postmodernism, or, The Cultural Logic of Late Capitalism* (Durham: Duke University Press, 1991, where it forms the first chapter,

8. See Ernest Mandel, *Late Capitalism*, trans. Joris de Bres (London: Verso, 1978).

9. On the problem of periodization, see Jameson, "Periodizing the '60s," in Jameson, *The Ideologies of Theory: Essays 1971–1986. Vol. 2, The Syntax of History* (Minneapolis: University of Minnesota Press, 1988).

models, leading to a focus on the surface of language instead of hermeneutical and/or dialectical interpretation, a schizophrenic proximity of things and images, the reconstruction of history as pastiche, and a new type of spatial disorientation. It is also with reference to this final feature, which Jameson details through an analysis of John Portman's Westin Bonaventure Hotel (Los Angeles, 1976),[10] that he proposes a cure in the form of a "cognitive cartography" capable of accounting for the unity of postmodern space-time by reconnecting its surface fragmentation to an underlying systemic order.

It is crucial for Jameson's theory that we must be able to separate and articulate relations between those dimensions that postmodernity folds together into an intense and seemingly intractable unity: subjective experience and objective structure, surface and depth, signifier and signified. In this sense, there is nothing postmodern about the analysis itself, and the distinction between postmodernity as a third phase in the capitalist mode of production, and postmodernism as a set of styles and modes of cultural expression, obeys a Hegelian logic, or more precisely the logic of essence, which was an integral part also of Marx's *Capital*. Appearance or semblance (*Schein*) is that which has to appear as a coming-apart of essence if essence is to realize itself, and the splitting up of phenomena into seemingly disconnected parts at the surface level testifies to the underlying unity—a unity which is not a substance, substrate, or thing, but precisely the principle governing the appearing and the solution of the contradictions, and which we can only grasp fully at the endpoint of the process.

10. It is obvious that Portman's architecture cannot represent the entire complex of postmodern spatiality, and Jameson's analysis has been criticized on many points. He returns in much more detail to the variety of architectural responses late capitalism in "The Constraints of Postmodernism," in Jameson, *The Seeds of Time* (New York: Columbia University Press, 1994), where Portman no longer appears at all. For a more thorough discussion of Portman, see Reinhold Martin, "Money and Meaning: The Case of John Portman," *Hunch* 12 (2009).

It is significant that this Hegelian model was already at work in Jameson's afterword to the influential anthology *Aesthetics and Politics* (1977), where he reconstructs the debates from the later part of the 1930s between Lukács and Bloch on expressionism, which at the time was used as a blanket term for modernism as a whole. To the surprise of many readers Jameson here partly resuscitates Lukács's position with its claim to grasp a dialectical totality, in a way that prefigures the theory of postmodernity: negative fragmentation of the surface occurs only because society in a state of crisis is drawn together around its central contradiction, whereas the normal state of affairs allows the different levels to co-exist in relative and peaceful autonomy. For Jameson, the different artistic and cultural expressions that we call postmodernism—whose multiplicity and divergences are, after all, not greater or more impossible to survey than those previous phenomena that we have become accustomed to call modernism—form a contradictory totality that in the end is dependent on the late capitalist mode of production.

On this point he was often misunderstood. There is no reason for him be to for or against the phenomenon called postmodernism, no reason for celebration or melancholy; rather postmodernism contains symptoms to be analyzed. Postmodernism, in its stylistically polymorphous appearances, offers a series of subjective articulations of the underlying structure of postmodernity, which often, and without contradiction (i.e., except the formative contradiction that traverses them as belonging to the logic of capital as such, whose late phase is a continuation and intensification of the earlier, but not the introduction of another logic), takes on the form of a second-order destruction of subjectivity and articulation. In this, these expressive forms—whose dismantling of the aesthetic depth-structure of expressivity, and this must be underlined, does not prevent them from being analyzed in Jameson's interpretative discourse as expressive of Capital, in fact, the first moment is the very *condition* of the second—perform the same task as once Balzac and Courbet, who gave us the keys to unlock the interlacing of commodity and artistic articulation in the nineteenth century,[11] or as the historical avant-garde, when it began to conjugate the arts according to the pattern of industrial and serial production in the first decades of the twentieth century. This why it makes perfect sense for Jameson to interrogate the possibility of a postmodern realism, with and against Lukács: it cannot be a question of returning to the narrative and mimetic techniques of the nineteenth century, or to the heroic undoing of these forms in the avant-garde, instead we must see the possibility of realism as bound up with the development of modern media and the way in which they transform discourse and its link to the referent. There is indeed a "reality effect" today that is different from the one Roland Barthes once described as the basic technique of classical realism,[12] which does not mean that the Real as such has evaporated, only that the means for letting it touch us, for letting it irrupt and explode in all of its weight and in all of the idiocy that it breeds in our complacent consumption of art, must be sought at the highest level of capitalist development.

The Hegelian tendency comes across in how Jameson understands individual works, expressions, and theories as translating a logic at work behind their back, and in how various philosophies are ingeniously marshaled in order to piece together the structure of postmodern thought are a series of surface effects, both in the sense that they negate dialectical depth models, and that this negation itself is a surface belonging to a depth that the

11.   For Jameson's most recent take on nineteenth-century realism, see *The Antinomies of Realism* (London: Verso, 2015).
12.   Se Roland Barthes, "L'Effet de réel", *Communications* 11 (1968), reprinted in Barthes, *Le bruissement de la langue: Essais critiques IV* (Paris: Seuil, 1984). See also the detailed discussion of Balzac and the code system of realism in *S/Z*, trans. Richard Miller (New York: Hill and Wang, 1974).

analysis must discover. In this way he reconstructs the postmodern sublime as an effect of a world system that has eradicated the last vestiges of nature, and as such constitutes the proper object of the sublime, as it appears for the subject in the form of various aesthetically mediated fractures in its experience. This is what for the individual is "unpresentable," and unlike Lyotard— for whom the sublime points to the ontological enigma of the event, of the "it happens" or "is it happening" that dispossesses the subject and opens onto a domain of touching, passibility, and a presence beyond the mastery of intentions, concepts, and systems[13]—Jameson instead draws on its phenomenological features in order to locate what he perceives as its proper cause, namely the system itself. For Lyotard, this reinscription would be a typically anti-postmodern figure of thought that suppresses the unpresentable within a master narrative that always ends up neutralizing the temporal twist of deferred action in a schema of cause and effect. The leitmotif of Jameson's work, "Always historicize!" which he takes to be "the one absolute and we may even say 'transhistorical' imperative of all dialectical thought,"[14] may be seen as placing the historian outside of any historicizing; on the other hand, Lyotard's modal postmodern as a continually recurrent and evasive *futur antérieur* would for Jameson

13. The term "passibility," which is developed in Lyotard's late work from the mid-eighties onward, originally stems from medieval theology, where it denotes God's capacity to be affected by the course of the world instead of simply remaining sealed in a state of impenetrable plenitude or "impassibility." For Lyotard, passibility gestures toward an intermediary zone, neither simply active nor passive—which in the theological register would amount to a divine middle voice of sorts—and opens an obscure domain of the in-between, neither first nor second, neither the stuff of givenness nor the forming concept, which is always withdrawn in knowledge and yet conditions it. For a discussion of this and other related terms in Lyotard, see Daniel Birnbaum and Sven-Olov Wallenstein, "From Immaterials to Resistance: The Other Side of "Les Immatériaux,'" in Yuk Hui and Andreas Brockmann, *Thirty Years after Les Immatériaux*.

14. Jameson, *The Political Unconscious* (Ithaca: Cornell University Press, 1981), 9.

appears as a nostalgic quest for a sublime in a world that has already devoured it and turned into yet another special effect. That these two versions of the postmodern, which can be called the Kantian and the Hegelian, in this way are able analyze each other and to inscribe the opponent as a symptom, indicates that we should not seem them as simply opposed, but rather as an oscillation inside contemporary thought, regardless of whether this contemporaneity is called postmodern or not.

Postmodernism and formalism

A third version of the postmodern—in fact, chronologically the first—emerges out of the arts themselves, and it belongs predominantly to the context of the American 1960s and the development of visual and the performing arts. This gave rise to many historical displacements and distortions when the term traveled across the Atlantic and entered into a productive alliance with, above all, French philosophical ideas that had been developed simultaneously, although mostly in connection with literary discourse, eventually forming the amalgamation "poststructuralism," in many respects just as misleading as "postmodernism," and sharing much of the same historical trajectory.

As has often been noted, the term "postmodernism" was used in art criticism for the first time, in a way that makes sense in relation to what would follow in its wake, by Leo Steinberg, in his 1968 lecture "Other Criteria."[15] Steinberg takes his implicit point of departure in the formalist vocabulary established by Clement Greenberg, and locates a decisive shift in the dialectic of modernist painting between illusionist depth and materialist flatness in the treatment of the surfaces in Robert Rauschenberg's works. Here, Steinberg proposes, surface and depth, figure and ground, have been erased in favor of a con-

15. Reprinted in Steinberg, *Other Criteria: Confrontations with Twentieth-Century Art* (New York: Oxford University Press, 1972).

ception of the surface as a depository for cultural debris, and the traditional hierarchies of painting have been broken down, which is expressed formally in the tilting of the upright vertical—the picture plane at right angle to the spectator's gaze, which since Alberti's window has defined painting as the art of illusory depth—by 45 degrees, so that it becomes a "flatbed," a reclining horizontal, more like the surface of a desk or a floor. The materials attached to Rauschenberg's surface—paint, photographs, cigarette ends—no longer calls forth a dialectic of illusionism, but are rather present as such, on the same level as the surface on which they are deposited. This, Steinberg concludes, places us in a situation outside of the gambit of modernist painting, for which the term "postmodern" might be used.

Steinberg's flatbed was perhaps little less than an ironic comment on the much elaborate discourse of flatness in Greenberg, and his use of the term postmodern incidental, but in hindsight it may be seen as part of a rethinking of the visual arts already well underway in 1968. For Greenberg, the trajectory of modernism was determined by an increasing emphasis on specificity, in a Kantian move that understood each art as oriented toward self-reflection on its constituent features, which in the case of painting was "flatness" and the "delimitation of flatness." While the terms are made explicit only in Greenberg's late programmatic statement "Modernist Painting,"[16] the underlying conceptual structure had been worked out already in 1940, first presented in the seminal essay "Towards a Newer Laocoon,"[17] where Greenberg locates his work in the legacy of Lessing. As

16. The essay goes back to a radio talk from 1960, and was first published in *Arts Yearbook* 1961. See Greenberg, *The Collected Essays and Criticism, Vol. 4: Modernism with a Vengeance, 1957-1969,* ed. John O'Brian (Chicago: University of Chicago Press, 1993), 85-94.
17. Reprinted in Greenberg, *The Collected Essays and Criticism, Vol. 1: Perceptions and Judgments, 1939-1944,* ed. John O'Brian (Chicago: University of Chicago Press, 1986).

American painters in the postwar period increasingly came to take these limits as the very content of their work, Greenberg was led to interpret them in a more narrow way. Even though the path from abstract expressionism to color-field painting seemed like a logical progression, with the late modern artist as a specialist in formal and technical problems, for Greenberg this was a development that contained several dangers, above all in presenting artist with a seemingly unidirectional path to follow, which eventually would ruin the claims of taste by making them dependent on a concept of art that could be extracted from historical analysis. Many of the artists that ended up on the other side of Greenberg's demarcation line of modernism seemed to be pursuing the same goals that he had himself set up, but in fact the reflection on the specifics of painting and sculpture led to a new form of insistent materialism that inevitably blurred those distinctions that were at the basis of the formalist interpretations of modernism. Moreover, they appeared to short-circuit the autonomy of judgment that is the other and equally necessary side of the formalist enterprise: formalism is not there for the sake of form alone, but "a kind of bias or tropism: towards esthetic value, esthetic value as such and as an ultimate," as Greenberg would say a decade later.[18] In the mid-sixties, a host of concepts—the specific objects of Donald Judd, the expanded situation of sculpture in Robert Morris that would eventually lead him to claim a position "beyond objects" in the fourth of his "Notes on Sculpture,"[19] both rejected as instances of "objecthood" by Michael Fried,[20] to cite only the three most

18. Greenberg, "Necessity of Formalism" (1971), in Richard Kostelanetz (ed.), *Esthetics Contemporary* (Buffalo: Prometheus, 1989), 191.
19. See Morris, "Notes on Sculpture, Part 4: Beyond Objects" (1969), in Morris, *Continuous Project Altered Daily: The Writings of Robert Morris* (Cambridge, Mass.: MIT, 1995).
20. See Fried, "Art and Objecthood" (1968), rpr. in Fried, *Art and Objecthood: Essays and Reviews* Chicago: University of Chicago Press, 1998). For an analysis of this rapid development, see Frances Colpitt, *Minimal*

famous instances in this rapidly evolving dialectical drama—were proposed in order to analyze this situation, eventually co-alescing into the terms Minimal Art and Conceptual Art. The general effect of these discussions was a disconnection from me-dium specificity and an opening up of the visual arts toward an indeterminate set of techniques, practices, materials, mediums, etc., which, given the particular identification of modernism as such with its formalist interpretation, for some critics made it irresistible to understand this as a shift towards postmodern-ism. "Within the situation of postmodernism," Rosalind Krauss suggested a decade later, in an essay that looks back to this ex-plosive development with a focus on the domain of sculpture, "practice is no defined in relation to a given medium—sculp-ture—bur rather in relation to the logical operations on a set of cultural terms, for which any medium—photography, books, lines on walls, mirrors, or sculpture itself—might be used."[21]

Similar tendencies were spread across all the other arts in the sixties, and particularly in dance, they seemed to herald a postmodern shift, which is no doubt also due to the proximity of the visual and the performing arts in the period. Against the theory of dance that perceived it in relation to an inner center, a psychological space subsequently externalized into outer space, a choreographer like Yvonne Rainer would propose "an alterna-tive context that allows for a more matter-of-fact, more con-crete, more banal quality of physical being in performance," and which could be materialized in everyday activities like to "stand, walk, run, eat, carry bricks, show movies, move or be moved by some thing rather than oneself."[22] Just as in the new limit forms

Art: The Critical Perspective (Seattle: University of Washington Press, 1993).

21.   Rosalind Krauss, "Sculpture in the Expanded Field" (1978), reprinted in _The Originality of the Avant-Garde and Other Modernist Myths_ (Cambridge, Mass.: MIT, 1986), 288.

22.   Yvonne Rainer, "A Quasi Survey of some 'Minimalist' Tendencies in the

of painting and sculpture, the emphasis was not on illusion, but on the material facticity of movements, and how they could be organized into open serial structures: "simply order, like that of continuity, one thing after another," as Donald Judd famously suggested,[23] "The series progresses by the fact of one discrete thing following another,"[24] in Rainer's version.

The polemic was largely directed towards the kind of formalist interpretation that had become hegemonic in certain parts of postwar American art criticism, which is why this type of postmodernism would be more accurately described as postformalism. In hindsight it can also be understood as a rediscovery of those parts of the European avant-garde that had been rendered invisible by formalist art-historical narrative (Dadaism, constructivism, the legacy of Duchamp), and thus a kind of repetition through deferred action, as Hal Foster has proposed,[25] or, in a more negative vein, as a repetition that turns the tragedy of the historical avant-garde's attempt to dismantle autonomy into a farce played out inside the institutionalized art system, as was suggested by Peter Bürger already in the early seventies.[26] For some, this historical distance from the heroic phase of the avant-garde signaled the latter's inevitable demise, and the entry into a posthistorical stage, where the linear time of modernism had come to an end, so that styles and techniques from the past were once more available, neutralized and divested of

Qualitatively Minimal Dance Activity Midst the Plethora, or an Analysis of Trio A," (1968), in Gregory Battcock (ed.), *Minimal Art: A Critical Anthology* (Berkeley: University of California Press, 1995 [1968]), 267f.

23. Donald Judd, "Specific Objects" (1965), reprinted in *Complete Writings 1959–1975* (Halifax: Press of the Nova Scotia College of Art and Design, 1975), 184.

24. Rainer, "A Quasi Survey," 271.

25. See Foster, *The Return of the Real* (Cambridge, Mass.: MIT, 1996).

26. See Peter Bürger, *Theorie der Avantgarde* (Frankfurt am Main: Suhrkamp, 1973); *Theory of the Avantgarde*, trans. Michael Shaw (Minneapolis: University of Minnesota Press, 1984).

their former historicist and teleological charge—it seemed, for instance, once more possible to be a Painter, and to redeploy expressionist and other now classically modern gestures, as in the case of the *heftige Malerei* in Germany, or the Italian transa-vantgarde.[27] For others, the disruption of linear history rather implied the imperative to continue the avant-garde with other means (which, as we noted, was the proposal of Lyotard), and the critical task of art remained as important as ever, although it now had to find other tools that were drawn from sociology, philosophies of language, psychoanalysis, and many other disciplines. In the first version, postmodernism thus seemed like a unabashed return of the intuitive artist, subjectivity, and styles, in the second it was an intensification of art's claims to constitute a kind of theoretical research in its own right, prolonging themes that had been formulated in the early phases of conceptual art. As we will see, these developments in the visual arts had close counterparts in architecture, sometimes antedating, sometimes postdating them: the relation between the eclecticism of Venturi and Scott Brown and the formal researches of Eisenman, and later the debate between Whites and Grays, display an obvious structural affinity to the somewhat later debate on the revivals of painting vs. the continuation of the avant-garde. At the time these cross-connections however appear to have gone largely unnoted: architects sometime gesture toward the other visual arts, so Venturi and Scott Brown's appeal to

27.   An intense and principally interesting polemic was triggered by Benjamin Buchloh's essay "Figures of Authority, Ciphers of Regression" (1981), which posed the question not only of the viability of expressionism in the present, but also, implicitly, whether painting, as a figure of art-historical authority, as such can be of relevance today. For Buchloh all the various returns to tradition that were proclaimed in the 1920s— the neoclassicism of Picasso, Cocteau's *rappel à l'ordre*, the Italian *valori plastici* and *pittura metafisica*—were bound up with a political regression ultimately ushering in Fascism, and he detects an echo of this in the revival of historical styles and techniques in the early eighties.

pop and Eisenman's at least implicit references to minimalism, whereas artists and art critics seem to have been largely oblivious of the parallel developments in architecture.[28]

The tension inside the concept between the populist and the avant-gardist version was there from the start, which is no doubt why it became less useful and eventually was discredited; what calls for an explanation is instead the *unity* of opposite claims that it once seemed to herald, even though it seems just as doubtful that this unity could be found inside one or several of the arts and their respective histories, just as it seems far too reductive to simply take the opposite turn and explain it from the outside, as a simple byproduct of the logic of capital. The link between the sociopolitical and the aesthetic was itself one of the key problems in the postmodern, not always for the practitioners, but consistently so for those who have attempted to theorize it, often in terms of a disconnect in relation to earlier models of critical theory, a break that in hindsight cannot be dismissed as just an ideological phantasm, although it surely often was this too. To the extent that we perceive the problems broached by the postmodern as still relevant, its insides and outsides must be linked in some other way—and perhaps especially in the case of architecture, which not only is the art that is most closely aligned with the mode of production in all of its economic, technological and social aspects, but was also used as an exemplary case, negatively or positively, in most of the early theorizations of the postmodern.

28. Some attempts were made to connect minimal art to architecture, but mostly in very general and unspecific terms. In Gregory Battcock's influential anthology *Minimal Art* (1968), only one out of the almost thirty contributions explicitly address the connection to architecture, Michal Benedikt's "Sculpture as Architecture" (1966-67), but does so in general terms, without giving any reference to actual architectural works of the period.

Histories of the postmodern

So far, we seem to be faced with three divergent stories. The first one (at least in the modal version) lays claim to a Kantian critique of reason that interrupts the historical narrative, although pushing the idea of critique far beyond the limits assigned by Kant. The second pursues a historical analysis in the wake of Hegel and Marx, and interprets postmodernity as the most recent, perhaps final, at least late phase of capitalism, and the question it poses on the aesthetic level is whether this phase can produce a realism, in the sense of an art that would be able to brings its contradictions together into a legible whole that makes the systemic order and subjective experience communicate. The third takes its point of departure in the undoing of a certain interpretation of modernism, and asks to what extent an avant-garde, or at least a radically transformative artistic praxis, is still possible, and in this sense it can integrate element from the first version (the continuation of the avant-garde with other means, as in Lyotard), or from the second (the dismantling of expressive forms, or pastiche as a posthistorical montage, as in Jameson).

In architecture, the debate around the postmodern became particularly intense, as if the fate of the concept of the postmodern would be inextricably tied up with architectural discourse. Even though, as we have noted, the sources of the term and is various cognates (postmodernism, postmodernity) may differ depending on what particular field that is taken as point of reference (philosophy, social theory, one or several of the arts), architecture seemed to be a pervasive theme, at least if one looks to by the early programmatic essays by Jürgen Habermas and Fredric Jameson. It is also within architecture that the term first congealed into a stylistic notion and postmodernism was transformed from a problem into a particular look: the return of ornament and disconnected parts of the classical heritage and the Beaux-Arts, various types eclecticism and iconicity that could lay claim to being a "vernacular" (Venturi) or return us to a comprehensible language of forms, often drawing on a humanist heritage. This was a look that obviously just as quickly could be superseded by others, and it immediately became just as dated as its predecessors, and shot through with a kind of irony and doubly invisible quotation marks. These markers were, it must be remembered, however also part of the postmodernism's own claim to dismantle ideas of originality, authorship, and authenticity, and it appeared as if the phenomenon postmodernism in some hyper-reflexive twist itself immediately became postmodern.

The reason for the early and massive impact of the postmodern in architecture must also be sought in the history of the discipline itself. The reactions against modernism began almost immediately after the Second World War, and one could even claim that architectural discourse had already entered into a postmodern phase, even if it was not named as such, just as the late modern formalist interpretations of the others arts were being consolidated. The discovery of everyday life, from Aldo van Eyck to Team X, and many other critical analyses, above all in relation to the urban form, which would eventually lead up to the symbolic dissolution of CIAM in 1959, predate the major symbolic publications in the mid-sixties, Venturi's *Complexity and Contradiction in Architecture* and Aldo Rossi's *L'architettura della città.*[29] A decade later these developments would be brought together into Charles Jencks's *Language of Post-Modern Architecture* (1977),[30] where the synthesis in terms of style, or rather a plurality of styles that co-exist in a neutral availabil-

29.   For more on Venturi and Rossi, see chap. 2, above.
30.   Charles Jencks, *The Language of Post-Modern Architecture* (London: Academy Editions, 1977. The book has since 1977 gone through many editions, and has become a standard reference, also because Jencks is one of the few who has consistently held on to the term "postmodern," in a long series of publications..

ity, became the guiding idea, which limited the analytic value of the concept, but also made it more useful and effective for journalistic polemics. From Jencks onward, the idea of break somewhere in the sixties had imposed itself, regardless of whether it is described as postmodern or not, and of what its basic reasons were supposed to have been. Ten years after Jencks, the term "postmodern" is still retained in Heinrich Klotz's ambitious *Moderne und Postmoderne: Architektur der Gegenwart, 1960–1980,*[31] while ten years further ahead, the equally ambitious anthologies edited by Kate Nesbitt, *Theorizing a New Agenda for Architecture: An Anthology of Architectural Theory, 1965–1995,*[32] and K. Michael Hays, *Architecture Theory Since 1968,*[33] settle in their titles for more neutral markers, "a new agenda," or simply "since," even though they too in their respective ways suggest a break sometime in the sixties after which things no longer remain the same.

Rather than to write the history of the rise and decline of

31. Klotz, *Moderne und Postmoderne: Architektur der Gegenwart, 1960–1980* (Braunschweig: Vieweg & Sohn, 1984); one can note that the English translation, published four years later, gives the title a backward-looking inflection: *The History of Postmodern Architecture*, trans. Radka Donnell (Cambridge, Mass.: MIT, 1988). Klotz aims to avoid purely stylistic criteria and the idea of eclecticism, and for him the postmodern is not so much a rejection of the modern as it is an attempt to integrate a moment of fiction in function.

32. Kate Nesbitt (ed.), *Theorizing a New Agenda for Architecture: An Anthology of Architectural Theory, 1965–1995* (New York: Princeton Architectural Press, 1996). In the introduction, Nesbitt notes, "While only the first chapter is so titled, postmodernism is in fact the subject and point of reference for the entire book. I hope to make clear that postmodernism is not a singular style, but more a sensibility of inclusion in a period of pluralism." (17)

33. K. Michael Hays (ed.), *Architecture Theory Since 1968* (Cambridge, Mass.: MIT, 1998). Hays notes that many point of chronological departure could be chosen, but that "in the long run, the coupling of Marxist critical theory and poststructuralism with readings of architectural modernism has been what has dominated theory in the main, subsuming and rewriting earlier texts; and 'since 1968' covers that formation." (xiv) In this sense, his conception of theory, unlike the one adopted by Nesbitt, is normative, which no doubt accounts for the otherwise bewildering absence of the term postmodernism from the introduction.

the term "postmodern," or to write a history of the different
histories that has been written about it, the task here is to ask
what such a historicizing of our recent past amounts to. In order
to do this, two recent examples will be extricated from this huge
and labyrinthine literature, each of which constitutes a profound take on this complex phenomenon as it was staged in architecture, and also because they provide paradigmatic versions
of what such a historicizing might entail: Jorge Otero-Pailos's
*Architecture's Historical Turn: Phenomenology and the Rise of the
Postmodern*, and Reinhold Martin's *Utopia's Ghost: Architecture
and Postmodernism, Again.*[34]
Otero-Pailos pursues what he calls a "polygraphic" historical
account, tracing both the development of a series of concepts as
well as individual trajectories and institutional shifts. Martin,
on other hand, surveys the postmodern phenomenon as a set of
theoretical problems, and develops a reading that perhaps could
be called "symptomal,"[35] in the sense that the visible evidence
is understood as conditioned by certain structurally necessary
blind spots. In this reading, such spots do not impair or obscure
vision, but *open* it, they render forms legible and visible, and
allow the surface conflicts and debates to unfold as if they were
propelled ahead by an inner and autonomous logic, whereas
they in fact belong to a larger discursive formation that they

34.   Jorge Otero-Pailos, *Architecture's Historical Turn: Phenomenology and the
      Rise of the Postmodern* (Minneapolis: University of Minnesota Press,
      2010), and Reinhold Martin, *Utopia's Ghost: Architecture and Postmodern-
      ism, Again* (Minneapolis: University of Minnesota Press, 2010). Hence-
      forth quoted as AHT and UG with page number.
35.   The idea of "symptomal reading" (*lecture symptomale*) stems from Al-
      thusser, and does not appear as such in Martin's book. For a systematic
      discussion, see Althusser's introduction to the collective volume *Lire le
      Capital*. (The book has since its first publication in 1965, with contribu-
      tions by Althusser, Étienne Balibar, Roger Establet, Pierre Macherey,
      gone through many versions; the current standard edition containing
      all variations and subsequent additions is the one edited by Etienne
      Balibar on PUF, 1996.)

both reflect and help to set in motion.

Otero-Pailos's polygraphic analysis provides us with a fairly recognizable historical trajectory; Martin is reluctant to "simply historicize," and instead chooses to emphasize the "untimeliness" and "asychronicity" of the postmodern with respect to the concerns of the present—in short, to read it as a phenomenon that refuses to be placed firmly within any kind of reassuring historical narrative. In this sense these two books exemplify two different methodologies: the first offers a reconstructive hermeneutic that remains largely respectful to intentions and projects, the second could be called hermeneutics of suspicion, which reads surface statements and claims as effects of underlying structural conflicts. These two histories might, to be sure with some caution, respectively be called internal and external: either the break is understood as effected by a series of questions proper to architecture, or as emanating from a displacement of the spatial or terroritial ordering of capitalism itself, for which architecture becomes not just an eminent cipher, but also a crucial agent.

Reading the inside: phenomenology and the return of history

In hindsight postmodernism has come to be reduced, and undoubtedly not without good reasons, to a superficial stylistic phenomenon: eclecticism, a free use of historical material, an exploration of contradictions, a mix of high and low. This emphasis on style, surface, and ornament has consequently generated accusations of aestheticism, political irresponsibility, anti-Enlightenment irrationality, and many other notoriously bad things. But while all of these features no doubt have played a role, a more intellectually ambitious genealogy also needs to unearth that which, given certain conditions, made the postmodern phenomenon not only possible, but perhaps also necessary as a moment in the reflection on the legacy of modernism.

Otero-Pailos traces the ascendancy of a new generation in the sixties, whose break with modernist ideology was conditioned by a fatigue with technological utopianism, the leveling of International Style to a universal corporate language, and the loss of historical traditions. Reconnecting to the past seemed to be a logical solution, and phenomenology as a possible philosophical ally, in its by that time well-established critique of abstract concepts of space and form, and in its attempts to ground them in more profound analysis of the "lifeworld" (Husserl), or of "being-in-the-world" and "dwelling" (early and late Heidegger). Through the impact of phenomenology, architectural history increasingly became a search for *sense*, a demand not just for history, but more profoundly for *historicity*, and to this extent it undoubtedly continued the modernist legacy of operative history, i.e., a writing of history that aspired to legitimize future production, as it was diagnosed in the same period by Manfredo Tafuri (whose rigorous divide between operative and critical history in hindsight, in spite of all the theoretical tools that it wields, on the methodological level may seem strangely antiquated in sometimes running the risk of repeating, albeit in a self-consciously tragic mode, the positivist distinction between fact and value).[36] This operative dimension, to the extent that it retained its philosophical aspirations, was however grounded in larger claims about the ground of sense, not just in theories of functional form, but in an understanding of empirical form as itself based in essences that lay at the foundation of human experience as such.[37]

36. For more on this division, see chap. 1, above.

37. Such claims, one must note, were just as decisive for someone like Giedion, whose *Space, Time, and Architecture* explicitly set out to reconnect the "new tradition" to the past, bridge the gap between "rational construction" and emotional needs; "in spite of the seeming confusion," he writes in the first preface dated 1940, "there is nevertheless

To account for the *depth of history* on the basis of an *experience of meaning in the present* in the end however formed a complex and eventually also contradictory task: on the one hand this was a new access to the dimension of history, which aspired to bypass the art historian's traditional reliance on written documents by appealing to the particular capacity of the architect to re-enact the past as a project of sense and embodiment, on the other hand this experientialist paradigm could just as much be taken as a rejection of theory in the name of the immediacy of meaning. The results of this double orientation proved to be nothing short of paradoxical: on the one hand, as Otero-Pailos shows, phenomenology was a key element in the emergence of what we today know as "architectural theory," which has moved far beyond the particular claims of phenomenology, on the other hand its intuitionism and experientialism fostered an anti-intellectual attitude, which became more pronounced as the wave of theory rose higher in the eighties, with Derrida as the first major reference, who would then be followed by many others, for which the experientialism of the earlier generation became an object of suspicion.

The reference to phenomenology must however not be taken to suggest that these debates were exclusively the result of a reception of certain philosophical works—in fact, seen in this way, they in fact appear as a strangely belated echo of phenomenology from the twenties and thirties (which in its own time seems to have gone wholly unnoticed in architecture), whereas those philosophers that pursued this tradition in the sixties, most visibly Derrida, were in fact profoundly questioning the rhetoric

a true, if hidden, unity, a secret synthesis, in our present civilization."
See *Space, Time and Architecture* (Cambridge, Mass.: Harvard University Press, thirteenth printing 1997), vi. For Giedion, this synthesis is however rooted in the new space-time conception that welds together elements from contemporary physics, contemporary art, and the new engineering sciences, rather than from the philosophical tradition.

of roots, soils, and foundations that were paramount in the first wave of architectural phenomenology. As Otero-Pailos shows, equally decisive were new uses of graphic design and photography, a whole new visual rhetoric that was instrumental in lifting the boundaries between scholarly work, previously relegated to the discipline of architectural history, and the "project," which now began to mobilize a vast array of sources—all of which by no means had been foreign to the period of the early modern masters, as is abundantly clear in the case of Le Corbusier. Just as in the case of the other visual arts, it would make more sense to speak of this as a retrieval of those aspects of the historical avant-garde that had been obscured by contemporary criticism. Breaking with the past thus often simply meant to return to a more full appreciation of it, just as the reading of philosophical texts on another level displayed a belatedness that made certain contemporary developments invisible; together, these two tendencies produced a strange amalgamation of avant-garde and arrière-garde attitudes that still remains a defining feature of architectural phenomenology.

Otero-Pailos focuses on four particular intellectual trajectories, each of which illustrates an important dimension of the postmodern: Jean Labatut, today largely ignored, but who as a teacher exerted a decisive influence on the generation that would later become known as postmodernists; Charles Moore, a student of Labatut, and one of the signal architects of postmodernism; Christian Norberg-Schulz, whose theoretical and historical work was pivotal in bringing phenomenological concerns into the architectural debate, and finally Kenneth Frampton, whose historical surveys and theories of tectonics and critical regionalism have contributed to the opening up of phenomenology to critical theory and many other strands of contemporary thought.

Phenomenology *avant la lettre*:
Labatut and Moore

Jean Labatut is treated under the rubric "Eucharistic Architecture," which points to the intertwining of a religiously tinted transcendence and bodily presence that is characteristic not only of Labatut (who in fact remained suspicious of phenomenology, partly for political reasons), but of large parts of phenomenology as such. Labatut was trained in the French Beaux-Arts milieu to which he always retained a certain loyalty, but he also drew important inspiration from his work on camouflage techniques during the First World War. This required a capacity for calculating and understanding the cultural, technological, and physiological dimensions of perception, and it would become the basis for Labatut's conception of architecture as a broader visual medium. Drawing on cubism as well as Bergson, this was an exploration of subjective experience as the unifying function with respect to the object's dynamic transformations, and in this sense Labatut's relation to phenomenology is indirect, more that of someone who opened a set of avenues for further questioning, and principally through his teaching rather than writing.

From 1927, Labatut's classes at Princeton continued the interrogation of circulation and movement, and his experience of camouflage of boats pushed him toward a conception of *water* as the modern element par excellence. Unlike architects from the Corbusean tradition, Labatut did not look to the steamliner as the model to emulate, but to water itself: it has no shape, it is all movement and flow, and his question was how architecture could achieve such a state of permanent fluidity and dissolve into pure motion and experience.

The 1939 World Fair became the setting for Labatut's first synthesis of this work, partly in his contribution to the commercial building fair, but above all in his design for the Lagoon of Nations, which turned into the fair's major public magnet. Using fountains and artificial lighting to create a dazzling spectacle, Labatut mobilized a vast array of commercial display techniques in order to forge an evanescent and perceptually based architecture.[38] But rather than a mere play on the senses, Labatut's version of abstraction, or the experience of movement as pure sensation uncoupled from figurative references through manipulation of perception, also involved the quest for a deeper spiritual dimension. This separated him from the Bauhaus conception of architecture as a science of construction and engineering, and he always emphasized the importance of a general liberal education that draws on historical experience, although understood in a particular way.

In the 1940s he began discussions with Jacques Maritian, who would play a decisive role in his future development. Maritain, a leading Catholic philosopher, had set out to rectify the modern Cartesian split between mind and body by going back to a philosophy that emphasizes the nexus between mind and world, which Maritain erroneously, maybe because of his politically motivated distaste for Sartre (who indeed also retained a substantial amount of Cartesianism), understood as being in opposition to Husserl and Heidegger. Both Maritain and Labatut instead looked to Bergson in their emphasis on intuition as a pre-conceptual access to reality, which for them was attainable not only through science, but also through poetry, art and various types of mystical experiences. For Labatut these conversations became the basis for an architecture that stressed

38. While acknowledged by journalists and music critics, Labatut's contribution was however largely ignored by the architects The important exception is Sigfried Giedion, who included Labatut's Lagoon among the attempts to create a new monumentality. As Otero-Pailos notes, this may be seen as a parallel to the spectacles of Speer, although Labatut "came down strongly against the univocal dimension of politicized art, searching instead for a more apolitical, spiritually uplifting, but still hypnotic architecture" (AHT 57).

embodiment as a source of meaning, and he aligned them with his own research into everyday sign systems and symbols as it developed in the Bureau of Urban Research, which he founded in 1941. The experience of mobility and speed in urban space, but above all as it emerged for the traveler on the new highways, the impact of night lighting and scenic vistas on the perceptual habits of a subject in constant motion, were the focus of a new kind of research (as Otero-Pailos points out, this emphasis on signs was to exert a massive influence on Labatut's student Robert Venturi, although the latter never acknowledged the importance of his teacher).

Maritain soon understood the possible implications of this research for the possibility of the invention of a new conception or religious buildings. In the wake of demands for a modernized church, catholic thinkers doubted the capacity of abstraction (rejected by the pope Pius XII in his 1947 encyclical *Mediator Dei* as the "illusion of a higher mysticism") to attract a wide audience, and Labatut seized the opportunity to create a new type of church that would integrate religious symbolism with the persuasive power of commercial architecture, establish a middle ground between high modernism and mass culture, and in this sense formulate a truly universal architectural language. In its first version, Labatut's projected Church of the Four Evangelists was to function like a movie-theater, with the congregation facing a large convex parabolic screen using the sun a source of light, while its exterior envelope would consist of sheets of colored glass allowing the sunlight to enter at the same time as it would project a dazzling display for the passersby; later he envisaged using figurative glass murals in order to stage a play of transparency and reflection, and to produce what he called a "truly twenty-four hour architecture" capable of affirming its place within the visual overload of the urban landscape while also retaining a dimension of aloofness and abstraction.

Labatut's conception of an experiential architecture as way to the unity of body and mind, the material and the spiritual, took concrete form in the school in Princeton, designed in 1961 for the Catholic Society of Sacred Hearts. Here Labatut develops the idea of an architectural transubstantiation as the "real presence" of the spiritual, an incarnation that aspires to become a "Eucharistic" architecture, and in this sense the theological quarrels over the meaning if transubstantiation were to take real physical form: it is the building itself which should give us the body of Christ, offered to the body of the visitors, so that they in turn can be directed back to their own incarnated soul and "feel the movement of immobile things," as Labatut claimed.

Charles Moore, the second case in point, has often been seen as something of a trickster character, but Otero-Pailos shows the extent to which his playful and occasionally whimsical projects emerge out of a set of distinct problems that took the teaching of Labatut one step further, specifically in sidestepping its theological dimension and bringing it closer to phenomenology (which in turn often displays a kind of non-confessional spirituality that has undoubtedly facilitated the encounter with certain types of art).

Moore soon found himself in opposition not only to the modernist establishment, but also to its art-historical counterpart, particularly in his crucial emphasis on the role of historical buildings in conveying an intuitive meaning that was itself transhistorical, so that history was both a point of entry and something that must be reduced or even forgotten in the future project, which is one of the key elements in the making of the architect-historian as a new kind of theorist. This was rooted in Moore's reflection on the material imagination of architecture, which pitted him against textual versions of history. While his dissertation on the role of water in architecture pursues the quest of Labatut, but through his constant reference to Bachelard, specifically the latter's *Water and Dreams*, he also brings phenomenological motifs to bear on architectural theory (whether Bachelard in any strict theoretical sense belongs to phenomenology, understood as a tradition beginning with Husserl, and which attempts to ground the sciences and experience in some more primordial access to things, is another question).[39] Crucial for this was the idea of an imagination that would "see matter beneath the object," as Bachelard puts it, which is what makes the element of water instrumental for the "task of de-objectifying and dissolving substances."[40] This imagination is not a mere projection of our mind, but *"projections* of a hidden soul"[41] that gives us a glimpse of a union of subject and object, poetic images emerging inside the subject as a primordial force through a state of reverie that cannot be grasped by logical judgments, or the "formal imagination," and yet are to be taken as "primitive and eternal," so that they "prevail over reason and history."[42]

Moore's thesis extracted such poetic implications from

39. Bachelard's work is often divided into two parts, the first relating to the philosophy of the sciences, where his theory of epistemological breaks and the constitution of theoretical objects, and the emphasis on "phenomenotechnics" as a way to produce phenomena, in many respects opposes him to Husserl, particularly on the issue of a possible grounding of the sciences in the lifeworld. The second part, where he addresses the material imagination, reveries, and the autonomous status of poetic fantasy, might at first hand seem to bring him closer to certain phenomenological motifs, although the break between imagination and sensibility on the one hand, and science and rationality on the other, which underlies his work, renders this proximity problematic. For a discussion of Bachelard's long-standing and complex relation to Husserl, see Bernard Barsotti, *Bachelard critique de Husserl: Aux racines de la fracture épistémologie/phénoménologie* (Paris: L'Harmattan, 2002). The recently published *Handbook of Phenomenological Aesthetics* (Dordrecht: Springer, 2010), edited by Hans Rainer Sepp and Lester Embree, has no separate entry on Bachelard, and he is only mentioned in passing, although the editors note that he is "related to phenomenology in the broader sense" (xvii).

40. Bachelard, *Water and Dreams: An Essay on the Imagination of Matter*, trans. Edith. R. Farrell (Dallas: Dallas Institute of Humanity and Culture, 1983), 12

41. Ibid, 17.

42. Ibid, 1.

works far apart in space and time, on the basis of what he called an experiential immediacy, which to be sure involves an essential moment of fiction, and in this it is in some respects not so far apart as one might think from the more strict procedures of someone like Husserl.[43] For Moore it is however not variation that gives us the essence, but memory, but as Otero-Pailos stresses, the memory in case was in fact there in order to be forgotten, or transformed into a creative act outside of history, and in this sense Moore can criticize his modernist predecessors for not being modern enough in relying on objective, pre-given forms handed down by an equally objectified history.

Escaping from the modernist box also implied a stance against the political McCarthyism of the time and a defense of the irreducibility of individual experience, and Moore's projects for additions to existing buildings, such as fountains at signature works like the Lever House and the Seagram building, provide a sense of breaking out. But as Otero-Pailos demonstrates, Moore's fascination for decoration and superficiality ultimately had in fact more to do with his understanding of the interior, which is the space of the human mind as such, with its layers of fantasy and memory, and here too his poetics of space comes close to Bachelard.[44] The aedicule became the vehicle for the

43. See, for instance, Husserl, *Ideas* I, § 70, where fantasy (*Phantasie*) is understood as the basis for the method of eidetic variation, and thus as the "vital element" (*Lebenselement*) of phenomenology. For Husserl fantasy takes us away from the singularity of experience toward the essence, whereas in Moore, it is the overlay of memory that reduces he immediacy of the thing.

44. Bachelard's *Poetics of Space* is almost exclusive dedicated to places that we once loved, to the exploration of "topophilia." His topo-analysis provides us with a profound account of intimacy and of the path to the house that takes us back in time, a regressive route that mobilizes a fantasy essentially predicated upon memories that are "housed" in our soul. We inhabit houses just as much as they inhabit us, Bachelard says, but in terms of tradition and memory, not as a transformation and opening toward something new. The house is our first universe, and Bachelard emphatically rejects those philosophers that "know the universe

material imagination, as in Moore's later book *Body, Memory, and Architecture* (1977, co-authored with Kent Bloomer), where water as the primary element has been replaced by fire: the miniature size of the aedicule brings the building into contact with the body, kindling an "inner fire." Here too Bachelard was a forerunner, particularly his *The Psychoanalysis of Fire*, which suggested that the origin of fire was not in some outer accident—

before they know the house, the far horizon before the resting-place." (Bachelard, *The Poetics of Space* trans. Maria Jolas [Boston: Beacon Press, 1969], 5) All subsequent worlds and spaces—and not least the city, which for Bachelard seems to have only a negative function as an agent of the dissolution of the house—are inscribed into this first non-geometric, non-objective space, and to this extent it can only be given to us as a remembered, or even dreamt space: "the house we were born in is more than the embodiment of home, it is also an embodiment of dreams [...] there exists for each of us an oneiric house, a house of dream-memory, that is lost in the shadow of a beyond of the real past. I called this oneiric house the crypt of the house that we were born in." (15). In this, the protective enclosure plays a decisive role, and in many detailed and intriguing reflections on secret spaces (closets, drawers), non- or proto-human dwellings (nests, shells) that already point in the direction of minute and intimate slices of space (corners, nooks), Bachelard wants to show how the "phenomenology of the verb to inhabit" (xxxiv) means to live intensively, to be in an enclosure; further on, he speaks of the "hut," whose truth derives from "the intensity of its essence, which is the essence of the verb 'to inhabit.'" (32) Bachelard here obviously comes close to Heidegger's essay on "Building Dwelling Thinking," although his own references are mostly negative remarks on the idea of "thrownness" in early Heidegger. In accordance with Bachelard's amalgamation of oblivion and modernity, this world is however always one that is on the verge of disappearing, it is a rural sphere threatened by modernity's disruption of interiority. If the world described by Bachelard is a crypt, it is also a melancholy introjection that would require a "working-through" or "perlaboration," a *Durcharbeiten* in the Freudian sense, and needs to ask the question whether we must take leave of the topophilia that chains us to the lost thing. Nothing would at first sight be more opposed to Bachelard's spatial poetics than Corbusier's vision of transparency, where the subject must take up a new relation to the thing and to visibility as such. Uwe Bernhardt, discusses Corbusier's housing project Cité Frugès, Pessac, and interestingly suggests that the changes eventually introduced by the inhabitants can be understood as attempts to "reestablish the dimension of 'dream' advocated by Bachelard in dwelling." See Berhardt. *Le Corbusier et le projet de la modernité: La rupture avec l'intériorité* (Paris: L'Harmattan, 2002), 105.

lightning striking, or two branches rubbing against each other, which, not incidentally, is also the first explicit myth of the origin or architecture in Vitruvius—but in bodies rubbing against each other in sexual intercourse and generating heat, a process that only subsequently was transferred onto nature. For Moore, the aedicule became not just an origin of sense, but was also endowed with the task of folding the cosmic vectors together, creating a secularized version of Labatut's Eucharist architecture, and which also communicated with a whole counter-cultural discourse of mind expansion through drugs and channeling of sexual energies, as in Reich's "orgone accumulators."

If this inward turn was still connected to a cosmic dimension, it also affected the surface, which perhaps is what is most commonly associated with postmodernism, in Moore's idea of "supergraphics." Visually closely aligned with pop art, this type of interior decoration soon expanded into an overall visual strategy for the implementation of Moore's subjective vision of architecture, applicable to all kinds of surfaces, even though it too in the end, just as the aedicule, aspired to achieve an inner experience. The language of advertising, cherished by Venturi, here converges with a phenomenology of inner experience, which indicates the malleability of these concepts, as was already the case in Labatut, whose Eucharist language frictionlessly can move over into the domain of consumer psychology.

As Otero-Pailos demonstrates, this inner experience, while nourished by references to phenomenological philosophy, eventually also produced an anti-intellectual stance. The emphasis on immediacy and on an intuitive access to history, bypassing critical analysis of sources and in the end relying on the authority of the teacher, gave architectural phenomenology a particular slant that one the one hand brought it far from the project that set phenomenology at its course as a philosophy, precisely because it pushing one of its implicit potentials to the extreme.

It is an experientialism that wants to have everything, including universals and essences, given to it in the flesh, that demands that everything be given in intuition, and thus only with great problems, and at a cost of extreme tensions, can account for the necessity of historical mediations that always introduce a moment of contingency in sense, just as it, seen from the other end, appears to drag essences down into the flux of subjective experience and thus deprive them of their universality. These problems will become even more pressing in the next two cases, where the philosophical stakes are placed at a much higher level, and where phenomenology's dual heritage in architecture—on the one hand a tool for accounting of experience in all of it vicissitudes, on the other hand almost always trading on more or less hidden, normative agendas—becomes explosive.

The images of truth:
Norberg-Schulz and Frampton

If Labatut's and Moore's relation to phenomenology in the more strict sense is indirect or unsystematic, Christian Norberg-Schulz was the one who provided its application to architecture with a systematic foundation. Beginning in Gestalt psychology (*Intentions in Architecture*, 1965), he soon moved on to more phenomenologically oriented concerns (*Existence, Space and Architecture*, 1971), which then were summarized in his *Genius Loci: Towards a Phenomenology of Architecture* (1980), where Heidegger becomes the major philosophical source.

Otero-Pailos chooses to bypass most of Norberg-Schulz's actual comments on Heidegger, and instead reads him through the way in which his books make use of photographs in order to construct a visual narrative that purports to give us "aletheic" images, i.e., images that claim a truth outside of both the works depicted and of the historical moment of their production. While this portrayal of Norberg-Schulz as "visual thinker," casting him

as someone who in the vein of Moore forged a kind of image pedagogy that also included graphic design and lay-out, does uncover
a neglected aspect of his work and demonstrates his crucial role
in the development of an experiential conception of history, it
also tends to obscure his phenomenologically inspired critique of
technological modernity, which is where his substantial relation
to phenomenology and Heidegger in particular must be located.[45]
As we will see, this has particular bearings not only on Norberg-
Schulz, but also on the role of phenomenology as such in "architecture's historical turn" and the "rise of the postmodern."

Otero-Pailos in fact analyzes Norberg-Schulz as a fundamentally modernist theorist, whose very project was to rescue modernism from its threatening relapse into mere repetition of historical models. The decisive influence on Norberg-Schulz's attitude
to history came from Giedion, both in the overall sense that the
present moment is one of crisis, and that the transition to the
new must be affected through a synthesis of art and science, as
well as in the more specific use of the method of *Metodengleiche*,
i.e., the juxtaposition of decontextualized images that were supposed to provide an intuitive access to formal essences (a move
that we also found in Moore, even though he drew on different
sources). Becoming an architect-historian meant to appeal to an
intuition of what Norberg-Schulz called "topology," i.e., formal
invariants that were themselves invisible but lay at the foundation of visual forms. The cultural task of the architect historian
is to restore meaning, which must come through visual order,
and not through the retrieval or invention of styles, and here too
Norberg-Schulz pursues Giedion's project, although he no longer aims to capture the dynamism of space-time, but to retrieve a
stable and underlying structural order.

45.   For a discussion of Norberg-Schulz's actual interpretation of Heidegger
       in more detail, see my *Essays, Lectures* (Stockholm: Axl Books, 2007),
       344–348.

In the first book, *Intentions in Architecture*, the theoretical sources for this task came from Gestalt psychology, particularly in the version of Rudolf Arnheim (a theory already that by that time had run its course in the visual arts and begun to be replaced with other models),[46] whose defense of the untrained eye had put him in opposition to the art historians and their analysis of disparate elements: to understand a work for Arnheim meant to grasp an intuitive whole, not to piece together distinct elements, each with their own meaning. For Norberg-Schulz this implied that historical analysis and design practice must proceed from the same premises of an a priori visual order. Oddly enough, the term "intention" does here not signify any allegiance to phenomenology, and Otero-Pailos notes that this might be due to Norberg-Schulz's awareness of the strong anti-psychological stance of Husserl (which in fact is the very condition of possibility of phenomenology as the ground of the other sciences, i.e., the uncovering of a dimension of constitutive consciousness that lies beyond any of the empirical sciences, not only psychology, but also anthropology, sociology, history, etc., and that later would lead Husserl to understand himself as the true heir of Kant's transcendental philosophy).

Psychology in the end however proved to be a shaky foundation, and from *Existence, Space and Architecture* onward Norberg-Schulz would rethink his relation to phenomenology. The privileged term for the invisible topological order now begins to shift towards the place or "existential spaces", of which architectural space is the "concretization." Here the concept *genius loci* appears

46. For the impact of Gestalt psychology on art education in the US, see Howard Singerman, *Art Subjects: Making Artists in the American University* (Berkeley: University of California Press, 1999). The first of Robert Morris's "Notes on Sculptures" engages in detail with this tradition, and while he continues to use its vocabulary, it is gradually being dismantled as the field of experience is understood in a more expanded sense. See *Continuous Project Altered Daily: The Writings of Robert Morris* (Cambridge, Mass.: MIT, 1995), 1-8.

for the first time, as a name for places saturated with objects that provide direction and centrality, ranging from the minute size of the hand to entire urban structures and landscapes, between which there is a continuity that architecture has to respect, allow to spring forth, and eventually concretize through its own artifacts.

Otero-Pailos provides a detailed analysis of how this conclusion is conveyed to the reader by means of a visual imagery, which gives a persuasive visibility to an order assumed to itself be derived from an invisible essence. Composing his books both as textual and photographic essays, Norberg-Schulz gave the final words to the images that provided the synthesis of the argument, but as such they were deprived of context, so that textual and visual rhetoric supplemented each other's lack. As Otero-Pailos notes, there is something deeply paradoxical in this photographic strategy, given Norberg-Schulz's dependence on Heidegger, for does not the latter's analysis of how the world become a "picture" (*Bild*) from Cartesian philosophy onward, and even more so when combined with his later analysis of modern technology as "framing" (*Gestell*), quite simply render any claim that photography—together with cinema a specifically modern art form, whose profound impact on the aura, aesthetics, subjectivity, space-time, desire, fetishism, etc. has been detailed by an infinity of theorists at least from Benjamin onward—might be "aletheic" in the sense suggested by Norberg-Schulz wholly impossible?

While such claims about the aletheic image are no doubt untenable, and belong to a historically dated phase of art theory—as Otero-Pailos rightly notes, it seems impossible to deny that the interpretation of any such image is always mediated through subjectivity as well as a set of historically specific conventions—Norberg-Schulz's issues with Heidegger perhaps lie elsewhere, which is also where the conflicted heritage of phenomenology

213

itself becomes visible, and of which his use of photography is an indication, though not the problem itself. His reading emphasizes the possibility of a return to an order already given in nature, beyond the mediation of history, for which the aletheic image is an instrument or mediator, but not truth itself: put briefly, the problem is not truth conveyed by an image, but truth itself. This comes across in the theoretically central introductory chapter in Genius Loci, "The Phenomenon of Place."[47] This time starting out not from photographs, but from Heidegger's reading of Georg Trakl's poem "Ein Winterabend" in *Unterwegs zur Sprache*,[48] Norberg-Schulz wants to show how space can be articulated by an architecture that follows the movement of nature's own spacing, locating itself as the mediating juncture between nature and culture, and thus preserving them in their difference and harmonious unity, i.e., in their *truth*. Picking up on the difference between the inside and the outside that structures the poem, and the image of the falling snow that sets up a relation between heaven and earth as a comprehensive environment, Norberg-Schulz reads the interiority as shelter and protection, and as opposed to the wanderer coming from the outside into the house, crossing a "threshold turned to stone" that

47. The essay was first published in 1976, and then reprinted in a slightly modified version as the introductory chapter in *Genius Loci: Towards a Phenomenology of Architecture* (New York: Rizzoli, 1980). Henceforth cited as GL.

48. Norberg-Schulz's reading proceeds to a rather literal interpretation of the poem, and effectively disregards what Heidegger in fact says about language and space. Elsewhere I have tried to elucidate this connection; see my "The Vicinity of Poetry and Thought," in Marcia Sá Cavalcante Schuback and Luiz Carlos Pereira (eds.), *Time and Form: Essays on Philosophy, Logic, Art, and Politics* (Stockholm: Axl Books, 2014). Cf. also the rather different interpretation of the current state of architecture developed four years earlier by Manfredo Tafuri and Francesco Dal Co in the final chapter of their *L'architettura contemporanea*; Heidegger's late work on poetry in *Unterwegs zur Sprache* her too provides the point of entry, although the emphasis lies on the absence of a relation between word and thing, and the impossibility of forging a stable language (for more on this, see chap. 1 above).

marks the "rift" between "otherness" and "manifest meaning" (GL 9). To inhabit the house is thus to inhabit the world from the point of view of a center, a focal point that gathers together the inside and the outside, meaning and otherness (and in this we can recognize motifs developed a few years subsequent to Heidegger's essay by Bachelard, and then by Moore). The landscape is never purely natural, but always on the way to culture, and is as it were completed by the intervention of artifacts: settlements, paths, and landmarks form focal points that "explain" the landscape, "condense" the natural environment into a meaningful totality, and actualize its capacity for sense. The *genius loci* is only achieved when all of these determinations—the natural and the man-made, the categories of earth-sky (horizontal-vertical) and outside-inside, and finally "character," the *how* of the presence of things—are brought together in terms of concentration and enclosure.

The interaction between landscape and settlement is repeated in the structure of the edifice: floor, wall, and ceiling, which condense and focus the triad ground, horizon, and sky, and a phenomenology of place and space, Norberg-Schulz says, thus necessarily comprises "the basic modes of construction and their relationship to formal articulation" (GL 15). In this way we can say that architecture *receives* an already given environment in order to *focus* it in buildings and things, and that things and artifacts thereby "explain the environment and make its character manifest" (16), i.e., they uncover the meanings potentially present in the given environment. For Norberg-Schulz the life-world is built up in a series of nested operations, in an ascending movement leading from a first *visualization* of our understanding of the place, through a *symbolization* that detaches signification from the immediacy of its context and turns it into a cultural object, and finally the *gathering* of all the parameters into an existential center (as the paradigm case, Norberg-

Schulz refers to Heidegger's discussion in "Building Dwelling Thinking" of the bridge that does not just *connect* banks that are already there, but lets them *emerge* as banks as it crosses the stream).

Through this we are supposed to reach back into a sphere of dwelling and re-establish contact with the world in a way that releases us from the demands of technology and the objectifying machinations of modern planning. "Human identity presupposes the identity of place," Norberg-Schulz states, and the priority accorded to transformation and movement as a key to freedom in modernity —we can here think of Giedion's "stream of movement" or the fluidity and malleability of "space-time" as the very element of architecture— must be reversed: "It is characteristic for modern man," Norberg-Schulz claims, once more picking up a figure from Trakl's poem, "that for a long time he gave the role as a wanderer pride of place. He wanted to be 'free' and conquer the world. Today we start to realize that true freedom presupposes belonging, and that 'dwelling' means belonging to a concrete place." (GL 22)

As Otero-Pailos points out, many readers have criticized Norberg-Schulz's reading of Heidegger for being simplistic, and while this may be true, it nevertheless brings out one particular dimension that is undoubtedly there in the phenomenological tradition: Norberg-Schulz's reading of Heidegger is one-sided and selective, but it is difficult to say that it is simply wrong. What he claims as the true heritage of Heidegger has been equally noted by readers of all kinds, from Adorno to Deleuze and Derrida (who always remained something of a paradoxically loyal heretic): the desire for absolute foundations, grounds, and certainties that would already, in their truth, be given in *physis*.[49]

49. While the Greek *physis* in Heidegger's interpretation cannot be identified with nature in the modern sense, it is the nevertheless the distant and obscured origin of all modern natures, as it were *the first name of*

This quest for origins was however always marked by the suspicion—perhaps even promise, at least in its later versions—that it would be infinite. This was already the case in Husserl's search for the depths and recesses of experience, and his understanding of transcendental subjectivity as necessarily embodied not just in a physical side, but also in intersubjectivity and history; in Heidegger, the quest for foundations is rejected in the early thirties, and yet returns in constantly new guises, one of which undoubtedly would be mythologically tinted "Fourfold" (*Geviert*) that organizes his understanding of world in the later texts, and is operative throughout the interpretation of Trakl. The tension between these two motifs, or better this tension between two sides of the same motif, cannot be resolved, and in fact should not be: it is constitutive of phenomenology as such, which is why any appeal to it as a figure of philosophical authority to be applied to another discipline necessarily involves a moment of deception, and even more so when it is called upon to deliver a normative aesthetic agenda, as is undoubtedly the case in Norberg-Schulz. This need obviously not be intended, rather it belongs to the phenomenological tradition as such, and beyond this undoubtedly to any philosophical tradition that eschews the search for empty generalities and pursues the exchange with artworks at the kind of depth where the issue is their *truth*, their capacity to reveal something hitherto *unknown* to thought, which is why it can be taken neither as an objection nor as a defense of phenomenology (or any other philosophical tradition), only as a constant temptation that must be accounted for.

For Kenneth Frampton, the last case studied by Otero-

being before all subsequent oppositional structures—*physis* as distinct from *techne*, *nomos*, *polis*, and all concepts that would derive from this split—or rather the name of being at that moment where it contained this difference within itself, in the movement of truth as *a-letheia*, as a duplicity of hiding and showing that only later, through the emergence of philosophy in Plato, was caught up in a series of external oppositions.

Pailos, these issues have become key elements for reflection, and the necessity of a historical meditation inherent in any grounding can be taken as the pivotal theme of his mature theory of critical regionalism and tectonics. The notion of experience, or "experiential surplus," here functions as the guiding thread, and Otero-Pailos follows it through Frampton's early engagement with Art and Crafts ideals, and traces the sustained importance he gives to manual labor and practice throughout his work, for a long time conceptualized under the rubric of "constructivism," until it eventually ushered in the vocabulary of critical regionalism and tectonics from the early eighties onward.

For Frampton too, the power of the image was important, which he developed during his year as en editor of *Architectural Design* (1962–65). But instead then seeking for "aletheic" images that would disclose a hidden topology, Frampton's editorial strategy, strongly influenced by Ernesto Rogers's *Casabella*,[50] was to use images to convey detailing, tactility, and materiality, which remain key term in his later work that often positions itself in opposition not only to the conventions of architecture photography as such, but also and more generally to the consumption of works through images and "information" that in turn feeds a particular kind of photogenic architecture. But rather than a general rejection of the image, Frampton's proposal was that these graphic techniques could themselves become a way to achieve a surplus experience, which is what transforms mere building into architecture, i.e., takes us out of the sphere of pure necessity into the space of freedom and reflection, and Otero-Pailos shows how this theme emerges in Frampton's early encounter with the works of Hannah Arendt, as well as his

50. Roger's own writings, which Frampton did not notice at the time, were in fact steeped in phenomenology, even though not in any technical sense of the term. See for instance Rogers, "The Phenomenology of European Architecture", *Daedalus* Vol. 93, No. 1 (Winter, 1964): 358-372.

exchanges with the phenomenological circles in Essex, which fostered a more anti-modern attitude.[51]

If Arendt's *The Human Condition* and its tripartite schema of labor, work, and action became decisive for Frampton, the question was how to translate this into architectural discourse, for which the triad of building, architecture, and, somewhat more vaguely, surplus experience—the extra dimension of experience that makes architecture into a liberating art—offered a solution. For Arendt labor was the toil of physical necessity, that which keeps us alive, work was the production of tools and technical forms with a continued existence of their own, or instrumental rationality, and action, finally, was the capacity for beginning, for bringing something new into the world in an act of freedom, which is essentially related to the possibility of an exchange between equals taking place in language. This exchange in turn requires a "space of appearance," i.e., a public sphere, which for Arendt is essentially made of intersubjective linguistic practices rather than material things, and as such has no existence over and above those who take part in them.

Frampton's transposition of these terms is not without problems, as Otero-Pailos notes, especially since he neglects Arendt's stress on language and identifies the sphere of action with the production of a particular kind of architecture, or sometimes with a particular dimension of architecture as such. But rather than seeing this as a misreading based on the "structurist notion that all human experiences could be constructed in material and visual terms" (AHT 226), it is probably more fruitful to read it as a necessary critique that attempts to correct the unmistak-

51. The Essex circle notably comprised Joseph Rykwert, Dalibor Vesely, and Alberto Péréz-Gomez, all of which have produced eminently erudite historical work. In this context the latter's *Architecture and the Crisis of Modern Science* (1983) must be mentioned, not least because it shows that a phenomenological analysis of conceptual history in no way implies an impressionistic treatment of historical documents and sources.

ably idealist tendency of Arendt's theory of the public sphere, whose emphasis on language neglects that it cannot do with specific and materially embodied institutions. If this sphere exists in a physical environment to which it undoubtedly cannot be *reduced*, its physical features can nevertheless not be entirely contingent in relation to the exchanges that take place within it; for what would "space of appearance" be, which simply lacked all spatial coordinates and features? The "act of human public appearance," Frampton writes in the essay "Labor, Work and Architecture" (1969), "depends upon 'work' as the sole agency through which relative permanence of the human world, testifying to human continuity, may be established."[52]

In the early theories of Frampton, put forward in the journal *Oppositions* that was at the crossroads of the theoretical debates of the period,[53] he presents architectural history as a conflict between building and architecture, passing though critical moments like the first separation between engineering and architecture in the mid eighteenth century, the subsequent assumption of power by the engineer a century later, signaled by Paxton's Crystal Palace 1851 (in fact largely designed by the railway engineer Charles Fox), and most recently the period around World War I and the introduction of industrial production. This last step, Frampton suggests, created a situation in which "the traditional cultural system is totally vitiated,"[54] and after which all that was left was a process in which building displaced architecture and eradicated the possibility of surplus experience.

52. Cited in AHT 226.
53. These debates significantly pitted Frampton against Eisenman, whose project was to restart modernism, emancipated from its humanist legacy, and for whom the historical attitude of Frampton was leading in the wrong direction. Later, in 2007 Eisenman would look back and say, "We were starting out to build a modernism in America, and unfortunately Postmodernism, as it came to be in this country, was one of the effects of *Oppositions*" (cit. in AHT 229).
54. "Industrialization the Crises in Architecture" (1973), cited in AHT 232.

This renders the concept of architecture systematically ambivalent: on the one hand it points to building, on the other hand to an experience beyond its own material facticity. In Frampton's subsequent work, the search for this kind of experience took two paths, one leading towards history and one towards politics. The historical option presented the task of retrieving the experiential dimension that had been repressed in a culture of engineering, which also, and somewhat paradoxically, meant to focus on constructive details, how units and elements are joined. But rather than opposing itself to politics, this seemingly formalist attention to details aspires to show how they condense history and politics in a form specific to architecture, in the *joint*, which for Frampton assumes a particular, even ontological significance, and is where he most fruitfully encounters Heidegger, as we will see.

The larger reflection on architecture's place in culture and history would in the early eighties come to be phrased in terms of "Critical Regionalism." While the term itself was borrowed from Alexander Tzonis and Liane Lefaivre, as Frampton is always careful to stress, he nevertheless gave it a much wider significance. First put forth in the programmatic essay "Towards a Critical Regionalism: Six Points for an Architecture of Resistance" (1983),[55] critical regionalism launches a six-point program as a strategy of aesthetic resistance, opposed to both a postmodern compensatory eclecticism and its remodeling of architecture as symbolism and scenography, and to a pure technological universality.[56] Drawing on Paul Ricoeur, the first three points sketch a general sense of modernity and its historical

55. First published in Hal Foster (ed.): *The Anti-Aesthetic* (Seattle: Bay Press, 1983). The following citations are from this version.
56. For a precise analysis of Frampton's simultaneous battle against these two opponents, and which also reads his strategy on the basis of Heidegger, see Deborah Fausch, "The Oppositions of Postmodern Tectonics," in *Any* 14, 1996.

trajectory, the first setting up a conflict between local culture and universal civilization, which has to be understood as a dialectical opposition with the regional as the mediating term. The second signals a farewell to the avant-garde as a viable model, an argument continued in the third, which speaks of an increasingly leveled and false "world culture" made up of media and its images, substituting information for experience (and even more so for "surplus experience").

The following three points contain the positive program, and here we find that which comes closest to what could be called Frampton's aesthetic. Point four proposes the idea of a resistance of the place-form, where Frampton derives his fundamental analytical tools from Heidegger (especially the 1951 essay "Building Dwelling Thinking") and with some reservations he shares the suspicion against the mathematical objectification of space, and the need for a return to the concrete and the communal as a way to resist the limitlessness of technology. After Heidegger, Frampton suggests, "we are, when confronted with the ubiquitous placelessness of our modern environment, [brought to posit] the absolute precondition of a bounded domain in order to create an architecture of resistance." (24) This also means to emphasize a series of concepts that all inscribe themselves in a tension between "nature and culture": topography, context, climate, light, and tectonic form. Connecting to local situations, critical regionalism marshals these tools in the name of *inertia*, and it professes to be a programmatic *arrière-garde* that mediates between local and specific traditions and an increasingly homogenized universal civilization. In this way it wants to protect us from a universal leveling by focusing on what is highlighted in the sixth and final point, physical and tactile elements, which work against what Frampton perceives as a one-sided emphasis on visual elements. Regionalism asserts such qualities that tend to get lost in an architectural culture increasingly permeated by images and reproduction technologies, it counters the "loss of nearness" by preserving the "place-form" against both modernism and its obsession with the *tabula rasa* as well as all forms of sentimental and populist counter-reactions—but in doing this, it must remain within what Frampton himself calls a "double mediation," for instance as in the interplay of the *"rationality* of normative technique" and the *"arationality* of idiosyncratic forms" (21–22).

This arational rationality is what comes to the fore in the idea of tectonics. Historically, the concept draws on a long tradition extending back at least to the mid-nineteenth century and the moment when a certain threshold of modern architecture was crossed, and the classical heritage seemed irrevocably dispersed. From that point onward there emerges a symptomatic, long, and inconclusive debate on the relation between the technical "core-form" (*Kernform*) and the aesthetic "art-form" (*Kunstform*),[57] of which Frampton is one of the last heirs. While this is obviously a fundamentally modern problem that translates a fundamental insecurity about the value of the inherited formal language, one can also note that the question that initiates the discussion, posed by Bötticher in his analysis of the "tectonics of the Greeks,"[58] bears on the possibility of retrieving the classical within the modern, i.e., if it is at all possible to re-create, within modern architecture, the natural and organic bond—the "juncture" (*Junktur*)—that in the Greek temple unit-

---

57. For discussions of the nineteenth-century discourse on tectonics and related concepts, see Werner Oechslin, *Stilhülse und Kern: Otto Wagner, Adolf Loos und der evolutionäre Weg zur modernen Architektur* (Berlin: Ernst & Sohn, 1994). For contemporary discussions, see for instance Hans Kollhoff (ed.), *Über Tektonik in der Baukunst* (Braunschweig: Vieweg & Sohn, 1993), and *Any* 14, "Tectonics Unbound."

58. See Karl Bötticher, *Die Tektonik der Hellenen*, 2 vol. (Berlin: Ernst & Korn, 1844–52). For an analysis of Bötticher's program, see Hartmut Meyer, *Die Tektonik der Hellenen: Kontext und Wirkung der Architekturtheorie von Karl Bötticher* (Stuttgart: Axel Menges, 2004).

ed statics and expression, technology and art. The discourse on tectonics that begins in the middle of the nineteenth century in this sense emerges as a melancholy reflection on the loss of the classical heritage, which in turn echoes in the idea of a loss of "surplus experience."

For Frampton, tectonics functions as a complex mediation between the autonomous dimension of formal compositional language and a given setting that is at once historical-cultural and environmental; it is not something purely technical, but rather the necessary basis for a structural poetic that would be able to inscribe the inevitable impact of modern technology while transforming it to a conscious expression of form. In an essay from 1990, *"Rappel à l'ordre*: The Case for the Tectonic,"[59] Frampton adds another distinction, which also highlights the Heideggerian background to his concepts: the tectonic object is not only opposed to its scenographic and technological counterpart, but is *itself* divided into an ontological and a representational aspect. These two aspects are associated to Semper's distinction between the tectonics of the architectural frame, and the compressed masses of stereotomy (i.e., a massing of similar elements like bricks), and the frame is now understood as tending toward the "aerial element," while the telluric mass-form descends downward into the earth. This duality for Frampton becomes an expression of "cosmological opposites" endowed with a "transcultural values" (95), which make up the founda-

59. Reprinted in *Labour, Work, Architecture* (London: Phaidon, 2002). The following citations with page number are from this version. Frampton's reference to Cocteau's neoclassical "return to order" should probably to some extent be understood ironically, and yet it unmistakably gestures, across the chasm opened up by modernism, in the direction of the classical tradition, even of the "orders" in architecture, which on the surface were precisely what appeared to be displaced by tectonics in the nineteenth century, basically from Semper onward and yet survive in the sense of an order that is already incipient in nature, and to which architecture constitutes a reflexive response.

tion of our life-world, and it is not difficult to understand these concepts as a somewhat demythologized version of Heidegger's Fourfold, which seeks to establish specific architectural interpretations of his seemingly religiously tinted notions

Following Semper, but in a certain way Heidegger too, Frampton proposes that the *joint* be understood as the essential element of architecture: it forms a fundamental syntactical transition from stereotomic base to tectonic frame, it provides an "ontological condensation" (95) of the very idea of *tikto* as bringing-together, and allows the other elements to come forth—the joint establishes connections *and* separations, first between stereotomic earth and tectonic lightness, then unfolding its operations throughout all the other constructional details. Sense, Frampton says, must be understood as an interplay between connecting and disconnecting, a "dis-joint" (102) that produces a gathering and assembling while also letting the different elements come forth in their *difference*.

These threads are finally drawn together in the massive *Studies in Tectonic Culture* (1996, curiously enough not discussed by Otero-Pailos), which develops the theory of tectonics in the framework of an encompassing analysis of the path of modernity. Through a series of extended in-depth analyses of paradigmatic architectural works that attempt to grasp how their overall significance as cultural objects are reflected and expressed in the smallest technical details of their construction, Frampton traces a "tectonic trajectory" leading from the origins of modernist architecture into the situation of late modernity. Here too he construes the dialectic of modern architecture as a tension between the representational and ontological, with tectonics as the meditating force that allows construction to assume the form of a poetic practice—it is what raises the technological into a form of art, and what conveys the surplus experience— that would have the power to resist technology's transformation of the earth into a depository of material, and its flattening of things, ultimately of space itself, into calculable entities devoid of density and presence. Tectonics would be that which allows construction to shine forth in a transfigured form as *truth*, in bringing forth the necessary difference and togetherness of things.[60]

The legacy of phenomenology

Finally, what is then the legacy of architectural phenomenology, and to what extent does it fit into the theme of the postmodern as a historical turn? In the epilogue Otero-Pailos points to the ambivalence and conflicted nature of this legacy. It introduced a new set of visual techniques and brought about an expanded sense of architectural intellectuality, but also set specific limits to theory, and eventually ended up opposing what it had made possible. The problem of how to link intellectuality, bodily experience, and history in a unity was as such surely not a new one, and it had a long genealogy extending back to the nineteenth century and the psychologizing of aesthetics. Connected to modern technologies of perception and representation it had however gained a new depth and intensity, as in Giedion, and through him to his students, notably Norberg-Schulz, whose aletheic image can be read as a development of the *Methodengleiche*.

60. For a reading not unsympathetic to such claims, but that nevertheless fundamentally problematizes the claim to *truth*, see Fritz Neumeyer, "Tektonik: Das Schauspiel der Objektivität und die Wahrheit des Architekturschauspiels," in Kollhoff, *Über Tektonik in der Baukunst*. Neumeyer shows that it is indeed the case that this truth is often an "image" of truth, a rhetorical display of structural honesty, more than organic relation between the demands of engineering and architectural expressivity. Even more emphatically than Frampton he also notes the extent to which the value of the tectonic, particularly in its constant referencing of the phenomenological body as a source of meaning, can only be defensive: its task is "not to once more make the disappearing body appear, but to prevent it from completely disappearing" (59).

226

If architectural phenomenology was an attempt to bring us back to authentic experience, its way of doing so was still through various means of representation (which does not exclusively mean texts, as Otero-Pailos stresses, but also graphic techniques layout, editing of images, the photographic essay in all of its guises): "Architectural phenomenology was not so much a representation of real architectural experiences. Rather, it was a discursive fabrication of a new sort of technologically mediated architectural experience." (AHS 255) In this it poses an explicit and highly conscious challenge to the protocols of art history, in proposing a different way of conveying experience, which in the end also introduced an element of anti-intellectualism into the new intellectuality that was the prerogative of the architect-historian.[61]

In relation to the modernist legacy, architectural phenomenology played a complex and sometimes even contradictory role: inside the postmodern turn to historical styles it upheld a modernist claim to an essential experience that would ground them outside of history, and thus was instrumental, Otero-Pailos suggests, in reconciling "the postmodernist fascination with history and the modernist repulsion from it." (AHT 256) In this sense it occupied a Janus-faced or transitional position, which is also why it toward the end of the eighties could be attacked from within by a new generation that turned against the whole idea of grounding and foundation, for which a new reading, or sometimes a rejection, of Heidegger could be instrumental (in these discussions, it seems to have been little noticed that Heidegger himself had rejected the idea of fundamental ontology more than fifty years earlier). Rather than a return to

61. At the same time as these new means were tested in architecture, they were being mischievously dismantled in the visual arts. Dan Graham's *Homes for America* (1966) is an obvious example, and even more so Robert Smithson's early photo-text-essays; on Smithson, see chap 6, below.

the essential structures of experience, the body, or nature as the ground of dwelling, the task now became to account for its impossibility in the modern world, for the irrevocable division between forms and grounds, and the detachment of language from its anchoring in some natural or pre-given order of perception.

In the end, phenomenology, both as a philosophical movement and as a particular form of architectural thought, seems difficult to place in the modern-postmodern schema, regardless of what content we choose to give the latter. Historically its first phase is coextensive with early modernism and the discovery of the temporal dynamic nature of subjectivity, which is why its influence sometimes may be seen as running parallel to that of Bergson (as Otero-Pailos shows to be the case in Labatut); the invention of consciousness as a transcendental field takes at the same time as the invention of abstraction in art, as can be seen in Husserl's early work,[62] long before phenomenology's postwar ascendancy, through the influence of Merleau-Ponty, to the role of one of the major interpretative paradigms for early twentieth-century painting and for at least certain parts of recent abstract art; it may no doubt be read as a resistance to the technologizing of perception, but just as much as an attempt to understand the ground of technology, as in the case of Heidegger, who can in no way be cast as merely a backward-looking opponent to modern art.[63] In this sense, to the extent that such labels at all make

62.   See Husserl's letter to Hofmannsthal from January 12, 1907, which sets up a close parallel between aesthetic autonomy and Husserl's own recently discovered phenomenological reduction. I discuss this in more detail in "Husserl's Letter to Hofmannsthal: Phenomenology and the Possibility of a Pure Art," *Site* 26–27 (2009), where there is also an English translation of Husserl's letter; German original in *Briefwechsel*, Husserliana Dokumente, eds. Elisabeth Schuhmann and Karl Schuhmann (Dordrecht: Kluwer, 1994), vol. VII, 133–36.

63.   It is well known that after the war Heidegger was planning to write a sequel to *The Origin of the Work of Art* that would start out from the work of Klee, and his meditations on the essence of technology are intimately connected to those on art, as can be seen in texts like "Bauen Wohnen

sense, phenomenology is a quintessentially modern and even modernist philosophy, in focusing on subjectivity and its relation to otherness (other human beings, the social order, history) as the nexus in which sense is constituted, rather than on ideal logical or linguistic structures, as in the first wave of analytic philosophy, which is no doubt why the former has been such an attractive ally for the modern arts in general, whereas the latter has only had a marginal influence.

The two moments, grounding *in* the subject and the ungrounding *of* the subject, are like the two facets of phenomenology, and if we take the first to be modern, the second postmodern—as in all the attempts that were made to understand the postmodern as a "decentering of the subject"—it belongs just as much to both, as is evidenced by the second phase of architectural phenomenology that Otero-Pailos situates in the late eighties. In this sense, this is more like an oscillation between two poles inside the same problem: no matter how we draw the line, the postmodern will always be inside the modern and inversely, as was suggested by Lyotard in his conception of the *futur antérieur.*

To some extent this strange and confusing crisscrossing of before and after is an effect of the non-synchronicity of philosophy and architectural thinking, which is further complicated if we include the thinking in and around the visual arts. There will be different genealogies depending on how we draw the lines, and the result is inevitably a story of projections, decontextualized and belated readings, willfully aberrant interpretations and applications that refuse to yield a unity. And if he term "postmodern" for a while offered itself as a common denominator for all of these trajectories, as if they all at a given point in time would had begun to move in lockstep and adjust their relative

Denken" and "Die Frage nach der Technik," which are the most frequently cited in the architectural reception.

speeds to one another, this was no doubt an optical illusion produced by a desire for interpretative mastery, no matter how much many (though not all) of these interpretations emphatically rejected such mastery.

The inverse solution would then be to reject the idea of an internal history, and instead opt for a theory of the postmodern not as a series of continuous problem given by a singe discipline, or even by the interaction of a multiplicity of disciplines, but by the outside, by the forces of Capital and the way it transforms the world which all of these theories and practices inhabit. This need not imply to see these disciplines as mere passive reflections, but rather as overdetermined responses, which however in the end cannot form a exclusive history of their own. Neither a mere symptom nor an autonomous force, architecture would then be situated at the limit, its particular competence and agency forming a kind of disciplinary interiority that reflects, monadically, that which surpasses it, in a topological twist; whether this restores its agency or even more effectively neutralizes it, can be taken as precisely the problem of the postmodern that still remains with us.

Reading the outside: globalization and the return of the repressed

This opposite route into the postmodern complex—and just as much out of it, in way that complicates the inner-outer divide—is the one taken by Reinhold Martin. In consonance with this move, instead of simply historicizing the concept as a past and sealed-off object offered up for dispassionate scholarly work, his claim is rather that the postmodern in relation to the present is characterized by a particular untimeliness itself in need of a new analysis. It is like a recent past that refuses to be aligned with the present just as much as it cannot be consigned to the past, first and foremost because it belongs to a larger socio-historical structure that we still inhabit in all of its ramifications, including those that concern the sense of historical sequences and order.

Postmodern architecture, Martin suggests, must first of all be understood as part of a transformed universe of production and consumption, and if it rejects the machine aesthetic of modernism, it is because it is itself part of a machine of a different order, which it however does not simply mirror, but also effectuates and sets in motion. Postmodernism must thus first be "translated out of" architecture (UG xii), but this translatability also makes it possible for its particular disciplinary knowledge to become a key for unlocking a more general context, which is why it is no coincidence that many of the earliest theorizations of postmodernity, from Fredric Jameson to Jürgen Habermas, picked architecture as their main exhibit. In relation to these predecessors, Martin's project is not to zoom in and narrate a more specific history of architectural theories or practices with one stage leading to another (as was the proposal in Otero-Pailos), but to study a set of concepts that by the end of the mid eighties had become a discursive formation called postmodernism, and which all clustered around architecture rather than emerging out of it as from an inner disciplinary dialectic. The method, he says, is not to contextualize architecture, but rather to decontextualize it in relation to established narratives in order find other connections and constellations. These constellations however do not form a set of parallel tracks that would simply reflect each other, but are related so that each of them generates its own outside, dispersed over contemporary history, from the close to the far away, which is also one of the pervasive ways in which postmodern architecture partakes in a certain territoriality, both conceptually and socio-politically, i.e. in the ordering of late capitalist space.

Ultimately, Martin's interrogation bears on architecture's immanence in a power that it remains barred from perceiving other than in the distorted mirror of its own autonomy, and on how its various modes of acting and representing, its *thinking* in the widest sense, also amount to an active *unthinking* of other possibilities, above all the idea of utopia. In its focus on auto-regulation and on its own history and language, postmodern architecture, through all of its many and seemingly contradictory shapes, was an embrace of the status quo, which in turn was obscured, Martin suggests, by a return to an idea of Architecture conceived as an act of freedom that claims to break with the teleologies and historical necessities of modernism. The newfound exercise of freedom and autonomy, with its unmistakable echoes of the historical avant-gardes, could engage in an almost endless variety of experiments with representation (some of which are detailed in Otero-Pailos book, although from a rather different angle) that all had in common a gradual severing of the ties to historical truth, eventually leading to the insight into truth's radical contingency, which itself, Martin proposes, must be seen as the product of the naturalized narrative of capital.

In this sense, the postmodern was a "cruel combination of freedom and servitude, truth and lies" (UG xv), and the role of its architectural avatar, as a fully materialized "immaterial production," both production and representation, was to reorganize the imaginary as well as space, or as Martin prefers to say, territory. Drawing above all on Agamben's theory of the contemporary generalization of the structure of the state of exception, Martin sees a new regimentation of territory at work, moving between the poles of the *network* and the *island*, on the one hand creating intense connection between all entities, on the other producing a proliferating set of boundaries that cut through social space, both in the form enclaves and gated communities, and of zones that divest their inhabitants of legal status as they slice through the fabric of everyday life. But if this new regimentation erases utopia as the thought of an outside and replaces it with immanent loops of auto-regulation, these in turn generate their own outsides on the inside: utopia's ghost that returns in the guise of outsides that haunt the inside from which it has been expelled, in a figure that runs through many of Martin's analyses. His often repeated claim that the further inside you get, and the more architecture folds back on its own specificity and competence, the further outside you get, is itself reversible: the more architecture is deterritorialized in the world, the more its own specific procedures can be read as a cipher of the totality.

In the world of late capitalism the ubiquity of corporate models calls for what Martin calls a "phenomenology of capital" (xvii), and while the term—itself picked up from Ernest Mandel, who speaks of the corporation as "the main phenomenal form of capital"—may be incidental in this context, it can nevertheless be placed in a significant opposition to the tradition delineated by Otero-Pailos. Rather than the search for an experiential take on architecture grounding itself in the discovery of formal essences or the depths of subjectivity (in fact, phenomenology aligns the two, since essences have sense only in relation to a subjectivity that apprehends them), phenomenality here seems to imply the opposite, i.e., the way in which an objective order not only appears before a subject, but also subjectivizes the subject, in a way that renders the latter's own level of agency problematic.

The postmodern obsession with the question of the discipline: is there at all *an architecture*—echoing Le Corbusier's old dictum, that we first must ascertain whether we are at all moving "towards an architecture," *vers une architecture*, before we interrogate its possible newness, belatedness, or timeliness— and the incessant claims to ground the discipline in history, some version of formal analysis, or some specific technology, surely testified to an almost neurotic anxiety. To some extent this is

233

reminiscent what Tafuri at the outset of *Progetto e utopia* claimed
to be "one of the principal ethical imperatives of bourgeois
art" characterizing the whole cycle of modern architecture: "to
dispel anxiety by understanding and internalizing its causes."
The many versions of this anxiety that traverse the postmodern
for Martin however all derive from a common problem, which
remained invisible in all the solutions that tried to overcome
it, and his many critical comments on Tafuri notwithstanding,
Martin's theory is in many respects an updated version of the
latter's analysis, the difference being that what Tafuri perceived
as an end for Martin appears as an intensification (which is
not entirely foreign to Tafuri, who instead of "postmodernity"
would speak of "hypermodernity"). So for instance the withdrawal into private games, the idea of a radical autonomy that
would amount to a resistance to reification, which in Martin's
reading, echoing Tafuri, signifies the exact opposite: "It is sometimes mistakenly thought," he writes, "that by stepping away
from functionalism, which by the late 1950s had been appropriated by the corporations, and into a renewed art for art's sake,
architecture steps away from capital. This overlooks the fact that
corporate capitalism had, by then, expanded into the aesthetic
realm to such a degree that architecture's claims to formal autonomy played right into the demand for a maximum of spectacularization (in what is now called 'signature architecture')"
(UG xx). That the step into self-reflexive language does not
shield architecture from capital and the corporate world, but in
fact opens it up to the latter's intensified power as it moved into
its aesthetic phase, is a claim that would seem to follow from
Tafuri's conclusion. Inversely, the populism that wants to merge
with mass culture still remains within a quest for autonomy, and
exists by virtue of a dialectical interplay with historical connoisseurship, as in the case of Venturi: the order of Versailles and
the A&P parking lot reinforce each other, and the erasure of

the high-low division becomes architecture's own loop as it attempts to ground itself.

Many of these features are obviously in continuity with modernism, which itself by no means constituted a monolithic movements, and any simple periodization will lead astray (in some respects, Martin notes, this comes close to the formal structure of Lyotard's *futur antérieur*, even though one must note that the latter was conceived precisely in order to avoid the kind of macro-historical hypotheses that underlie conceptions like that of late capitalism, which still informed Lyotard's earlier book *The Postmodern Condition*). The "post-" in postmodern does not refer to any chronological marker, but rather to a defining feature, the "quasi-consensual ban on utopian projection" (xxi) that however only leads the repressed to return, this time in the form of the ghost. Postmodernism is on one level simply what later came to be known as globalization, even though Martin wants to avoid the before and after, and speaks of a "progressive circularity" (xxii). If postmodernism in inseparable from the discourses of the cold war, consumer culture, and eventually globalization, it becomes neither before nor after such terms, Martin stresses, and he wants to avoid the language of economic causality; his proposed vocabulary is instead that of the feedback loop, elements that enter into resonance with and reinforce each other, becoming input as well as output.

This idea of the loop organizes the argument as well as the book as a whole, which moves in circles, coming back to similar figures from different perspectives. But while it has the obvious advantage of avoiding the reductionist language of base and superstructure, the loop also performs a bit of magical *actio in distans*: it allows elements far apart to be related without specifying their more precise relation, and even though causal relations may be suspended in order to avoid reductionism, they cannot in the end simply be evacuated. If one would want to retain the image of the loop, one must also bear in mind its acoustic result: it eventually renders the elements that initially enter into it indiscernible. In this sense, feedback and all of its kindred terms (control, self-regulation)—and in this they belong to same order as those features singled out by Jameson (collapse of depth models, the waning of affect, history returning as pastiche)—are phenomenal characteristics of the cultural logic of late capitalism, and they belong to its own self-image, to its appearance (*Schein* in Hegel's sense, which must not be conflated with mere illusion; appearance is perfectly real, although not the *all* of the real), but are equivocal and slippery when understood as analytic or epistemological tools.

Or, to put it as simply as possible, there is an imminent risk that the analysis of the postmodern absorbs the features of its objects so as to eventually merge with it, *that it itself becomes postmodern*, which is no doubt a problem that any analysis that wants to remain in the Marxist tradition (which surely applies to Jameson) must face—it is a risk that one cannot avoid running, if the analysis is to reach the same level of sophistication and self-reflexivity, the same level of Hegel's "cunning of reason," as its object, which is needed if there is to be a possibility of going beyond or break away from it. Martin's vocabulary retreats from the affirmative Beyond, instead his attention to the recurrence and return of ghosts of utopia, to the way in which all carefully sealed and safeguarded disciplinary insides just as insistently as unconsciously produce their own outsides, testifies to the need to find a different exit, one that remains faithful to a kind of immanence, both practically and theoretically. That network are never closed, but always contain moments of reversal, and that the topology of globalization is never a simple extension outwards, from center to periphery, but that every inclusion also excludes, is both a threatening No way out and a promise of a return that would not simply present us with ghosts.

As Martin's analysis moves through the seven distinct concepts that also make up the chapter headings, Territory, History, Language, Image, Materiality, Subjects, and Architecture—all of which can be taken as a set of multiple entries, so none of them should be seen as the foundation of any other—the loop continually becomes more dense. But it also unfolds between two poles that mark beginning and end, Territory and Architecture, which taken together pose the problem of the *place* and *agency* of architecture, both in the material world and in the discursive formation that we still inhabit: what does architecture *do*, and to what extent can what it does, at the place, site, or territory that it occupies, signify something other than a system that continually folds back on itself? Is the promise of an architecture that would reinvent utopia just another ghost in the machine, or does it have some other purchase on a seemingly monolithic real?

From Territory to Architecture

Territory, first of all, is not *space*, which may seem like a small terminological displacement, but in fact signals a crucial shift. Instead of the category that since its first emergence as a generic term in architectural thought at the end of the nineteenth century, and through its various versions from Giedion to Zevi and onwards, eventually became "sacrosanct," as Venturi once quipped (and who significantly wanted to replace it with the concept of sign),[64] territory wants to point to "the oscillation between the territoriality of thought—its epistemic delimitation—and thought concerned with the city and its territories" (UG 1). Unlike space, as the infinitely malleable element of architecture, the territory is bounded, it is produced through acts of territorialization that always relate to an outside.

64.   For the emergence of the category "space," see chap. 3, above.

In keeping with this conception, Martin displaces the standard reading of the classical documents of early postmodernism: what they propose is a not a decentering or unhinging of the modernist signifier, but rather a reterritorialization of modernism's urban imaginary. From Rossi to Venturi and Scott Brown, from Banham to Archigram, the general claim was in fact a call back to order, to various forms of *architecture parlante* that would "re-semanticize" (in Tafuri's words) architecture and produce a new immanence. At stake for Venturi and Scott Brown was thus less a populism and a dissolution of the low-high division than normalization, i.e., an adjustment to the methods of social science, filtered through the models of Levittown and Las Vegas. Rossi on the other hand takes the route via a deeply embedded cultural memory and a collective will inscribed in the city and its artifacts, but in the end he approaches the same problem as Venturi and Scott Brown, although from the opposite angle, i.e., how to represent unity. Venturi and Scott Brown must attempt to extract a "difficult whole" out of the seeming random order of the Strip and Main Street, Rossi an underlying diversity out of the seeming permanence of the city.

Following a second axis, no longer that of *representation* of insides and outside, but that of their *production*, leading from the center-suburbia division to the gated communities and their negative foil in poor residential areas, Martin takes the 1972 destruction the Pruitt-Igoe housing complex—emblematized by Charles Jencks and innumerable subsequent publications as "death of modern architecture"[65]—as a prism through which he reads the unfolding of a territorial discourse on security. The Pruitt-Igoe complex had the same year as its demolition become the object of an analysis in Oscar Newman's *Defensible*

---

65. Jencks, *The Language of Postmodern Architecture*, 9. The photograph of the event also appears on the back cover, which even more contributed to making it into an iconic event in all senses.

Space, which pointed to the efficiency of fences and boundaries for the enhancement of security, and to the need to develop architectural techniques for what also in Newman's vocabulary is termed "territoriality." Parameters like density and cost efficiency were here correlated to the variation of crime rate in order to produce a concept of "defensible space" as the "last stand of the urban man committed to an open society" (Newman, cit. in UG 18). In Newman's discourse, which forms the other side of postmodern claims for the liberation of style and aesthetic complexity, urbanism essentially becomes a problem of risk management, and security issues an integral part of a neoliberal form of governing that in its archipelago structure realizes the utopian diagram on the interior, instead of projecting it onto a distant, exterior, and non-existing (*ou-*) *topos*, in a double movement that is "[a]ctively *unthought* by postmodernism" (21). The island or enclave becomes a basic unity of the postmodern city, mirroring the slum and the refugee camp; it is however both closed and open, just as the Utopia once imagined by Thomas More.[66] There is not simply an opposition between the island and the network, but a mutual implication that organizes the topological structure of postmodernity.

Considered as an ending of modernism, this topological twist similarly impacts on *History*, the second of Martin's chosen points of entry. Starting out from Tafuri's diagnosis of the exhaustion of the avant-gardes, as they were being replayed in the seventies, specifically in the debate between "Grays" and the "Whites," and continuing through Fukuyama's "end of history" proclaimed

66.　Martin here draws on Louis Marin, *Utopiques: Jeux d'espaces* (1973) and Fredric Jameson, *Archaeologies of the Future: The Desire Called Utopia and Other Science Fictions* (2005). Curiously enough he here (as well as in the reference to literature on utopia, UF 208 note) omits Françoise Choay's *La règle et le modèle*, which derives a systematic and specifically architectural theory of utopia as a "model" on the basis of More, and follows its ramifications up to early modernism. See also chap. 6, below some fifteen years later, Martin refuses to see these figures in terms of an end, neither as the tragic endpoint of the avant-garde as in Tafuri and Dal Co's reading of Mies's Seagram building,[67] nor as the triumphant fulfillment of liberalism, but as a mutation on a different level, unwittingly captured by Fukuyama's image of the end of history as the "victory of the VCR." What this image signals, is rather a sense of history as reruns and bootleg copies, rewind and fast forward, which for architecture implies that it is no longer faced with media from the outside, but has itself become one of them and forms part of a continual modulation. Tafuri's assessment, "the war is over,"[68] i.e., that the battles of the avant-gardes no longer make any sense given their exhaustion as possibilities for a radical change, is for Martin premature; in fact it marks a moment of transition to a situation where Tafuri's "plan"—the project aiming to plan and control the future that after the 1929 crash was absorbed into the State-Capital complex, depriving modernism of its founding illusion—gives way to a different kind of game, the two sides of which are the simulations of nuclear war and risk, and Buckminster Fuller's more benevolent version in the World Game whose stake is the fate of "Spaceship Earth." Both of them play with "the very *idea* of the graspable" (UG 34), and indicate the extent to which history is remodeled as a permanent instability that calls for preemptive risk management strategies and displaces the modernist utopias of form as a blueprint for the future.

The famous reading of John Portman's Westin Bonaventure Hotel in downtown Los Angeles proposed by Jameson is thus

67. This interpretation, which suggests that Mies's late work should be understood in terms of silence and a withdrawal of language, has generated a long series of responses. For a discussion of the idea of silence as negation, see chap. 1 above, and in more detail, my *The Silences of Mies* (Stockholm: Axl Books, 2008).

68. See Tafuri, "The Ashes of Jefferson," in *The Sphere and the Labyrinth The Sphere and the Labyrinth*, trans. Pellegrino d'Acierno and Robert Connolly (Cambridge, Mass.: MIT, 1990), 301.

only half of the story, and Martin proposes that the spatial dislocation characteristic of late capitalism's cultural logic on another level gives way to integration in a flexible system of pattern-based networks. As it is made visible in gridded surface of the curtain wall, which can be taken as an epitome of post-war corporate architecture's remodeling (rather than betrayal) of prewar modernism, the organizational complex, of which the later postmodernism is a continuation and intensification, constitutes an *organicism*, rather than a denaturalization and a disenchantment of an earlier auratic experience; the aura that once signaled the autonomy of art is neither falsely perpetuated nor destroyed, as was once Benjamin's alternative in the face of mechanical reproducibility, but dispersed and spread out on a systemic level that operates by way of integration through images, patterns, and a technique for handling stimuli and affects. As such, this complex is equally a *biopolitical* machine, and it does not work by substituting ornament for structure or image for substance, as was initially argued in Venturi and Scott Brown's opposition between the duck and the shed, and then repeated in countless analyses, but through a technology of organization that makes all such oppositional terms ceaselessly trade places in a "total flow" (Jameson) of modulation, which in turn is integrated in a network of networks.

These shifts, Martin suggests, fundamentally depend on the translation of all variables to an ecology or environment of (proto)-linguistic unities, a concept that extends from the natural to the political and the aesthetic, which is also how he proposes to understand the third parameter of the postmodern, *Language*. Once more referencing the Gray-White debate, which opposed the proponents of autonomous form, purified of its social mission, to those opting for a content derived from history or mass culture, Martin proposes that it "made no difference that one side spoke of semantics while the other spoke of syntactics, because these two levels ultimately converge—again, quite pragmatically—in architecture's new home within an ecology and an economy of signs" (UG 66). Just as the domain of History, this ecology or economy is a space of risk that must be stabilized and contained through techniques that draw on the "arts of the environment," a concept that goes back to Kepes and the project to establish a language of vision as the basis for a universal semantics. The discovery of architecture as a language with its own rules provides it with an illusory disciplinary autonomy inside a more general sign ecology, at the same time as it also turns it into a key for the deciphering of this totality, which is no doubt the reason why it lends itself so easily to becoming a monadic representation of the postmodern as a whole. Martin traces this development through several steps up to Eisenman's project for a pure architectural syntax, which on the one hand wanted to emancipate itself from the legacy of humanism, on the other hand can be read as its most far-reaching affirmation, as an inquiry into the deep structure or general grammaticality that a priori conditions all possible architectural statements. It is, Martin suggests, a "preemptive effort [...] to retain sovereignty over an environment that attains to existence only as a signifying system," which is also "a very real global economy naturalized as a global media-ecology" (66f), and in this sense the search for deep structures is also a language of power, a unity of language that is fundamentally political.[69]

"We shall emphasize image," Venturi and Scott Brown once declared, and ever since, the idea of postmodernism as a reign of images without anchoring, of free-floating simulacra that strike back at and undermine the real, copies without originals that

69. Martin here draws on the polemic against Chomsky's linguistic tree-structure in Deleuze and Guattari's *Thousand Plateaus*, which asserts that language is fundamentally as transmission of slogans, but also orders or "order-words" (*mots d'ordre*).

subvert the hierarchy from which they nevertheless derive, has become deeply engrained. For Martin, this fourth parameter, *Image*, must however not be understood in terms of an opposition, dialectical or not, to reality, where one of the two in the end must take precedence over the other, but as a problem of what we could perhaps, following Deleuze's analyses of cinema's movement-images and time-images, call the *space-image*: how architecture organizes the real precisely through its capacity to become and generate images that themselves are part of it rather than disembodied simulacra floating in a general imaginary.

An interesting case of this would be the decorated shed of Venturi and Scott Brown, which famously opposed itself to the duck in terms of surface and ornaments supposedly emancipated from the demand to express and render legible the inner structure, and in this sense could be taken as paradigmatic examples of free-floating signifiers. But as Martin shows,[70] this cannot be simply identified with an opposition between authenticity and inauthenticity, truth and illusion, as is often the case. Later on, Venturi and Scott Brown would sometimes invert their former claim and ascribe truthfulness and authenticity to the sign, as opposed to the false and illusionary transparence of modernist buildings: truth now belongs to signage and decoration that simply say what they need to say, it belongs to surfaces and images that are rooted in everyday understanding, not to arcane experiences of modernist space and structure that in fact are mere illusions.

For Charles Jencks, who a decade later claims to draw the correct conclusions from these earlier debates, the populism

---

70.   And in fact, already the shed-duck opposition is unstable on its own
terms. Martin here draws on the analyses of Aron Vinegar; see Vinegar
I Am A Monument: *On Learning from Las Vegas* (Cambridge, Mass.: MIT,
2008), 49–92, and chap. 2, above.

of Venturi and Scott Brown is inadequate in that it simply inverts the elitism of modernism, and what is required is instead a more comprehensive understanding of architecture as language, which he too develops along the lines of Kepes, eventually proposing an "evolutionary tree" of architectural styles leading up to the natural conclusion of the "radical eclecticism" of a realized postmodernity. But as Martin notes, radicality here means assurance that nothing radical will ever happen, that styles will come and go without ever disturbing the fluctuating yet permanent ecology of global consumerism, which is Jencks's version of the end of history, and in this close to Fukuyama's later proposal. Here too there movement toward dispersal and diversity is just as much integration into a continually recreated systemic equilibrium that feeds on local stylistic innovations.

On the level of *Materiality*, the thesis that any attempt to reach a secure inside will only takes us further out is brought to bear specifically on the relation to the oil industry. Starting out from Philip Johnson and John Burgee's Pennzoil Place (1976) in downtown Houston, Texas, Martin asks how the architectural works partakes and helps to produce the fetish "oil" (itself composed of many parameters), by placing itself at the intersection of finance, technology, aesthetics (the theory of the corner, from Mies onward, by which "architecture can be judged," as Johnson proposed), and organization.

Architecture has, Martin suggests, following David Harvey, something of a premonitory function in signaling the development of capitalism at the same as it, acting in the role of a visual fetish, covers up its real effects: "wherever capitalism goes," Harvey writes, "its illusory apparatus, its fetishisms, and its systems of mirrors comes not far behind."[71] In the case of architecture, this illusory mirroring apparatus materializes the work

71.   Harvey, *The Condition of Postmodernity* (Oxford: Blackwell, 1990), 344.

of ideology, and the ubiquity of reflecting surfaces seems like a perfect illustration of a visuality that in fact conceals by virtue in its spectacular specularity.[72] But as Martin proposes, maybe we should look *at* the mirror instead of *in* it,[73] if we are to grasp what it in fact performs as an architectural device. What these surfaces stage is precisely the ubiquity and placelessness that overtook modernist universality, and their essential character is the modular structure, reflection upon reflection, which provides "the materiality of flexible accumulation" that for Martin is less the "time-space compression" of Harvey than the "quasi-stasis" of the feedback loop (UG 105f) doubling back of the surface onto itself. Rather then mimetically rendering late capitalism, the mirror *belongs* to it, so that culture becomes immanent to capital instead of remaining an exterior reflection. Extending, but also inverting, Jameson's famous and now canonic analysis of the Bonaventure Hotel (its status almost having become equal to Tafuri and Dal Co's interpretation of the Seagram building), which suggests that "the distorting and fragment-

72. In some respects, the architectural image as it has come to be used in postmodernity intensifies a situation already diagnosed by Benjamin. Drawing on a quote from Brecht—"The situation is complicated by the fact that less than ever does the mere reflection of reality reveal anything about reality. A photograph of the Krupp works or the AEG tells us next to nothing about these institutions"—Benjamin suggests that what is needed is a new visual literacy that reads images in search of their hidden social conditions. See Benjamin, "Little History of Photography," *Selected Writings*, vol. 2 (Cambridge, Mass.: Harvard University Press, 1999), 526; for the citation from Brecht, see "Der Dreigroschen-prozess: Ein soziologisches Experiment," in *Werke,* eds. Werner Hecht, Jan Knopf, Werner Mittenzwei, and Klaus-Detlef Müller (Berlin: Aufbau, 1988), 469.

73. Interestingly, the *at* that displaces the *in* implies that we should try to discern something else than the subject as it consolidates and assembles itself by identifying with its mirror image, which in a tradition from Lacan to Althusser has been an influential version of the theory of ideology as an imaginary solution to a real problem, and also situates the subject as caught in the imaginary. There are however also other resources in the Lacanian theory of the gaze and the visible; see note 76 below.

ing reflections of one enormous glass surface to the other can be taken as paradigmatic of the central role of process and re-production in postmodernist culture,"[74] Martin proposes that what is reflected is not the distorted images of the surrounding, the city as an Other that in this doubling becomes dislocated and unreal, as Jameson contends, but the mirror itself, dupli-cating itself to infinity in the feedback loop that replaces the vertigo of the doppelgänger with a seriality recursively turning back onto itself, which Martin associates with the use of serial compositions in minimal art and Warhol.

Such self-reference in one sense seems to prevent there from being anything to discover behind the surface, and yet we must proceed to another level, at which the mirror in inscribed in a larger order, and where its role is to render the outside world invisible: rather than hiding something in its interior, its con-ceals the exterior, which is the modus operandi of postmodern architecture's particular fetishism. The illusion that it produces, Martin suggests, is precisely *that there is just illusion*, that materi-als have become unreal and dematerialized, and in order to per-form this trick, it requires materials organized and assembled in a particular way.

But if the mirror in all of its illusionistic and concealing functions is the paradigmatic object of postmodernism, what or who is then the *Subject* that looks into or at it? Bypassing the Lacanian legacy in most of its ramifications, Martin once more looks at architecture's reflective surfaces, first in order to discov-er how they dissolve subjects as well as objects, but then to ask who this subject is that disappears and then reappears, particu-larly in the form of a new subject of mass-customized consump-tion: a subject whose personality is continually constructed on the basis of available choices and modulations in digital produc-

74.   Jameson, *Postmodernism*, 42.

tion and reproduction, but at the same time becoming invisibly visible in the play of mirror as a second subject on the outside, a bare life that is not recognized, counted, and valued, and yet inextricably intertwined with the first so that the form two sides of the same figure.

Analyzing the prehistory of this development, Martin interrogates two corporate headquarters built for Union Carbide in 1960 and 1982. The first, designed by SOM and Gordon Bunshaft, set in midtown Manhattan, was explicitly intended in order to provide a "striking corporate image," the second, designed by Kevin Roche John Dinkeloo and Associates, located in the rural setting of Danbury, Connecticut, instead turns inward and assumes a stealth mode towards the exterior, which however return as a haunting reflection, a ghost, on the inside. The Park Avenue building can on the one hand be taken as an epitome of the postwar corporate architecture as it entered its generic phase, with its modular, gridded curtain wall, standard office partitions, and rationalized design all the way down to its drinking fountains and light switches. On the other hand it was already deeply marked by the new discourse of human relations, as comes across in the stress of flexibility; intended for the "Orgman," the emerging corporate subject baptized by William Whyte, it also signals a shift inside the organizational complex toward the idea of the corporation as a family and its employees as sentient beings in need of psychological monitoring and support.[75]

In the second building these incipient features have become essential; intended to be as invisible from the exterior as possible, the new headquarters was to be a world closed in upon itself, with each of the 3300 identically sized office rooms fur-

75.   On Whyte and the Organ, see Martin, *The Organizational Complex: Architecture, Media, and Corporate Space* (Cambridge, Mass.: MIT, 2003), 121.

nished and decorated according to the individual taste of its occupant (with a limited choice among thirty preset styles). Based on extensive analyses of interview material gathered from employees in the former building, the design flattened spatial hierarchies and eventually turned into a snowflake structure, developed with the help of computers, that would provide all offices with views and adjacent parking facilities, diminishing the need to spend time outside the building. Through this personalizing strategy, each employee becomes an individual subject, equipped with a particular taste and capacity for choice, all of which was fed into computer banks to ensure optimal quality and fit between form and individual.

Two years after the completion of the building, the catastrophe at the manufacturing plant in Bhopal, India, took place, resulting in more than three thousand casualties. Martin details the efforts of Union Carbide to avoid legal and financial responsibilities, and what emerges is first the moral disconnect between the architectural inside, designed for maximum comfort of those in the "family," and the almost complete indifference toward the victims for a disaster that most likely was caused by negligence and cost-cutting. Between these two sides, the inside and the outside, there is however not a relation of mere externality, but a mutual implication that belongs to the logic of corporate action on a globalized world. On the level of architecture, Martin projects this connection back into one of the central sections of the building, containing the cafeterias or "living rooms" adorned with mirrors, where the postmodern Orgmen were surrounded by scintillating reflexes of themselves. These mirroring surfaces, while performing a perfect closure where the corporate subject meets only fragments of itself, also indicate something like a gap, a breach or tear in the screen,[76] where the ghosts of

76.   The use of the term screen may be incidental here, but can be extended in the direction of a different Lacan than the one of the mirror stage,

Bhopal can be glimpsed. This generates a double result: first the hyper-individuated subject, a "dividual" in Deleuze's term, continually fashioning itself through new choices and through the production of infinitesimal differences in taste; then, as its ghosting double, a subject that is not counted, a "bare life" that remains outside while still being the precondition and material base for the production of the inside, from its architectures to all other technological, social, and economic assemblages that uphold the division between the two. In this sense, the architecture in Danbury can be said to be haunted by the victims in Bhopal already before the event as such; it is a "counter-memory," an "inverted memorial" or a "memorialization in advance" (UG 143) of the deaths that it must attempt to exclude in order to secure the innermost interior of the corporate world.

And finally, the question of *Architecture*—or, put more straightforwardly, "What is to be done?" (UG 147) Is there a possibility of acting in another way than to register and multiply symptoms, an agency of architecture that would provide it with a way of both moving inside itself and yet taking a stance outside of its illusory autonomy? Towards the end Martin calls upon the idea of utopia as projection in a way that once more

who would also be contemporary with the initial stages in Martin's version of postmodernism. The 1964 seminar on *The Four Fundamental Concepts of Psycho-Analysis* develops an interpretation of the gaze as *objet a*, which takes several steps beyond the mirror stage and the earlier theory of the Imaginary, in fact comes close to the theory of the breach on the visual field sketched out in Martin's analysis of the second Union Carbide headquarters (even though Lacan's theory has no explicit political connotations, nothing prevents us from adding them from our present vantage point). What dispossesses the subject, Lacan suggests, is gaze that does not belong to the subject, but comes from the outside, from the visible as such, and the artwork is set up as a screen, or a "taming of the gaze" that allows the subject to play with the threat emanating from the visible, although always with the risk that the screen will be pierced through. For a reading of Warhol, particularly the *Disaster* series, along these lines, see Hal Foster, *The Return of the Real* (Cambridge, Mass.: MIT, 1996).

draws him close to Tafuri's damning analysis of modernism as "project and utopia," and yet wants to stake out a different path.[77] The first step in this is that the real, in the sense of various cynical "realisms" that have been opposed to modernism's utopias, must be "derealized," dislodged from its seeming massivity and inevitability, which however cannot mean to simply opt for utopia as the simply unrealizable other, but rather, Martin suggests, means to learn to live with its ghosts.

As a concept that signals the limit between the real and the unreal, the present and the haunting of the past (even of the future, if we follow the reading of the second Union Carbide headquarter), for Martin the ghost harbors the possibility of projection that re-arranges past, present, and future, not by replacing what exists with something entirely new that often stands in for the lost Whole, but by extracting something other from a past that remains non-actualized.[78] If the postmodern moment was a crisis of projection as the possibility of a practice envisioning radical alternatives to the status quo, it also rendered utopian thought unthinkable, against which Martin proposes not a simple revival, but more something like an attentiveness to how certain figures of thought will not go away, but ceaselessly return inside that which is meant to exorcize them, calling upon a different use of our imagination, first in order to

77. The terms *progetto* and *progettazione* are highly polysemic in Tafuri, as Martin notes, especially if one also looks at the earlier book *Teorie e storia*, and it is doubtful that it can be reduced to something that would be a mere "ideological phantasm" (UG 149). See also chap. 1, above, note 16.

78. Martin here comes close to what Deleuze has called the virtual, which cuts through the divide between possible and real, and introduces another sense of temporality. The absence of a reference to Deleuze here is probably due to Martin's implicit polemic against how he has been appropriated in certain strands in contemporary architectural theory, notably as a precursor of the digital. There is however no need to restrict the relevance of Deleuze's thought to this particular reading; for more on this, see chap. 6 and 7, below.

simply see them in architecture's mirror, and then possibly to break out of it.

Surveying a series of cases, meandering from the mid seventies to mid eighties, from Paolo Portoghesi's Venice Biennale and the historical props of the Strada Novissima (1980), via James Stirling's Neue Staatsgalerie (Stuttgart, 1983), Oswald Mathias Ungers's project for the Wallraf-Richartz Museum (Cologne, 1975) and his Deutsches Architekturmuseum (Frankfurt am Main, 1984), Charles Moore's Moore-Rogger-Hofflander condominium complex (Los Angeles, 1978), and up to the Internationale Bauausstellung (Berlin, 1984), Martin traces the ghost of a utopia that returns inside structures whose claim is to *not* add up, and *not to do so once and for all*, as if inadvertently obeying utopia's call for a future beyond which only more of the same is to be expected (the same in postmodernism being the surface fluctuations of styles that only confirm the homeostasis, as in Jencks). So for instance do the various forms of the *promenade architecturale* proposed by Stirling and Ungers no longer lead to synthesis: the Neue Staatsgalerie stages a "narrative of passage with no end " (UG 157), while the gridded forms of the Wallraf-Richartz Museum, in their seemingly classicizing axiality and symmetry, intensify the desubjectifying traits of a functionalist like Hilberseimer, effectively dislocating the subject that appears in the drawings only to be excluded. The most obvious derailing of the *promenade* takes place in Moore, whose Los Angeles condominium excels in passages and stairways that "lead nowhere, but with great precision" (161). Martin's suggestion is that there remains something utopian in this very *refusal*—which itself is carefully constructed, it must be remembered—to add up, a refusal of the project that itself takes on the form of a project: it is the forever deferred possibility of arrival that lends these works their aesthetic significance, and they are always haunted by the modernist specter that they are trying to exorcize, in the process becoming like props or frames for the return of the undead (the "visor effect").[79] Similarly, it is a ghostly presence that is conferred onto the props of the Strada Novissima, just as Ungers's Architekturmuseum, with a house set inside the house, acts as kind of memory of architecture—a house haunted by Architecture as it comes to frame itself the space of the museum.

But if the path of haunting leads inwards, into Architecture and its memory, what routes would take us out? Maybe, Martin proposes, there is something deep inside architecture that can be retrieved for other purposes, although his final suggestions remain insecure and tentative. As we have seen, in the territorial form of the island there survives something like an echo, to be sure ghostly, of utopia, precisely in its otherworldly aspirations, and Martin looks to, among others, two projects for Berlin, John Hejduk's Berlin Masque (1981) and Cities within the City (Ungers, Koolhaas, Riemann, Kollhoff, and Olaksa, 1977). Hejduk's project is an image of the divided city: two blocks separated by a twelve foot hedge and only connected by a small bridge, each inhabited by only one person, the east one looking toward the future, the west one toward the past; they are wait-ing, disconnected, for a history that would allow them to cross the bridge, but at present seems unthinkable, like a forbidden exit or entry. Cities within the City, "the most comprehensive diagram of postmodernism's topological cascades" (UG 173), instead works by an internal multiplication, redrawing Berlin as an interior archipelago of enclaves (a theme treated the year after in Koolhaas's *Delirious New York* with the Manhattan grid as the organizing geometric parameter, splitting each lot from

79. Derrida develops this on the basis of a reading of *Hamlet*, of how the ghost always requires a technical supplement, a material device in order to appear at the very limit of appearing; see Derrida, *Spectres de Marx* (Paris: Galilée, 1993), chap. 1.

the other while ascertaining an overarching order). Its utopian gesture is not divisive but conciliatory, in attempting to provide for as variegated architectural spectrum as possible—a multitude of small utopias, which, as Martin note, however runs the risk of wholly fragmenting all collective identities into so many private spheres, neighborhoods, and gated communities.

The promise of a rethought postmodernism, thought through to its innermost contradictions and beyond them, the task of "learning to think the thought called Utopia once again" (UG 179), is poised at the precise point of this reversal, where the retreat into the interiority of Architecture would not take us back to an illusory *autonomy of forms*, but perhaps to a different *form of autonomy* that would restore architecture's emancipatory agency; a way of bringing together inside and outside that would render them legible precisely in their contradiction, a critique of ideology that provides an agency to forms by allowing them to signal their own incompletion, rather than presenting them as a compensatory fantasy. The recent past, read in such a way, would be not be consigned to a past offered up for an analysis that scans its shortcomings in order to know better, but rather constitute a recentness that impacts just as much on the present by splitting it, estranging us from its simple thereness and solidity.

5. Looping Ideology

Architecture, media, and materiality

The relation between architecture and media is intimate, to the point that is seems true that architecture has simply become an integral part of the culture industry of late capitalism. It projects images of cities, regions, and countries, it generates a star system of its own, and it continually feeds contemporary visual culture with a never-ending flow of desirable photogenic material. While this spectacularization on one level is undeniable and forms the general condition of modern aesthetic experience—the same culture of the spectacle pervades the other arts to such an extent that a moralizing critique almost seems redundant, since it often tends to merely duplicate the vocabulary in which the products themselves are couched—other reactions may be more productive than lamenting or welcoming the liquidation of autonomy, and other ways of responding to this situation more fertile than the alternative between rejection and submission.

If the relation between the built environment and the spatialization of power in the electronic media age is to be grasped at a more fundamental level, we must investigate how architecture not only symbolizes or represents media logics on the iconic level, but also how it integrates them into its very tectonic and organizational structure. This integration is not a specifically modern feature, although it is probably the case that our contemporary perception of it has been sharpened, and has made it possible to locate our own position in an unfolding of the media-architecture nexus going all the way back to the invention of the architectural treatise and the new relation between printing and building in the Renaissance, or, depending on the generality at which one defines media, even back to Antiquity.[1] But today architecture also undergoes an inverse movement, where it reaches out to include an urban environment that increasingly appears as a media- or even brandscape,[2] inserting itself into a city that more than ever consists in the production and circulation of desirable images, to the effect that it in the end becomes one more image, perhaps in terms of what Edward Soja has called a "postmetropolitan" condition where old urban forms only remain as an aestheticized scenography.[3] The question seems unavoidable: What would it would mean for architecture to respond critically to this process, not just in terms of a rejection or refusal (such strategies are not infrequent, and not necessarily regressive, although they fall outside of the question here), but in the qualified sense of taking on this process in order to introduce a moment of suspension, division, and reflection?

While pressing, such a question might also be too general and diffuse for any singular answer to be appropriate, and instead of pursuing it on a purely conceptual level, we might do

1. See Mario Carpo, *Architecture in the Age of Printing: Orality, Writing, Typography, and Printed Images in the History of Architectural Theory*, trans. Sarah Benson (Cambridge, Mass.: MIT, 2001), and *The Alphabet and the Algorithm: Form, Standards, and Authorship in Times of Variable Media* (Cambridge, Mass.: MIT, 2011).

2. Pioneering efforts in this area have been in the last decade and a half by, among others, Beatriz Colomina, *Privacy and Publicity: Modern Architecture as a Mass Media* (Cambridge, Mass: MIT, 1994), Bart Lootsma and Dick Rijken, *Media and Architecture* (Amsterdam: Berlage Institute, 1999), Reinhold Martin, *The Organizational Complex: Architecture, Media, and Corporate Space* (Cambridge, Mass.: MIT, 2003), Kester Rattenbury (ed.), *This is Not Architecture: Media Constructions* (New York: Routledge, 2002), Mitchell Schwarzer, *Zoomscape: Architecture in Motion and Media* (New York: Princeton Architectural Press, 2004), Omar Calderón, Christine Calderón, and Dorsey Peter, (eds.), *Beyond Form: Architecture and Art in the Space of Media* (New York: Lusitania Press, 2004), and Scott McQuire, *Media City: Media, Architecture and Urban Space* (Los Angeles: SAGE, 2008), to name but a few.

3. See Edward Soja, *Postmetropolis: Critical Studies of Cities and Regions* (Oxford: Blackwell, 2000).

better to interrogate particular works. This is not because any individual work or body of works would answer it by presenting methods or strategies that could subsequently be generalized—the confidence in the general, generic, and ubiquitous is in fact part of the problem—but because some of them intensify this condition, render it legible in the form of a specific constellation, and in this force us to think the intersection of concepts and particulars, general structures and individual experiences. The trajectory of Rem Koolhaas and the OMA (Office of Metropolitan Architecture) in this respect seems exemplary,[4] and the particularly exemplary example that will guide us here is the new television center in Beijing. At present still unfinished and not in use, it condenses in a singular gesture many of those issues that seem ambivalent and undecidable, which also means that it detaches itself from the present moment in ways that engage the sense of time, and the limit or framing of what is contemporary. In an obvious sense, the current incompletion, even though accidental, is one such dimension, and writing about a work that presently only exists in part poses problems of method.[5] But in this case it also highlights the relation between me-

4. To be "exemplary," Kant says in the *Critique of Judgment* (§ 46), *exemplarisch*, is not the same as to an "example" (*Beispiel*) of a general concept. The exemplary work does not depend on imitation or on the following of a rule, but it can serve as a *rule for the judgment* of other artists. The reference to Kant's aesthetics may seem to skip over far too many historical mediations and take us back to a historical moment that is irrelevant to present concerns, but it still points to a valid intuition of what it means for any type of artwork to be *singular* and non-deducible from any preceding determinations, and yet call upon a *judgment*, both in the spectator as well as in another artists that picks up predecessor's problem and in this necessarily transforms it. For Kant, judgment refers to taste, which first seems to enclose it in a particular sphere severed from cognitive and normative issues, and in the sense the judgment provoked by works like OMA's would be thoroughly different; on the other hand, as Kant also suggests, judgments of taste have a profound bearing on cognitive and moral issues, precisely because of their autonomy.
5. During a visit in Beijing in November 2008, the author and a colleague, Helena Mattsson, were granted access to the building site. The outer

dia and architecture: the material that will be examined consists largely of texts, statements, and images, and in this sense it is an architectural work that for most people still exists only in a mediated form. And finally, as we will see, the interpretation also engages the work's own future social and political performance, which is still in the balance in a non-trivial sense.

The imbrication of architecture and media, in the widest sense of the term that includes images and the transmission of information in general, is a recurrent theme in Koolhaas, and it calls for a type of questioning and reflection that transcends approaches that focus primarily on the formal aspects of buildings. In fact, as we will see, the need to rethink the formal perspective in architecture, both with respect to production and analysis, is a constant theme in his writings and projects, from the early texts on Manhattanism, through the ideas of bigness and the generic city, and up to his present work. As an "incubator" or "condenser" of new social forms, he suggests, architecture must actively approach a positive condition of formlessness that displaces perceptual wholeness and integration, and attain an intractability to formal decoding that does away with traditional legibility and aesthetic analysis.

It is however equally true that such a refusal of legibility in itself produces a different type of image quality, which has been projected in a long series of publications and exhibitions that undoubtedly are one of the reasons why the work of Koolhaas

shells of the buildings were at the time in principle ready, while the floors and interiors, i.e., most of those aspects belonging to the organizational logic that the present essay addresses, were still under construction. Since then one of the three buildings in the complex, the TVCC (Television Cultural Center), was partly devastated by fire in 2009, and has been undergoing repair. The main building was ready in 2012, and today [at the moment of the final revision of this text: January 2016], the Center is completed, and many of its projected features have turned out differently. I have however left those parts of the text that relate to the Center's unfinished state as they are; rewriting them today would amount to writing a different text.

258

and the OMA has gained such immense visibility also outside the architecture world. The projects, writings, and books of Koolhaas and OMA have succeeded in straddling the divide between theory and practice, sophisticated thinking and popular culture, presumably because the sense of urgency they radiate, and because of their refusal to take commonplaces for granted. From the seventies onwards, he has ceaselessly asked the question—which to many might seem to border on the senseless, since it appears to defy the codes of intellectual responsibility as such—why we perceive our present, our cities and architectures, as *lacking* something, as *imperfect*, and why we expect architecture to provide us with this missing thing that would once more make the socius whole. In this there is an unmistakable affinity to the reversal of inherited judgments undertaken by Robert Venturi and Denise Scott Brown in the sixties and early seventies, closely linked to the emergence of pop art, which was one of the defining earlier moments when the culture of media and electronic images came to disrupt the order and hierarchy of the fine arts, including architecture.[6] The idea of a transformed perception of the architectural lowlands however no longer relates to Las Vegas and the disdained commercial landscape around Route 66, but to urban forms outside the Europe-America axis, and it no longer defines itself in relation to the divide between the modern and the postmodern, even though traces of this can be mobilized for ironic purposes.[7] The shift in perception proposed here however only marginally thrives on formal ambiguities of architectural language, and instead engages the multiva-

6.   For the relation to Venturi, see Rem Koolhaas and OMA, *Harvard Design School Guide to Shopping* (Cologne: Taschen, 2001), 590–617.
7.   See, for instance the "Generic City," in Koolhaas and OMA, *S, M, L, XL* (New York: Monacelli Press, 1995): "The style of choice is postmodern, *and will always remain so.* [...] Instead of consciousness, as its original inventors may have hoped, it creates a new unconscious. It is modernization's little helper." (1262)

lence of programs and social forces, ultimately the very place of architecture in the socio-political world. In a way that is much more radical than Venturi, Koolhaas challenges us to perceive, feel, and think differently, in order to see whether this could release a new of inhabiting social space, and from the analysis of Manhattanism to the work on shopping, and Asian and African urban forms, the task he as set has been to trace a genealogy of urbanity as a radically unfounded experience, liberated from traditional humanist, moral, and aesthetic values.[8]

These more overarching claims about urbanism and politics are then reflected back onto the architectural level, where the condition of non- or aformality that extends from the perceptual to the tectonic, on the one hand rejecting traditional ideas of form, one other hand approaching a kind of formal extreme, seems to be able to tell us something about our present cultural condition, not just about a particular stage in the development of design discourse, but also about our desire for an architecture that would articulate the contemporary moment in its very illegibility and its contradictory qualities.

From the vantage point of media studies, the relation to architecture may seem fairly straightforward and pragmatic. The

8.   The beyond-good-and-evil perspective often adopted by Koolhaas may have a background in Nietzsche, although he is to my knowledge never mentioned in Koolhaas's writings. This connection may seem far-fetched, but in fact Nietzsche's writings had a profound influence on many of the early modernists (Corbusier, Behrens, Mies,, etc.), for whose large-scale projects Koolhaas shows a great sympathy; he may even be said to be one of the few to continue modernism with other means, in the transformed socio-political space of a globalized postmodern capitalism. For Nietzsche's influence on early modernism, see Alexandre Kostka and Irving Wolfarth (eds.), *Nietzsche and "An Architecture of Our Minds"* (Santa Monica: Getty Institute, 1990), and Fritz Neumeyer, *Der Klang der Steine: Nietzsches Architekturen* (Berlin: Gebr. Mann, 2001). For a critical discussion of Koolhaas's writings on urbanism as an attempt to retrieve a Nietzschean position, see William S Saunders, "Rem Koolhaas's Writings on Cities: Poetic Perception and Gnomic Fantasy," *Journal of Architectural Education*, Vol. 51, No. 1 (1997).

discourse of media architecture has largely occupied itself with questions of organizational, political and financial conditions, whereas the buildings that house them have appeared more as practical solutions, although sometimes as part of a symbolical surplus value and marketing strategies. And yet, here too there is a possible convergence that might take it into the heart of the problem at stake. Precisely because of the global nature of media, and of the ubiquity of identical images and info bits that encircle the planet, there has been a recent emphasis on issues of how media, in the increasing detachment of their mode of production from a national level, organize a perception of transnational space that in turn impacts both the national and the local levels. They are instrumental in producing, and not simply mirroring, a geo-political order of the near and the distant, the relevant and irrel-evant, danger and safety, into which the subject and its agency are inscribed, an order that then through local institutional systems on a descending scale exert a profound influence on our experi-ence of everyday space. This "spatial turn"[9] within media studies thus emphasizes location as an active creation of place, as a pro-duction of a system of centrality and periphery through which differences in the social order (political and public vs. private and individual, corporate vs. public facilities, public vs. restricted ac-cess) are negotiated. Ranging from the individual experience in front of the screen to the way in which society as whole is ex-perienced and organized in terms of spectacle and participation, enjoyment and repulsion, identification and alienation, the space creation of media is operative on all levels.

In this process, physical architectures may seem peripheral and merely as outward symbols of networks that shape space

9.   For a discussion of this, see the introduction in Staffan Ericson och Kristina Riegert (eds.), *Media Houses: Architecture, Media, and the Produc-tion of Centrality* (New York: Peter Lang, 2010), where a first version of this chapter was originally published.

on a more diffuse and yet decisive level. But as works of architecture, they also give a specific materiality and concrete localization to the nodal intersections that tie together vast informational networks that seem independent of spatial form. Architectures bind immaterial networks to locations, and while each one of them is contingent and expendable from the point of view of the media system, they sometimes produce a surplus of sense that make them into instruments of thought instead of just reflexes of an order that transcends them.

In this sense we may say that the two modes of analysis evolve toward what perhaps could be called a "zone of indiscernibility"[10] where they are entangled, but also undergo transformation: the spatialization of media necessitates a different take on materiality, a kind of immaterial materiality, just as the informatization of architecture loosens if not severs it ties to the obdurate identity of the physical object. The introduction of the architectural object into this more extended form of spatial analysis implies that it too be understood as a part of a flow of information that it both reflects and attempts to control; inversely, it also means that flows of information must always have forms of spatial anchoring, points of centrality that are produced through particular technologies.

As have been shown by Saskia Sassen in a series of works,[11]

10.   I borrow this term from Deleuze, who often employs it to designate an interstitial dimension where two seemingly opposed terms: human-animal, body-soul, image-virtual image, etc., enter into a mutual "becoming" that transforms both of them without establishing a third synthetic term. The term can be taken as a transformation of Leibniz's thesis on the "identity of indiscernibles," i.e., that two entities that have all internal properties in common are identical, an argument that Leibniz sometimes uses to refute the objective reality of space and space and time; for Deleuze, indiscernibility does not imply identity, but rather proliferation of infinitesimal differences, so that the two indiscernibles does not become one, but are opened toward a common multiplicity.

11.   Among Sassen's many writings, see "The Topoi of e-space: Global Cities and Global Value Chains", in *documenta x: Politics Poetics* (Stuttgart: Cantz, 1997), *Globalization and its Discontents: Essays on the New Mobility*

globalization in no way implies that place and space simply lose their significance, instead it depends on a new spatial system with centralized nodes that control flows of money and information, and organizes certain types of financial, legal, and technical skills and competences. These places constitute points of intersection in the "global value chain," and while they on one level may break out of the national system and their surrounding hinterland, they are nevertheless dependent on national policies as frameworks for the production of centrality. For Sassen this means that we must reconceptualize the very notion of *locality* or place-boundedness, which also has consequences for our understanding of architecture as built form. Objects like buildings and various forms of real estate, in fact all types of concrete environments, are in the process of becoming liquefied, both due to the invention of new financial instruments and to the increasing presence of electronic communication that these instruments presuppose. The city becomes an amalgamation of various informational circuits that loop through it, and Sassen proposes that we should think of these spaces as *topological* (connecting that which in normal metric space is remote) rather than *topographical*. Instead of a dematerialization or a general loss of place, this is a *production* of new forms of centrality: worldwide dispersal of financial and corporate operations requires central managements with their specific corresponding material structures, hypermobility always has an irreducible physical side, and the important issue is what *kind* of materiality and place-boundedness this imbrication produces, how it engenders differently organized space-times that also makes possible other forms of political acting. Architecture is one such means of production, and furthermore one that in privileged moments may be able to

of People and Money (New York: New Press, 1998), and *Territory, Authority, Rights: From Medieval to Global Assemblages* (Princeton: Princeton University Press, 2006).

reflect and express these processes, prying them apart and making them into objects as well as moments of critical thought.

Inserting the building into a network structure, where it is no longer solely a form that can be characterized by morphologically based concepts drawn from the history of art or architecture (is it still modernist, or postmodernist, or something else?), or simply a reflection of external functions, but a conduit for information, behavior, actions, and perceptions that works equally by way of its material structure, the image quality that it projects, and the abstract machine or diagram of power relations that it actualizes, thus requires a different kind of theoretical approach. The materiality of architecture is in this sense only to a limited extent equivalent to the matter that it contains, and if the technological framing that enables matter to hold together in a particular configuration pervades matter itself into its innermost fibers, the idea of architecture as an art that in essence deals with gravity, with matter as opacity, weight, and resistance, must be rethought.[12] On the other hand, this does not simply eradicate form, but pushes it in a different direction, so that it comes be generated from a much wider set of parameters, of which Koolhaas's "informal" may one important indication, as long as we don't take it as simply a negation, but rather a way of taking form to the limit.

The founding work for any such analysis remains Beatriz Colomina's analysis of architecture as a mass medium, which was instrumental in taking architectural history beyond its nor-

12. Hegel seems to have been the first to develop a systematic analysis of gravity and opacity as the foundation of architecture, which is why it for him is the first, but also lowest art form, destined to be superseded by other forms that gradually detach themselves from matter and weight. For a discussion of this, and of Hegelian motifs inform the nineteenth-century discourse of tectonics, see my "Hegel and the Grounding of Architecture," in Michael Asgaard och Henrik Oxvig (eds.), *The Paradoxes of Appearing: Essays on Art, Architecture, and Philosophy* (Baden: Lars Müller Publishers, 2009).

mal confines and sources.[13] Drawing on close readings of buildings and plans, texts and statements by Le Corbusier and Adolf Loos, but also on a rich material of images from the archives, she theorizes the architectural object as only one part of an entire cycle of representation that aims to generate a global effect on the perceiving subject. The look of modernity achieved in different ways by Corbusier and Loos was fundamentally invested with desire, it called for an affective response, and mobilized a whole structure of fantasy. In producing a set of distinctive images of what architecture could be, traversing all available media, they also launched a pedagogy of vision in several senses. Their works wanted to teach us a way of looking and perceiving, also in the sense that the buildings themselves were intended as machines for viewing, as Colomina shows in Loos's self-contained and theatrical interiors, and Corbusier's framing of the exterior through the building itself understood as a camera. Finally, in presenting us with vistas framed and edited by architecture, they made the subject enter into visibility as itself an image—a possibility for a "publicity" of the subject that would later be theorized in varying fashions, from the expanding sense of an involvement in and a grasp of the social, to the objectively paranoid structure of a gaze emanating from the world itself as a terrifying Other,[14] which still echoes in many debates on the

13.   Another aspect of such a "look" would lie in how it mobilizes a discourse on fashion, which is no doubt also relevant for Koolhaas, and not only because of his work with Prada. For a discussion of fashion and early modern architecture, see Mark Wigley, *White Walls, Designer Dresses: The Fashioning of Modern Architecture* (Cambridge, Mass.: MIT, 1995).

14.   This is developed in Lacan's model of the gaze as *objet a*, in his 1964 seminar. For Lacan the gaze (*le regard*) comes primarily from and belongs to the visible as such, which means that it threatens the subject, which in turn uses the image as a "screen" (*écran*) to protect itself, which is the function of art as "gaze tamer" (*dompe-regard*). He develops this with reference to Baltrusaiti's analysis of Holbein's painting *The Ambassadors*, in which the anamorphous pictorial structure plays a central role, which allows the subject to hold death and finitude at bay while still acknowledging it. See Lacan, *Les quatre concepts fondamentaux*

nature of public space.[15]

If we concieve of the architectural object in terms of a uni-laterally understood late modern theory of autonomy (which is often, too simplistically I think, attributed to Adorno),[16] this type of reading may seem to simply dissolve it into an set of cultural determinations that deprives it of its status as work, and thus of its capacity to negate, resist, and make a difference in the world. Material forms are increasingly defined in relation to their communicative potentials, which is interiorized into their very fabric, and architecture morphs into what was once called "electrotecture,"[17] in a process which could be traced into the minute details of architectural production, from building materials to designer software and the virtual ubiquity of the computer, not only as tool, but as a generative instrument in its own right. Some theorists and architects, no longer arguing

de la psychanalyse (Paris: Seuil, 1973). The paranoid (a term not used by Lacan) dimension of this theory is underscored in Norman Bryson, "The Gaze in the Expanded Field," in Hal Foster (ed.): *Vision and Visuality* (Seattle: Bay Press, 1988). See also chap. 4 above, note 76, for a similar use of the screen in Reinhold Martin's analysis of the Union Carbide Headquarters.

15. I discuss this further in "The Antinomy of Public Space," in Maaretta Jaukkuri (ed.), *Art and Common Space* (Trondheim: The Trondheim Academy of Fine Art, 2013).

16. While such an attribution is obviously not simply false, it does not exhaust the possibilities of continuing his problem into the present, in a way that reframes some, thought not all, of his philosophical presup-positions. In architecture, this would bear specifically on autonomy as an effect of the *frame* (see the Introduction above for more on this): architecture in the most general sense frames things and events, and to this extent is would be the precondition for autonomy; but at the same time, it has the capacity of turning this framing condition into a work in its own right, which thus would inhabit the limit of autonomy. Such a "parergonal" (Derrida) status would indeed withdraw it from aesthetic theory in the traditional sense, which is why it is becomes particulary pertinent for the kind of aesthetic reflection I am trying to develop here.

17. See the pioneering discussions in ANY 3, 1993, *Electrotecture: Archi-tecture and the Electronic Future,* and Mark Taylor and Eesa Saarinen, *Imagologies: Media Philosophy* (New York: Routledge, 1994).

from the point of view of historical research, but from a standpoint closely associated with certain strands in contemporary image production in media and publicity, have suggested that this mediatization implies that we must take leave of an older model of critique and theory, even that the very idea of critique as such is obsolete, and that we have to move on to a purely affirmative stance. For, given this type of implication of the architectural object into a larger set of parameters,[18] which introduce themselves at the most basic physical level, what sense could there be in talking of autonomy, let alone resistance?

Today the development seems to follow two tracks (which obviously often cross in any given case, sometimes reinforcing, sometimes contesting each other): in the first, the structure of electronic capital is interiorized into the design process itself, and becomes a type of generative aesthetic, and in this it can be seen as a sequel to the industrial look, the machine aesthetic, of early modernism, which is now being redeployed on another technological plateau.[19] While many of its proponents

18. The term "parameter" has become a key term in what is today understood as "parametric design," which, apart from its obvious practical usefulness, in many cases appears to pursue a quest for an all-encompassing scientific discourse from which design solutions could be generated. If parametric design, at least according to one of its most vocal proponents, Patrik Schumacher, is a "New Global Style," or the "autopoiesis of architecture, which is the self-referential, closed system of communications that constitute architecture as a discourse in contemporary society" (Schumacher, cited in Staffan Lundgren, "The Digital Dissolution of Disegno," *Site* 33 [2013]: 279), then the pushing of form to the limit I think points in the opposite direction, and shows the self-reference and closure of the system of communication to be a technological and ideological fantasy.

19. The key theorist in this development was for a long time Greg Lynn, whose writings and projects were instrumental in developing a new kind of morphogenetic aesthetic. Lynn was also significantly enough the first, at least to my knowledge, to introduce Deleuze in a more productive fashion in the debate on architecture; see Lynn, "Forms of Expression: The Proto-Functional Potential of Diagrams in Architectural Design," *El Croquis* 72 (1995), and the essays collected in *Folds, Bodies & Blobs* (Brussels: La lettre volée, 1998).To some extent this was also

stress the objective, scientific, and even deductive nature of such work, it is however still part of *aesthetic* based in a reading of form, with all the limitations that this implies. The second option, which I think is the proposal by Koolhaas and OMA (even though metaphors and tropes from the first version are frequent here too, I find this less important for what is at stake), is to address the new form of capital on the level of urbanism. In this version, aesthetics is usually repudiated in favor of politics, even though it is a politics that is often understood in a very broad sense—which, to be sure, is not in itself a guarantee that this does not amount to yet another aestheticized version of politics, this time transferred to the levels of infrastructures and urban systems, or that it avoids the risk of becoming another version of the technological sublime, where the marvels of engineering and computational power foreclose all critical questions. The particular quality of the work of Koolhaas and OMA, is that it willingly and explicitly meets those risks head-on, and to the extent that it is successful, it also allows us to understand why such risks can be neither simply avoided nor embraced. The critical in this sense has to do with the production of *divisions* and conflicts in the real itself, rather than with assuming an external stance outside of the system in order to pass a judgment. The image of surfing, or riding the crest of a wave sometimes us by Koolhaas has not surprisingly led him to be perceived as advocating cyni-

an emphasis on form as non-semantic, diagrammatic, and as resulting from the application of a highly specialized technological design expertise. For Koolhaas, the emptying out of the semantic in favor of an idea of pure performance and operation misses what is actually happening: "Semiotics is more triumphant than ever—as evidenced, for example, in the corporate world or in branding—and the semantic critique may be more useful than ever." Rem Koolhaas and Sara Whiting, "Spot Check: A Conversation Between Rem Koolhaas and Sara Whiting," *Assemblage*, No. 40 (1999): 46. For a general discussion of how Deleuze was introduced into architectural theory, see Marko Jobst, "Why Deleuze, why Architecture" in Hélène Frichot and Stephen Loo (eds.), *Deleuze and Architecture* (Edinburgh: Edinburgh University Press, 2013).

cism and opportunism, but it may also be understood as pointing to the moment when things are about to break up, where they unleash those forces whose cohesion can make something at one moment emerge as entirely solid, another moment as consisting of myriads of disjointed parts—none of which is an illusion, but belong the wave itself.[20]

The image of the crest, then, rather than implying a simple affirmative stance, or an outright acceptance of the powers that be, can be read as an attempt to insert a prismatic wedge into the light of the present, so that it is split up in several possible directions and paths; it makes it possible to think the present as an intersection of many times, pasts, and futures, and it releases an unmistakable critical and *reflexive* potentiality, precisely by suspending the kind of judgments that we normally make.

CCTV: Program and image.

The CCTV center in Beijing is a key work in the contemporary discussion of media and architecture: it combines a superb visibility and an iconic status with a highly complex architectural treatment of the program, and it claims to integrate the development of digital media into the structure itself, which in turn is assumed to project a different mode of behavior. There is no doubt a split here between the fascination with the achievements of technology and engineering, and an underlying political agenda: OMA themselves sometimes take pride in

20.   See for instance the retrospective comments on *Delirious New York*, where Koolhaas speaks of Manhattanism as a "divorce between appearance and performance: it keeps the illusion of architecture intact, while surrendering wholeheartedly to the needs of the metropolis. This architecture relates to the forces of the Grossstadt like a surfer to the waves." "Elegy for the Vacant Lot," in *S, M, L, XL*, 937; see also "New York/ La Villette," in *OMA-Rem Koolhaas: Architecture 1970–1990*, ed. Jacques Lucan (New York: Princeton Architectural Press, 1991), 160. For the non-cynical reading of "surfing" adopted here, see Jacques Lucan, "The Architect of Modern Life," in ibid, 37.

describing it as "the world's most advanced postmodern build-ing," whereas they on other occasions stress the political role, presenting the building as a possible blueprint for a more demo-cratic and transparent society.[21]

The complex is set on a 10-hectare site in the new Central Business District in Beijing, and comprises two high-rise build-ings and a service center. The main headquarters is 230 meters high, with a floor space of app. 400.000 m2 (which makes it into the world's second largest office building, and no doubt also the most complex: all the 55 stories have individual floor plans), and is intended to house more than 10.000 employees. It contains administration, broadcasting, and various production facilities, with the intent of integrating the whole production process in a "singe loop of interconnected activity."[22] OMA describes it as two structures arising from a common production platform partly located underground: one dedicated to broadcasting, the other to research and education, both of which merge at the top to create a cantilevered headquarters for the management. On this sense the building forms a loop not just in terms of pro-gram, but also in a physical sense, comprising horizontal and vertical sections whose aim is to "establish an urban site rather

21. "We are engaged," Koolhaas says, "with an effort to support within [China's] current situation the forces that we think are progressive and well-intentioned [...] We've given them a building that will allow them to mutate." *Time Asia*, May 2, 2004. To some extent the split between these two agendas is due to the context of presentation, as we will see, but it also corresponds to a deeper problem lodged within architectural practice and theory as such. This problem is obviously not particular to Koolhaas, although his projects tend to make it acutely visible in a reflexive form, which is why he becomes an easy target for criticism, but also the reason why, as the present essay argues, his work indeed consti-tutes *works* in a qualified sense, and call upon, even demand, a response not just from within the architectural profession.

22. These and the following quotes relating to the CCTV project are all taken from one of OMA's official websites, as accessed January 22, 2009. The same text, with small variations, can be found in Koolhaas, *Content* (Cologne: Taschen, 2004).

than point to the sky," eschewing the two-dimensionality of the "soaring tower" for a "truly 3-dimensional experience."

Beyond this visual impact, the loop structure is also intended to have a behavioral effect on the employees: the adjacency of different functions is intended to produce an awareness of the activities of the co-worker and foster a spirit of collaboration, materialized in the structure of the building, inwardly as well as outwardly. The third and perhaps most striking dimension of the loop is that the building, although a high-security complex, is planned to allow for a path of public access that runs through the entire structure, and offer views not only of Beijing CBD, but also of the production process itself. Through glass partitions the visitors are to be able to inspect the making of television, at least ideally speaking in all of its details, thus producing a sense of transparency, literally as well as metaphorically. As we will see, this loop is what brings together, in a contradictory unity, the program and the (still conjectural, it must be remembered) reality of the building's modus operandi: it projects the idea of transparency and openness while at the same time making legible and visible the current constraints on this idea, holding these two aspects together without erasing the difference between them.[23]

The second major building, the Television Cultural Center (TVCC), is a more traditional 115,000 m2 high-rise (although designed to comprise a number of variations, ranging from the irregular façade to the hotel rooms, which all have an individ-

23. My proposal here intersects with the analysis proposed in Shannon Mattern, "Broadcasting Space," *International Journal of Communication* 2 (2008), from which I have drawn many valuable insights. My accent however falls slightly differently; for Mattern, the fact that the building embodies contradictions runs "contrary to the designer's claims" (869); in my reading, the point is that the embodiment, even exacerbation, of such contradictions has been part of Koolhaas's different projects from the outset. The strategically planned introjection of social conflicts is, I would argue, what makes it possible for them to achieve the status of "works" in a qualified sense, and this is what warrants my understanding of them as allegorical.

271

ual layout), and includes a five-star hotel, a visitor's center, a large public theatre, and exhibition spaces. Unlike the CCTV, this second building is meant to be freely accessible to the public, and it has a more conventional layout. These two buildings, together with the third low-rise structure containing technical facilities, are set in the Media Park, which is intended as a landscape for public entertainment and outdoor filming areas that will form an extension of the central green axis of the CBD, all of which indicates the extent to which the complex is itself intended as a spectacle or amusement park, and forms part of a kind of "spectacularization" of media production itself.[24]

The location of the CCTV in the urban fabric of Beijing is also understood to be a decisive factor in the production of a new image of centrality. From the point of view of the symbolical geography of Beijing, it is an efficient way to forge a different Chinese identity, more oriented towards economic growth than party power, or, more precisely, a projection a particular type of state-run capitalism. Located on the West-East axis defined by the Chang'an Avenue, and not the North-South axis of impe-

24.   Helena Mattsson has analyzed how the corporate takeover of public spaces tends to transform architectural boundaries between interiority and exteriority, public space and workplace, through the creation of "event zones," where production and spectacle come together, also as a means of compensating for the gaps and losses in our understanding of the real processes of production and consumption on a global scale. Specifically in media institutions, these assemblages are geared towards the production of a public, a public that, precisely, is seen more as consumers of a spectacle. These architectural structures, she argues, should not be understood as disciplinary, but rather as "spaces of security" in Foucault's sense of the term: instead of regulating everything by clear-cut spatial divisions, they "let things happen," even though they entail new forms of discipline that operate through desire and affect instead of regulation, and in fact can be reconnected to certain aspects of Bentham's Panopticon overlooked by Foucault. See Mattsson, "Staging a Milieu," in Jakob Nilsson and Sven-Olov Wallenstein (eds.), *Foucault, Biopolitics, and Govermentality* (Huddinge: Södertörn Philosophical Studies, 2013), and, on the particular spatial strategies used in the BBC headquarters in London, Mattsson, "The Real TV: Architecture as Social Media," in Ericson and Riegert, *Media Houses.*

rial power, where we find the Forbidden City and Tien'an Men Square, the building symbolically redraws the map of Chinese power, by opposing itself to the old television center located close to the centers of political administration. Built a Soviet style in the early 1980s, the old building is a fairly anonymous high-rise, heavily guarded and allowing for no public access, and it can be taken as an epitome of all the qualities from which that new leadership in China is attempting to move away.

On the level of imagery, the new CCTV building has a clearly iconic status (the idea of an icon is also embraced by OMA, who regularly use the term in their publicity). The iconic function also comes across in the way in which the building has already long since been used in advertising, as a symbol for a new Chinese modernity that is opening up towards a global mediascape. On the local level, its impact can be measured by its frequent present in cartoons, and it has come to form part of common jokes, where it is compared to a pair of trousers. But as a political brand, it must also unite several contradictory features: the emphasis on openness and communication flows must co-exist with an image of centrality and authority, above all because of the role played by CCTV as a unifying mechanism in Chinese media culture, This iconic quality can thus obviously also meet with negative reactions, even a sense of fear, since the building is sometimes understood as an image and embodiment of governmental power and repression.

The role of the CCTV headquarters as a window to the world is however just as insecure as its status in the quickly changing domestic Chinese mediascape.[25] There is at present only one English-language channel being broadcast by CCTV,

25. For an analysis of the Chinese media system as it appeared in the initial stages of the CCTV project, see Zhengrong Hu, "Towards the Public? The Dilemma in Chinese Media Policy Change and Its Influential Factors." Research Paper, John F. Kennedy School of Government, Harvard University, 2005.

and it is debatable to whom this test probe is in fact directed: presumably not to the Chinese population, but just as little to the foreigners, who would undoubtedly choose other means to acquire information. The Chinese-language channels are mostly perceived as mouth pieces of the government, and have little credibility, and especially so since the dominance of CCTV goes hand in hand with many recent attempt to thwart local media, and to integrate them in a system of central command.

Furthermore, an additional question posed to any centralized media system, and CCTV in particular, is how to make the shift into the digital age. The current phase of growth may be seen as a way to meet the challenge of new media through expansion and diversification. This attempt is however not unlikely to fail, which would mean that a project like the CCTV is doomed in advance, and that the creation of a symbolical and highly prestigious architectural gem may in fact be read as an act of desperation. Given the insecurity of the current media situation, and the role of central television in an increasingly digitalized media environment, there is a fatally ironic sense in which the building may be understood as the future tomb of CCTV, a way of embalming the past—and in this sense it would, in a curious twist, corroborate Adolf Loos's claim, made at the beginning of the media age, and by an architect who wanted to resist the modernist culture of images and representation, that the only authentic architecture is the *tomb*.

Inside/outside

The CCTV project picks up many formal characteristics from Koolhaas's previous works, some of which can be traced back to his earliest works, the projects at the AA, *The Berlin Wall as Architecture* (1972), and *Exodus, or the Voluntary Prisoners of Architecture* (1972, together with Elia Zenghelis, Madelon Vriesendorp, and Zoe Zenghelis), above all the idea of split between inside and outside that is not there to be overcome in terms of an underlying or projected unity to be achieved, but rather exacerbated to the highest degree so that it itself becomes a reading instrument of sorts, almost like an optical tool that allows us to see in split fashion.

The student work on the Berlin wall, while staying within the limits of an interpretation of an already existing structure (as was the requirement for the AA "Summer Study"), proposed a reading of the wall as form, or rather as a cut at the limit of form, a "formless modern,"[26] which announces several of the themes that would later occupy Koolhaas. The title is obviously provocative, and its neutral, or even indifferent and cynical ring seems to place it a no-mans-land beyond good or evil. But, as Koolhaas would later say, it also recorded a moment in his own development that hinges on the question of architecture's place in the world: confronted with the reality of the wall, it was "as if I had come eye to eye with architecture's true nature," and "the sixties dreams of architecture's liberating potential [...] seemed feeble rhetorical play. It evaporated on the spot." (225–26) The division, exclusion, and imprisonment produced by the wall, was it not "the essential stratagems of *any* architecture?" (226), and a "warning that—in architecture—absence would always win in a contest with presence" (228)?

Connecting the shifting morphologies of wall as it meandered around West Berlin to minimalist sculpture, Japanese gardens, Sol LeWitt, Frank Gehry, John Hejduk, Schinkel, and many others, Koolhaas was struck by its "*total mockery of any of the emerging attempts to link* form *to* meaning *in a regressive chain-and-ball relationship*" (227). Discovering that its meaning changed almost by the hour, that it reflected events and decisions far away

26. Koolhaas, "Field Trip: A (A) Memoir (First and Last...)," in Koolhaas and OMA, *S, M, L, XL* (New York: Monacelli Press, 1995), 22. The following quotes with page number are all drawn from the same text.

and "forever severed the connection between importance and mass" (228), implied that one must cease to "believe in form as the primary vessel of meaning" (227). Rather than a form or an object to which a stable meaning might be ascribed, the wall should be approached as a "situation" (219) that evolved from moment to moment, precisely because it itself was only an "erasure, a freshly created absence," a "first demonstration of the capacity of the void—of nothingness—to 'function' with more efficiency, subtlety, and flexibility than any object that you could imagine in its place" (228).

But beyond this experience of the ultimately vacuous nature of any discourse that would settle for mere form, there was another discovery that blurred the line between different types of judgments in an even more disturbing way: "The greatest surprise: *the wall was heartbreakingly beautiful* [...] it was the most beautiful remnant of an urban condition, breathtaking in its persistent doubleness. The same phenomenon offered, over a length of 165 kilometers, radically different meanings, spectacles, realities. It was impossible to imagine another recent artifact with the same signifying potency." (222) And furthermore, as if to suspend, or corrupt, the ethical-political aspect of this beauty, the wall "suggested that beauty was directly proportional to its horror" (226).[27] But rather than an aestheticizing of politics and violence, as seems to lie implicit in the title—which in a sense could be also read in reverse: *architecture as a Berlin Wall*—the project implied a radical questioning of architectural aesthetics. The void produced by the wall, the violence and death that it inflicts, belong to ar-

27. In a later text on "The Terrifying Beauty of the Twentieth Century," Koolhaas returns to the Berlin Wall project and proposes that "the interpretation of the Berlin Wall as a park enlivened by a Zen sculpture made it possible to imagine the villas along with it" (S, M, L, XL, 208). The association to terror would of course traditionally be understood in terms of the sublime rather than beauty in the line running from Burke to Kant and onward. Many of the characteristics that Koolhaas later would ascribe to "bigness" also echo the traditional sublime.

chitecture's founding moments, and there is no way architecture can extricate itself from it, just as the "attraction" it generates, precisely when it in its most violent and terrifying moments becomes "hypnotic" (229), must be analyzed as a moment in our desire, and not as an unfortunate accident that could be undone.

Exodus, the second and more ambitious project, develops the theme of separation and violence, although at first in a seemingly benign inversion of the Berlin Wall. It does not deal with an architecture whose disastrous ethical and political implications are beyond doubt, instead, in opposition to a wall that positions architecture as the "guilty instrument of despair," it asks whether it is "possible to imagine a mirror image of this terrifying architecture, a force as intense and devastating, but used instead in the service of positive intentions."[28] If the Berlin Wall was an imposed structure, *Exodus* was based on free choice—but in the end, both of them however lead to dystopian results that, even though not equal, yet have a disturbing proximity.

The basic gesture of *Exodus*, presented in a sci-fi language that both mimics and mocks the rhetoric of the project description, was the creation of a gigantic architectural enclosure, formally akin to the earlier typology of megastructures,[29] to be placed over the whole of central London. The residents would freely

28. From the project description in *S, M, L XL*, 5. The following quotes with page number are all drawn from the same text.

29. As Reyner Banham noted, the idea of megastructure had by the early seventies lost much of its appeal, and the flexibility that it earlier had promised now appeared as part of a control society; see Banham, *Megastructures: Urban Futures of the Recent Past* (London: Thames and Hudson, 1976). Koolhaas would later set his idea of bigness apart from the idea of megastructures, and suggest that the latter was only "a very safe Bigness" that "never lands, never confronts, never claims its rightful place—criticism as decoration" ("Bigness," *S, M, L, XL*, 504). *Exodus* may be read as an attempt to bring out the dystopian implications of this idea by pushing it to the limit; the ironic take on megastructure surfaces already in the notes to the Berlin wall project, where "'Famous' students present megastructures made of sugar cubes to universal approval of grinning Archigramesque teachers." (*S, M, L XL*, 215)

decide whether they would choose to live inside the structure, in a life of luxury, lacking nothing, but without the possibility of ever leaving, or outside, in a life of misery and deprivation, but with the freedom of movement. Thus, here too were find "Division, isolation, inequality, aggression, destruction: frontline of architectural warfare" (11), and the transformation from guilt and despair to a secluded and enclosed happiness proves to be almost entirely reversible: the exodus only takes us into the heart of the world's irresolvable contradictions.[30]

The attempt to solve urban problems by radical planning was here turned on its head: the creation of two "totally desirable alternatives" becomes a brutal division that reinforces the logic of incarceration, which is implicitly revealed to have been an integral part of the architectural utopianism of the preceding decade, and one might add, in turn reflects the projects of revolutionary architecture in the late eighteenth century.[31] The

30.   As Felicity D. Scott points out, the idea of exodus has strong parallels in the Italian Autonomia movement from the same period, which may have indirectly influenced Koolhaas through the work of Superstudio; see Scott, "Involuntary Prisoners of Architecture," *October* vol. 16 (Autumn 2003). The theory of exodus, as it has later been presented in a systematic fashion by Paolo Virno, implies a step out of the capitalist logic that draws on its most advanced forms and sets up an alternative social form; see Virno, "Virtuosity and Revolution: The Political Theory of Exodus," in Michael Hardt and Paolo Virno (eds.), *Radical Thought in Italy: A Potential Politics* (Minneapolis: University of Minnesota Press, 1996). The strategy of Superstudio can however be read in many ways, and as Pier Vittori Aureli suggests, it can also be understood as a way of exacerbating the spatial logic of capital to the point where it breaks up from within, although this in the end proved to be a mere duplication of the same logic; see Aureli, *The Possibility of an Absolute Architecture* (Cambridge, Mass.: MIT, 2012). To me this seems to be the underlying proposal in *Exodus*, which in this sense can be read as grim parody of the idea of radical autonomy. The idea of autonomy obviously contains all these possibilities, from immanent intensification to a radical step outside, and many of the projects of the period are characterized by this polyvalence. For an overview of the context of the Italian left, see Aureli, *The Project of Autonomy: Politics and Architecture with and against Capitalism* (New York: Princeton Architectural Press, 2008).

31.   *Exodus* antedates Foucault's reading of the Panopticon by three years,

interiority produced by the exodus from the deteriorating outside—which in turn would lead to the latter degenerating into a
"pack of ruins"—sealed off by the prohibition against receiving
messages from without by the "Jamming Station" (9), in the
end proves to be not the infinity of pleasure, but imprisonment

In a series of variations, *Exodus* calls this upon to the radical
utopianism of infinite desire—the inhabitants of this "strip of intense metropolitan desirability" are those that are "strong enough
to love" architecture, they are "ecstatic in the freedom of their architectural confines," and will be provided with "collective facilities that fully accommodate individual desires" and offer an "or-
namental frenzy and decorative delirium, an overdose of symbols"
(7).[32] This theme culminates in the final section, "Avowal," where,
in order to "express their everlasting gratitude the Voluntary

and may be read as developing, *avant la lettre*, the possible transformations of panopticism in late capitalism. As Felicity D. Scott suggests,
"The 'voluntary prisoners of architecture' would reside in a postdis-
ciplinary structure, but one haunted by an archeology of disciplinary
society as it gave way to a logic of control" ("Involuntary Prisoners of
Architecture," 86). This can be seen in OMA's 1979–81 study for the
renovation of the Koepel prison in Arnhem, Netherlands. The prison
was based on the Panopticon principle and solitary confinement, which
today have been reversed, even though this, paradoxically enough, has
not meant that the Koepel has suffered the same fate as other and later
model prisons, since its "spatial surplus" in the end has proven more
open to flexibility than later architecture with its claim to a form-
function fit. If no particular spatial order, OMA argues, as such seemed
capable of allowing for the new and unpredictable uses that inevitably
would become necessary due to shifting ideas about detention, the proposal must instead be a "prospective archaeology, constantly projecting
new layers of 'civilization' on old systems of supervision," so that the
"sum of modifications would reflect the never-ending evolution of systems of discipline." See "Revision," *S, M, L, XL*, 234–252, cit. at 241.

32. Jonathan Crary, who crossreads Koolhaas and the urban futures of J. G.
Ballard, interprets Koolhaas on the basis of Tafuri's claim that the recurring problem in modernism was how to deal with the anguish of urban
experience: Koolhaas's proposal in *Exodus*, Crary suggests, is neither to
cherish speed, freedom, and the expansion of perception brought about
by technology, nor to lament the richness and depth of experience obliterated by modernism, but the creation of an anachronistic interstice. See
Crary, "J. G. Ballard and the Promiscuity of Forms," *Zone* 1/2 (1986).

Prisoners sing an ode to the architecture that forever encloses them." (20) In the end, the hedonist utopia however proves to install a circuit of pleasures and desires that merely revolves endlessly around an empty satisfaction, as in the section "Allotments," which is poised as an place of quiet and repose, where the voluntary prisoner may "recover in privacy from the demands of intense collectivism," and yet seems to summarize the whole of the underlying logic: "Time has been suppressed. Nothing ever happens here, yet the air is heavy with exhilaration." (19)

If these early student projects are suffused with a critique of the innocence of the utopianism of the sixties, and call for an understanding of the "ambiguous and dangerous" power of architecture,[33] they are also testing grounds for ideas that would later become central in Koolhaas's later work. Both in the *Berlin Wall* and *Exodus*, there emerges the idea of an architecture that breaks free from traditional legibility by its sheer size (which he later would speak of in terms of "bigness"),[34] a fascination for ar-

33. Koolhaas, "Sixteen Years of OMA," in *OMA-Rem Koolhaas: Architecture 1970–1990*, 162. Here Koolhaas explicitly takes on some of his predecessors, notably Archigram, Archizoom, and Superstudio: "The tone of these productions was anti-historical, relentlessly optimistic and ultimately innocent. 'Exodus, or the Voluntary Prisoners of Architecture' was a reaction to this innocence: a project to emphasize the power of architecture is more ambiguous and dangerous." Continuing through *Delirious New York*, this was a "polemic with the aspect of European Modernism" (ibid). There are to be sure also many links and allusions to early utopianism, notably Thomas More's *Utopia*, whose spatial implications became the object of an extended analysis a decade later by Françoise Choay, in *La Règle et le Modèle: Sur la théorie de l'architecture et de l'urbanisme* (Paris: Seuil, 1996), 171–213.

34. As seems to be the case in the theory of the skyscraper as "automonument," presented later in *Delirious New York*: "Its physical manifestation does not represent an abstract ideal, an institution of exceptional importance, a three-dimensional readable articulation of social hierarchy, a memorial; it merely is itself and through sheer volume cannot avoid being a symbol—an empty one, available for meaning as a billboard is for advertisement." Koolhaas, *Delirious New York: A Retroactive Manifesto for Manhattan* (New York; Monacelli Press, New York, 1994 [1978]), 100; henceforth cited in the text as DNY with page number.

chitecture as a practice that acknowledges and even exacerbates divisions and contrasts, and perhaps also, in a germinating form, the idea of a loop or Möbius strip: a figure with two sides that run in parallel and never intersect, two separate worlds in an infinite division: inside and outside, East and West, affluent and poor, where freedom and restriction are not opposed as plus and minus, but are shown to be implicated in a structure that folds back on itself. The theme of an inside and an outside that are both autonomous and joined together to form a contradictory whole has continued to be operative in Koolhaas's subsequent work, and we will see its both structural and metaphorical, or, as the term will be, "allegorical," implications for the CCTV center.

The work that first gained Koolhaas international fame was the book *Delirious New York* (1978), where many of the ideas that still influence his work were first developed, even though they later may survive only in a displaced or inverted form. Here we find a radical farewell to any idea of a an urban form that would be rooted in nature, and a celebration of a "culture of congestion" that radically accepts and even attempts to intensify those traits in modern urban culture, which in so many of the postwar recantations of modernism appeared as its disastrous result. Koolhaas's is a different modernity, opposed to the version provided by Corbusier and early CIAM, excavating other names and resources; it is a "history of the fantastic,"[35] which is also the history of fantasy and desire, which takes us from the city to the idea of Metropolis.[36]

35.   Jean-Louis Cohen, "The Rational Rebel, or the Urban Agenda of OMA," *OMA-Rem Koolhaas: Architecture 1970–1990*, 9. The retroaction proposed by Koolhaas, Cohen writes, "measures and slices the body of architectural history with his retroactive scissors," and "transforms, by detaching them from their contexts, grand simplifying paradigms which characterize certain projects of the German *neues Bauen* or the Russian constructivists into complex and pertinent structural agendas" (ibid).

36.   Among the many predecessors to the idea of Metropolis, the case of Hilberseimer is rarely cited, even though his book on *Grossstadtarchitektur* (1927) in many respects seems an important ancestor of *Delirious New York*. The "cell," which in Hilberseimer's Metropolis is what through its

This rewriting takes the form of an inversion of the classical idea of the manifesto, which attempts to program, project, and control a not yet existing future,[37] and Koolhaas instead proposes a "retroactive manifesto" for Manhattan: Given that "to exist in a world totally fabricated by man, i.e., to live *inside* fantasy" is what we desire, and that what fuels our imagination is a vision of a "hyperdensity" and the city as a *"paradigm for the exploita-*

repetition dislocates the traditional urban form, may be taken as an early version of the parceled structure that the grid makes possible.

37. This would confirm to the temporal logic of the plan, as analyzed by Tafuri (see chap. 1, above). Koolhaas's relation to Tafuri's critical history is complex: on the one hand, his way of reading history, decontextualizing it in order to find material for his own projects, is in many respects eminently operative; on the other hand, he sometimes appears to subscribe to Tafuri's dismantling of the amalgamation of project and utopia, i.e., of any idea of an architecture that would proscribe the future and anticipate a liberated society, and instead embrace the idea proposed in *Teorie e storia dell'architettura* that "the only possible way is the exasperation of the antitheses, the frontal clash of the positions, and the accentuation of contradictions." From Tafuri's point of view, *Delirious New York* seemed to have appeared too late to become part of his reading of American modernism, and the references to "the cynical play of Koolhaus" (sic), and the "'jokes' of Koolhaas" in the essay "The Ashes of Jefferson" (written between 1976 and 1978) seem incidental; see Tafuri, *The Sphere and the Labyrinth*, trans. Pellegrino d'Acierno and Robert Connolly (Cambridge, Mass.: MIT, 1990), 279 and 300. Interestingly, the text which begins by locating itself at the precise moment in time when Koolhaas's book was published, and points to a blockage: "New York, 1978: few large buildings under construction [...] while an economic crisis of uncommon proportions grips the 'capital of the twentieth century.'" (ibid., 291) The general matrix for Tafuri's reading of New York is however close to several of Koolhaas's proposals. Citing Nietzsche's fascination with Venice, Tafuri speaks of "the prophecy that the city of lagoons launches to the future: the city as a *system of solitudes,* as a place wherein the loss of identity is made an institution, wherein the maximum formalism of its structures gives rise to a code of behavior dominated by 'vanity' and 'comedy'" in a "metropolis of total indifference and *therefore* of the anguished consumption of multiplied signs." (ibid) Perhaps one could say that Koolhaas is the most conscious, monstrous, and yet paradoxically loyal disciple of Tafuri, who cannot be accommodated within the latter's conceptual and historical schemata that he as it were observes from the other side, from the vantage point of what he often refers to as a modernism without *guilt,* which applies particularly to the archeology of Manhattanism proposed in *Delirious New York.*

tion of congestion" (DNY 10), what *would* a manifesto have looked like, which would have produced exactly this result? In this he obviously opposes, but also inverts Le Corbusier's famous criticism of Manhattan for lacking a generating idea: the point is to find this idea *post factum*, a "*theoretical* Manhattan, a *Manhattan as conjecture*" (11).

This inversion of the temporal logic of the manifesto requires a different form of analysis, and Koolhaas, assuming the role of "*Manhattan's ghostwriter*" (DNY 11), provides us with a missing story, from the first settlements to the skyscraper, which also highlights names that had been if not erased, then at least marginalized in official architectural discourse (notably Wallace Harrison, Raymond Hood, and Hugh Ferriss, who emerge as the true heroes of Manhattanism). The developmental line he traces was unconscious, and necessarily so: it results from a logic that was never planned, but is more akin to a natural process. The retroactive dimension however also contains a projective part, which surfaces in the "Fictional Conclusion, " which presents a number of architectural projects as the bearers of a future Manhattanism that still remains to be practiced and elaborated. The theory is thus retroactive in the sense that it unearths a possibility that was lost, or at least obscured, in the postwar period, when Manhattanism began to dilute and eventually abandon its principles. The grid structure of "Manhattanism" was only a transitory phenomenon—and in fact, as Koolhaas suggests, the subject of *Delirious New York* "passed into premature senility before its 'life' was completed" (DNY 11; see also the "Postmortem," 283–292, that leads over to the fictional conclusion).

What, then, are the basic tenets of Manhattanism, developed in a particular place and time, and yet endowed with a power that will allow them to mutate into other urban forms? The founding concepts, the *grid*, *lobotomy*, and the *schism*, all follow from a first division that is never an explicit theme and yet guides all the subsequent formal moves: the absolute distance from nature, which is then repeated as we descend further into the urban structure.[38]

The first explicit principle, the grid, develops the split between inside outside in terms of a radical discontinuity between buildings that all negate each other and their context. This division is made possible by the grid structure remaining indifferent to the content that it distributes, so that it allows maximum stylistic and programmatic freedom inside a given enclosure, and provides maximum regulation through an overall structure. In "The City of the Captive Globe," one of the projects that make up the fictional conclusion, Koolhaas pushes this to the extreme: each lot contains a heavy base of polished stone, constituting a series of "ideological laboratories" from out of which "each philosophy has the right to expand indefinitely toward heaven" (DNY 294). The competition for the sky is generated by the grid structure, originally comprising a set amount of lots

38. Marco Tabet reads this divide from nature as an echo of Worringer's analysis of the twin roots of art: empathy derives from a sense of belonging in the world that is developed in the Greco-Roman tradition, abstraction from a sense of fear and terror in the face of a hostile nature, and a corresponding need to create a world of autonomous form, which was developed in the Northern tradition. See Tabet *La terrifiante beauté de la beauté: Naturalisme et abstraction dans l'architecture de Jean Nouvel et Rem Koolhaas* (Paris: Sens & Tonka, 1996), and Wilhelm Worringer, *Abstraktion und Einfühlung* (Dresden: Verlag der Kunst, 1996 [1908]). As Tabet notes, Worringer's book was published by Piper Verlag in Munich, which four years later would publish *Der Blaue Reiter* and Kandinsky's *Über das Geistige in der Kunst*, and even though Worringer had no interest in the art of his own time, and his theory of empathy in fact was opposed to the long tradition that made the discourse of empathy one of the passageways towards modernist abstraction, his book nevertheless may have exerted an important influence in the artistic milieus of expressionism. In Koolhaas's case, this divide however seems to me to result much more from the radical *auto-affirmation* of architecture, in opposition to all pre-given models, whether derived from nature, the sciences or any other source. To be sure, the emphasis on program, events, and social forces can be understood as a step back from claims of autonomy in a simplistic sense, but it does not make architecture subservient to any formal model.

with no possibility of lateral expansion, so that the race for the sky becomes the only solution, producing the skyscraper morphology as a logical outcome. This is an "archipelago" of "Cities within Cities" that each celebrates its own values and develops its own folklore while still reinforcing the system, creating a "city where permanent monoliths celebrate metropolitan instability" (ibid.).

This division is then reflected in an analogous discontinuity inside the building itself, where an act of "lobotomy" disconnects the outside from the inside, so that the skyscraper comes to form a universe of its own: the exterior is only formalism, the interior only functionalism. Finally, in turning each floor into a separate world, the "schism" makes each skyscraper-universe into a multiverse of different uses: "From now on each metropolitan lot accommodates—in theory at least—an unforeseeable and unstable combination of simultaneous activities, which makes architecture less an act of foresight than before and planning an act of only limited prediction." (DNY 85)

These and many other similar early statements were at first sometimes seen as provocations, and to some extent they were; but on another level we can read them as attempts to rethink the basis of architecture, above all, the idea of the city as it morphs into the Metropolis, which has more and more become predominant in the work of Koolhaas and OMA. The analysis of Manhattanism can thus be read as first systematic attempt (prefigured on the earlier student projects, which however still largely remained within the sphere of critique and irony) to emancipate urbanism from a certain idea of planning whose foundational power still determines our imaginary. It would be followed by many other similar although less systematic writings that explore other phenomena normally relegated to the disdained margins of architectural culture: the sprawl of the edge city, the blandness, boredom and neutrality of suburbia, the extensive research projects at Harvard, which have resulted in several publications dealing with emerging urban forms in Asia and Africa, as well as forays into the world of shopping. These investigations may seem unrelated and even opposed, and yet they should no doubt be understood as derived from a central issue, which is the question of how we should conceptualize the urban form of the future without nostalgia.

A decade and a half after the initial analysis of Manhattanism, the central essay "Generic City," which can be understood almost as a kind of cinematic fantasy,[39] would push the decentering of urbanism to one possible conclusion. This is a city beyond any question of historical identity, made up of simulated history, without distinctions between center and periphery, always ready to be reconstructed according to current needs, also on the level of its self-understanding. Those values that once pertained to the European city, and then to its various extensions and dialectical reversals in the US—the delirium of New York being a kind of second beginning of modernity, haunting the consciousness of a European modernist like Le Corbusier—have here mutated into a post-historical state: "the generic city is a city liberated from the captivity of center, from the straitjacket of identity. The Generic City breaks with this destructive cycle of dependency: it is nothing but a reflection of present need and present ability. It is a city without history."[40]

In its fascination with grand scale mutations, the idea of the generic city in a certain way joins the planning visions of the

39. See for instance the final sections in "Generic City," which are shot through with sexual imagery (*S, M, L, XL*, 1263–64). It is perhaps not entirely coincidental that Koolhaas, before embarking on a career as an architect, attended film school and co-wrote *The White Slave*, a 1969 Dutch film noir, and subsequently wrote a script for legendary soft-porn director Russ Meyer, which was never shot. In the first project, the Berlin wall at one point is likened to a "script, effortlessly blurring divisions between tragedy, comedy, melodrama" (S, *M, L, XL*, 222).

40. "Generic City," S, M, L, XL, 1251f.

modernism of the 1920s and '30s, from avant-garde urban theories of Russian "disurbanism"[41] to the *Ville radieuse*, although
with the decisive difference that it now aspires to dislodge the
Planner in favor of a process that integrates chance and contingency. Already in the book on New York, hyperdensity and
the lobotomy of the skyscraper were meant to ensure "perpetual
programmatic instability" (DNY 87) and later, in relation to
the project for the Eurolille terminal, Koolhaas speaks of a "dynamique d'enfer"[42] that replaces overview with a process that
inevitably links parts together into a new kind of aleatory unity
that can only be surveyed and controlled at a meta-level.

These theoretical investigations into large-scale urban structures however also have their parallel in singular projects that
attempt to articulate them in individual objects, and one way to
approach the CCTV project would be to see it as such a point
of crystallization between different lines of research. Here I will
just briefly look at two earlier projects, both from 1989, where
we can see the ideas germinating that would eventually be developed in the CCTV headquarters.

In the project for the new National Library in Paris, Koolhaas
addresses the issue of how to conceive of a building whose main
role is to contain and transmit information, and which in a

41.   The project that first took Koolhaas to New York in the 1970s and the
      Institute of Architecture and Urban Studies led by Peter Eisenman, and
      eventually led to the publication of *Delirious New York*, was the writing
      of a thesis on Russian constructivism and Ivan Leonidov. Parts of this
      material were eventually published as, "Ivan Leonidov's Dom Narkom-
      tjazjprom, Moscow," co-written with Gerrit Oorthuys, *Oppositions* 2
      (1974).
42.   The phrase was coined in a lecture from 1993 entitled "Beyond
      Delirious," where Koolhaas reflects on different ways to organize the
      planning process, and proposes a "a dynamic from hell, which is so
      relentlessly complex that all the partners are involved in it like prisoners
      chained to each other so that nobody would be able to escape." Cited
      from the reprint in Kate Nesbitt (ed.), *Theorizing a New Agenda for
      Architecture: An Anthology of Architectural Theory, 1965–1995* (New York:
      Princeton Architectural Press, 1996), 336.

certain way encloses a whole world within itself. The concrete question of how we can rethink the idea of a library in the present of course resounds with the CCTV project, and the technological transformations since 1989 have indeed only sharpened the problem.[43]

The first answer in the Paris library was to understand the rooms in the building as empty spaces hollowed out of a dense cube comprised of information, and then to work with a high degree of "cross-programming" that would render the traditional divisions of labor within the library insecure and unstable. The rooms hang like suspended organs within the translucent cube, while they at the same time may be described as voids: "In this block," Koolhaas says, "the major public spaces are defined as absences of building, voids carved out from the information solid. Floating in memory, they are like multiple embryos, each with their own technological placenta."[44]

As Fredric Jameson suggests, the emphasis on formal non-legibility (the "block" that contains all the interior organs seems to lack specificity) may be seen as a typical attempt to evade aesthetic perception, just as it opposes Corbusier's idea of the outside as an expression of an inner organization, and instead

43. Already in 1989, Koolhaas writes: "At the moment when the electronics revolution seems about to melt all that is solid—to eliminate all necessity for concentration and physical embodiment—it seems absurd to imagine the ultimate library" (*S, M, L XL*, 606). For a discussion of the other entries in the competition (which was won by Dominique Perrault), see Anthony Vidler, "Books in Space: Tradition and Transparency in the Bibliothèque de France," *Representations* 42 (1993). Vidler suggests that "Koolhaas' mistake was to configure information under the sign of translucency and shadowy obscurity; the politics of the moment insisted, and still insist, on the illusion that light and enlightenment, transparency and openness, permeability and social democracy are not only symbolized but also effected by glass" (131f). As we will see, the play with transparency in the CCTV center takes this idea one step further, and shows how transparency as such can be a means of hiding, and how visibility can become a means of obscuring.

44. *S, M, L XL*, 616

proposes an idea of "incommensurability."[45] But the condition of "non-" or "aformality" here also results from the program itself, of rather from the impossibility of defining and circumscribing the program: the information solid (the image of the network was here only on the horizon, and it would undoubtedly have modified the spatial schema: depicting information as a "solid" today appears counter-intuitive) only allows for embryonic spaces that do not come together into a structural totality.

Something similar takes places in the Seebrügge Sea Terminal project, which, as Jameson notes, even further highlights the quality of a "container" and the co-existence of radically discontinuous activities. Heterogeneity may be to weak a word to capture what is happening here, Jameson suggests, since the co-existence created here implies a "radical absence of ground,"[46] a new groundlessness that begins to produce a category of its own, opposed to the schema of totality vs. part, and instead must be understood in terms of "replication,"[47] i.e., a way to interiorize the split between object and urban fabric that was characteristic of modernism.

The work of allegory

Coming back to the CCTV project, we can see how it inserts these themes—producing and maintaining divisions and yet allowing for an overlap of previously compartmentalized functions—into a new and highly charged ideological context, where the formal

45. In his discussion of Koolhaas, Jameson points to the analogy between Corbusier's idea and what Althusser in a rather different context called "expressive causality," i.e., the conception of society as a totality that expresses itself in all of its minute details and all of its levels, against which Althusser pits the theory of a "structural causality" that allows each level to have a semi-independence, while still hanging on to the idea of a determination in the final instance: see Jameson, *The Seeds of Time* (New York: Columbia University Press, 1994), 135.
46. Ibid., 139.
47. Ibid., 140.

layout of the building constitutes a complex allegory of the role of media in contemporary China, but also and on a more general level, the role of media in the culture of current capitalism. But rather than just conforming to a set of predefined protocols, it stages their inner contradiction, delivering promises that it at the same time cancels, materializing repressive mechanisms while at the same allowing us to see through them in a in oscillation between metaphor and reality, imaginary solutions and actual conflicts, all of which, as we will see, amounts to a kind of ideological operation that also operates *on* ideology.

The project in its current state is in fact the second of two proposals: the first, a traditional *hudong* structure, was rejected, and the second one claims to incorporate the first, and to project the traditional labyrinthine low-rise building into a new spatial configuration Both of these proposals were directed against the idea of the skyscraper, which, as we have noted, was a recurrent typological idea in Koolhaas's and OMA's previous theories, from the grid, lobotomy, and schism that were at the basis of the culture of congestion celebrated in the late seventies, to the idea of the high-rise as the "only remaining typology" in the mid nineties, as is claimed in the essay on the Generic City. Instead, we are now faced with what OMA on their official website baptize the "tragedy of the skyscraper." Today, they suggest, this typology is caught up in a pointless "race for ultimate height" that can only be lost as time goes on, and although it claims to mark the place as significant, it produces repetitive banality, and is unable to act as "Incubators of new cultures, programs, and ways of life." The location of the CCTV center at the heart of new Beijing CBD, replete with high-rise buildings, makes this statement more significant; many comments, also critical ones, have been made about the grand scale of the building, which is probably an effect of the way is presented on websites and in publicity, as a kind of luminous icon that hovers over the cityscape, detached from its surroundings. Seen its actual urban context it in fact appears neither overbearing nor grandiose; it indeed actively challenges and attempts to deal with the chaotic surroundings of the CBD, but not through the exertion of power or by attempting to dominate the environment.

But if the earlier praise of the skyscraper is now rejected, the idea of the container building as a city of its own remains, as a transformed "bigness" and a renewed emphasis on iconicity. This iconic quality is longer achieved through phallic erection, but through a pliant form, which we might understand as a *collapsed skyscraper*, or a structure that refers back to traditional *hudong* typologies, although it must in the end obviously be seen as something new, also in the sense in which it organizes what I here propose to call an allegorical operation.

The organizing structure of the building, which establishes both its outer form as well as the inner trajectory, is the loop. As we have seen, this loop has three senses: the *first* is the physical lay-out the building itself, which loops around itself or forms a kind of knot; the *second* is the production process as a "loop of interconnected activity"; the *third*, and for my proposal most essential aspect, is the loop as a continuous transparency implemented in the structure of the building, a Möbius strip that allows a public pathway through the edifice to co-exist with a closed and sealed-off section for the employees, thus creating a continual sense of public space and communication while at the same time marking the division by impenetrable glass partitions. In this way, production and consumption of media remain separate, and yet they are united in the structure of a building that itself claims to constitute a common space as a spectacle, or a viewing machine that produces the sense of a political unity while at the same time prohibiting it at every level.

Throughout all of its programming, the CCTV complex can thus be taken as part of a general process that shifts the parameters of commodity fetishism by transferring the logic of the spectacle back onto production itself: the commodity no longer being a material object that crystallizes labor, but itself an immaterial entity called information, this transferal is as it were the loop of ideology itself as it transforms its own production into a spectacle. If Marx's analysis in Capital I: 4 proposed that the material production process was concealed in order to endow the commodity with a spectral and mysterious life of its own, making it into "a very strange thing, abounding in metaphysical subtleties and theological niceties,"[48] it is now the process that is displayed, often couched in a vocabulary of participation and interactivity. While this process is not particular to media, it is here that it reaches its highest point of visibility, precisely by folding this visibility back on itself. In the rhetoric and reality of transparency—which should not be distinguished as the false and the true, but rather as two moment of the same process—the production of images is laid out before us a spectacle to be enjoyed, consumed, and in which we are called upon to verify our own participation and agency. Even though certain essential features of this machinery will remain hidden, it would be too simple to say that nothing has changed, and that the workings of ideology production would remain just as concealed as before: the fetishizing of the means of production does not abolish fetishism, but pushes it to a new level, that of a fetishism unfolding through the visible and transparent, in which the desire that holds the subject captive is the desire to itself become part of this very visibility; to monitor and to be monitored, in the end to assure itself of its own existence by applying to the panoptic machinery to itself.[49] It as if the analysis of ideology once pro-

48.   Karl Marx, *Capital*, vol. 1, trans. Ben Fowkes (London: Penguin, 1976), 164.
49.   See Žižek, *Enjoy your Symptom! Jacques Lacan in Hollywood and Out* (New York: Routledge, 1992). Certain strands of Hollywood cinema, particularly during the seventies, developed the theme of conspiracy to the

posed by Marx—the mechanism of a *camera obscura* that gives us the image of the world turned upside down, so that ideas, endowed with an agency of their own, would be the source of reality instead of reality the source of ideas—would have been transformed into a theater of sorts, in which the desire to have the real thing is what drives the illusion.

The CCTV project can be read as an allegory of this co-implication of openness and closure, and in this way it can be said to already display and unmask its own ideological operation, precisely as an occultation at the same time produced and denounced immediately in what it gives to see. The work of Koolhaas is in this sense not so much *beyond* good or evil—a position that he, as we have seen, often seems to assume, as in his statements about the necessity for architecture to ride the crest of the wave, the necessarily "uncritical" stance that must be assumed for there to be any architectural creation at all, or the creation of a "dynamique d'enfer" that empties out the subjectivity of the architect—as it is *both* good and evil in an inextricable double-bind. It carries out the task of projecting an image of openness while at the same time rendering physically legible the current constraints on this promise; it displays its own symptom

level of specific visual paranoia: the surveying gaze that everywhere has to be identified and rejected can, ultimately, be duplicated and directed at the surveyor, as in Coppola's *The Conversation* (1974), in which, in the final scene, the surveillance expert Gene Hackman takes his entire apartment apart in order to find the hidden surveillance camera, but without discovering it, with the ultimate implication that it is the *film itself* that is surveying him, or on the role figure's subjective level: that the entire visual field has become a single gaze that threatens him, a Gaze from nowhere that is no longer human, but which belongs to the system's elusive order. Thomas Y. Levin reads this inversion as an extension of Guy Debord's theory of society of the spectacle, and as a desire for the reality of the image as index; see Levin, "Rhetoric of the Temporal Index: Surveillant Narration and the Cinema of 'Real Time'," in Thomas Y. Levin, Peter Weibel, and Ursula Frohne (eds.) *CTRL-[SPACE]* (Cambridge, Mass.: MIT, 2002), but it can no doubt equally well be understood in Lacanian terms, as the threat emanating from the gaze as *objet a*, i.e., from the order of the visible as such.

in its very structure, and perhaps it can even be said to enjoy its symptom, in the sense that the particular joy that it produces is always and necessarily entwined with fear, violence, and repression, also in a political sense, so that "beauty" becomes "directly proportional to horror," as in the case of the Berlin wall project.

The alternative between a reading that ultimately finds compliance and submission, and one that sees a subversive and emancipatory potential, is also reflected on a more straightforward level in a difference in the communicative strategies employed by OMA. In their various public appearances, they tend to emphasize different things in the Western and the Chinese context, so that the idea of openness seems be aimed at Western intellectuals, whereas in China the technical complexity and the sophisticated engineering solutions are highlighted. While undoubtedly an effect of the different intellectual and ideological contexts of Chinese politics and a Western audience of architecture critics and intellectuals, this can also be taken as symptomatic of a split in the role of the architect, of which Koolhaas would be a paradigmatic case at the present moment: is he a provider of high tech solutions and a seductive imagery that in the end must accommodate themselves to the political order,[50] or a producer of political or social visions that may have the capacity to challenge this very order? On the one hand, the complex publicity maneuvers of the OMA testify to the delicacy of these issues, and to the limitations of architectural work. But

50.   A significant amount of criticism has been leveled against the building from the point of view of engineering, most vocally in a speech at Harvard University in March 2008 by Alfred Peng, who can be seen as representative a more traditionally "official" view of architecture. This stress on technological efficiency also comes across in Peng's statement that the architect has no responsibility for the organization of the building in terms of social structures (interview conducted by Helena Mattsson and the author in Beijing in November, 2008). The source of this conflict is obviously two wholly different ideals of the architect, where Peng and OMA can be located at the extremes of the spectrum.

on the other hand, the materialization of ideology is also the becoming-physical of its contradictions, which allows us to read the work precisely as a *work* in the emphatic sense, in the same way that we read other works of art not just as passive reflections of an existing order, but as interventions, as resistance and transformation.

The work of Koolhaas has been labeled as "postcontemporary,"[51] and maybe this term (which in Jameson's case seems to displace the idea of the "postmodern" in a somewhat obscure manner) can provide us with a clue to the reading of this strange work that is the CCTV headquarters. On the one hand it remains sealed in the contradictions of the present moment, on the other hand it points to a future that it projects, but also *embalms* already in advance, and in this sense it constitutes a point of intersection between different times and histories, between ideological masking and unmasking, which is what I have here attempted to grasp in the term "allegory." It makes our present readable precisely by staging the conflicts inherent in any attempt to grasp it.

51.   Jameson, *The Seeds of Time*, 134.

6. Imagining Otherwise

Utopia and heterotopia

The desire to invent artistic practices that not only intervene in everyday life, but also point to a different form of existence, is at least as old as the avant-garde. Such a desire has often been labeled utopian, but then often in order to be just as quickly dismissed in the name of a return to the safe haven of established institutions and normalized practices, which offer the prospect of normal procedures, predictable outcomes, and consensual communities. Utopia seems discredited: it either takes us away from our immediate tasks, and seals us in an imaginary and even compensatory fantasy, or, worse, it becomes realized in a violent and coercive fashion, and in fact turns out to be the most repressive of systems, since it, to the extent that we understand it as an actual state, by definition must exclude any transcendence.

In architecture, utopian fantasy has a long legacy, and as Françoise Choay has argued, it can even be taken as one the two founding moment of a modernity beginning in Renaissance architectural theory. The architectural treatise provided a set of rules with general applicability, with Alberti's *De re aedificatoria* as the paradigm, in which the eclectic and merely aggregated form of Vitruvius's *De architectura* was subjected to a radical restructuring, becoming a generative logic that starts out from general axioms, descends to particular applications, and finally aspires to create and all-encompassing spatial logic. Utopia, on the other hand, whose initial moment Choay locates in Thomas More, provided both "a critical approach to a present reality and the spatial modeling of a future reality," and an "instrument for the a priori conception of built reality, at the level of the imaginary."[1] The rationalist theory organized around rules however had a complex relation to its utopian counterpart, and for Choay it is the tension between these two conflicting views have organized architectural discourse up to the mid-nineteenth century, where the invention of "urbanism"—with the work of Cerdá as the essential turning-point—brought them together and set modern architectural theory on its course.

Starting from a different perspective, we can note that the late eighteenth century marked the beginning of an almost infinitely ramified discourse of the "project," the unrealized and often unrealizable conception of buildings, cities, and environments, encompassing spatial structures that straddled the divide between architecture and all the other arts, and that it aspired to form the blueprint for a coming society. The title of Manfredo Tafuri's classic 1973 study, *Progetto e utopia*, points to the intimate link between the projective and the utopian moment, and to the fact that their conjunction can be taken the basic structure of modern architecture from the Enlightenment to its eclipse, which Tafuri locates in the interwar period.[2] In this interpretation, utopia is not primarily an invention of the Renaissance, but belongs to the dialectic of enlightenment, beginning somewhere in the middle of the eighteenth century, when the architectural project assumed the function of covering over the conflicts between nature and the emerging capitalist order embodied in the city, as in Abbé Laugier's famous claim that we should understand the city itself in terms derived from landscape painting and the theory of the picturesque, i.e., as a new nature.

1.   Françoise Choay, *La Règle et le Modèle: Sur la théorie de l'architecture et de l'urbanisme* (Paris: Seuil, 1996), 21. For more on Choay's interpretation of Cerdá, see chap. 2, above.
2.   For more on Tafuri, see chap. 1, above.

While the outer limits of both Tafuri's and Choay's chronologies may be debatable—and they cannot be superimposed so as to form a single coherent narrative—it has become a commonplace to say that the projects of modernism pursued utopian goals, fueled by advances in technology and the social sciences. Consequently, the rejection of modernism that would follow may be taken as an anti-utopian quest for the everyday, the already given forms of language, tradition, sense, history, etc. From the various postwar rediscoveries of the classical language of architecture as a continually available depository of forms, ornaments, and styles, to the return to the foundation of meaning in the phenomenological dimensions of place and space, to the acceptance of semiotic flows of Las Vegas as the vernacular of modern culture, the historical depth of Rome or Venice, or the resistance of the regional culture to the false universality of corporate civilization, the rejection of utopia seemed like a common denominator for the postmodern in all of its contradictory guises. While all of these moves obviously cannot be summarized under a return to some imagined past as it was assumed to have existed, but must rather be understood as various ways of remodeling and reinventing architecture's relation to its history—one of the results being the creation of the new figure of the architect-historian who claims a different access to history than the one practiced by earlier art historians, another one Kenneth Frampton's professed "arrière-gardist" position, which can understand itself as strategy for mobilizing history as a resistance against a false theory of progress, and thus as opening a more reasonable path towards true progress—this nevertheless signals something like a waning of utopian energy in the face of a contemporary world increasingly hostile to any radical challenge to the prevailing order.

And yet, beyond the rejection of utopia in its more emphatic forms, the question whether artistic practice can be understood as a site for the emergence of alternative ways of "worldmaking,"[3] of a production of sense that would eschew pre-conceived protocols, refuses to go away. The repression of utopia may lead to its return as a "ghost,"[4] or to the re-channeling of its energies through other conduits, and the project,

3.   "Worldmaking" does here not refer to the form of the creator-God of medieval metaphysics who engenders a universe *ex nihilo*, nor to the form of the Platonic demiurge, who takes on a cosmos threatened by chaos and restores it to a beautiful order, but rather to the idea of philosophy a creation of concepts, that we encounter both in the analytical and the continental tradition of philosophy. There is something to be discovered as soon as we begin to overhear a resonance between the work of philosophers that one many levels are as far apart as, say, Nelson Goodman and Gilles Deleuze. For Deleuze philosophy must in no way be understood as approaching its exhaustion or its end, but ought to reassume its task of creating and constructing concepts. Philosophy, Deleuze suggests, indeed has an autonomy of its own, and should not settle for a mere "reflection" on other spheres of experience (science, politics, art), just as little as the other disciplines need to wait for philosophy in order to reflect upon their own activities. In the case of Goodman, philosophy must accept not only the loss of the ultimate given and the fact that there will be no "unified science" in the sense envisaged by positivism, but also that this was a myth that fundamentally impeded our understanding of the sciences and the arts as "ways of worldmaking." The raw material of this worldmaking must be understood as already existing other worlds, Goodman stresses, and not some brute stuff that would be simply available outside of our categorical schemes. There is no "one" world awaiting us at the end of science, art, or philosophy, although this is no reason for despair. The attitude proposed by Goodman and Deleuze instead implies a constructivism not only with respect to theories, but also of the movement of experience itself—experience is always a kind of *experiment* before it is the interpretation of something given, it is the capacity to transform oneself and to think of a multiplicity of centers, grounds, and worlds. See Goodman, *Ways of Worldmaking* (Indianapolis: Hackett, 1978), and Deleuze and Guattari, *What is Philosophy?*, trans. Hugh Tomlinson and Graham Burchell (London: Verso, 1994), chap. 1. For the link between Deleuze and Goodman, see Nikolas Rose, *Powers of Freedom: Reframing Political Thought* (Cambridge: Cambridge University Press, 1999), 31ff, where he interestingly enough discusses it in term of "governable spaces," i.e., in relation to Foucauldian themes that will be in focus in the following.

4.   As is suggested by Reinhold Martin, in *Utopia's Ghost: Architecture and Postmodernism, Again* (Minneapolis: University of Minnesota Press, 2010). For more on the details of Martin's interpretation of postmodernism, see chapter 4, above.

although now in the guise of a transformed sense of the projective, has indeed returned in architectural discourse, although often in a sense that seems to simply adjust to the imperatives of commodity culture and marketing.

But other avenues should also be possible, ways in which the critical force of architecture could be reinvented, although in a sense that must also imply a transformation of the idea of critique; perhaps we need to reinvent the moment of division, splitting, and shifting—the very etymological root of critique, in the Greek *krisis*—so as to reclaim the force of difference, of that which tears the present apart and shows its layered temporal structure, instead of solidifying it into a monolithic contemporaneity that sees he future as only more of the same. It may be that we need to invent some other vocabulary than that of utopia to grasp these possibilities, and that we need to free the imagination from the alternative between the utopian and the real, in order to think the *work* done by work, the action performed by works on our perceptual habit. In short, to *imagine otherwise* may be tantamount to a profound rethinking of the domain or site of the imaginary as the realm in which artistic practice is supposed to be located. Neither simply the a priori conception of built reality (Choay), nor a covering over of insoluble contradictions of reality (Tafuri), the imaginary could instead be taken as the space of an indetermination that is not simply opposed to a fixed order, but rather uncovers the transformational capacities or virtualities inherent in any ordering.

To ask for the *site* of the imaginary may seem less than obvious, but is has the advantage of already locating the question in a proto-architectural domain, which also, somewhat paradoxically, means to resist, at least initially, theories that locate it in a specific modality of consciousness, or in the relation to the unconscious, even though the question of how, or if, these different versions of the imaginary are ultimately entangled must remain open.[5] To intervene in the site might consist in linking its actual presence to a certain *double*, so that they together enter into an incessant oscillation where they pass over into each other,[6] a virtual place in the sense of an as yet undefined capacity for transformation, linking it in new ways to the past—which obviously may, but need not, involve representation in digital media that rather tend to impose a reified and technological idea of the virtual that too simply and quickly codifies and seals the rich philosophical tradition extending from Deleuze back to Bergson and Leibniz.

Freeing practices, things, and situations from their normal use, either by decontextualizing and rendering them "inoperative,"[7] but in this also preparing for a different use, or by re-

5. The rethinking the imaginary is postwar phenomenology and psychoanalysis, above all Lacan and Merleau-Ponty, provides essential steps in this discussion, and they form a matrix for the discussions of Foucault's later interventions. Lacan's trajectory is exemplary, from the early classic theories of the mirror stage, through the discussion on the "topic of the imaginary," in *The Seminar of Jacques Lacan: Book 1, Freud's Papers on Technique 1953–1954*, trans. John Forrester (Cambridge: Cambridge University Press, 1988), where he still understands the imaginary in terms of a "lure" that ensnares the ego, up to the later work on the Borromean knots. A similar path can be traced through essays of Merleau-Ponty from the 1950s, where he is gradually moving away from the phenomenology or perception based in Husserl toward and ontology of the visible and of the flesh based in Heidegger.

6. The imaginary, Deleuze writes in 1972, is defined "by games of mirroring, of duplication, of reversed identification and projection, always in the mode of the double." Deleuze, "How Do We Recognize Structuralism?," in *Desert Islands and Other Texts, 1953–1974*, ed. David Lapoujade, trans. Melissa McMahon and Charles J. Stivale (New York: Semiotext(e), 2004), 172. The productivity of this theme is indicated by Deleuze's later exploration of the "time crystals" in cinema; see *Cinema 2: The Time-Image,* trans. Hugh Tomlinson and Robert Galeta (London : Continuum, 2005). In a recent study, Jakob Nilsson develops the dimension of untimeliness in the cinematic image in the direction of a theory of utopia that comes close to many of my proposals here; se Nilsson, *The Untimely-Image: On Contours of the New in Political Film-Thinking*, diss. (Stockholm: Acta Universitatis Stockholmiensis, 2012).

7. This is a theme developed by Giorgio Agamben in the final chapter of his *Il Regno e la Gloria: Per una genealogia teologica dell'economia e del governo* (Vicenza: Neri Pozza Editore, 2007). Such an "inoperativity" (*ino-*

trieving a potential that lies hidden inside them, by prying them apart through a kind of spectral analysis, might then be a way to allow such practices to act as a transformative power. This need not rely on a defined projection of the future, but determines the place to be reached as a site constituted in a now-and-here that is also a *now/here*, or, if we read this term backwards, as Samuel Butler once proposed in a visionary novel, as an *erewhon*.[8]

References to the various theoretical ramifications of these ideas of site, space, and virtuality could be multiplied infinitely, but instead of pursuing such an undoubtedly endless task, it might be useful to return to a moment that within, or least at the margins of, modern architectural discourse, was one of decisive articulations of the place as *same* and *other*, as a no- (*ou*) or other (*heteros*) place (*topos*). Such a place was be the co-implication, interweaving, and perhaps even confusion of *utopia* and *heterotopia* in Foucault's early work, which since the late sixties has been a continually present reference, with many divergent

perosità) does not imply a passive or contemplative stance, but rather opens up the possibility of a different mode of action that Agamben determines as "groundless" and "anarchic," and it no doubt belongs to what he in an earlier work calls a "coming community," although the more precise political implications of this remain fairly vague.

8. Deleuze suggests that we should see the ideas invented by philosophy (which here indeed bear a striking resemblance to artworks) as "nomadic and phantastical notions"; they are "not universals like the categories, nor are they the *hic* et *nunc* or *now here*, the diversity to which categories apply in representation. They are complexes of space and time, no doubt transportable but on condition that they impose their own scenery, that they set up camp there where they rest momentarily: they are therefore the objects of an essential encounter rather than of recognition. The best word to designate these is undoubtedly that forged by Samuel Butler: *erewhon*. They are *erewhons*." Deleuze, *Difference and Repetition*, trans. Paul Patton (London: Continuum, 1994), 356. This proximity to the space-time of art, at once virtual and wholly actual, seems to be somewhat downplayed in Deleuze and Guattari's later theory of art, where the role of art is circumscribed as a way of rendering composites of affects and percepts autonomous, which separates it from the conceptual creations of philosophy. See the chapter on "Percept, Affect, Concept," in Deleuze and Guattari, *What is Philosophy?*

and even contradictory ramifications. As we proceed, these concepts, which on one level seem simply opposed, will themselves
appear to be entangled in multiple and productive ways, and
they form a constellation that often has gone unnoticed, and
while heterotopia has become the object of many commentaries, which have made it into a reference just as pervasive as it
is diffuse in many contemporary artistic practices,[9] utopia has
remained in the background, even to the extent that Foucault
has been understood as simply rejecting the concept as such.

On a more general level, the work of Foucault overlays present concerns and a both distanced and passionate archaeology of
the past, and it has itself become something like a "site" that can
be excavated in many different ways, and from which many current intellectual movements and critical practices can draw their
energy. In the present context, it is particularly relevant that
Foucault's quest for a different form of materialism that would
cut through the divisions between bodies (actions, things) and
minds (thoughts, texts), and open up a questioning of established conducts and disciplines, also implied a rethinking of the
imaginary in terms of space and materiality, even though this at
first may have seemed like a marginal problem. This rethinking
also made possible a different understanding of the "event,"[10]

9. For a collection of texts that trace the influence of the idea of heteroto-
    pia with particular emphasis on the transformations of public space, see
    Michiel Dehaene and Lieven De Cauter (eds.), *Heterotopia and the City:
    Public Space in a Postcivil Society* (New York: Routledge, 2008).

10. Foucault understands the event as a non-corporeal entity, and yet not
    as something mental. What he proposes is a non-corporeal material-
    ism that accounts for the "dispersal of the subject" due to the "chance,
    difference, and materiality the very roots of thought." See Foucault,
    L'ordre du discours (Paris: Gallimard, 1970), 58–62. Foucault's concep-
    tion of the event as an autonomous dimension parallel to that of the
    series of bodies and ideas comes very close to the theory of Deleuze
    in *Logique du sens*, a book that Foucault reviews the same year as the
    introductory lecture at the Collége de France; see Foucault. "Theatrum
    Philosophicum" (1970), in *Dits et écrits* (Paris: Gallimard, 1994), vol.
    II. The idea of "event" has recently been brought into focus by Alain

both in terms of ontology and of practice, an *"event infiltrated by other events,"* as Molly Nesbit says in an essay where she connects Foucault's work from the late 1960s to the counter-cultural practices of the period, evoking a time when "philosophy and art stay separated, sharing a situation shaken by incongruity and shift,"[11] but in this also suggesting that today we are precisely in the midst of such an incongruous and shifting moment.

Impasses

The concept of heterotopia plays a complex and even contradictory role in Foucault's early work, and some interpreters have seen it as their task to restore order, either by constructing a systematic theory, or by criticizing what they perceive as Foucault's confusions.[12] But perhaps what is needed is neither to dispel the confusion by showing it to be a surface illusion that can be corrected at a deeper level, nor to understand it as merely a case of inconsistency, but rather to enter into the contradiction as such, i.e., to see it as that which demands and even "gives" something to think. As Deleuze suggests in his interpretation, that Foucault's trajectory leads him into a series of impasses is not a sign of inconsistency, since these impasses are more like

Badiou, whose conception however is that of major and unprecedented shifts in thought, and the event is for him unique and wholly extraordinary, whereas Deleuze's idea, which I think applies to Foucault as well, is oriented towards taking hold of a different dimension of the ordinary. I discuss these differences in more detail in my "Framing the Event," in Ingrid Gareis, Georg Schöllhammer, and Peter Weibel (eds.), *Moments: A History of Performance in 10 Acts* (Karlsruhe: ZKM, 2013).

11. Molly Nesbit, "Light in Buffalo," in Joseph Backstein, Daniel Birnbaum, and Sven-Olov Wallenstein (eds.), *Thinking Worlds: The Moscow Conference on Philosophy, Politics, and Art* (New York and Berlin: Sternberg Press, 2007), 108.

12. The systematizing tendency prevails in Edward Soja's influential *Thirdspace: Journeys to Los Angeles and other Real-and-Imagined Places* (Oxford: Blackwell, 1996). For Soja, Foucault is part of a general "spatial turn" in the humanities and social sciences, which for him also includes thinkers as different and Benjamin and Heidegger, as well as many others, which in the end renders the concept too fluid and imprecise.

objective illusions forced upon thought by reality itself; they must rather be endured and traversed, and not simply avoided as if they were mere subjective mistakes.[13]

Heterotopia has at least two distinct meanings that we must begin by recognizing: the first, presented 1966 in *The Order of Things*, relates to the order of language and discourse, the second, first presented in a radio talk in 1967, to lived social space. As we will see, this distinction does not preclude these two senses from being knit together at another level, within the space of a problem that however requires an act of invention on the part of the reader. And furthermore, a closer examination of the emergence of these two versions of heterotopia will show them, in each case, to be bound up with contrasting ideas of utopia. The two utopias and the two heterotopias thus form an unstable and contorted quadrant, but also engage in a continual exchange in which they will prove to reflect and presuppose each other.

It is true that these and many other analogous tensions may be seen as resulting from the fact that Foucault in the early years was trying various avenues of thought that did not necessarily cohere—but this he in fact pursued throughout his life, and few thinkers would to such an extent live up to the motto of another great historian of the present or even the immediate future, the architectural critic Reyner Banham: "the only way to prove you have a mind is to change it occasionally."[14] Rather we should

13. See Deleuze, *Foucault*, trans. Séan Hand (London, Athlone, 1988). Deleuze reads the archeology of knowledge in Foucault as a continuation of Kant's *Critique of Pure Reason*, and suggests that the shift to the analytic of power is akin to Kant's move to the pure practical postulates in the second Critique. Perhaps there is a further echo of Kantianism in Foucault at the point of intersection between these two domains—theory and practice in Kant, knowledge and power in Foucault—and the problem of a transcendental illusion as something that we must see through although without ever being able to dispel it, is something that they share.

14. Banham, cited in Nigel Whiteley, *Reyner Banham: Historian of the Immediate Future* (Cambridge, Mass.: MIT, 2002), xv. Foucault develops the theme of a "history of the present" in his later writings, in particular in

see it as resulting from the *matter of thought itself*, from the dense interplay of language and space that ties together the fabric of the early works.

It is equally true that both versions of heterotopia, whose relation Foucault curiously enough never discusses, as if they would simply be a case of mere homonymy, are presented in opposition to utopia, and can be understood as yet another case of a critique of utopian thinking. Such an opposition would be in line with Foucault's later genealogy of knowledge and power, which often implied a resistance toward what he felt to be the all too facile themes of utopia and transcendence as they had been bequeathed to us by a long tradition. But this resistance is obviously a complex and delicate task; a counter-history, if it is to generate possibilities for acting differently, and operate as a strategic history of the present or an ontology of actuality, also requires that we are able to free a virtual becoming, or a becoming-virtual, *inside* the present in its relation to a past that is no longer simply past, in relation to a future that is not just an extension of the present. It calls upon us to release a swarm of other pasts and futures that constitute a proliferation of doubles, so as twist free from the historicist version of history as a burden that enforces an already formed, and thus in a sense past future upon us. In this sense we may take heterotopia as a reformulation of utopia, or as attempt to excavate an untimely moment *inside* utopia, for which the other, the *heteron*, at a cer-

his comments on Kant. The most systematic explication can be found *in Le gouvernement de soi et des autres: Cours au collège de France (1982–1983)*, ed. Michel Senellart (Paris: Seuil, 2008). For a discussion of Foucault's shifting attitudes towards Kant, which extend from his translation of and long preface to the *Anthropology*, to the last texts that in a certain way takes him back to the initial problem, although now seen in much more positive fashion, see my "Governance and Rebellion: Foucault as a Reader of Kant and the Greeks", *Site* 22–23 (2008). For investigations of the temporal structure of Banham's history, see Anthony Vidler, *Histories of the Immediate Present: Inventing Architectural Modernism* (Cambridge, Mass.: MIT, 2008).

tain point appeared like a more apt term than the negative *ou*, the negative "non-" of place in u-topia.

Such a counter-memory, in its attention to what has been effectively said, to the specific dimension that Foucault tried to circumscribe in the concept of "statement,"[15] must thus not shut us off from the space and time of actions—a foreclosure of practice that for many readers, if not for Foucault himself, seemed like an unavoidable effect of the dispassionate and distanced gaze of the archeologist. The work on the "order of discourse" must also make it possible to interrupt a discourse that issues orders that we are assumed to obey and accept. In Foucault's later work, the many analyses of power and resistance, of processes of subjectivation and the complex of governing that came to the fore from the mid seventies onwards, obviously take on this task. This also means that the earlier work in some sense may be retroactively understood as an impasse that would trap us in discourse as *opposed* to things, which would amount to a highly sophisticated form of modern idealism, from which Foucault in fact always sought to break away.

Tracing the concept of heterotopia in its relation to utopia would be one way to see how these problems were already germinating in the early texts, but also, in a certain sense, to understand the extent to which this impasse (if it is one) remains valid even for us, today. To some extent this means that it would be misleading to ask whether Foucault succeeded in undoing,

15. The *statement* (*énoncé*) which forms the proper object of archeology, must be distinguished from the *phrase*, which relates to the depth of the subject and is an object of interpretation, and the *proposition*, which can be formalized and inserted into an axiomatic system. Whereas the phrase is dialectical (one phrase represses another), and the proposition generates a typology (they form hierarchies and may include each other), the statement belongs to a topology. The statement is essentially "rare," Foucault says, and should be related neither to the subject nor the object, and the uncovering of such an autonomous dimension is decisive for the archeological method. For an analysis of these three levels, see Deleuze, *Foucault*, chap. 1.

traversing, or overcoming them—for in this case success would inevitably also imply failure, not so much in the sense that the formative contradictions would have been left behind, but above all that the solutions would have congealed into precepts that we would be called upon to repeat. The task must rather be to enter into these impasses, to struggle with them, and it must always be begun anew, just as Nietzsche once said that each thinker must pick up an arrow shot from some obscure past and pass it on into some equally dim future, not on the basis of knowing what future time *means*, but by reaching out into the dimension of the "untimely," that which suspends meaning by unhinging time from its repressive and depressive cardinal axes.

The quadrant

The idea of a systematic analysis of "other places," what Foucault not without a certain irony calls a "heterotopology"—for a science, a *logos* of the *topos* of the *other* as a disruptive force, seems paradoxical through and through—initially appeared in the first of two radio talks broadcast in December 1966, "Les Héterotopies" and "Le Corps utopique." The two talks were part of a series of radio shows entitled "Utopia and Literature," and in the first of these two brief excursions Foucault presents the basic outlines of heterotopia as a spatial otherness. This would be further developed in the public lecture from 1967 known under the name "Des espaces autres,"[16] which has become the principal

16. This text, which forms the basis for most discussions of heterotopia in Foucault, for a long time remained unpublished. There was a partial translation into Italian as early as 1968, but the integral text was published only in 1984, the year of Foucault's death, when it translated into German in the catalog to the Internationale Bauausstellung in Berlin, where it could pick up obvious resonances from the particular status of the city as a no-place between East and West. Since then is has been republished many times. The French text can be found in *Dits et écrits* (Paris: Gallimard, 1994), vol. IV, 754f; trans. by Robin Hurley as "Different Spaces," in *Essential Works*, ed. Paul Rabinow and James D. Faubion (London: Penguin, 2001), vol. 2, 177ff. Henceforth cited as EW, with pagination.

source for contemporary discussions of the concept of heterotopia in terms of social space.

The conjunction of these two presentations must however caution us from understanding utopia and heterotopia as simply exclusive terms, which is an interpretation that results when one moves directly from the first radio talk to the lecture in 1967. The second radio talk in fact takes the opposite route, and in addressing what Foucault calls the "utopian body" in terms of an inner ego-oriented space, it retrieves many of the phenomenological themes that Foucault was struggling with at the time. In close parallel to Merleau-Ponty he here wants to show how a utopian desire emerges out of a body that is riveted to an irreducible and ineluctable facticity, in a fantasy of another and glorious body, or of a soul that would be able to wholly escape the body. From within a certain phenomenology, but also by brushing it against the grain, Foucault here provides what we could call a genealogy of transcendence. This brief exposé has many important connections to Foucault's other essays from the period, above all those that draw on certain forms of literature as resistance, and they indicate the centrality of his rethinking of the idea of the imaginary.

As already noted, this initial divide between heterotopia as connected to social space and utopia as connected to the phenomenology of the body is however complicated by the fact that the idea of heterotopia had already appeared earlier in 1966, before the radio talks, in a rather different way in the introduction to *The Order of Things*. Unlike in the later radio talk, heterotopia is here not presented, even playfully, as the outline of a science or a taxonomy—in fact, if anything, it is rather the *limit* of science and taxonomy in several senses. And even if the concept as such plays no part in the subsequent analyses carried out in the book, where Foucault goes on to propose an archeology attempting to uncover the rules (the "episteme") that have organized knowledge in the Renaissance, the Classical age, and post-Kantian modernity, it occupies a highly strategic place in the introduction, in pointing to that which makes *thought itself* possible. Heterotopia, he here suggests, is an experience of order and structure as a groundless event that itself must remain extra-epistemic, but as such it is also what allows us to see the taxonomic structures from a certain *outside*; it is a kind of quasi- or hyper-transcendental sphere, a void of reason that at the same time is the place of emergence for all forms of reason. It is the limit of reason, first in a twisted Kantian sense of making thinking possible,[17] and then in the much more radical sense of resisting any kind of discursive appropriation.

When Foucault in *The Order or Things* sets up an opposition between heterotopia and utopia, it is thus not because the latter would transcend the body in its material facticity, as in the second radio talk on the utopian body, but, he says, since it unfolds in the dimension of fabulation and myth, which was not altogether absent from the radio version, although it mostly remained on the horizon as one possible development of the space of the imaginary.

In the following 1967 lecture on other spaces, Foucault returns to the version of heterotopia suggested in the first radio lecture the year before, and does not draw on any of the quasi-transcendental implications ascribed to it *The Order of Things*. So, all in all we have two different versions of heterotopia (if we here disregard the rather small differences between the first

17.   In the first Critique Kant explicitly places the question of how the
       faculty of thought itself is possible outside of the scope of transcenden-
       tal philosophy (A xvi), since this would be either an empirical question,
       or overstep the boundaries of what can be known and take us into the
       sphere of the noumenal. Foucault's project to uncover a dimension of
       the a priori that at the same time would be historical in this sense con-
       stitutes a kind of anti-Kantian (in appealing to empirical and historical
       changes) Kantianism (in claiming to locate conditions of possibility for
       empirical experience).

radio talk and the public lecture), both of which seem to reject utopia, although the meaning of the latter concept seems far from unequivocal. We seem to be have entered into something like a conceptual quadrant: in the first pair, heterotopia is opposed to utopia as real social space is opposed to the phenomenological dialectic of the lived body; in the second, it is opposed to utopia as a radical experience of ungrounding is opposed to the false security provided by myth and fabulation. What are we to make of this constellation, this rapid succession of seemingly incompatible statements presented in the space of less than a year? In what sense, if at all, could they be taken as different aspects of the same investigation into the multidimensionality of the *topos*? In order to grasp the dynamic of this enigmatic quadrant, we must look at the successive versions in more detail.

Heterotopia and the condition of possibility of archaeology

Foucault famously opens *The Order of Things* by citing Borges's imaginary Chinese encyclopedia, the encounter with which he also points to as the origin of his own investigation. Borges's text seems to defy all normal logic, although the precise epistemological function of this amusing literary example—or better, the tension that it both acknowledges and helps to conceal—has not been sufficiently acknowledged. As we have noted, it is not just an example of taxonomic contingency, but points to the other place, the *heteros topos*, *from* and *to* which Foucault's analyses claim to proceed: it is the experience of the limit of order and reason that makes it possible for archeology to begin, as well as the limit toward which it moves, in designating the possibility of another form of thought than the present one.

Animals, the encyclopedia says, should be divided in categories like: "(a) belonging to the Emperor, (b) embalmed, (c) tame, (d) sucking pigs, (e) sirens, (f) fabulous, (g) stray dogs, (h) included in the present classification, (i) frenzied, (j) innumer-able, (k) drawn with a very fine camelhair brush, (l) et cetera, (m) having just broken the water pitcher, (n) that from a long way off look like flies."[18] The categories proposed are not simply incongruous but also involve classical set-theoretical paradoxes ("included in the present classification"), which is why Borges's text, Foucault suggests, creates a self-reflexive and impossible taxonomy that can only exist in the non-place (*non-lieu*) of lan-guage. In this non-place—which will soon be identified with the other place, the *heteros topos*—the impossibility of co-existence is suspended, and in this, it destroys the "table upon which, since the beginning of time, language has intersected space" (MC 9/ xvii). This table is the surface on which categories may co-ex-ist and distribute their respective content, and its destruction first produces an absolute *disorder* from which nothing would come. But in this it also proves to be the condition of possibil-ity for the crucial experience that there is a contingent *order* of things and words, and that the link between them is the result of an event that eludes the acts of consciousness as normally understood, and must be sought at level of an archeology. This is why Borges's encyclopedia, Foucault claims, should not be understood as a utopia, which he now describes as a place sim-ply located *somewhere else*, beyond the vicissitude of time, in the space where myths and fables can unfold in the eloquence of a discourse that rests confident in its power to name and signify, and thus also in its power to "intersect space" at some later mo-ment in time. Instead, Foucault refers to the encyclopedia as a heterotopia that runs against the grain of language, "desiccates" it by destroying in advance the syntax that holds words and things together and safeguards the power of naming; it allows

18. *Les mots et les choses*, (Paris: Gallimard, 1966) 7; *The Order of Things*, trans. Alan Sheridan (London: Routledge, 1989), xvi, Henceforth cited in the text as MC with pagination (French/English).

the other to irrupt *inside* the same, but in this it also renders these otherwise fixed oppositions fluid and mobile, and makes them available for archeological analysis.[19]

This experience of otherness is where Foucault finds the point of entry to his own archeological project, i.e., the possibility to uncover a interstitial dimension that he would lie *between* the basic codes of a culture that determine what can be understood as "empirical," and those scientific or philosophical theories that account for the existence of order in general. The idea of a between introduces a certain ambiguity into the argument, as if this dimension would both underlie and be juxtaposed to the others. This is not incidental, and it already points ahead to a crucial question that will at least be hinted at in the spatial concept of heterotopia, i.e., if the epistemic rules do not themselves already presuppose some other form of ordering that cannot be discursive, and if so, how these two moments are to be articulated in relation to each other. The heterotopia created in Borges, Foucault says, opens onto an archeological space, an

19.   It is indeed true that this heterotopic non-place in Borges's text still bears a concrete geographical name: *China*, the mythical other, which functions as "a precise region whose name alone constitutes for the West a vast reservoir of utopias," as Foucault remarks, whose "culture is the most meticulous, the most rigidly ordered, the one most deaf to temporal events," and whose writing "does not reproduce the fugitive flight of the voice in horizontal lines," but rather "erects the motionless and still recognizable images of things themselves in vertical columns"—all of which, in our "dreamworld," makes China into the "privileged *site* of *space*" (MC 10/xix). While undoubtedly part of an Orientalist projection that designates the East as the other of the West, and whose philosophical roots lead back to Leibniz and his fascination for the kinship between non-phonetic writing and the idea of an universal characteristic, this also indicates the unavoidable link that binds alls "others" to a "place," indeed to an imaginary and ideological place: see Leibniz, *Discours sur la théologie naturelle des chinois*, ed. Christian Frémont (Paris: L'Herne, 1987). But it also points to an unavoidable *embodiment* of the heterotopic, although it would be reductive to claim that this makes heterotopia something purely *imaginary*. Accounting for the necessary co-implication of these moves is one of Foucault's major problems, also beyond these particular texts from the 1960s.

obscure region that is at once intermediary and fundamental, where a culture deviates from its codes in such a way that they become visible in their naked existence and contingency, and in this way it forms the limit of culture. But as a limit situated on this side of words, perceptions, and gestures, as well as on this side of the subject that would comprehend or constitute them, it is also the place of critique and transformation, in a way that picks up certain motifs from the Kantian critique while also displacing others, most famously in the term "historical a priori" that inscribes the transcendental subject and its unity of experience as one possibility among many.

At first this seems to amount to a rejection, or better, a bracketing of the subject, which is carried out in a non- or counter-phenomenological fashion: it is a reduction *of* meaning, and not *to* meaning, a reduction of constitutive intentionality to an anonymous event of ordering. Instead of a consciousness that would ground the various classes or regions of objects, as in Husserlian phenomenology, there is something like a structuring without an agent. And yet, Foucault enigmatically still suggests that archeology approaches this limit as a kind of *experience*, a "pure experience of order" (MC 13/xxiii) that would allow us to uncover and describe the historical a priori conditions that make it possible to see and enunciate in an orderly and regulated fashion inside a given epistemic order. If archeology lays bare a "ground" (*sol*), then the form and nature of this ground, and even more so the possibility of experiencing it, seem difficult to locate and circumscribe. As we have seen, this *sol* is neither a subject that relates to the world in meaning-bestowing acts, but nor can it be located within a phenomenology that moves beyond the subject, as the ground of fundamental ontology in Heidegger's sense, where the regions of objects are determined in relation to ecstatic temporal projections of Dasein. Both of them for Foucault still retain the structure of subjectivity, which also entails continuity between the object of knowledge and the ground that cancels out the ruptures of history. In emphasizing discontinuity, he first seems close to Bachelard's analysis of epistemological breaks, which attempts to locate the threshold at which a science takes leave of its prehistory by constituting a new object irreducible to immediate sensory experience.[20] But discontinuity for Foucault does not set up a relation to an ideality or objectivity that breaks with prehistory, only to a discursive object that is itself a moment in history, and in this sense his alliance with Bachelard is only momentary.

This vacant space, encountered in an experience that does not belong to a consciousness, points ahead to many of the transformations that would follow: first, the discovery of power relations as the informal element in which the forms of discourse and knowledge take on stability as archives, then the various forms of self-relation that moulds a provisional subject capable of governing itself and others. The silent ground of our culture, "the same ground that is once more stirring under our feet" (MC 16/xxvi), is shot through with displacements and fault lines, and the possible experience of its ungrounded nature at first needs to circumvent the form of the subject, which encloses this experience in a form that neutralizes it in advance. The ground laid bare is thus on the one hand a set of rules that remains fixed when seen from within a given empirical order,

20. For a brief and concise discussion of Bachelard's theory of science, see Domique Lecourt, *L'épistémologie historique de Gaston Bachelard* (Paris: Vrin, 2002 [1967]). The essential difference is that the epistemological break for Bachelard constitutes an object of science by severing it from its "prehistory" in sensuous experience, whereas the break for Foucault simply takes us from one discursive object to another, all located on the same level. His constant resistance to the term "ideology" is rooted in this, and the concept of *savoir* is intended to suspend the opposition between science and ideology, a distinction that at the time was crucial for Althusser's use of Bachelard to establish an epistemological break in Marx. These two readings of Bachelard developed in parallel, although with diametrically opposed results.

but on the other hand, when seen as a limit, it displays the cracks and fissures that provide mobility to the historical conditions. At this point, Foucault however seems more bent on rejecting traditional solutions to the problem of change, and his proposals remain largely negative, in that they leave open a space for transformation without determining it more precisely.

In this sense, the heterotopia that we encounter in the encyclopedia of Borges would be the provisional name for this site, the Outside, that from out of which thought emerges and which opens the possibility of thinking the Other as the void that always inhabits the Same. This *heteros topos* is neither dialectically nor logically *opposed* to the topology of everyday language, to its orders, categories, and linkages, but situated below or in between them—to once more repeat the symptomatically ambiguous formula that Foucault provides— so as to form the condition of possibility of any stable signifying order, while simultaneously showing all such stability to be situated and local, and thus, at the limit, always struck by a certain impossibility. It is only on the basis of this non-ground, or of a ground that immediately breaks open, that archeology can begin to articulate itself as an experience in search of a subject and an object, and of the tenuous and instable link that for a certain period will bind them together.

Utopia as transcendence

As we have noted, the two versions of heterotopia given by Foucault—the first pointing towards the abyssal condition of language and classification, the second, to which I will return in the next section, toward the spatial ordering of society—are however as it were syncopated by the reappearance of utopia. To be sure, the second radio talk from 1966 may be taken as a reminiscence of older themes, or as a hesitation with respect to the rejection of phenomenology and humanism in *The Order of*

Things (or possibly, given the context, simply as a concession to a rubric that Foucault had not himself set). But it may also, and more productively, be seen as an indication of Foucault's attempts to rethink the imaginary at the limit of the inside and outside, or as the intersection of space and language, heterotopia and utopia.

In this context it is essential to note that the imaginary is also the domain of art, and particularly so in the trajectory of modernity that was initiated by the invention of aesthetics in the first half of the seventeenth century, which however is a development that in Foucault's archeology of the human sciences curiously enough receives no attention.[21] The problem of the imaginary is particularly relevant since Foucault in this period appears to have perceived the possibility of transgression as essentially connected to modern literature and art, as he suggests in the final sections of *The History of Madness*, with its references to Nietzsche, van Gogh, and Artaud. Madness, he proposes, is the *absence of work*,[22] not in the sense of something simply negative, but as the truth of the modern work, a moment of unreason that opens the pathway to what *The History of Madness* calls the undivided experience of the division between reason and madness. Here we find the traces of another experience, a resistance that articulates itself by with-

21. This is perhaps because artworks, in *The Order of Things* but also elsewhere in the early writings of Foucault, seem to be endowed with a capacity to, if not entirely step out of their historical frame, then at least achieve a reflexive transcendence in relation to it, and in this way they are like "operators" of the historical analysis. Their function seems to be to herald, but also embody, and even point beyond, their epistemic location, as in the case of Velázquez, but also Cervantes, who marks the threshold between Renaissance and the "prose of the world," and the analysis of order of the Classical Age. For the idea of artworks as operators, see Jean Starobinski, "Hamlet et Freud," preface in Ernest Jones, *Hamlet et Oedipe* (Paris: Gallimard, 1967), and my "The Place of Art in Hegel's Phenomenology," in Brian Manning Delaney and Sven-Olov Wallenstein (eds.), *Translating Hegel: The Phenomenology of Spirit and Modern Philosophy* (Huddinge: Södertörn Philosophical Studies, 2012).
22. See "La folie, l'absence d'oeuvre" (1964), DE, vol. 1.

drawing into silence, into the margins of discourse. At the same time that Foucault sees madness as an entity constituted by being placed in various moral and medical institutions and discourses, he draws on an idea from romanticism: art as the bearer of another truth that is somehow open to madness, a non-dialectical negativity or experience of limits that cannot be reduced to rational ordering. The infinity and excess of language transgresses reason and order, it scrambles and disassembles the law of the Father, and literary writing is positioned as the primordial reservoir for this resistance.

This motif unfolds in a of series texts, "Hölderlin and the Question of the Father" (1962), "Preface to Transgression" (1963, on Bataille), the book-length study of Raymond Roussel in 1963, "Fantasia of the Library" (on Flaubert, first published as a postface to the German translation of Flaubert's *La tentation de Saint Antoine*, in 1964), and "La prose d'Actéon," on Pierre Klossowski, 1964).[23] Foucault's literary essays may seem as asides in relation to his historical work on madness, the clinic, and the emergence of the human sciences, and yet, in all their diversity and circumstantial quality, they display a cumulative movement, which can be taken to culminate in the text from 1966 on Blanchot, "La pensée du dehors."[24] In the latter he explicates the underlying idea of literature as the relation of language to the Outside (*le Dehors*), a dimension of emptiness that dissolves the subject into a space of pure dispersal. This concept would also later become crucial for Deleuze's interpretation, which traces it in its various forms throughout Foucault's work, not just as a negative void and absence, but as space of openness out of which thinking emerges, and in this sense it belongs to

23. All of these are reprinted in DE, vol. 1; the essays on Hölderlin, Bataille, and Flaubert are translated in Foucault, *Language, Counter-Memory, Practice*, ed. Daniel Bouchard (Ithaca: Cornell University Press, 1977).

24. In DE, vol. I; Eng. trans. in Foucault/Blanchot, *Thought from Outside / Michel Foucault as I Imagine Him* (New York: Zone Book, 1987).

the same order as the heterotopia of language that underlies the archeological analyses.

Just as in the case of heterotopia, this idea of a resistance inherent in certain types of literature is however complicated by many other of Foucault's statements from the period that inscribe it as a situated and finite possibility, which shows his hesitation in front of the theme of the imaginary. The same year as the essay on Blanchot, *The Order of Things* provides an account of the archeological possibility of literary counter-discourse, which to some extent deprives it of its radical quality by inserting its thrust in a historical narrative. The experience of literature as a limit, he here suggests, is conditioned by the modern epistemic order, it is born out of the same conjuncture, and constitutes an integral part of its metaphysical contortions. Emerging as the obverse side of modernity's anthropological humanism, literature harbors an experience of the being of language that already from the beginning will haunt modernity and signal its limit, but as such it also belongs to it as an internal oscillation.[25] While this on the one hand continues to give literature a singular place inside the episteme, it also seems to reject its claims for an exorbitant position. A possible conclusion of this would be that insurgence inside language, even though indispensable, is not enough, and requires to be prolonged into a dimension that transcends the discursive. For the Foucault of the late sixties, who begins to orient his work towards the new question of power, literature gradually

25. The return of language as a historical opacity is what heralds the breakdown of the system of representation that characterized the classical age, although language is now spread out in many functions, from the formalist attempts at finding a pure universal language to the celebration of its infinity in literary writing. For modernity, Foucault suggests, the problem of language unfolds in the distance between Nietzsche's question "Who speaks" and Mallarmé's answer: the being of the Word itself, to which the intransitivity of literary writing testifies in the highest degree. See *MC* 314–318/303–307. For a discussion of this, see Tilottama Rajan, "The Phenomenological Allegory: From 'Death and the Labyrinth' to 'The Order of Things,'" *Poetics Today*, 19:3 (1998).

ceases to appear as an ontological phenomenon, and increasingly comes to be understood in terms of a particular type of discursive regulation; "literature" becomes a way of delimiting texts, in which the function of the author plays a crucial role in the order of discourse by indicating a particular kind of origin that sets it apart from scientific and other types of texts. Later on, Foucault would even appear entirely to be dismissive of his early texts and the search for an ontology of literature.[26]

In the lecture on the utopian body, the theme of literature remains in the background. Utopia, Foucault suggests, should not be reduced to a motif inherited from history or simply sealed within the domain of "fabulation" (which is precisely what he had suggested the year before in *The Order of Things*), but is rooted in the doubling of the body itself, in its capacity to transcend itself into a virtual dimension. The question of the imaginary however forms a bridge to the literary essays, in the sense that a certain experience of the body can be understood as the origin of a utopian fantasy that is particularly present in writing.

The contours of the imaginary are traced with reference to the body's constant quest for going beyond itself into an oneiric dimension, which is also what the initial scene of the text locates an a kind of immediate past, which is also the only literary reference: the narrator in Proust's *Recherche*, anxiously awakening in each new place, once more finds himself relocated to his own body. In spite of the potentials of the Proustian virtualization of space and time (of which Deleuze's *Proust et les signes* had provided a striking analysis only three years earlier), we are here brought back to a place from which we "cannot escape" (9),[27]

26. For the role of the author, see "What is an Author," in *Language, Counter-Memory, Practice*; for the rejection of the earlier texts from the sixties, see, for instance, "Structuralism and Poststructuralism," in EW 2.

27. Page references in the following are to the text in Foucault, *Die Heterotopien, Der utopische Körper: Les hétéropies, Le corps utopique: Zwei Radiovorträge* (Frankfurt am Main: Suhrkamp, 2005).

and Foucault sets out by painting a rather negative and restrictive picture of an objective body, understood as a limitation on my freedom. I am *chained* to my body: "I cannot move around without it, I cannot leave it where it is to go somewhere else" (ibid). It is an inescapable or pitiless place, the "topia" (*topie*), to which the subject is riveted, as when it seems itself in the mirror every morning, "shortsighted, bald: not beautiful, to be sure" (10), thus the very "contrary of a utopia" (9).[28]

It is against this that a first utopian movement emerges: fairy-tales that depict a different, glorious body, moving at the speed of light, becoming invisible at will, capable of all kinds of tricks and transformations, or images of a soul that ascends, hovers outside the body, and even may survive it. These fantasies are however themselves rooted in the body, in the "fantastic" relation it is capable of having to itself outside of its objective constitution, which also means that it cannot know itself in any exhaustive way: "It also possesses places without place, more profound places, places more insistent than the soul, than the tomb, than the enchantment of magicians." (12) It is an entity with many dimensions, it is both open and closed, visible and invisible; it is always outside of itself, and as such also the origin of all utopian fantasies.

This ecstatic capacity is then externalized and inscribed back onto the objective body, as in tattooing or other ritual practices

28.   Even though Foucault makes no reference to his philosophical predecessors, these initial description seems less related to the classical Husserlian opposition between *Körper*, the body seen as an objective physical entity from a third-person perspective, and *Leib*, the body lived from within as the source of my spatial orientation and the point where kinesthetic processes are knit together, which is the point of departure for Merleau-Ponty. Without pressing these brief passages to much—they are no doubt intended as a rhetorical contrast to the subsequent movement of transcendence, which is shown to be more originary—it seems reasonable to say that this description is in fact surprisingly close to the Cartesian conception of the body as an inertia in relation to the for-itself of the ego that we find in Sartre and the early texts of Levinas.

that prolong the virtual doubling already present in our first self-relation, and transform it into a "fragment of imaginary spaces that will communicate with the universe of divinities or with the universe of the other" (15). Rather than something added onto an objective being, this vertiginous virtuality now proves to be primordial, and the place of the body is at once here and nowhere: "The body is as the heart of the world, this small utopian kernel from which I dream, I speak, I proceed, I imagine, I perceive things in their place, and I negate them by the indefinite power of the utopias that I imagine. My body is like the City of the Sun. It has no place, but it is from it that all possible places, real or utopian, emerge and radiate." (18)[29]

This movement is however also always brought back to my facticity, as the moment of restriction or finitude that it also what reestablishes identity: the mirror that gives my reflection back to me, and the experience of death where I once more will be reduced to my objective body. And finally, in the last words of the text, the act of making love shows me that "the body is here" (20), i.e., it shows how the body of the other puts a definite limit, although no longer in a negative sense, to the utopian movement, perhaps thereby restoring a different dimension to facticity in relation to an other that is another subject.

Other spaces

If we now pass on to the second instance of heterotopia, presented in the public lecture from 1967, "Of Other Spaces," we immediately notice that it opens up a rather different perspective than the linguistic version offered in *The Order of Things*, but also takes a route that at first seems opposed to the meditation on the utopian body. Heterotopia now appears as connected to

29.   The reference here is to Tommaso Campanella's classic utopian work *La città del sole* (1602), although Foucault does not develop any of its architectural implications.

the production and reproduction of social space, it is like a negative foil to discipline (even though this concept still remains on
the horizon), and the order that it at once mirrors and subverts
is less a question of classification and taxonomy than of *command*. These two themes, discourse as structure and command,
will be joined together a few years later, and it becomes an explicit theme in the inaugural lecture at the Collège de France
in 1970, *L'ordre du discours* (rather misleadingly translated into
English as *The Discourse on Language*, which obliterates the problem of order by covering it under the blanket term "language").
Here the order of things appears more as an *ordering*, a relation
of power where inclusion and exclusion are not just classificato-
ry terms on a discursive level, but also, and even predominantly,
institutional relations that make possible and prohibit varieties
of movement, passage, and circulation. Ultimately, as Foucault
will say in 1970, any such order of discourse rests on the exclusion performed by the will to truth—which, he adds, is the most
enigmatic of exclusions since it makes *truth* itself into a problem,
a result of a battle or struggle rather than something emanating
from the good will or spontaneous rectitude of the subject's faculties.[30] In *L'ordre du discours* Foucault suggests that we should
look to the initial stages of Greek thought in order to discover
the emergence of this division, an analysis that he then begins
in the 1970–71 lectures on the will to knowledge.[31] In the lecture

30. This is one of the many points that would connect Foucault to Deleuze's work of the period, for instance to the analysis of the "image of
thought" in the third chapter of *Difference and Repetition*. In *L'ordre du
discours*, Foucault sketches the outlines of an analysis of the transformation of the idea of truth (*aletheia*) in ancient Greece, whose basic features
had recently been investigated in Marcel Detienne's 1967 study, *Les
maîtres de vérité dans la Grèce archaïque* (Paris: Maspero, 1967), on which
Foucault draws heavily. This transformation would occur roughly with
the advent of Platonic philosophy, where truth no longer depends on a
figure of mastery and authority, as in the sixth-century poets where the
one who speaks is an index of truth, but is transferred to the statement.
31. See Foucault, *Leçons sur la volonté de savoir: Cours au Collège de France*

from 1967, this theme is still only implicit, and while the analysis of the way in which a given society orders its categories and its social relations remains at a tentative and largely descriptive level, it nevertheless engages a whole set of material and spatial issues that would not reenter his work until much later.

The 1967 lecture begins by noting that if the nineteenth century was obsessed with history and chronology, with the problem of the originary and the derivative, today we imagine ourselves in a space of simultaneity, of networks and interlinking. And when structuralism acknowledges this, Foucault notes, this is not simply in terms of a negation of temporality and a predilection for some frozen eternal order—which at the time were commonplace accusations in the wake of the debate between Sartre and Lévi-Strauss—but a way to rethink the interlacing of time, space, and event, which is also how we might understand Foucault's own positive connection to structuralism, rather than in terms of the strange idea that historical change would somehow be impossible to understand, which was often ascribed to him.[32]

Space indeed has an entangled history of its own, and Foucault parenthetically gives us a few hints of what such a history might look like, from the ancient and medieval hierarchy of

(1970–1971), ed. Daniel Defert (Paris: Gallimard/Seuil, 2011). Here the perspective shifts somewhat, and Foucault traces the idea of a "will to truth" through several agonistic juridical forms from Homer through Hesiod and up to Sophocles; the debate between Plato and the Sophists however fades from sight, and it is now Aristotle's analysis of the apophantic proposition that signals the decisive step in the expulsion of the sophists and the creation of a purified knowledge (*connaissance*) that aspires to transcend the disruptive forces of "knowing" (*savoir*).

32. The allegation often directed against Foucault's early work, that he would deny change, seems misguided. While it is true that some of the analyses performed in *The Order of Things* have a structuralist leaning, above all in the emphasis in rules that would govern the formation of statements inside a given episteme, it us just as true that there is no *general* theory of language, structuralist or other, and the book is just as occupied with change between the epistemic order as their respective inner structure.

places, which remained operative in everyday life as well as on a cosmological level, and then was pried open by the intrusion of the infinite, in a series of upheavals leading up to the Cartesian *extensio* that renders all sites equivalent in the mathematical projection of the coordinate system. This historical background is however less important, and Foucault soon passes over to the present: today, he claims, we tend to think more in terms of sites, nodal intersections understood in relation to series, networks, and a vocabulary derived from information theory. Our space has thus once more become a relation between sites, although not in the sense of the Aristotelian analysis of *topos* that inscribes places within a stable order, but rather, Foucault somewhat enigmatically adds, in a way that forms the basis of our modern anxieties.[33] Bachelard and phenomenology, he continues, has taught us that space is not simply a homogeneous extension, but always fantasmatic and projective (as was the case in his own preceding lecture on the utopian body); there is however also another type of space, which is what will introduce us to the new definition of heterotopia: a place that "eats and scrapes away at us," where "the erosion of our life, our time, and our history takes place"; places that resist the operations

33.   Maybe such an intuition also lies behind Heidegger's remark in one of his last texts, when he, in the context of a discussion of how modern technology transforms space, notes that the latter must be understood on a pair with Goethe's *Urphänomen*: it cannot be derived from anything else, it is neither subjective nor objective, but precede this alternative—and, he adds, this impossibility of reducing or turning away from the phenomenon toward something else is what produces *anxiety*. See Heidegger, "Die Kunst und der Raum" (1969), in *Aus der Erfahrung des Denkens, Gesamtausgabe* vol. 13 (Frankfurt am Main: Klostermann, 1983), 206. This brief essay was originally conceived in dialog with the work of the Basque sculptor Eduardo Chilida; for discussions of this encounter and Chilida's work, see Otto Pöggeler, *Bild und Technik* (Munich: Fink, 2002), 225–31, and Andrew J. Mitchell, *Heidegger Among the Sculptors: Body, Space, and the Art of Dwelling* (Stanford: Stanford University Press, 2010), 66–94, none of which however address the question of anxiety.

of consciousness, even subvert it; places that relate to all other spaces in the sense that they "suspend, neutralize, or reverse the set of relations that are designated, reflected, or represented by them" (EW 2, 177f).

It is true that these spaces could be called both utopias and heterotopias, and Foucault proposes that we should differentiate them in the following way: utopias are inverted or perfected imaginary forms of present society, and they cannot be localized inside of it; heterotopias, on the other hand, are *real* places[34] that are formed in the very founding acts of society; they are *contrary* locations that on one level represent, question, and invert all other spaces, but in this they also form a coherent system together with their opposites (and here we may recognize a typical feature of cybernetics, to which Foucault referred earlier, namely the idea of self-regulation). One could even imagine a "heterotopology," Foucault says, a systematic description, if not a science (and here he retracts the claim in the radio talk the year before) of such places, and he proposes six principles for this type of analysis.

1. These places exist in each society, but can be divided into two major groups: heterotopias of *crisis*, as in the case of sacred or forbidden places, or places of passage like the boarding school, military service, or the honeymoon trip, and het-

---

34. Foucault suggests that an intermediary form would be exemplified by the mirror, which brings us closer to aesthetic issues: in producing an imaginary double, the mirror shifts my identity so that I am both here and not-here, both there and not-there. This brief aside may be read in conjunction with the figure of the mirror in the famous analysis of Velázquez in *The Order of Things*, where the gaze of the painter, the royal couple, and the spectator are superimposed so as to form a "metathesis of visibility." This interpretation of *Las Meninas* in fact forms another introduction to the book, located *after* the Borges citation, and unlike the literary example it forms an essential part of the narrative of the text itself, by prefiguring the close of the classical episteme of representation and the birth of Man, who will come to occupy the place left vacant in the painting.

erotopias of *deviation*, as in the case of rest homes, hospitals, and prisons, places which, Foucault notes, may have become more common today.

2. Their functions may change due to the structure of society, for instance the cemetery, whose location is dependent on the varying perception of death; once at the center of society, it has today been pushed to the margins and rendered invisible.

3. They may juxtapose incompatible sites in one place, like the theater, the cinema, or the garden.

4. They are linked to particular slices of time, "heterochronies" that break away from the flow of everyday events, as in the case of museums and libraries that accumulate past time, or fairgrounds and festivals that are connected to the transitory nature of time; and finally there is the case of the vacation village that brings together both of them in a time that stands still.

5. They constitute systems of opening and closure, they are not generally freely accessible like public space, and require a function of gatekeeping. Some may even include and exclude at the same time, and create a kind of spatial pocket (for instance the Brazilian bedrooms where the visitor could enter without meeting the family, or the American motel room).

6. Finally, they have two extreme functions: either to expose all of normal life as illusory, or to create another and more perfect space. In this they are places of illusion and compensation; the first can be exemplified by the brothel, the second by certain colonies, for instance Puritan societies in North America.

This is obviously a rather loose and improvised description, which takes us from graveyards and libraries to museums and brothels, from cinemas and motels rooms to rites of passage and initiation. It would be easy to criticize Foucault for certain inconsistencies—but maybe, just like Borges, he is making fun of our desire to classify, of our desire to create precisely a *logos* of the *heteron*. This notwithstanding, the fundamental feature of all these places is that they have a productive *and* a subversive relation to everyday spaces. A heterotopia is a place where we can find rest and withdraw (the holiday resort, the convent, the library), but it also allows for a certain overturning of the rules of everyday conduct. But precisely because of this duality, it operates as an integrated and functional part of the spatial cycle of (re)production, or of "the production of space," as Henri Lefebvre would say. To go on holiday is already to envision returning to work—but it also produces fantasies of subversion that both form part of the cycle or reproduction and destabilize it: heterotopias always threaten to overflow their boundaries, they are a source of uprisings and unrests that the social order attempts to contain and even integrate as disciplinary mechanisms.

Heterotopias thus function both as an instrument for the reproduction of the social order, and as a constant source of disorder and contestation that has to be contained within precise limits. They can be taken as materialized instances of order as ordering, but also as materialized experiences of the contingency of order—they are conditions not of an archeology of epistemic rules, but of spatial and temporal boundaries that in any given culture determine what should and what should not be done, when to do or not to do it. In this their otherness may seem less radical and more straightforwardly empirical than the vertiginous non-ground of the epistemic orders excavated in the archeology of knowledge, but they are also what provides these orders with a physical instantiation and practical application: the heterotopias of language and space are different, and yet knit together in the fabric that binds words, things, and actions together, and constitute the normality of knowing and acting in a given epoch.

Limits of heterotopia

The idea of heterotopia was early on picked up in a critique of Foucault, proposed from a Marxist perspective by some of the key figures in Venice School in the late 1970s. These polemics tend to assume that Foucault not only wanted to reassess Marxism, but in fact to simply discard its lessons in favor of an idealism that dissolves all material specificity of the social order. In the collective volume *Il dispositivo Foucault* (1977, with contributions from Franco Rella, Manfredo Tafuri, Georges Teyssot, and Massimo Cacciari), Foucault's conception of power was scrutinized in a highly critical but ultimately misleading fashion.[35] But while it was misguided, the polemic can still be seen as instructive, since it provides a negative relief against which Foucault's conception becomes clearer, and also because it articulates parts of its polemic in terms of architectural issues.

In the introduction Franco Rella proposes an interpretation that sets the tone for the following discussions, in which Foucault's rejection of the juridical (prohibitive, negative) and unitary concept of power leads to the idea that power would be nothing but a plurality of *dispositifs* that attempt to "suture an empty center," something wholly "other," a blank or a void in being (DF 10 note).[36] For Rella, Foucault's understanding of

35.   *Il dispositivo Foucault* (Venice: Cluva, 1977)). Henceforth cited as DF with pagination.

36.   In the following I will focus on the texts by Rella and Teyssot, which are the most rewarding. Cacciari aligns himself with Rella's claims, and suggests that "The anarchical dispersal of power, understood simply as disciplinary techniques, coexist with a fetishistic conception of power" (DF 61), to the effect that Foucault's analysis is claimed to ultimately rest on "mystical-ideal" (62) dialectic between Unity and Multiplicity. Tafuri's contribution is strangely enough the most disappointing, since one would have expected more: after a few interesting although tangential remarks on the relation between word and image in *The Order of Things*, he too succumbs to idea that power in Foucault would wholly dispersed, ungraspable, even mystical. He ends up equating it with an equally misguided interpretation of Derrida's idea of dissemination: "a kind of private game without rules whose social effects can be verified"

power would be that of a non-place, a "mysterious noumenon" (DF 12) that transforms all concrete spatial orders, even space itself, into a heterotopia: "Space is always 'other,' always heterotopic" (ibid). For Rella this also means not only that the concept of ideology is rejected (which is indeed Foucault's thesis), but also that in the end analysis itself becomes useless, which is far from Foucault's claims: "Transparence is absolute. Thus there is nothing to dissolve. Nothing to analyze." (13) Power, Rella suggests, is for Foucault a "non-place" that can only be grasped through its "infinite heterotopic localizations" (ibid), which is an exact inversion of Foucault, for whom power is always localized, specific, and belongs to a precise constellation, rather than being diffuse phenomenon that permeates everything in the same manner. For Rella, Foucault cannot reach the level of determinate contradiction—which is simply another way of saying that he does not subscribe to a traditional class analysis—and his concept of power in the end becomes useless and counterproductive. In his own subsequent essay in the book, "The Political Economy of the Body," Rella draws the even sharper conclusion that Foucault's discourse, by virtue of its mystifying quality, "in the end becomes not a critical discourse *on* power, but the discourse *of* power itself" (55, my italics), a kind of idealist veil

(45). While other writings by Tafuri are more appreciative of Foucault's genealogies, especially the essays gathered in *The Sphere and the Labyrinth* (1980), they ultimately remain at the same impressionist level and show little sign of any sustained reading. The absence of a productive encounter between Tafuri and Foucault is indeed one of the missed opportunities of postwar architectural theory, and it was no doubt to the detriment of both. Tafuri could have given Foucault a much sharper perception of architectural history, which always remains slightly out of focus in his research on spatial and urban assemblages, and Foucault might have forced Tafuri to rethink the philosophical eclecticism that, while not a problem in itself, led him into problems that for a while may have been essential on the personal level—in this not unlike the "objective impasses" in Foucault—but sometimes generated false solutions, such as the massive and, I think, untenable divide between operative and critical history. For more on this, see chap. 1, above.

draped over reality so as to hide its true contradictions.

It is ironic that Rella's criticisms on one level seem almost identical to Jean Baudrillard's diagnosis presented the same year in his *Oublier Foucault*. Baudrillard is however less interested in correcting Foucault in the name of Marxism than to intensify his claims so as to pass beyond, or "forget," him (in the infinite, not imperative, it must be added, *oublier* and not *oubliez*; the suggestion is that we ask ourselves what if would *mean* to forget Foucault, not that we *ought to* do it, even though this distinction is of course inaudible in French). For Baudrillard—who largely supports his reading on *Discipline and Punish* and the first volume of *The History of Sexuality*, rather than on the idea of heterotopia—the ubiquity of power and sex that allegedly results from Foucault's analysis means that these have ceased to be applicable concepts, which however does not imply that we should return to more traditional formulas, but that the "principle of reality" that still guides Foucault's use of them must be abandoned. Since power and sex are everywhere in Foucault's analyses, Baudrillard suggest, they are in fact nowhere, they have imploded, and the path we must choose is not to rectify Foucault, but to intensify those features that in Rella's reading made him problematic.[37]

It is important to note precisely how and in what respect both of these readings are misleading. First, on the general level

37. "It may be that Foucault only speaks so eloquently of power (and, let us not forget this, in *real* and objective terms, as dispersed multiplicities, but in terms that do not question the objective perspective he assumes on them—an infinitesimal and pulverized power, but whose reality principle is not put into question) because power is dead, and not just irreparably dead through dispersal, but quite simply dissolved in a way that still escapes us, dissolved through reversibility, by having been annulled and hyperrealized in simulation." Baudrillard, *Oublier Foucault* (Paris: Galilée, 1977), 13. Immediately before this Baudrillard also states, similarly to Rella, that "Foucault's presentation is mirror of those powers that de describes" (11). Rella inversely connects Foucault to Baudrillard and the "nouveaux philosophes" (*DF*, 17, note 16).

of the question of power—which, it must be remembered, is not yet explicitly in question in the essays on utopia and heterotopia—it is simply wrong that Foucault in his later writings would have presented it as a "non-place" or a "mysterious noumenon," or that it is simply everywhere in the sense of a fleeting and atmospheric phenomenon. While is true that he wanted to move away from what he saw as the far too massive dualisms of Marxism, and that this move was perhaps never sufficiently reflected except than on the level of personal reactions, he did this in order to investigate the realities of power through a more differentiated analysis that pays attention to complexity of singular and local conditions.[38] Far from dissolving the power relations into a non-localized noumenon, he wants to understand the materiality and spatiality of power in the most concrete possible manner, as it takes on form in prisons, schools, hospitals, factories, etc. Power is always specific, particular, and it is exerted in singular *dispositifs* with their singular objectives (to teach the student, to cure that sick, to correct the deviant, to discipline the soldier, to render the worker productive, to make the delirious reflective and reasonable, etc.), and the problem, if there is one, is not the noumenal character of Foucault's concept of power, but inversely its extreme specificity and locality, an almost nominalist quality that makes it hard to make general claims outside a particular context.

It is true that Foucault resisted the division between science and ideology, but this too he did not in order to turn his own

38. For a discussion that attempts to combine Foucault with Marx, see Richard Marsden, *The Nature of Capital: Marx after Foucault* (London: Routledge, 1999). In this reading, Marx explains the "why," the structures that limit social action, but not the "how," the mechanisms that make these structures operative, whereas Foucault explains the "how" of power mechanisms, but not the ultimate goals of disciplinary power. While to some extent attractive, this solution however introduces precisely the crucial moment of teleology that Foucault rejects, and for him the "why" will always be a shifting and unstable effect of the "how."

analyses into some ungraspable and atmospheric discourse on the void in being, but to interrogate a different level, that of *savoir* (a term that only with great caution can be translated into the English "knowledge"), a neutral term that encompasses both the talk of the delinquent, the madman and the pervert as well as that of the prison warden, the psychiatrist, and psychoanalyst.[39] This does not mean that everything in the end becomes the same and that all distinctions are obliterated, only that a genealogical analysis of the formations of knowledge of power should not take the teleology of truth as its guiding principle, and that there is conflict, asymmetry, reversal, and contestation involved in any relation. Truths about human beings, their crimes, insanities, and desires, are always caught up in struggles, which does not simply falsify them, but shows that any establishing of such truth will entail asymmetry as well the possibility of reversal.

39. On this point, there is an encounter between Foucault and Lefebvre. The relation between them seems to have been highly antagonistic, at least on Lefebvre's part. They however share the interest in how mechanisms of power and knowledge intersect with everyday life, and how subjective experience is at both an effect and the locus of resistance. A Foucauldian-style critique of Lefebvre would single out his belief in the "given," and his overemphasis on subjectivity as a free and spontaneous; Lefebvre on his part explicitly charged Foucault with blindness to the contradictory and dialectical dimension of everyday life, and suggested that he somehow deduced them immediately from a transcendent structure of power. This is also the point where Lefebvre underscores the distinction between *savoir* and *connaissance*, and claims that Foucault symptomatically does not pay any attention to the second with its connotation of skills and concrete practices, thus forfeiting the dialectic between the sphere of epistemology and the world of practice. But as we have noted, the use of the term "savoir" is not intended to render everyday life invisible, but rather to suspend the opposition between ideology and science, which is a motif Foucault shares with Lefebvre. Edward Soja's attempt to bring them together in terms of "thirdspace" provides a good analysis of the idea of space in Lefebvre, but remains confusing on Foucault, not least since he connects hetero-topia directly to the space of discipline. As Łukasz Stanek notes, the term "heterotopia" in fact figures in Lefebvre too, although it refers to the sense of being excluded from central urban space, with reference to the Nanterre University; see Stanek, *Henri Lefebvre on Space* (Minneapolis: University of Minnesota Press, 2011), 178.

334

The concepts of "heterotopia" and "non-place" proposed by Rella are in fact derived from the version of heterotopia proposed in *The Order of Things*, and as Daniel Défert points out,[40] what all the authors in *Il dispositivo Foucault* curiously enough miss, with the exception for Georges Teyssot, is that other concept of "heterotopia" that indeed relates to real and material places in the world. Teyssot's contribution to *Il dispositivo Foucault*, "Eterotopie e storia degli spazi,"[41] is the only one that takes note of Foucault's different uses of the term heterotopia, but he too still understands the term basically in a taxonomic way, and his main reference is *The Order of Things*. But in spite of the rather foreshortened reading of Foucault, Teyssot extracts a highly productive question. He applies the heterotopic model of classification to a hospital from the eighteenth century, and in the first step his analysis seems merely to confirm that the taxonomy of patients from our perspective appears as wholly arbitrary. But then he proceeds to another question: does architecture belong to the *episteme* of its age, to a set of rules that under a given time would regulate the visible and the sayable? Or must architecture be understood essentially as a hybrid entity, a result of many conflicting interest, a composite that analysis must decompose? This second question points to the passage between the linguistic and spatial versions of heterotopia, in the sense that the ground that is "once more stirring under or feet" must necessarily also be a *material* ground, the physical instantiation of taxonomic structures that regulates the interplay of the heterotopic and the "autotopic" (the "same" and not "other" space, to coin a term that Foucault himself did not use). If the concept of heterotopia points to specific places where our everyday life is subverted and where something "oth-

40. See Défert, "Foucault, Space, and the Architects," in *Documenta x: Poetics/Politics* (Stuttgart: Cantz, 1998).
41. Teyssot's essay has been translated by David Stewart as "Heterotopia and the History of Spaces," in K. Michael Hays (ed.,) *Architecture Theory Since 1968* (Cambridge, Mass: MIT, 1998).

er" or "different" appears in the cracks in the fabric of normality, they must also be seen in relation to the "sameness" of spaces and language that uphold this very normality.

Reinventing the site

Returning to our initial question, we can now see how art practices that intentionally situate themselves outside the divisions between the aesthetic and the everyday sphere, between the temporal layering of time as it appears in institutions and the horizontality of mundane life, may be connected to the idea of heterotopia. Abandoning its pretenses to utopia in the sense of an other place radically outside of the sameness of space, and asking for that which is other *in* the same, that which ruptures the present without being elsewhere, in what sense do such moves entail a different understanding of the site of the work—both in the sense of its physical setting, as well as in terms of its place in the imaginary? Or more generally, how does this impact on the place of the imaginary as such, in between what has been traditionally called the faculties (reason and sensibility), or in psychoanalytic parlance, as an order that precedes—even while remaining inside—the symbolic, and is farthest away from the real?[42]

The desire to return to the concreteness of the site, as in the various claims about "site specificity" that were opposed to the alleged abstraction of modernist visual art, emerged in the various practices in and around minimal art. Independently, and yet in parallel to the visual arts, the rediscovery of place in architecture, notably in the theory of genius loci and its various cognates, appeared as an equally radically challenge to the technological universality of postwar building. While these dif-

42. Those of my comments in the following that draw on Lacan intersect in several respects with those of K. Michael Hays's *Architecture's Desire: Reading the Late Avant-Garde* (Cambridge, Mass.: MIT, 2010), even though my conclusions differ somewhat from his.

ferent reactions do not form a unity on the level of the forms produced, or that of theoretical programs, we might see it as responses to an underlying worry that the physical sensorium was in the process of dissolving, thus the sense of a return to something overlooked or lost, a longing for concreteness and embodiment, which at least in architecture was directly linked a critique of technological modernity

As Fredric Jameson suggests, "We need rather to take into consideration the possibility that the renewed attention to the problem of the site is itself a function of the imminent extinction of the very category in question: an urgency and a desperation that then washes back over this theme to lend it a kind of second-degree historical content in its own right, the return of 'content' itself as a new event."[43] The theorist of *genius loci*, Christian Norberg-Schulz, similarly proposes that the "loss of place" is the basic experience of our era,[44] just as Kenneth Frampton, although with more emphasis on the necessity of historical mediation, launches the idea of critical regionalism and the "tectonic" as a mediation of the autonomy of the formal language of architecture with its cultural context.[45] Regardless of the considerable differences between these theories, they share an experience of loss that must be countered by a restoring praxis; but maybe such a loss of place is simply a necessary consequence of what has been called our "supermodernity,"[46] where other forms of places, largely modeled on transit, have become part and parcel of everyday life, and in fact must be de-

43. *The Seeds of Time* (New York: Columbia University Press, 1994), 165.
44. See Christian Norberg-Schulz, *Genius Loci: Towards a Phenomenology of Architecture* (New York: Rizzoli, 1980), above all chap. 1.
45. Se Frampton, "Towards a Critical Regionalism: Six Points for an Architecture of Resistance" (1983) and "Rappel à l'ordre, The Case of the Tectonic" (1990), both reprinted in Frampton, *Labour, Work and Architecture* (London: Phaidon Press, 2002).
46. See Marc Auge, *Non-Lieux, Introduction à une anthropologie de la supermodernité* (Paris: Seuil, 1992).

337

scribed in terms of the new experience they give rise to. And furthermore, intentional re-creations of places may seem like a resistance to the emptiness of universal placelessness, but are in fact and integral part of global spatial system that works precisely by diversification, localization, and regionalization. The various claims for the place made in art and architecture, fragmentary and contradictory as they are, cast a particular light on this process.

In many respects, contemporary artistic practices, especially in claiming to intervene into the fabric of everyday life and to detach our perceptual and mental habits from an unquestioned anchoring, aspire to release a heterotopic energy belonging both to language and space, and particularly to the interstitial element that articulates them upon each other. Foucault's inclusion of the museum as a heterochrony that accumulates past time points to one aspect of this process, in which the horizontal flow of events is folded back upon itself, twisted out of joint, and laid out before us in order to be evaluated anew. The estranged gaze on the contemporary moment made possible by the museum and similar institutions of accumulation shows our current practices in a different light, reveals the contingencies and necessities that permeate them, and in this it also asks to what extent we could do things otherwise.

The crucial issue seems to be to retrieve a sense of mobility, of inventing a capacity for displacement that would not simply congeal into objects of appreciation, but release a similar energy in whoever encounters such events. And perhaps it is not coincidental that the last example Foucault provides us with at the end of the 1967 lecture on other spaces is the *boat*. It is presented as the heterotopia par excellence that condenses all the ambivalences of the preceding examples, and it is difficult not to recall the glorious description of the Ship of Fools, at the outset of *The History of Madness*, located at the moving frontier between inner and outer, *as* the inner of the outer and inversely—as a figure of freedom and enclosure at once. In the final lines of the lecture this limit begins to resonate even more with the idea of movement and displacement, with the oneiric and the imaginary, and it points to the possibility of a heterotopia of resistance: "In civilizations without ships the dreams dry up, espionage takes the place of adventure, and the police that of the corsairs." (EW 2, 185).

Coming back to these texts by Foucault from the late sixties, partly in order to read them as impasses, or perhaps better prismatic points of intersection from which many of his later interrogations would unfold, might we not also follow the suggestion by Molly Nesbit and see them as "event infiltrated by other events," i.e., as engaged in a subterranean dialog with many of the radical artistic movements of the period, which themselves form equally prismatic points of intersection with respect to the present? The site-specific practices that emerged in the 1960s were surely not on Foucault's horizon when he gave the lecture in 1967, and yet the questions he posed appear particularly relevant when read through this connection. His own writings on the visual arts at the time were mostly engaged with problem of painting and representation, as in the book-length study of Magritte (and most famously in the reading of Velázquez *Las Meninas* placed at the beginning of *The Order of Things*), or the series of lectures on Manet and the origin of modernist painting. The latter he interprets in way that in hindsight is surprisingly close to the formalist criticism developed by Greenberg and Fried, unlikely as it may be that Foucault would have understood the Manet lectures as a contribution to this debate, which was focused on the issue of the flatness, materiality, and "objecthood" of painting, i.e., the demarcation line between an art that would continue a modernist quest for autonomy in terms of a residual illusionism, and one that collapses autonomy into the world of real objects.[47] From our vantage point, the productive link is however not to the status of late modernist painting, but to the emerging artistic practices in which the ideas of site and space were radically transformed, precisely in terms of a heterochrony and a heterotopy that overlays time, space, and language in a new way. Locating them within Foucault's heterotopia-utopia quadrant will to be sure not provide them with a general grid of intelligibility, but rather give rise to a set or resonances, sometimes collapsing concepts into each other, sometimes breaking them apart. In this, it remains faithful to the idea of impasses that are not there to be surmounted, but explored as that which gives thought mobility, pushes it ahead, from one place to another.

Varieties of sites and non-sites

The artist who more than anyone else embodies these shifts, and whose investigations run parallel to the researches of Foucault that have been in focus here, is no doubt Robert Smithson, whose work soon expanded beyond the vocabulary of minimal art precisely because of his understanding of the site as a complex of same and other, of language and space. Working in remote places, often incorporating geological and natural processes in a way that displaces the parameters of aesthetics and the art object, he still refused any understanding of the land of land art as a lost Arcadia; there is no originary place to be recreated. Nature for Smithson is rather a time of oblivion and erasure, a process of entropy that bars any identification of it as our true home; his quest is not for a return to some prior state of sanctity, but for a state of "dedifferentiation," an oceanic state where words, things, and images begin to fuse. This also why it

47. For a discussion of these different readings of Manet, see Carole Talon-Hugon, "Manet ou le désarroi du spectateur," in Maryvonne Saison (ed.). Michel Foucault, *La peinture de Manet* (Paris: Seuil, 2004).

is difficult to distinguish his theoretical statements from his artistic practice, his criticism from his art, which is a consequence of his multivalent understanding of the site of the work.[48] If there is "a museum of language" in the "vicinity of art," it is not because any of the terms would be reducible to the other, but because they share a similar condition of dedifferentiation that will eventually lead all stable structures to collapse.[49]

Just as little as the insistence on the site implies any claim about a return to the originary does his move toward the blurring of boundaries exclude the problem of reality and representation in favor of a direct presence; in fact it intensifies it to the point that it transforms the institutional frame into an means of aesthetic production.[50] So for instance in his 1969 *Yucatan*

48. It is true that Smithson himself did not consider his writings as part of his art; posterity has however not hesitated to see his texts and works as a single continuum. So, for instance, in Craig Owens's often-cited review of the posthumous collection of Robert Smithson's writings, where he famously suggests that we in the case of Smithson can observe a fundamental displacement of visual art from the visual to the field of language. In Owens's perspective, Smithson's work with texts and images, ranging from the early non-sites and text-photo essays to the later monumental projects, constitutes a kind of Baroque practice that allows for a return of the repressed unconscious in late modernist art, the "eruption of language into the field of the visual arts." See Craig Owens, "Earthwords," *October* no. 10 (Fall 1979); reprinted in Owens, *Beyond Recognition: Representation, Power, and Culture* (Berkeley: University of California Press, 1992), 45. For a discussion of Smithson as a critic, see Lars-Erik Hjertström, "Robert Smithson and the Importance of a Sovereign Criticism", *Site* 26–27 (2009). For a discussion of Smithson's philosophical views, which equally emphasizes the importance of language, see Gary Shapiro, *Earthwards: Robert Smithson and Art after Babel* (Berkeley: University of California Press, 1995).

49. See Smithson "A Museum of Language in the Vicinity of Art" (1968)," in *Robert Smithson: The Collected Writings*, ed. Jack Flam (Berkeley: University of California Press, 1996).

50. In a discussion with Dennis Oppenheim and Michael Heizer, Smithson responds to the question how he understands the relation between gallery spaces and nature: "I think we all see the landscape as coextensive with the gallery. I don't think we're dealing with matter in terms of a back to nature movement. *For me the world is a museum*. Photography makes nature obsolete." See "Discussions with Heizer, Oppenheimer, Smithson," *The Collected Writings*, 246, my italics.

Mirror Displacements (1–9), which together with the essay published the same year in *Artforum*, "Incidents of Mirror-Travel in the Yucatan," in this respects constitutes one of his most significant works.[51] Moving between texts, photographs, and a series of actions all existing at different times and places, the work "itself" is impossible to access outside of the multiple sites of entry that it creates (or, which amounts to the same, infinitely accessible), none of which are more correct or true than any other. In the concluding section in the essay that constitutes one layer of the work, Smithson writes: "If you visit the sites (a doubtful probability) you will find nothing but memory-traces, for the mirror displacements were dismantled right after they were photographed. The mirrors are somewhere in New York. The reflected light has been erased. Remembrances are but numbers on a map, vacant memories constellating the intangible terrains in deleted vicinities. It is the dimension of absence that remains to be found. The expunged color that remains to be seen. The fictive voices of the totems have exhausted their argument. Yucatan is elsewhere."[52]

Mirror Displacements embodies in a more complex form fashion the dialectic between "Site" and "Nonsite" that Smithson had begun to investigate the year before his trip to Yucatan. Inspired by a visit to the slate quarries of Bangor-Pen Argyle, Pennsylvania, Smithson had initiated an exploration of the boundary between inside and outside, nature and art, by return-

51.　The same things could undoubtedly be said about Smithson's most famous work, *The Spiral Jetty*. Here too the work can be accessed through photographs, films, and texts, as well as through its physical manifestation. The latter has however come to overshadow the other dimensions of the work, transforming the "elsewhere" into a physical difficulty of actually getting to the site, or into a kind of ironic *Fort-Da* game because of the sinking and rising of Great Salt Lake, which in certain periods have made the work invisible.

52.　Smithson, "Incidents of Mirror-Travel in the Yucatan," *The Collected Writings*, 132f.

ing materials picked up at the quarry to the gallery and presenting them together with maps, photographs and geological information, which together formed the "Nonsite" that reflected and
undermined the integrity of the "Site" as both were drawn into
a process of mirroring and imbrication. This was, Smithson re-
marked in a statement accompanying the exhibition, a "course
of hazards, double path maps that belong to both sides of the
dialectic at once."[53]

The site-nonsite dialectic was however still caught up in a binary play of inside and outside, which in the *Mirror Displacements*
is taken further and becomes more like a trajectory meandering
though time and space. The latter work brings together many of
his basic themes: a fascination with the prehistory and geological past of modern society, which still remains lodged inside our
modern systems and artifacts,[54] the mirror as model for art that
duplicates and dislocates itself in infinity, both of which point to
a particular structure of temporal reversibility and duplication;
of crucial important in this context is however also the fact that
the movement out of the gallery space ends up taking us back
to he institution, so as to transform the site itself into a mobile
construction. The "elsewhere" that both is and is not Yucatan
is framed, by photography and writing, by the gallery space and
the pages of the magazine, and all of these parts are swept along
in a transversal movement that shows the instable and fundamentally mediated character of the place that the critical art of
the period wanted to retrieve beyond the abstractions of modernism.

53. Cited from the reprint in *Robert Smithson: Sculpture*, ed. Robert Hobbs
    (Ithaca, NY: Cornell University Press, 1981), 110.
54. For Smithson, the monuments of modernity are monuments of entropy
    and decay, and upon closer inspection they prove be "ruins in reverse."
    See for instance the reading of minimalist sculpture in "Entropy and
    the new Monuments" (1966) and "A Tour of the Monuments of Pas-
    saic, New Jersey" (1967).

Closer to architecture we find works like *Hotel Palenque* (1969), *Partially Buried Woodshed* (1972), which each in their particular way draws out the implication of the temporal layering of the sites and spatial structures, how they come to be inhabited, even haunted, by events that not only pre- but also antedate them. *Hotel Palenque*, conceived during the same trip to Mexico that was at the origin of the mirror displacements, constitutes what Smithson sometimes talked of in terms of a "ruin in reverse." Here too issues of representation and temporal layering are crucial: during the trip Smithson took a series of photographs of a hotel where he was staying, and which seemed to be undergoing a continual renovation that only furthered its dilapidation; additions were made that only contributed to the disorder, repairs that lead to even more damage, in an endless cycle of self-deconstructing restoral. Subsequently these images served as the basis for a lecture to architecture students at the University of Utah in 1972, at the occasion of his last completed and most famous large-scale project, *Spiral Jetty* in Great Salt Lake, where the "de-architecturalized" site of Hotel Palenque was presented as a meditation on the co-implication of entropy and structure (the work today exists the typically mediated and yet congenial form of a slide installation with a tape recording of the lecture). Instead of marveling at the Mayan ruins that have made the site famous—which could be glimpsed from the window, as Smithson notes in passing—he meditates on the hotel's emptied pool, the deserted dancehall, and various architectural oddities, as if the depth of prehistory had to be released from its grandiose and picturesque dimension, and brought back into the ephemerality of the Instamatic to be experienced.[55] The task of hotel restoration becomes as infinite as

55. As Jeff Wall points out, Smithson engages in a kind of parody of photo journalism, beginning in text-image works like the essay on the monuments of Passaic, where the travel description at first hand seems

time itself (or, from another perspective, just as finite, since it is doomed to perpetual incompletion), it is ceaselessly begun anew and just as quickly abandoned, allowing the architectural mishaps to unfold in a rhythm that belongs to an order outside of our plans and projects.

Partially Buried Woodshed (1970) is a more direct take on decay and the presence and power of the earth to dislodge our architectural quest for stability and permanence. Located at the campus of Kent State University, Ohio, it consisted of an abandoned woodshed on which twenty cartloads of earth and dirt hade been poured, until the central beam cracked. Smithson wanted the work to remain on site and be subjected to natural decay, and it stayed there until the final remains were removed in 1984.[56] A couple of months after the completion of the work, on May 4, four students were killed and nine wounded by the Ohio National Guard during a protest on the campus against the American invasion of Cambodia. While this event as such obviously had no direct link to the work—which at the time had been little noticed—associations could easily be made between the cracking of the house and the cracking of the political system, "infiltrating" one event with another, most visible in the anonymous message "May 4 Kent 1970" painted on the woodshed during the summer, which brought the work to public attention.

just as meandering and directionless as his photographs are devoid of the qualities of "professional" photography; see Jeff Wall, "'Marks of Indifference': Aspects of Photography in, or as, Conceptual Art," in Ann Goldstein and Anne Rorimer (eds.), *Reconsidering the Object of Art: 1965–1975* (Los Angeles: Museum of Contemporary Art, 1996). But while there is undoubtedly an element of "deskilling" involved here, one must not overlook the particular poetic of Smithson, which is precisely to invest the sites that he documents with a temporal and existential depth that is largely absent from the dialectical narrative of conceptual photography that Wall constructs.

56. For a thorough documentation of the work's genesis and subsequent historical fate, see Dorothy Shinn, *Robert Smithson's Partially Buried Woodshed*, exh. cat. (Kent, Ohio: Kent State University School of Art Gallery, 1990).

Such contingencies are however from the outset part of the conception of the work: the accelerating process of dilapidation is proportional to the profusion and weight of accumulated meanings. Entropy is on the one hand a loss of information, but on the other hand just as much an increase, in the sense that the structure becomes inhabited by otherness, chaos, and de-structuration, "de-architecturized," in a movement which is not simply opposed to architecture as an external contingence, but in Smithson's version belongs to its temporal nature. Similarly, the task of restoration or preservation of the work (a question that became increasingly acute as its fame grew) brings out the multi-layered dimensions of this temporality: how can one preserve that whose purpose is to disintegrate, to what point in time should the work be brought back so that its disintegration and eventual disappearance become possible to experience at the right speed, at the right parallax between the work's own temporal trajectory from beginning to end and the point of intersection of the spectator?[57] *Partially Buried Woodshed* is at once a directly palpable breaking up of architectural form through the intrusion of nature, and a receptacle of sorts for other stories that can and will be woven around it approaches the state of a final formlessness.

These multiple relations to the site can be understood in terms of the development of minimalist and postminimalist sculpture, as it has been analyzed by Miwon Kwon.[58] She distinguishes three stages, in all of which we might locate particular works and texts by Smithson. The first is the *phenomenological*

57.   In this, Smithson's reflections on the (anti)-monuments, from his first writings on the industrial landscapes of Passaic onward, only bring out the temporal paradox that was inherent in the discourse on preservation from its start in Viollet-le-Duc. On the paradoxes of preservation, see Thordis Arrhenius, *The Fragile Monument: On Conservation and Modernity* (London: Black Dog, 2012).

58.   See Kwon, "One Place After Another: Notes on Site Specificity," *October*, Vol. 80 (Spring, 1997).

place that we encounter in early minimalism, for instance in Robert Morris, where the sculpture is related to the qualities of the surrounding physical space and the movements of the spectator. This, Kwon suggests, is a "radical restructuring of the subject from an old Cartesian model to a phenomenological one of lived bodily experience," which furthermore is an attempt to "resist the forces of the capitalist market economy, which circulates art works as transportable and exchangeable commodity goods." [59] The second is the institutional place, defined by all those ideologies, theories, and symbolical orders that make up the frame of the artwork's legibility, and which in turn are part of a network of places (the studio, the museum, the gallery, the private collection, the art market, the public space of criticism) within which it circulates. It is here that we encounter the de-materialization and de-aestheticizing of the work and place in conceptual art; producing art is no longer essentially the producing of an object (though it can be that too), but more of an investigation into is framing conditions, all the "parergonal" apparatuses that make up to institution, and that also at the time began to be examined by thinkers as different as Danto, Dickie, and Derrida. [60] In the third step, this network is expanded so as to become a discursive site, understood as a "field of knowledge, intellectual exchange, or cultural debate," [61] in which the preceding interrogations of the specific mode of production of

59. Ibid, 86.
60. The two classic cases are Danto's pioneering essay "The Artworld" (1964) an Dickie's "Defining Art" (1969). Derrida's extended meditation on the structure of the "parergon" in Kant may seem wholly remote from these discussions, which at least in the case of Danto had a close connection to current art practices, but in fact, in its interrogation of the dynamic role of the frame for the determination of what should count as properly belonging to the work and what not, it draws out precisely those questions of limits that were ay the center of conceptual art. See Derrida, *The Truth in Painting*, trans. Geoff Bennington and Ian McLeod. (Chicago: University of Chicago Press, 1987)
61. Kwon, "One Place After Another," 92.

347

the art institution give way to mobile interventions in the real world. Rather than a physical and phenomenological site correlated to the body and its kinesthetic field, or the inside/outside dialectic of the art institution, this third site is a linking together of different physical localities, texts, and all possible forms of documentation. Its model, Kwon suggests, is "not a map but an itinerary, a fragmentary sequence of events and actions through spaces, that is, a nomadic narrative whose path is articulated by the passage of the artist"[62]—a series of "transitive places," "one place after another," with a paraphrase of Donald Judd's famous program for a non-hierarchical aligning of "one thing after another" in the new domain of "specific objects" that would supersede the syntactical anthropomorphism of traditional sculpture, but which here has come to signify the detaching from the physical site rather than its rediscovery.

Dislocating the site

Similarly to Smithson's expanding dialectic of site and nonsite, Peter Eisenman's "artificial excavations" open the question of the space-time of work in a way that dislodges most of its traditional parameters.[63] In the terms defined by Kwon, Eisenman's works would just like Smithson's traverse all three levels: his early architecture is formally close to minimalist sculpture, while operating with categories that aspire to subvert any grounding in a phenomenology of the body; the part of his sub-

62.   Ibid, 95.
63.   Or, we might say, in fact continues and radicalizes the kind of exploration that we find adumbrated in someone like Giedion, from the idea of "interpenetration" to the "space-time" drawing on physics, cubism, and a host of other sources in his 1941 magnum opus *Space, Time and Architecture*—which would be in line with Eisenman's claim that we have still not become truly modern, and that the promises of the avant-garde must finally be fulfilled in architecture in the same way that it had been in music, literature, and the visual arts. For more on Giedion, see chap. 3, above.

sequent work that will be in focus here examines the concept of architecture as both an institution and a discursive site, but also draws on an idea of fiction that is difficult to reconcile with the claims to disclosure and truth that still form the regulative idea of institutional critique in the other visual arts; it thrives on an indeterminacy, a kind of drift that is particular to the third level understood as a discursive site.

This phase of Eisenman's work is often read in close connection to deconstruction, but while it is true that this term and his various encounters with Derrida have generated a lot of attention and a huge literature, what will be understood here as the motivating thrust of his development is rather that the question that animated his work from the start, i.e. whether architecture at all can become a modernist art, in the sense that it would be able to autonomously interrogate its own forms, its site, and its structural parameters, developed in a way that "textualizes" the site and eventually pushes all of these terms to their limit.[64] Already from the outset this placed Eisenman in opposition to all types of historicism, revivalism, and eclecticism that aspired to recreate "meaning" in architecture. While his linguistic and semiotic analogies assume that architecture is language throughout, it is a language that has ceased to communicate a content exterior to itself (symbols, functions, references to nature, the body, etc.), at the same time as this "self"-reference always entails an otherness inside this self, a perpetual dislocation rather than a regained self-sufficiency.[65] If this disloca-

64.   For the idea of textualization of the site, I draw on Hays, *Architecture's Desire*, 51–89. Hays places Eisenman's work at the endpoint of a logic of commodification and reification, at which the only remaining possibility would be a self-reflexive staging of the depletion of all architectural signs. While this reading is entirely consonant with many of Eisenman's own statements, and has a (perhaps too) powerful logic of its own, the path I choose here is somewhat different, as will become clear in the following.

65.   The ultimate question here of course being what this otherness implies:

tion leads to the discovery of the other of the discursive place of architecture—i.e., in the first of Foucault's formulas for heterotopia, to a disruption of "table upon which, since the beginning of time, language has intersected space"—then it seems just as true this language, freed from its semantic ties to the world, must itself be infiltrated by a material otherness, if it is not to simply revert to a crystalline order of pure forms; it must somehow be affected by time, where, in Foucault's second formula, "the erosion of our life, our time, and our history takes place." The question would then be what might account for the relation between the two heterotopias, the one of language and the one of space-time, without reducing one of them to the other. For the Foucault of the late sixties, this was still an open question, and it was not until the relation between the discursive and the non-discursive—at what point language, after having been freed from its essentiality, *in fact* intersects space in historically variable ways—began to be framed in terms of power as a spatial and temporal ordering that a new understanding of this relation become possible. Eisenman's path never reaches this conclusion, or possibly evades it, which has not prevented his interpreters from filling in this gap for him, above all in proposing History (which here generally means late capitalism) as the absent cause.

The initial steps taken in Eisenman's early projects and texts from the sixties are in one respect close to minimal art and what Michael Fried, to be sure not a sign of appreciation, called "objecthood,"[66] i.e., a purely material presence of the work that

the ultimate groundlessness and abyssal of architectural language as such, or a much more determined other, such as the pressure exerted upon architecture by the mode of production of late capitalism. As Reinhold Martin proposes, the more one attempts to penetrate into the inside of architecture, the further out you end up. See Martin, *Utopia's Ghost: Architecture and Postmodernism, Again* (Minneapolis: University of Minnesota Press, 2010), and my discussion of this in chap. 4, above.

66. See Fried, "Art and Objecthood" (1967), in Fried, *Art and Objecthood: Essay and Reviews* (Chicago: University of Chicago Press, 1998).

short-circuits any metaphorical reading. Just as the new sculpture, architecture must in Eisenman's version be understood
as direct physical presence, or signs referring to themselves—
which, one must note, introduces an imperceptible difference
and dislocation that is essential, precisely because the structure
of referral is what lets the "self" appear. This, Eisenman argues, is the lesson of modernist pioneers like Terragni and Le
Corbusier,[67] whose legacy he sets out to retrieve for the present.
But there is also a decisive difference in relation to minimal art
and its exploration of presence and objecthood, since Eisenman
wants to displace the phenomenological model and the body
as a source of meaning, which in his interpretation is what
impeded architectural modernism from becoming truly modern: "When conventions and external references are stripped
from an object, the only reference remaining is the object itself. Hence, all those extraneous meanings like the column as
the surrogate for a man's body, doors and windows oriented in
relation to man's verticality, rooms scaled to his size, ordering
principles and plans in conformance with the classical hierarchies—all of which, however, remained disguised in the work of
modernism—have been suspended."[68]

That which here severs the object from the bodily system of
references, is that it is ultimately understood as part of a linguistic act akin to the one Foucault's archeology proposed to call an
enoncé,[69] which is also how one might understand Eisenman's
idiosyncratic take on generative grammar. For Chomsky this
was an attempt to locate, underneath the surface of language,

67. For Eisenman's relation to Terragni, see the texts assembled in Eisenman, *Giuseppe Terragni: Transformations, Decompositions, Critiques* (New
York: Monacelli Press, 2003). Corbusier is treated systematically for the
first time in "Aspects of Modernism: 'Maison Dom-ino' and the Self-
Referential Sign", *Oppositions* 15–16 (1979).
68. Peter Eisenman, "Misreading", in Eisenman, *Houses of Cards* (New
York: Oxford University Press, 1987), 172.
69. For Foucault's *enoncé*, see note 15, above.

those mechanisms or syntactic deep structures that would allow for all types of meaningful surface statements (whereas it would exclude statements like the famous "colorless green ideas sleep furiously"). For Eisenman, the idea of deep structures became an instrument for breaking away from a phenomenological essentialism that assumes the meaningfulness of architectural and sculptural objects to be rooted in the body's primordial relation to the world. The discovery of such structures instead make possible, as Eisenman sometimes suggests in a move that would hardly make sense in generative grammar, a suspension of the semantics of the architectural sign, a severing of its meaningful relation to the world in terms of function or symbolism, in favor a pure syntax, i.e., those rules for forming and connecting that make a statement acceptable as pertaining to architecture without yet ascribing any particular architectural meaning to it.

When he in the essay "Postfunctionalism" (1976) suggests that architecture has yet to become a truly modernist art, it is because its language in his view remains tied to a Renaissance paradigm that puts man at the center and organizes all of its signs in relation to an ultimate vanishing point, which in this general sense would also include the category of function.[70] The particular context of this text, published as en editorial in *Oppositions*, is a debate on the idea of typology that pitted "neorationalists" against "neorealists,"[71] but it also makes sense to read it as a reflection on Eisenman's own long-term projects to work through the formal language of modernism (beginning in 1967 in the series *Houses*, and extending up to the end of the seventies) and to continue the avant-garde with other means. As we have noted, this may on a purely formal level have brought

70. Eisenman, "Postfunctionalism," reprinted in Kate Nesbitt, *Theorizing A New Agenda for Architecture: An Anthology of Architectural theory, 1965–1995* (New York : Princeton Architectural Press, 1996).

71. See Hays, *Architecture's Desire*, 10.

him close to certain features of minimal art, while his ultimate aims were something else. Rather than being unique works that emphasize a material presence in the world, their "cardboard"[72] version of materiality gives them a paradoxical status, and the houses in fact more take on the guise of thought objects than objecthood: they are instruments of reflection. It is this ideal, immaterial materiality that allows them to operate as tools for a historical anamnesis or reactivation, while the attempt to begin modernism anew by a fundamental reorientation of its own social claims is made possible by their self-reflexive, inward turn that aims at the individual subject, but finally in order to dissolve it: "The houses herein proposed the converse of modernism's ostensible social project. They attempted to deal with modern alienation by inverting the outward thrust inward, toward the individual and his house [...] Thus they emerged from a discourse informed by modernism, but were ideologically distanced from its concern with changing outward surroundings and circumstances of life. They turned the discourse upon itself and, in that sense, began again the project of modernism. In this sense they used the idea of autonomy as an attempt to dislocate the metaphysics of architecture."[73]

The dislocation of the house above all has to do with its various symbolic functions: sheltering may remain indispensible, but need no longer be expressed or symbolized, since such symbolisms have become "meaningless and merely nostalgic," not least as they appear in the form of postmodern attempts to restore a meaningful language from the past: "The estranging vector moving out from the center is not subject to man's volition, and no postmodern retreat into simulated symbols of benign

72.   See Eisenman's programmatic 1965 essay "Cardboard Architecture," in *Five Architects: Eisenman, Graves, Gwathmey, Hejduk, Meier* (New York: Oxford University Press, New York, 1975), 15-17.
73.   Eisenman, "Misreading," 172.

past can mask it."[74]

In the House series, the focus lies more on the formal organization of the structure, less on the way in which it interacts with its surroundings—it is as if an attention to site and context would inevitably entail some kind of recreated unity and continuity of sense, whereas the inward turn would be a precondition for the act of dislocation. The last works in the series however form a transition to the phase that will occupy us in the following, and here we find a renewed interest in concrete topographic organization, for the terrain as point of departure that now, after having been divested of its stabilizing and naturalizing connotations—the genius loci that already whispers sense to us and prefigures the order we are extract out of it—can incorporate earlier formal ideas and push them further ahead. House 11 a picks up the L-shape from the preceding House X, but transforms it into a descent into the earth, so that half of the building is located under ground, half above, with the surface as a mirroring plane; House el Even Odd takes yet another step by being entirely under ground, as a total inversion of the idea of house as such, which now achieves a state of almost complete concealment, even though this is further complicated by the play of transparent and opaque surfaces, which renders the under/above distinction fluid and insecure. Just as the earlier houses drew on the elements and primordial relations of architectural language (the wall, the stair, the floor, the relation between load and bearing), the integration of topography here uses the physical environment as an abstracted raw material divested of it spatiotemporal specificity, and as a source for further transformational moves.

This is what is at stake in the series of projects entitled "Cities of Artificial Excavations," comprising eleven works that

74.   Ibid.

extend over more than a decade. If the Houses start off from the isolation of syntactic features in order to attain a state of self-reference that also lets the formal other, form's otherness, irrupt inside autonomy, the excavations take the opposite route and present us with a formidable semantic profusion that overlays systems of representation and draws on a vast array of literary, scientific, and historical references, in order to attain a maximum density; the "palimpsest" is not by chance one of the recurrent concepts. Here, three of these works will be in focus: the project for Cannaregio (1978), for Parc de la Villette (1985–86), and for an art museum in Long Beach (1986).

In the Cannaregio project, three different forms of memory traces are superimposed: the plan for hospital that Le Corbusier had projected for the area; the writings and speculations of Giordano Bruno, who resided in Venice in the 1590s, and was burnt at the stakes in 1600; and finally a general reflection on memory as such, which each in their respective ways produce a temporal loop that Eisenman contrasts to the nostalgia for the future in modernism, for the past in postmodernism, and for the present in contextualism.[75]. Eisenman's proposal consists of three brief textual statements ("Three texts for Venice"), and an overarching plan in which echoes of Le Corbusier's hospital and forms drawn from House 11 a are overlaid on the topography of Cannaregio. The encounter between the first text, "The Emptiness of the Future," and the site generates a series of voids, zones of absence that indicate the ghostly presence of Corbusier and early modernism. The second text, "The Emptiness of the Present," produces a diagonal line across the plan, like a cut that partly uncovers a deeper layer, partly activates the series of L-shapes drawn from House 11 a, all of which operate as

75. Eisenman, "Three texts for Venice", in Jean-Louis Bédard (ed.), *Cities of Artificial Excavations: The Work of Peter Eisenman, 1978–1988* (Montreal: Centre Canadien d'Architecture & Rizzoli, 1994), 47.

scalar displacements of a "normal house." The third text, "The Emptiness of the Past," draws on Bruno's mnemotechnics and alchemical works, and proposes to transform "the gold of Venice" into a memory of a "loss of memory," a seemingly "rational project" that pushes rationality toward its limit. Together these three texts, Eisenman proposes, produce a dislocation of the idea of the house, and thus of the limit condition of architecture as such. He writes: "The question is, Which object is the house, if in fact one of them is a house? Which one is the correct size? [...] These three objects together stand at the limit of architecture, in terms both of their scale and of their naming."[76]

These shifts brought about by shifts in "scaling" once more deprives the body of its central referential role, but even more so the site as something that would determine the architecture: the objects are divested of their spatial and temporal identity so as to become capable of migrating from one system to another and be grafted onto each other according to a non-linear and non-causal linking. There is no proper historical connection between the different systems, no suggestion of a deeper underlying unity that would make them into surface manifestations of a more profound order, but rather a suspension of the idea of the proper and the affirmation of a seemingly limitless possibility of grafting one thing onto another.

The subsequent project for Parc de la Villette (which marks the first collaboration with Derrida) pushes this logic even further. Here, the structures generated in Cannaregio are once more rescaled and transferred to a new site. Eisenman compares this multiple overlay of overlays, superimposing places, plans, and texts, to Freud's dreamwork, but as we have noted, an equally pertinent model would be Kwon's theory of the third, discursive site, made up of "one thing after another," a "frag-

76.   Ibid, 48.

mentary sequence of events and actions through spaces, that is, a nomadic narrative whose path is articulated by the passage of the artist."

In the third case under consideration here, the project for the Long Beach Art Museum, Eisenman once more refers to the idea of a palimpsest of superimposed narratives. Spanning two centuries—from 1849 and the settlement of California, 1949 and the creation of the campus, and finally the fictive rediscovery of the museum in 2049—as well as superimposing six different maps that relate to geological, political, and scientific structures, the museum wants to dislocate the scale that would be commensurate with the subject. It produces superpositions that "reveal relationships that were never visible when some things, such as social delineations, were given more importance than, for instance, the site of a riverbed"; it is "about the telling of stories, and this stone text that is being written, this fiction, might tell a very different story about Long Beach than has ever been recorded before."[77]

Rather than a phenomenological given or a permanent physical location, in all of these three cases the site is the object of a particular type of production,[78] and its identity is nothing else than a plurality of stories that may be told; there is however none that has any *truth*, which in the end runs up against the figure of thought that both Eisenman and even more so some interpreters of his work has assumed, drawing on psychoanalysis and critique of ideology, i.e., that the new text produced is an uncovering of something previously repressed that in some way or another may be brought out from its latency or concealment.

His commentators are however divided on this point. At one

77. Eisenman, project description, *Cities of Artificial Excavations,* 132.
78. For an analysis of the idea of place as produced, see Ignasi de Solà-Morales, "Place: Permanence or Production," in Solà-Morales, *Differences: Topographies of Contemporary Architecture*, trans. Graham Thompson (Cambridge, Mass.: MIT, 1997).

end point, we find Fredric Jameson, who speaks of the artificial excavations as a "the return of history, via the discontinuities of the site itself: the layerings are now historical, ghosts of various pasts, presents, and futures, which may in fact be alternate worlds but whose tensions and incompatibilities are all mediated through some larger absent cause, which is History itself."[79] At the other end, Yve-Alain Bois sees these narrative structures as little but an excuse, finally an unnecessary one— "shrewd" but "far too metaphorical"[80]—for he creation of new abstract forms. Both of them seem to exclusively focus on one particular aspect, and thereby miss the essential tension that exists between abstraction and historical and narrative references. Jameson, confident in the power of History, tends to understand the actual form of the works as a mere appearance, an ideology, or even a "scam," in which "a batch of disparate materials—a kind of lumber room of all kinds of different contents, partial forms, linguistic phenomena, social and psychological raw material, semi-autonomous ideological fantasies, local period concepts, scientific spare parts, and random topical themes—are forcibly yoked together and fused by the power of aesthetic ideology into what looks like an organic whole. What used to be considered a 'work' therefore is now to be treated as best as a kind of anthology of disconnected parts and pieces and at worst as a kind of dumping ground for objective spirit."[81] This seems too reductive, and largely bypasses the problem of accounting for the unity that in fact is there; not all piles of junk or juxtapositions of incongruent fragments are works in a quali-

79. Fredric Jameson, *The Seeds of Time*, 174.
80. Bois, "Surfaces," in *Cities of Artificial Excavations*, 41.
81. Jameson, *The Seeds of Time*, 168. The idea of organic unity as an ideological illusion is derived from Pierre Macherey (*Pour une théorie de la production littéraire*, 1974), ultimately from Althusser. While Jameson somewhat distances himself from it, it nevertheless leads him to downplay the actual work produced in favor of a "symptomal" reading that quickly moves to the level of "History."

fied sense that would merit our interest. And when Bois takes the opposite direction and reduces the narrative poetic that gives these works their specific fragmentation to techniques for achieving a "moiré effect"[82] this transforms them into a version of late modernist painting, which evacuates their claim to still be works precisely at the limit of architecture, located in a particular tradition that they both question and affirm (and, one might add, reduces them to a painting that at the time would hardly have merited such extended exegetical efforts).

Beyond this alternative, and perhaps also as synthesis of their respective claims, the reading of Michael Hays proposes that these works are emblematic of the predicament of the late avant-garde, precisely in amalgamating the acknowledgment of the impact of history (or History, in an emphatic sense) and the flattening of historical depth brought about by the universal reification brought about by late capitalism. What Eisenman does, so Hays, is to inscribe these effects of loss, render them readable and palpable, and so allow us to reflect on them in a critical way. Neither a mere surrender to the collapse of objective spirit (the Symbolic, in Hays's Lacanian vocabulary), nor a flight into the aesthetic pleasures of abstract forms, his work forms a last line of resistance that upholds Architecture in the face of its imminent impossibility, as it were oscillating between a negativity that is still a determined negation of this world, this phase in history, and an infinite negativity for which there is no more determined content to be grasped.

The question might be put in slightly simpler terms, which however soon enter into a vertiginous self-reflection: in what sense can these artificial excavations lay claim to uncover something repressed, if this still excludes any access to a real that would precede it? In an essay on the status of the rhetorical fig-

82.   Bois, "Surfaces," 41.

ure, written one year after the Long Beach project, Eisenman, with reference to the techniques of scalar displacement and superposition, writes: "Because elements along each of these axes are relocated, they began to also superpose on other elements to reveal unexpected correspondences which in their former reality would have remained unintelligible. What is revealed from the initial superpositions cannot be predicted. These are the so-called "repressed texts" that are found by reading these new rhetorical figures [---] This repressed text is a fiction which recognizes its own fictive condition. In its way, it begins to acknowledge the fictional quality of reality and the real quality of fiction."[83]

Eisenman would sometimes speak of this fictive reality and/or real fiction in terms borrowed from Derrida, as a "logic of grafting,"[84] where the grafted elements produce new and incalculable rhetorical effects that cannot be calculated in advance. Time, narrative, and the history to be recreated are all results of operations without any proper ground, and architecture's memory is fabricated in the present so that whatever is preserved and recollected is nothing but the result of a stratigraphic overlay that modifies what is visible underneath as the sheets on top are moved around—all of which would once more locate Eisenman's work at the third level of Miwon Kwon's typology of sites, i.e., the discursive site that emerges from a superimposition of times and spaces: a fiction in the sense of being made and produced, rather than discovered.

And yet, as Kwon notes, there would still remain a question to be asked: "What would it mean now to sustain the cultural and historical specificity of a place (and self) that is neither a

83. Eisenman "Architecture and the Problem of the Rhetorical Figure," reprinted in Nesbitt, *Theorizing a New Agenda*, 180–81, my italics.
84. For Eisenman's use of grafting, see Eisenman, "The End of the Classical: The End of the Beginning, the End of the End" (1984), reprinted in Nesbitt, *Theorizing a New Agenda*.

simulacral pacifier nor a willful invention?" The answer she gives draws on Kenneth Frampton's idea of a necessary mediation between the local and the universal, and the necessity of "a terrain between mobilization and specificity," the "relational specificity" that addresses "the differences of adjacencies and distances *between* one thing, one person, one place, one thought, one fragment *next* to another, rather than invoking equivalencies via one thing *after* another."[85] To this Eisenman's answer, at it emerges from his artificial excavations, would probably be that any such finding must be an invention, and to this extent yet another fiction of a ground, no matter how shifting and unstable, to which we could return. To this one must however add that fiction is not just simply what is imaginary in the sense of unreal or contained in the space of mental interiority, but is something made, and in this it draws along with it a whole complex of spaces and times; it folds the heterotopias of language and space together, and in tearing apart those inherited forms in which "since the beginning of time, language has intersected space," it also renders possible a thinking otherwise, so that the site as fiction is not just, and to the extent that we remain open to its virtuality, not even primarily, a story of the depletion and loss of forms, but of that which calls upon creation to be experienced.

85.   Kwon, "One Place After Another", 109, Kwon's italics.

7. Noopolitics, Life, Architecture

Retrieving the philosophy of life

There has been a recent urgency to connect architecture, and more generally visual culture as a whole, to a strand of thought that in a somewhat antiquated vocabulary would be called vitalism, *Lebensphilosophie*, or philosophy of life, and which is still seeking an adequate name.[1] But regardless of what terminology we choose, this shift may be said to occur in opposition both to the linguistic turn that seemed to place everything under the aegis of language, and whose high point was the advent of structuralism and its various aftermaths in the mid to late sixties, as well as to a long tradition of critical theory based in negation, negativity, and contradiction, i.e., the legacy of Hegelian dialectics. Displacing the model of consciousness and negativity, as well the obsessions with signs, language, and discourse, this neovitalist thinking once more looks to the body, affectivity, and "presence" as something that addresses us below the threshold of interpretation and reflection, and that requires that we remodel our theoretical tools, even the idea of theory as such.

1.   For a collection of texts addressing this topic, and where the present text was published in a first version, see Deborah Hauptmann and Warren Neidich (eds.), *Cognitive Architecture: From Bio-politics to Noo-politics: Architecture & Mind in the Age of Communication & Information* (Rotterdam: 010, 2010). In media theory, the idea of vitalism has been put forth most eloquently in the writings of Scott Lash, who extends its genealogy back to Tarde, Bergson, and Simmel, and inscribes it in a general movement towards a new philosophy of life; see Lash and Celia Lury, *Global Culture Industry* (Cambridge: Polity Press, 2007).

This line of research in many cases draws explicitly on earlier philosophies based in traditions of vitalist thinking from the turn of the former century, for instance Henri Bergson and Gabriel Tarde, but it also rethinks these themes in the context of contemporary global capitalism, whose production of ideology and consent is increasingly geared towards the dimension of affectivity and corporeality,[2] attempting to penetrate into a dimension that underlies our conscious mental operations and extends all the way down to our biological existence. In this sense it differs significantly from earlier vitalist thought, which often positioned itself in opposition to the disruptive effects of modernity, capitalism, and technology, and aspired to retrieve an originary stream of life, supposedly untouched by alienation and instrumentality. Current vitalisms break with this type of anti-modernism, and instead claim that it is only by immersing ourselves in the transformative processes of technology that we can fully grasp our being-in-the-world; it no longer opposes the organic and non-organic, the self-possession and interiority of living subjectivity and its externalization in various *hypomnemata* and mediating circuits, but rather understands them as facets of one continual process of differentiation.

On one level, this seems like a highly unexpected break with the past. Vitalism and *Lebensphilosophie* for a long time remained

2. The literature on affect and the affective turn—which can be considered as a particular aspect of what is here referred to under the more general rubric vitalism—has been growing the last decade, and it has already become of field of research in its own right that cuts across the borders of the social and human sciences. See, for instance, Brian Massumi, *Parables for the Virtual: Movement, Affect, Sensation* (Durham: Duke University Press, 2002), Nigel Thrift, *Non-Representational Theory: Space, Politics, Affect* (Milton Park; Routledge, 2007), Patricia Ticineto Clough and Jean O'Malley Halley (eds.), *The Affective Turn: Theorizing the Social* (Durham: Duke University Press, 2007), Paul Hoggett and Simon Thompson (eds.), *Politics and the Emotions: The Affective Turn in Contemporary Political Studies* (London: Continuum, 2012), Iain McCalman and Paul A. Pickering (eds.), *Historical Reenactment: From Realism to the Affective Turn* (Basingstoke: Palgrave Macmillan, 2010).

an anathema in much twentieth century philosophy, not only in analytic philosophy, with its early and formative emphasis on idealized systems of language and logic, but also in traditions that claim a proximity to the movement of experience, such as phenomenology and the current of critical theory emanating from the Frankfurt School. It was consistently rejected as part of an irrationalist attack against reason and the capacity for theoretical reflection, and often the simple association to *Lebensphilosophie* would count as refutation of an opponent.[3] In hindsight such polemics should however not prevent us from interrogating the proximity between these various figures of thought and the kind of contradictory unity they form; rather than opposing a philosophy of life to a philosophy of reason, we should attempt to understand their imbrication, and the circulation of philosophical motifs that form the underlying matrix of the period, and which returns today, albeit in a form that subverts many of the earlier motifs.

For instance, it is clear that the idea of life, as a counterpoint to the abstractions of certain parts (though by no means all) of the philosophical tradition, plays a crucial role in the writings of Benjamin and Adorno, first and foremost for the obvious reason that their persistent appeal to a *true* life as opposed to a *false* one—no matter how tenuous, dim, and obscure this life may be, at present even almost unthinkable, hidden behind the "black veil" of utopia—would make little sense outside of a basic intuition of what life might mean outside of the administered world. Rather,

3.   The accusations of a life-philosophical irrationalism was perhaps one of most frequent allegations exchanged throughout postwar twentieth century philosophy, and it seems like a successor to psychologism from the turn of former the century, although the mistake is no longer merely a theoretical one, but has profound ethico-political dimensions. This is how Adorno reacts against Simmel, then Lukács in turn against the Frankfurt School and a whole tradition dating back to Schelling, then Habermas and several of his followers against Heidegger, certain parts of Adorno, and most postwar French philosophy.

their claim would be that the life imagined by other strands of *Lebensphilosophie* is a disfigured one that remains caught up in a blind and non-reflected opposition to the instrumental rationality that it merely parodies, as becomes clear in Adorno's recurrent critique of Bergson. To extract a different sense of life that would go beyond instrumentality, while not discarding the latter's contributions to the necessary disenchantment of modernity, is fundamental for Adorno as well as Benjamin, even though this idea undergoes different inflections, for Adorno passing through the mediation of art and aesthetics, for Benjamin, although less clearly, through a messianic disconnection from the law.[4]

---

4. This seems to be the direction in which Giorgio Agamben's reading of Benjamin would lead, i.e., towards a "form of life" (*forma-di-vita*) that would disconnect from the subjugation of life to sovereignty. It is arguably in this context that one should understand the recurrent rubric "Threshold" in Agamben's books: it is not just an element that links chapters and sections, but also a conceptual move. In the early volumes of the *Homo Sacer* series, we often encounter expressions such as "threshold of indifference," "threshold of non-discernability," "threshold of non-differentiation," etc., all of which seem to indicate a state where those oppositions that have structured political philosophy from Greek thought to the present have entered into a confusion because their internal logic has been fully played out, but in this also indicating a possibility of thinking otherwise. The threshold is a place of extreme confusion and obscurity, where all things seem to become blurred, but also the place where thought may begin anew. For Agamben, this possibility is intimately bound up with a new relation between politics and ontology, which is also the place where he encounters Heidegger. In the last pages of *Homo Sacer I* he calls upon "the analogies between politics and the epochal situation of metaphysics," a state of exhaustion where we return to "the task and the enigma of Western metaphysics," that is to the question what constitutes "simple being," *to haplous on*, but also naked life, the "form of life" that "is only its own bare existence." See Agamben, *Homo Sacer*, trans. Daniel Heller-Rozen (Stanford: Stanford University Press, 1998), 105. At the end of *State of Exception*, where the question of praxis displaces the role of life, he similarly suggest that to "show law in its nonrelation to life and life in its nonrelation to law means to open a space between them for human action," and that to "a word that does not bind, that neither commands nor prohibits anything, but says only itself, would correspond an action as pure means, which shows only itself, without any relation to an end." See Agamben, *State of Exception*, trans. Kevin Attell (Chicago: University of Chicago Press, 2005), 88.

In hindsight, it is equally obvious that the way in which Husserl throughout his philosophy connects life, experience, and the living present (*Leben, Erlebnis, lebendige Gegenwart*), or the analyses pursued in his late works of the grounding of ideal objects in the life-world (*Lebenswelt*), have intimate links to a philosophy of life.[5] Thus, in Husserl too, it cannot be a question of erasing life from philosophy, instead the challenge would be to understand life from a transcendental point of view. When Husserl once claimed, "We are the true Bergsonians,"[6] this was a gesture that seemed to both acknowledge the necessity of the opponent's claims and point to their philosophical inadequacy. Similarly, the theme of life forms a pervasive reference in many of Heidegger's works, from the early pursuit of the problem of facticity and factical life, through the later explorations of Dasein's complex relation to animality, up the problem of body and perspectivism in Nietzsche.[7]

5. This theme was first emphasized by Klaus Held, *Lebendige Gegenwart* (The Hague: Nijhoff, 1966), and has since then been a central theme in much phenomenological research. The concept of "drive" (*Trieb*) is in fact central in many of Husserl's manuscripts, and points to the entanglement of the transcendental sphere, once it is understood as a genetic dimension, with concepts of will, desire, and affectivity, and to his encounter with many Freudian themes. For a recent discussion that attempts to ground psychoanalysis in such an expanded idea of phenomenology, see Nicholas Smith, *Towards a Phenomenology of Repression: A Husserlian Reply to the Freudian Challenge*, diss. (Stockholm: Department of Philosophy, Stockholm University, 2010).

6. So Husserl is supposed to have said to Alexandre Koyré; see Bernhard Waldenfels, *Phänomenologie in Frankreich* (Frankfurt am Main: Suhrkamp, 1987), 21.

7. The pioneering systematic study is David Farrell Krell, *Daimon Life: Heidegger and Life-Philosophy* (Bloomington: Indiana University Press, 1992), and it has been followed by many others, for instance Timothy C. Campbell, *Improper Life: Technology and Biopolitics from Heidegger to Agamben* (Minneapolis: University of Minnesota Press, 2011), Havi Carel, *Life and Death in Freud and Heidegger* (Amsterdam: Rodopi, 2006), and in a way that establishes a link to Hegel, Susanna Lindberg, *Entre Heidegger et Hegel: Éclosion et vie de l'être* (Paris: L'Harmattan, 2010). Many of these studies are implicitly indebted to Derrida's many analyses of the theme of *Geschlecht*, animality, and sexual and ontological

From the vantage point of the present, we might say that the problem of life was always there, and without attempting here to undertake the massive task of tracing an encompassing genealogy of *Lebensphilosophie* in the twentieth century,[8] it can still be safely conjectured that the relations to be traced between its past and its current return would not obey the simple schema of repression and return, rejection and reappraisal, but would rather constitute a set of complex retrievals and repetitions, bringing other constellations of the past to bear on the present, and discovering subterranean links between past moments where a congealed polemic only perceived massive oppositions. Furthermore, the way in which the concept of life re-enters the scene today, through the works of Foucault, Deleuze, Agamben, and many others, is in crucial respects conditioned by recent transformations in the life sciences that have opened a set of new issues in ontology, politics, ethics, and aesthetics, which in turn may incite us to re-read earlier positions as already engaging such questions as they appeared, consciously or not, to the thinkers of the early twentieth century.

In relation to architecture and visual culture, the re-emergence of themes from vitalist philosophy sometime seems to be conditioned by a transformed understanding of the *image*. Today, visual objects are increasingly understood as having an agency of their own, a capacity to act on us in unforeseen ways. This is undoubtedly on a more straightforward level due to their sheer ubiquity. At what we can take as the historical limit of classical critical theory, they were theorized under the rubric of "simulacra," a concept that still betrayed an unmistakable yet

difference in Heidegger, which can be found in several of his essays and books from the early eighties onward.

8.   For overviews of the history of *Lebensphilosophie*, see Karl Albert, *Lebensphilosophie: Von den Anfängen bei Nietzsche bis zu ihrer Kritik bei Lukács* (Freiburg: Alber, 1995), and Karl Albert and Elenor Jain, *Philosophie als Form des Lebens: Zur ontologischen Erneuerung der Lebensphilosophie* (Freiburg: Alber, 2000).

rarely acknowledged nostalgia for a Real beyond representation, and which in turn may be related to the earlier concept of the fetish, both in its Marxist and even older ethnographic sense: an inert object that through some magical operation of the mind has been endowed with *mana* or "theological niceties,"[9] a capacity to *move on its own* that in reality does not belong to it. Today, the image in its unfettered state has instead become an autonomous power that neither reveals nor conceals, but *is itself fully real*.[10] This cuts through its status as a mere representation, and also renders questionable the classical concept of "ideology," which ever since Marx's somewhat simplistic use of the *camera obscura* model in many cases has been modeled on a rather reductive view of consciousness as a deformed and distorted representation of an objective given.[11] Today, it is claimed, images are *presentations*, and even if any trust in a clear-cut distinction

9. The classic discussion can be found in Marx, *Capital* 1:4. The untainted Real that haunts Marx's claim is that of a pure and direct use-value, as has been pointed out by many commentators, most recently Jacques Derrida, *Les spectres de Marx* (Paris: Galilée, 1993), 253ff.
10. One of the most significant and philosophically far-reaching cases of this would be Deleuze's work on film, in *Cinéma 1: L'image-mouvement* and *Cinéma 2: L'image-temps* (1983 and 1985). Deleuze wants to move beyond both a phenomenological realism, rooted in Jean Bazin's theories, and the linguistic theories of Christian Metz (to name two very influential models) since both of them reduce the images of cinema to something else, a theory of the subject and perception, or of language and the unconscious, eventually as part of a cinematic apparatus that produces subjectivity as ideology. For Deleuze we have to liberate ourselves from the idea of a natural bearer of perception that would unify all images in an intentional consciousness, or in the suturing of the imaginary and the symbolic, and instead understand this partial bearer as itself constructed through the movement- and time-images. These images can be grasped in themselves, as belonging to things or matter, or as related to a subjective center, but none of these two have priority, and in this sense experience does not necessarily coincide with subjectivity. The task of philosophy (and cinema) would then be to discover these other dimensions, or as Bergson says in *La pensée et le mouvant*, philosophy should be an attempt to go beyond the human condition.
11. Which obviously does not imply that this model exhausts the possibilities of the concept of ideology. For further discussions of this, see the Introduction, above.

between presentation and re-presentation, for instance in the form a massive split between some immediate access to reality and its linguistic mediation, seems naïve on the philosophical level and should be treated with caution, the claim that we must retrieve the efficacy of the visual, its visceral and physical effects and affects, as a problem *within* theory itself, is however highly significant. The emphasis on reading the world may to some extent have blinded us to its being, as Hans-Ulrich Gumbrecht suggests (although this is indeed too a distinction that must be subjected to scrutiny). There is, he claims, an intentionality within the objects themselves, a way in which they produce presence effects that must be accounted for.[12]

But even though these debates obviously become highly complex as soon as one enters into the details, on a more general level they tend to split up along axes that remain distinctly recognizable. On the one hand, there are those who understand the return of the affect and the visceral dimension as pointing towards the necessity of an affirmation that would reject theory as an obstacle to experimentation and production, on the other hand those who perceive affectivity as a renewed possibility of resistance that would be based in the hidden potential of the body itself, beyond or beneath the conscious level.[13] Ideas of a

12. Hans-Ulrich Gumbrecht, *Production of Presence: What Meaning Cannot Convey* (Stanford: Stanford UP, 2004). It must be noted that Gumbrecht's idea of presence both draws heavily on Heidegger and argues for the continued relevance of Derrida (in close connection to the idea of "birth to presence" through touching in Jean-Luc Nancy, to which Derrida's *On Touching* constitutes a thoughtful response), which should make the distinction between being and reading difficult to uphold. In fact, already in Merleau-Ponty any sharp divide between being and reading seems impossible, if the latter is understood as diacritical movement of spacing and temporalization that engages our being-in-the-world to the fullest extent. For the idea of presence in architecture, see the special issue of *Archplus* 178 (2006), "Die Produktion von Präsenz."

13. These claims to some extent appear to return us to certain aporias within earlier versions of (the death of) critical theory, for instance in the fascination with intensity in Lyotard's work from the early seventies

post-critical or projective architecture have been used to under-score the necessity to move beyond inherited models of resis-tance, negativity, and rupture, sometimes even as a rejection of the idea of theory as such, in order to invest in a more fluid and affirmative attitude. The affective turn within the humani-ties and social sciences cannot but have profound implications for how we think theoretical work as such, and that the way in which our contemporary sensorial and noetic environment impacts on our existence renders must imply a questioning of the categories that were once used to underwrite the claims of critical theory seems warranted; the claim that they must simply be rejected seems less convincing.

Thus, while the return of vitalist philosophy on one level translates a general and widespread fatigue with, and even a re-jection of, inherited models of critique that are based on fixed models of experience and subjectivity, it seems more productive to understand it as a call for a more malleable and flexible way of understanding the way our sensorium is constructed. It would be misleading to claim that the noetic, affective, and biopoliti-cal dimensions of power would render theory as such unneces-sary or useless; rather they demand that we invent a theory that

(and in fact, Lash and Lury place their investigations into the contem-porary culture industry under the rubric "libidinal economy"). For Lyotard, the idea of intensity was opposed to Hegelian dialectics and its modern avatar in the critical theory of Adorno, and then to theory in general, in what seems like a consciously self-defeating move, or perhaps as in instance of a death drive inherent in theory as such, which seems to be implied in some of his statements. For Lyotard's initial responses to Adorno, see my *The Silences of Mies* (Stockholm: Axl Books, 2008), 68–80. After these first and dismissive remarks, Adorno in fact became an insistent if not always acknowledged presence in Lyotard's attempt to formulate a systematic aesthetic theory, and the renewed attention to affectivity and "passibility" in his writings from the mid eighties onward in many ways crosses my final proposal here. For a discussion of Lyotard's work in this respect, see Daniel Birnbaum and Sven-Olov Wallenstein, *Spacing Philosophy: Jean-François Lyotard and the Philosophy of the Exhibition* (forthcoming).

371

would be able to analyze the modes of affectivity and subjection that occur within this new formation of power. In this sense the problem of how to analyze politics, capitalism, and the possibility of resistance, have not disappeared, but have become increasingly acute, and perhaps need to be reformulated at a depth that goes beyond inherited models of mind and consciousness.

The claim for a presence of the visual, that there is a life lodged within images to which we must respond, indeed flies in the face of a certain type of interpretation that seals the visual object within an analysis of ideological formations whose representation it would be, and that consequently calls for a mode of deciphering that eventually uncovers the true meaning, a truth that in turn becomes all the more compelling by breaking away from the surface order of phenomena. A critique of images that reduces them to mere ideological reflections seems to deprive them of life, in transferring all of the movement and intelligence to the one who reads them; against this, the theory of presence demands that we restore the violence and force of the encounter, the way images confront our bodies with a physical texture, in a movement that belongs both to surface and depth, although organized differently than in a model of outer envelope and inner recesses. In some respects it may be true that the surface is what conditions depth—for the deepest in man is his skin, "Ce qu'il y a de plus profond dans l'homme, c'est la peau," as Valéry famously said.[14] This does however not imply that we should simply discard depth in favor of a simple immediacy, instead it should make us aware of the in-

14.   *L'Idée fixe* (1931), in *Œuvres* II (Paris: Gallimard / La Pléiade, 1960), 215. Gilles Deleuze cites Valery's statement in *Logique du sens* (Paris: Minuit, 1969), 18, and reads it in terms of his theory of the event as an "extra-being" distinct from the interactions and states of bodies. Similar to the dimension of sense in language, events are incorporeal entities that cannot be reduced to their material instantiation, although they are always connected to them as that which actualizes them. Events belong to a virtual temporality of the Eternal, the Aion of the infinitive verb, whereas actualization belongs to the finite tenses of Time, Chronos.

tricacies of the surface/depth model, as is abundantly displayed by the surfaces, folds, and crevices of art, from painting and poetry to the "hypersurfaces"[15] of modern architecture.

To some extent, it has seemed as if the emphasis on presence and affect would attempt to relocate the object and/or subject of critical theory—presuming that term critical theory should be preserved, as I do—to a new region, where the entanglement of the subjective and the objective is more acute, and where the conception of an appropriating hermeneutics must come to an end. But we must note that this may be a struggle against a non-existent enemy, provided that we not weaken the case of the alleged adversary beyond recognition. Indeed, few thinkers have emphasized the power of the musical work to undo our conceptual schemes to such an extent as Adorno, which for him too signals that there is a decisive limit of hermeneutics,[16] and few have highlighted the capacity of the visual art object to question all inherited views of perception more than Merleau-Ponty—all of which indicates that the difference between interpretations that seal the work in pre-given categories (of art history, literary history, cultural studies, critique of ideology), which undoubtedly do not only exist but in fact make up the mainstream of academic discourse, and those that put these categories themselves at risk, runs within these traditions themselves, and should not be used to force us to make premature decisions in favor of one or the other.

15. See for instance the volumes of *Architectural Design* on "Hypersurface Architecture", ed. Stephen Perrella (London: Academy Editions, 1998 and 1999). This would undoubtedly necessitate a rethinking of the too simplistic depth–surface divide that organizes Fredric Jameson's by now classic analysis of postmodernism and late capitalism.

16. We must note Adorno's emphatic resistance to at least a certain concept of hermeneutics: "The task of aesthetics," he claims, "is not to comprehend artworks as hermeneutical objects; in the contemporary situation, it is their incomprehensibility that needs to be comprehended." *Aesthetic Theory*, trans. Robert Hullot-Kentor (London: Continuum, 1997), 157.

Foucault, Deleuze, and the power of life

In order to get a perspective on these entangled issues, a good way to start out is from the research of Michel Foucault on bio-politics and biopower, which constitutes a common point of reference for most of the later theorizing. As we will see, Foucault's investigations however take him in different directions, and conflicting readings of his legacy are possible, perhaps even on the level of terminology: at first, Foucault does not seem to make any distinction between the power and the politics of the *bios*, and when the gradual (and never thematized) shift towards the latter term takes place, the theoretical frame changes too.

When the term is introduced, the power and/or politics of the *bios* generally refers to those mechanisms and forms of power that invest the human body as a locus of productivity and action, thus as a fundamentally living entity that obeys laws of its own, which must not only be respected as an external limit for what can be accomplished, but must be integrated into politics itself as the source from which it draws its energy. As his investigations unfold, Foucault begins to stress that this dimension of a living and unpredictable force is also what will eventually position the subject as free, or at least endowed with a certain agency. From this point onward, he will more speak of biopolitics, a concept that gradually severs its ties to theory of subjection or disciplining of the subject, and instead comes to denote a more subtle, gentle, and strategic governing that uses freedom as a leverage.

These theories, developed by Foucault in the latter half of the 1970s—first on the basis of a reading of the transformations of political theory in the eighteenth century and the emergence of the population as the physical and natural substratum of politics, but then also drawing on discussions of twentieth century liberal theory—have generated a highly complex reception across many disciplinary fields, from philosophy and the social sciences to ar-tistic practices and researches in the history of sciences. Foucault's relation to the life-philosophical tradition is however by no means simple; if his initial formulation of biopower may be taken as a way to reinvent the notion of life as resistance, his subsequent lectures on biopolitics seem to downplay this possibility, or rather see it as a surface effect of underlying shifts in modern forms of governing, or "governmentality." Beyond shifts in Foucault's own intellectual biographical, this ambiguity can be understood as belong to the problem of the *bios* as such: is there a different potential inherent in the idea of life, or is it simply an effect of shifts in power relations, not in the sense that would be something unreal, but in the sense that its reality is precisely what modern forms of governing tap into in order to become operative?

Foucault develops these concepts at a crucial juncture in his work, where he begins to doubt the explicative force of the disciplinary model of power that he had developed systematically in *Discipline and Punish* (1975). From this point onward his research begins to diverge in a prismatic fashion, which also means that the rather clear-cur division of his work into three parts that we find for instance in Deleuze's elegant and coherent reading,[17] must be questioned, at least with respect to the last phase. In Deleuze's interpretation, an archeological phase, focused on the regularities of discourse, is followed by a genealogical period where Foucault investigates the mechanisms of power in their interplay with discourse, eventually leading up to a third stage, revolving around the theory of subjectivation, where Foucault returns to Greek and Roman material in order to reinscribe the subject, although in a more historically flexible and conditioned way than in traditional philosophies of consciousness.

This division is based on Foucault's published works, where

17.   Gilles Deleuze, *Foucault*, trans. Séan Hand (London: Continuum, 2006). For a discussion of the place of biopolitics in relation to the other themes in the later work, see the introduction in Jakob Nilsson and Sven-Olov Wallenstein (eds.), *Foucault, Biopolitics, and Govermentality* (Huddinge: Södertörn Philosophical Studies, 2013).

there is large gap between 1976, the year of the first volume of *The History of Sexuality*, and the subsequent two volumes on sexuality published shortly before his death in 1984—a long caesura which was a time of reflection but probably also of crisis (the "inability to cross the line," of which Foucault speaks in the important preface to the second volume), that seemed to have ended with the return to a modified reflection on subjectivity, ethics, and freedom. Today however, this eight-year gap has been filled with the published courses from the Collège de France, and reading these texts we can see how Foucault already around the time of the 1976 lectures series *"Society Must Be Defended"* in fact began to re-orient himself in multiple and not necessarily coherent ways. From this point onward he develops the idea of a history of forms of governmentality, he works on the idea of the technologies of the self and on the idea of candor and truth-telling (*parrhesia*) in Greek and Roman texts, he returns to Kant and the enlightenment, and claims to pursue the question of modernity as a question of the "ontology of actuality," in the wake of Weber and the Frankfurt School—all of which can only with great difficulty be brought together into a unified set of problems that would amount to a distinct third phase. And it is in this context that the idea of biopolitics emerges, sometime between 1976 and 1977, and in Foucault's own development it in fact appears more like a transitional idea than a sustained theme.

When the idea emerges in the first volume of *The History of Sexuality*, it first seems like an extension of the analysis of discipline. *Discipline and Punish* had already pursued this in terms of the inscription of the body into an institutional field: the army, school, hospital, prison, etc., and this is where Foucault could be said to undertake a kind of proto-architectural analysis, most famously in the case of Jeremy Bentham's Panopticon. The investigation of disciplinary power had traced a transformation from the naked violence of visible punishment to a form of correctional techniques that assembled around the body, and generated a form of political technology that produced a *soul* as a new object of knowledge—the soul, which in this sense also becomes the prison of the body. Discipline, Foucault famously says, is not primarily about prohibiting, just as power in a more general sense is not essentially repressive, but works in terms of a positive organization of space and time, a partition and creation of segmented unities, and a breaking down and analysis of movements down to their smallest detail, as in military exercise, control of body postures in school, etc. Space, time, and bodies are parceled up, and then reassembled so as to become parts of larger and more efficient unities.

Military camps, prisons, hospitals, school, factories each in their respective ways thus become places for the creation of "docile bodies," and in conjunction with this, there is a development of corresponding discourses on military regulations, criminal law, pedagogy, political economy, etc. Discipline encounters new types of discourse, and together—in a kind of circular causality, or rather resonance, which displaces the base-superstructure model— they form a complex of power and knowledge complex that however does not simply produce homogeneity, but rather draws on its own limits, and unfolds through the proliferation of that which *escapes* it. Instead of a binary structure of law and transgression, the emphasis on norms produces an infinity of possible deviations that do not pre-exist the norm, but emerge as infinitesimal fluctuations around it, and the object of the legal as well as sexual apparatus can thus be understood as the production of various forms of illegality, criminality, and perversion, which they then integrate into larger wholes.

This at least begins to answer the question often posed to Foucault as to where the possibility of resistance could be located. If power and knowledge, although without being reducible to each

ARCHITECTURE, CRITIQUE, IDEOLOGY

other, form an interlocking structure, they always do so in relation to an outside that provides thinking and acting with an unruly mobility. The archive of knowledge is itself shot through with fractures that the mechanisms of power stabilize, but only by themselves being virtual and fleeting, since they exist in a field of action and reaction defined by reversibility and overthrows. This field is like a general externality, an outside that forms element or milieu in which the creation of docile bodies, becomes possible, but which then also subsists under any such body as a virtual double, a multiplicity of non-bound forces.

The theoretical model for such a resistance can undoubtedly be found in a Nietzsche's genealogy of consciousness and conscience, in his reflections on the amount of "pre-historical work" that is required for the formation of a responsible agent, on which Foucault draws implicitly. Here he may have been particularly influenced by the ideas of Deleuze in *Nietzsche and Philosophy* (1962), where Deleuze suggests that Nietzsche's genealogy should be understood as a critical analysis of power relations that takes the *body* as a focal point of analysis, not in the sense of phenomenological ground of living sense (the *Leib* as lived from within subjectivity, in opposition to the external and objective *Körper*),[18] but a constantly undone and reconstructed assemblage of affects and responses. To propose a model for philosophy in a new understanding of the body is also one of the key themes in Deleuze's later readings of Spinoza, which

18.   Foucault sometimes appears close to the phenomenology of Merleau-Ponty, with its "vertical" or "savage" being outside of institutionalized and sedimented forms of experience and discourse. He however always rejected this link, undoubtedly because of the teleology inherent in phenomenology, where the ante-predicative layers often seem to be acknowledged only in order to be taken up in signifying acts and brought to consciousness. As Deleuze notes, for Foucault there is an "archeological break" rather than a continuity between the discursive and the non-discursive, at least in his early work. Foucault's later lectures on the hermeneutics of the subject however re-open many of these issues again, and would require a discussion than I cannot undertake here.

develop the idea that the soul, or more precisely a certain interpretation of the soul, constitutes the prison of the body, and that we are not aware of what a liberated body might be capable of outside of its relation to the soul understood in terms of its Aristotelian form. As Spinoza famously writes in the *Ethics*: "in fact, no one has been able determine what a body is capable of (*quid corpus possit*), that is, experience has not yet enlightened us as to what the body—to the extent that is not determined by the soul—can or cannot do according to the laws of nature, if the latter is considered solely as corporeal."[19] But, Deleuze cautions us, we should not understand this as a simple reversal that subjects the soul to the body. Spinoza's famous parallelism does not settle for a mere inversion of the hierarchical schema, but instead configures its parts into a new dynamic interrelation: "the body surpasses the knowledge we have of it, *just as thought surpasses the consciousness we have of it*," and if the "model of the body, according to Spinoza, does not imply any devaluing of thought in relation to extension," it is because it, more importantly, "implies a devaluation of consciousness in relation to thought: a discovery of the unconscious, which is an *unconscious of thought* no less profound than the *unknown of the body*."[20] This unconscious of

19. Spinoza, *Ethics*, Book III, Theorem 2, Remark. This capacity is crucially linked to the idea of affects, which must be distinguished from psychological states such as emotions. Affects are both confused ideas in the mind and a corresponding increase or decrease in the body's vital force or power to act, its *potentia agendi*. As *potentia*, affect is both the capacity to affect and to be affected; it is an openness to the world that cannot be reduced to mere modifications of consciousness, instead our conscious relation springs from a deeper affective level.

20. Deleuze, *Spinoza: Philosophie pratique* (Paris: Minuit, 1981), 29. The theme of a "mere reversal" is a well-known leitmotif in Heidegger's reading of Nietzsche, and one of the main reasons why Nietzsche would have been unable to escape Platonism, and Deleuze may be taken to respond here to an objection of the Heideggerian kind. However, for Deleuze, neither Spinoza nor Nietzsche can be understood as failed attempts to step out of an epochal structure called "metaphysics"; they do not announce, however imperfectly, its end or overcoming, but rather perform transformations that can be picked up by us and developed in

thought opens consciousness and the body to a domain that exceeds them, in Spinoza's case the infinite substance of God-Nature, which in Deleuze's own ontology will receive various names: chaos, the outside, exteriority. In his interpretation of Foucault, this is the outside (*le Dehors*), an "abstract storm" from which thought emerges, and thinking is an event that *happens to*, *comes to*, thought.[21]

This domain that in Deleuze's metaphysics underlies the formed body, of which he has provided many versions, drawing on Nietzsche, Bergson, Spinoza, and Leibniz, but also writers and painters like Proust, Kafka, Artaud, and Bacon, is also what he uncovers in microphysical domain of power in Foucault. It is precisely because of its instability—virtual relations are a kind of "extra-being" that while being perfectly real yet go beyond the actual and envelop it in a "becoming"—that power relations remain unstable and that a "distant roar of battle,"[22] as Foucault says, can always be heard behind the official eloquence of institutionalized discourses of knowledge. This does not mean that there is some true or authentic corporeal life beneath the discursive order, a life that would be deformed by an external force and to which we finally could return, only that this unbound multiplicity remains

new ways. The end of metaphysics is, as is well known, a Heideggerian theme that is rejected throughout all of Deleuze's writings.

21. In the reading of Foucault, the parallelism does not relate to thought and extension, but to speaking and seeing, the "sayable" and the "visible," but here too their interplay is not that of a synthesis, but a violent struggle, developing through "captures" that make them encroach upon each other, and thinking is what occurs outside of and between them: "To think is to reach the non-stratified. Seeing is thinking, and speaking is thinking, but thinking occurs in the interstice, or in the disjunction between seeing and speaking. [...] thinking belongs to the outside insofar as the latter, an 'abstract storm,' is thrown down into the interstice between seeing and speaking. The appeal to the outside is a constant theme in Foucault and signifies that thinking is not the innate exercise of a faculty, but must come to thought." Deleuze, *Foucault*, trans. Séan Hand (London: Continuum, 2006), 76, mod.

22. *Discipline and Punish*, trans. Alan Sheridan (London: Penguin, 1977), 308.

a source of resistance, which indicates why resistance that *comes first*, as Foucault often said. The "diagram" of power relations can only be actualized if it at the same time releases a multiplicity of forces that eventually may become integrated, but which as such fundamentally oppose themselves to integration.

This proximity notwithstanding, there are important differences between Deleuze's (and Guattari's) philosophical constructivism and Foucault's analytic of power.[23] Foucault's interrogates how we have *become* the kind of subjects that we are (sexed, normalized, deviant), i.e., what kind of self-technologies, discourses, and mechanisms of power that have been taken up and used in this process of self-fashioning, and in the latter part of the seventies his investigations tend to become more and more historical in a traditional sense. Deleuze and Guattari on the other hand are engaged in the construction of synthetic and universal-historical models. Their project is to discern those lines of flight that always open up in every assemblage, on the basis of a general theoretical model: a society, they suggest, is not held together but its solid parts, but by what flees and leaks out of its segmentations and grids. Initially, this structure was theorized under the name of "desire," although other concepts would follow. Foucault, on the other hand, becomes increasingly critical of all such a priori, transhistorical and ontological conceptions, and for him a term like desire cannot be understood as a general productive force, only as a specific product of modern confessional technologies.

And in fact, it is in relation to the issue of biopolitics that we may in a productive fashion understand the divide between Deleuze and Foucault. Regardless of what other reasons, political and personal, there may be for their split in the later part of the seventies, the question of the metaphysics of life seems

23.   See Deleuze, "Désir et plaisir," in *Deux régimes de fous* (Paris: Minuit, 2003).

the philosophically most interesting one to examine. We should thus look more precisely at this point of divergence between them, which is also where Foucault begins to question his earlier work on discipline and his inquiries begins to proliferate in many divergent directions.

Foucault's first presentation of the theme of biopolitics, in the final section of the first volume of *The History of Sexuality*, still remains largely within the disciplinary model. In this version it can understood as operative according through a three-tier model: on the micro-level it works by individualization, by *producing individuality* in the form of sexed and desiring subjects that are increasingly endowed with a depth to be deciphered, which can be taken as a culmination of a long development. On the macro-level we see the emergence of *population*, which is a statistical phenomenon, individuals as they appear in terms of collective health, birth and mortality rates, etc. Between them there is an intermediary link, the *family* as the site of exchange between individuality and collectivity, the relay through which all individuals have to pass in order to become members of the reproductive body politic. On all three levels, life becomes the object of regulation and discipline, but at the same moment there emerges an opposite power inside of life that resists. This is the condition of possibility of all kinds of philosophical vitalism, from Nietzsche onward, each of which will attempt to extract a different life from the monitoring and correctional apparatuses within which it is made to appear as a calculable entity. In this sense, the power exerted *over* life, Foucault suggests, is also an emancipation of a resistant force *inside* of life, just as the disciplinary diagrams could not be deployed without creating a swarm of virtual actions and reactions that overflow them. The first model of biopower can in this sense be taken to develop the analysis of discipline on another level, not with reference to possible actions, but to modes of life and experience. Even though this remains peripheral in Foucault's published work, this theory also has architectural implications, for instanced in the discussion of the role of the hospital and the medicalization of urban space, where the mimetic paradigm comes to an end, and architecture begins to be understood as an ordering and production of space instead of as an representation of a pre-existing order, natural, cosmic, or other.[24]

But—and here we can see how Foucault's research at this moment breaks up in a prismatic way—this line of thought is precisely what he will question in following lecture series, *Security, Territory, Population* (1977–78) and *The Birth of Biopolitics* (1978–79). In addition to the idea of population, Foucault here also points to the emergence of a new concept of *security*, which becomes central since threats now emanate from *within*, from the population itself and its inherent tendency to create imbalances, deviations, and unpredictable crises, whereas the old model of sovereignty, which aimed to seize and preserve control over a territory, predominantly understood dangers and enemies as coming from *without*. In the lectures from 1977–78, biopolitics thus comes to be connected to security, and it is explicitly dissociated from discipline, which is tantamount to a fundamental self-critique, as Foucault himself notes.

Using the question of theft as a paradigm for transgressive behavior, Foucault discerns three possible avenues. First, theft can be understood as an infraction that must be punished according to a predetermined scale of punishment, i.e., as a *juridi-*

24. A document of these researches can be found in *Les machines à guérir (aux origines de l'hôpital moderne)* (Brussels: Mardaga, 1977). See also Foucault's condensed statement of these themes in "The Politics of Health in the Eighteenth Century," and "The Birth of Social Medicine," in *Essential Works*, eds. Paul Rabinow and James D. Faubion (London: Penguin, 2001), vol. 3. I have attempted to discuss some aspects of this shift in *Biopolitics and the Emergence of Modern Architecture* (New York: Princeton Architectural Press, 2009), and *Essays, Lectures* (Stockholm: Axl Books, 2007), chap. 8.

cal problem with a basis in law. Second, it can be taken as a form of deviant behavior that must be corrected through various techniques, i.e., as a *disciplinary* problem. But third and finally, it can also be theorized as a statistical phenomenon, where one must balance the losses and gains of disciplinary measures, and perhaps allow for a certain latitude of crime, which is a way to formulate the problem in terms of *security*. This a model based on probabilities, a calculus of cost within which the task is to attain an optimal balance, and not simply to make the transgressive phenomenon go away once and for all.

While these shifts first appear as merely small displacements inside the analytic of power in place since *Discipline and Punish*, as Foucault explores the theme further, it becomes increasingly clear that he is moving in a new direction. If sovereignty is exerted over a territory and a multiplicity of political subjects, and discipline is applied to singular bodies, to their affects and passions, then security can be said to work with a set of fluid conditions, constantly fluctuating quantities, and future probabilities. Posing the problem in terms of security means to invent a multifunctional order, and to calculate the negative and positive outcome of any given measure: security does not apply to a fixed state, but relates to a series of future events. If sovereignty monopolizes a territory and locates a central command, while discipline structures a space and sets up a hierarchy, then security attempts to plan an environment or a milieu in relation to a set of possible events. Discipline is centripetal, it isolates spaces and creates segments, it focuses and encloses; apparatuses of security, on the other hand, are centrifugal, and they aim to integrate new things in ever widening circuits. Discipline strives toward a regulation of details, whereas security allows things to run their course at a certain level, it "lets things be," and in this sense biopolitical power is what is truly at stake in the doctrine of laissez-faire of early liberalism. Discipline, Foucault says, divides things into licit and illicit, and to this extent it is still based on a law that is to be increasingly specified. In law, order is what is remains once everything prohibited and disorderly has been removed, all of which is intensified in discipline, since it also tells you what to do, which is why the convent can be taken as its the ideal form.

In all of this, we can detect an important shift away from the earlier work, where the juridical conception based in binary divisions was *opposed* to the attention to detail and modulations in discipline; here they sometimes appear as two stages of the same process, whose opposite would be security, which in turn as its correlate has an idea of *freedom*, not as some abstract faculty of quality of the will, but as that which is always presupposed as the other side of apparatuses of security, the vital condition that they must learn to master and from which they draw their own force.

In the apparatuses of security, the question is not panoptic *surveillance*, but how to take a step back and *observe* the nature of events, not in order to attain some immutable essence of things, but to ask whether they are advantageous or not, and how one can find a support in reality itself that makes it possible to channel them in an appropriate direction. In this respect we can say that the law operates in the *imaginary*, it imagines something negative; discipline is applied in a sphere which is *complementary* to reality; security, finally, operates within *reality itself*, in order to make its components interact and cohere in a more profitable fashion—which is what the physiocrats meant, Foucault suggests, when they said that economy in fact is a physics, and that politics still belongs to nature.

If the idea of life as a multiplicity of unbound forces set free by biopolitical power earlier was the source for a theory of resistance, the later lectures shifts the perspective: the process of life and nature becomes a correlate to security, which means that the vitalist ontology that subtended the work on discipline is put in question, if not entirely jettisoned. The correlation between security and freedom is not that of a formed segment to an unformed element, but much more of a functionalist co-existence, where the two sides reinforce each other in order to achieve a greater result, and as such it belongs to the order of governing and calculation. As a consequence of this, the ontology is life is replaced by a more thoroughgoing historicizing, which also comes across in Foucault's rejection of the implicit theory of an underlying multiplicity that provides the body with a surplus of resistance.

To this it may be objected that any account of the idea of vitalism as a general philosophical question must provide a much more encompassing history than the one beginning somewhere in the eighteenth century, and needs to take us back to Greek philosophy. In order to understand the depth of the question we would need, for instance, to revisit the divide between Plato's forms, based in mathematics and geometry (the *mathemata*, the "knowable things" that precede individual objects), and Aristotle's individual substances, modeled on the living being who strives to sustain itself, overcome obstacles, and reach its maximum state of actuality, the *entelechia*.[25] In this longer perspective, the *mathema* and the *bios* and/or *zoe* form a couple whose mutations traverse the history of western metaphysics as a whole, and their effects cannot be limited to, or meaningfully accounted for within, modernity.[26]

This frame may be established in very different ways: the history of metaphysics, as understood by Heidegger, would be one possible avenue, which finds its echoes in some of the works of

25. This division between the *bios* and the *mathema* is emphasized by Alain Badiou in his review of Deleuze's *Le Pli*, in *L'annuaire philosophique* (1988–1989), which is a much more nuanced confrontation that the more known, although rather one-sided reading proposed in his *Deleuze: "La clameur de l'Être"* (Paris: Hachette, 1997).
26. This is one of the basis claims in the first volume of Giorgio Agamben's *Homo Sacer* series. For a critical discussion of Agamben's proposals, especially the sharp distinction between *zoe* (qualified life) and *bios* (mere life in general), see Jacques Derrida, *Séminaire: Le bête et le souverain*, vol. 1 (2001–2002) (Paris: Galilée, 2008), 419ff.

Giorgio Agamben, who sometimes sets out to correct Foucault, or provide his analysis of modern biopolitics with a larger frame, but takes a fundamentally different direction. Foucault too would in the last lecture series, from *Du gouvernement des vivants* (1979–1980) onward, return to Greek, Roman, and early Patristic thought in order to analyze the problem of governing as a shaping of conduct (one's own and that of others), and here too the theme of *bios* returns at the end, although now in terms of a modeling of an existence that lays claim to a truth, or a courage to truth, opposed to the prevailing order. Beginning in Plato's hermeneutics of the subject and the metaphysics of the soul, continuing through the governing of oneself and others in public life, the Cynical reinterpretation of the teachings of Socrates, Christian asceticism, and eventually pointing toward the figure of the modern revolutionary, Foucault's lectures trace a genealogy of the *bios* that bypasses the traditional stations of the history of metaphysics, or approaches them from a very different angle. His ultimate suggestions for further research however remain open-ended, and extracting a systematic theory from them seems just as baseless as it runs against the very grain of what he was attempting. It is nevertheless clear that the term "governmentality," initially proposed to denote a crucial shift at the threshold of modernity, gradually sheds its first chronological specificity, and eventually, to the extent that it is retained at all, becomes a term denoting any kind of shaping of conducts and practices. In this sense, rather than developing through radical shifts and breaks, it is now part of those long temporal chains, in which, as he suggested already at the time of *The Archeology of Knowledge*, the "rhythms become broader," and which point to "apparently unmoving histories."[27]

27.   Foucault, *The Archaeology of Knowledge*, trans. Alan Sheridan (London: Routledge, 2004), 3–4. For Foucault in 1969, this slower history is still exemplified by "the history of sea-routes, the history of corn or of

387

Vitalism, noopower,
and the philosophy of life

But while it is true that the ubiquitous references to Foucault in most contemporary discussions of biopower and biopolitics necessarily involve a highly selective reading, the relevance of a philosophy of life, or more generally, of theoretical work that takes the contested nature of the living being as its problem, can not be settled simply by discussing the merits of various exegetical investigations of Foucault's work, especially so given the inconclusive and tentative character of his last researches. Many avenues of thought were left undeveloped as Foucault progresses, and some of them have been pursed by others, regardless of whether this contradicts Foucault's own trajectory or not.

As we have noted, in the first take on biopower, Foucault suggested that in modernity life not only becomes the object of a science that discovers that it has a history and a depth (evolution), it also appears as a multiplicity that must be surveyed and channeled, both on the level of the individual (sex) and the collective (population). And as the other side of this new mode of knowledge and power, there also emerges a life that resists, a series of counter-definitions that extend at least from Nietzsche, through pragmatism (James, Dewey), the ontologies of Bergson and the sociology of Tarde, but also important strands of phenomenology from Husserl through the early Heidegger and Merleau-Ponty, and up to Deleuze. And indeed, many others have, in parallel to Foucault or as an explicit transformation of his work, understood this type of vitalism as his essential legacy.

gold-mining, the history of drought and irrigation, the history of crop rotation, the history of the balance achieved by the human population between hunger and abundance" (4), i.e., basically those features that had been explored by the historians of *longue durée* from the Annales school, whereas his own interested lay in the rapid shifts on a higher level. The later work tends to, if not obliterate then at least question these temporal divisions.

In fact, the ideas of biopower and biopolitics have been developed in so many directions that the differences between the various versions seem to outweigh the similarities, even though Foucault, as we noted, rightly or wrongly remains a central reference in most of then.[28] Here I will just cite one particular version, which draws freely on both Foucault and Deleuze, the work of Maurizio Lazzarato.

Lazzarato begins from Foucault's analysis of disciplinary societies, which he develops further by drawing on Deleuze's brief sketch for a theory of the "societies of control."[29] In this essay Deleuze suggests that discipline and panopticism are precisely what we have left behind, and his account, while obviously not referencing Foucault's at the time still unpublished lectures, crosses many of themes addressed by Foucault in the second half of the seventies, above all in analyzing the relation between a situated agency and a flexible space of security. The structure of individuation and localization once brought about by discipline today works through the "dividual," Deleuze proposes, a waveform that supersedes the old individual as a basic unit. The centralizing function (the Panopticon tower with its

28. Other competing versions of biopolitics would, apart from Giorgio Agamben's *Homo Sacer*, also include Antonio Negri and Michael Hardt, *Empire* (Cambridge, Mass.: Harvard University Press, 2000), Roberto Esposito, *Bios: Biopolitics and Philosophy*, trans. Timothy Campbell (Minneapolis: University of Minnesota Press, 2008); Andrea Cavalletti, *La città biopolitica: Mitologie della sicurezza* (Turin: Mondadori, 2005), to cite but a few. The reference to Foucault is common to them all, although they interpret it in highly different ways.

29. "Postscript on the Societies of Control," trans. Martin Joughin, in Gilles Deleuze, *Negotiations: 1972–1990* (New York: Columbia University Press, 1995). Written in 1990, Deleuze's text is located at the beginning of a formation of power-knowledge whose current intensity and complexity could of course only be glimpsed twenty-five years ago. Its basic schemata however remain just as pertinent, and the main difference lies in the profound level at which they have penetrated into the formation of subjectivity, so that the techniques of control and the production of dividuality have themselves become the means of the subject's desire and *jouissance*.

unidirectional visibility) has been fragmented into a multiplicity of flexible monitoring instances, and a structure of universal *modulation* has replaced the disciplinary mold. In discipline we moved from one closed segment to another—from the school to the factory, from the factory to the hospital, the prison, and so forth, but today these compartmentalized milieus have been replaced by new, smooth functions. Control, on the other hand, is exerted over open spaces; it locates an element in an open environment, as in the case of an electronic bracelet worn by a prisoner, which provides or denies access to a given segment of space at a certain point in time. If the carceral system produced independent but analogous subsets, control spaces are interconnected and numerical, like sieves whose mesh constantly shifts its permeability. Unlike the former disciplinary matrix, the new structures operate through passwords that regulate access to information banks, and that can be recalled at any moment. What all this signals, Deleuze suggests, is a fundamental mutation of capitalism: the enclosed factory has been replaced by a service economy characterized by dispersal. The disappearance of the factory as the model of production in advanced capitalist societies is reflected in similar transformations of other spaces, for instance in offices, and increasingly also in academic institutions, where older forms of spatial hierarchies have been or are being replaced by flattened structures that promote an ideal of flexibility and participation, and reinvents a whole "psy-" vocabulary, from William Whyte's "Orgman" to Deleuze's laconic observation that the corporation has acquired a "soul."[30]

30. See William Whyte, *The Organization Man* (New York; Simon & Schuster, 1956). It is just as striking as symptomatic that Deleuze's idea of control has also been used in ways that appear to be more "generative" than critical. This symptomatic malleability, even reversibility, of critical concepts is one of the underlying motifs of the idea of the post-critical, but must be understood as a necessary condition of all concepts that are as advanced as the system they are describing (it is coincidence that many of Foucault's concepts suffered the same fate in architectural

For Lazzarato, these brief remarks by Deleuze form the starting point for his theory of "noopolitics," which also draws deeply on the sociology of Gabriel Tarde, whose micro-sociological
analyses of imitation and invention, and of the individual as a
monadic (in Leibniz sense) entity or a society of its own, are
only beginning to be appreciated.[31] Contemporary capitalism,
Lazzarato suggests, no longer has its base in labor, the factory,
and the institutions that regulate the relations between them,
but in a "collaboration of brains,"[32] i.e., the networked intel-

theory). See, for instance, the analysis of shopping facilities as "control
space," in Rem Koolhaas, Stefano Boeri, Sandford Kwinter et al., *Mutations: Rem Koolhaas, Harvard Project on the City* (Barcelona: Actar, 2000),
which, without mentioning Deleuze, transform his concept into a
technique for the planning of malls.

31. The reemergence of Tarde in theoretical work is a significant phenomenon, and many aspire to be the true interpreters of his legacy;
for an overview of the recent reception, see David Toews, "The New
Tarde: Sociology After the End of the Social," *Theory Culture Society*,
2003 (20(5). It seems likely that the context for Tarde's return is the
necessity to rethink our inherited conceptions of individuality and
collectivity in the light of current modes of exertion of power in the age
of telematics and electronic space. Here too, there is a link to Deleuze,
and many have pointed to his footnote in *Difference and Repetition*,
where he, already in 1968, rejects the psychologistic reading imposed
on Tarde by Durkheim and his followers, and suggests that "the little
ideas of little men" and the "interferences between imitative currents"
constitutes a "*microsociology*" already at the level of the person: "hesitation understood as an 'infinitesimal social opposition' or invention as
an 'infinitesimal social adaptation.'" *Difference and Repetition*, trans. Paul
Patton (London: Athlone Press, 1994), 313–314, note 3. Equally important—although for some reason often overlooked—references to Tarde
can be found in Deleuze, *Le Pli* (Paris: Minuit, 1988), 147 (on the relation between the ontology of "being" and the "echology" of "having"),
and in the monograph on Foucault, where Deleuze locates Foucault's
analysis of power in the wake of Tarde's appreciation of "diffuse and
infinitesimal relations, which are not those of large sets of great men
but are rather the tiny ideas of little men, a civil servant's flourish, a
new local custom, a linguistic deviation, a visual twisting that becomes
widespread." (*Foucault*, 142, note 7)
32. See Lazzarato, *Les Révolutions du capitalisme* (Paris: Empêcheurs de
penser en rond, 2004). Lazzararo's recent ideas have grown out of his
earlier work on "immaterial labor," although I will here stick to the
theory as it is formulated in the later writings.

ligence that we find for instance in contemporary software development, which the capitalist mode of organization taps into
and over which it attempts to seize control, at the same time
generating a plethora of countermoves that it both fears and
condemns, and needs in order to expand. Generally, the concept
of noopolitics implies that capitalism not so much exploits our
labor as our cognitive capacities, i.e., the new productive forces
that it must contain and channel into the corporate network,
but in this also forges a proliferating array of tools to resist it.

In order to achieve this, modern capitalism has long since
operated by creating a consent through images, sound bites,
brands, and various visual technologies that impact directly on
our brain, bypassing the censorships and reflective mechanisms
of consciousness—all of which demands that we reflect on the
way in which images act, but also on what kind of "image of
thought" that this makes possible, not just as a passive causal
effect, but as an active and constructive response.[33] Is there
something like a resistant form of subjectivity that can be constructed, more fluid and less constrained by inherited models of
autonomy, authenticity, inside-outside etc., and that would allow for a "being-together of the diverse" (Adorno) in what that
neither subsumes nor merely affirms its own dissolution?[34] In a

33. Deleuze and Guattari develop the idea of "noology" as a study of the
     various images of philosophy that lie before the development of any
     specific theories, particularly in *What is philosophy?* The theme is how-
     ever announced already in works from the late 1960s, for instance *The
     Logic of Sense* and *Difference and Repetition*. Perhaps we could understand
     noopower and noopolitics in the same vein, i.e., as way to shape our
     sense of what it means to act and exist politically, before we make any
     particular political choices.
34. See Adorno, *Negative Dialektik, Gesammelte Schriften*, vol. 6, 153. Such a
     task would at the same time be a question of *metaphysics* and *epistemology*
     (what would the ontological status of the non-identical be to the extent
     that it is freed from identity, and how can we know it), *ethics* (what
     would it mean to relate to others without making them into versions of
     myself, and yet without giving up the quest for equality and universal-
     ity), *politics* (which political forms would allow for a polity that respects

certain way, this remains close to what Foucault said about early liberalism: it is first and foremost not an ideology in the sense of a false, distorted, or imaginary representation of reality, but a new form of governing by affecting and channeling conducts, i.e., a way to work *with* reality; liberalism does not simply provide us with an theoretical and/or ideological smoke-screen behind which other and more real things (actions, practices, material events) are taking place; instead, itself a practice, it is a way to make certain things real by working with and intensifying, tempering, or redirecting processes already underway in reality itself. And furthermore, it even more acutely poses the problem of resistance: where would we locate an outside that could be a resource for experiencing, thinking, and acting in some other way than those that are not even imposed on us, but emerge as if out of our own most spontaneous preferences?

In a wider context, visual arts, architecture, advertising, and media in general can be seen as part of the same process, whereby our minds are governed (in the Foucauldian sense of "conduct of conduct," and not as repression or coercion) in order attain new levels of action and reaction, and the noetic has in a sense that by far transcends the traditional analysis of ideology become a site of conflict, even of political struggle, at a level which extends below that of human subjectivity and integrates consciousness in a process of transformation which is neither nature nor culture. This power and this politics would inscribe themselves on the most fundamental level of mental life, at which our most basic affects and ideas are organized, where memory, fantasy, and intelligence emerge, and which recently has come to be described in terms of a certain "plasticity."[35] The connection to visual arts

the singular and yet forms a community), and, finally, *aesthetics* (to what extent can this being-together be prefigured in works of art, without becoming an already defined content that is enforced upon them).

35. For the philosophical idea of plasticity, which on the one hand has its roots in Hegel, on the other hand in neuroscience, see the extended

ARCHITECTURE, CRITIQUE, IDEOLOGY

is here particularly relevant: if the position they occupy in this transformation concerns not only images as we normally apprehend them through media or in institutionalized spaces of art, but in fact extend into the sphere of what used to be called the unconscious, the articulation of life and consciousness on a pre-subjective level, would it be possible to attempt to provide pockets of resistance, residual modes of experience that yet remain to be colonized by technology, or must they be content with simply recording and reflecting a process whose determining factors are located elsewhere? The question is whether we still need to think the capacity of the work of art, for instance the architectural work, to open up a space of freedom in the same way as we have been doing since late modernist theory—basically, in a figure of thought that has been most succinctly formulated by Adorno, as an internalizing of the formal contradictions of society, which in the second moment produces a critical distance (transcendence, reflection, negation, or whatever vocabulary we might use)—or if the rethinking of critical theory that has been underway at least since the seventies in fact entails a dismantling of the very idea of resistance and the critical.

Lazzarato's proposals move in the direction of a possible "General Intelligence" that must be conquered, and in this they are similar to ideas that have been developed by Paolo Virno in his analysis of post-Fordist labor as subjectivity and the development of a new "virtuosity."[36] Virtuosity here has connota-

reflections of Catherine Malabou, beginning in *L'Avenir de Hegel: Plasticité, Temporalité, Dialectique* (Paris: Vrin, 1996), and continuing through a series of works that increasingly focus on epigenetics. In her recent research she has developed a critique of both Foucault's and Agamben's conceptions of life for lacking a support in scientific biology, which, while misguided in relation to their respective claims and philosophical projects, is highly indicative of the current desire to find a new point of articulation between nature and mind.

36. See for instance his *A Grammar of the Multitude* (Los Angeles: Semiotext(e), 2004).

tions not just of skill and dexterity, but also of the Machiavellian *virtù*, which in his time was largely (though no exclusively) the prerogative of the prince, but today can be made into something common: it is the capacity to seize the moment, to adjust to situations and shifts in the balance of power, in order to extract a new force, even and perhaps even primarily, by extracting something from the opposing forces and turning them against themselves. Such a mutation should be understood as transcending the sphere of art as well as politics on the inherited sense, and it affects the very fabric of life, the underlying substructures of the mind. The political challenges of such a shift are of course formidable: how should we conceive of an ethics or a politics, how should we account for a possible formation of a possible ethical or political agency, when the "multitude" that it must organize and integrate—without reducing it into the all-too classical form of a subject, individual or collective—extends beyond what we normally circumscribe by the use of our inherited political categories? Whether such a turning around, or stepping out— "Exodus," as Virno calls it—is the kind of radical shift that it claims, or a mirage produced by the powerful logic of Capital itself, as many of those who uphold the ethos of the traditional Left have argued, remains to be seen.

Critique and beyond:
the case of architecture

If we accept the claim that the current mode of production has moved not only beyond the level of material goods, but also beyond the one of information and communication, and entered into the space of the noetic and affective, that it invests our mind as a plastic entity before all reflexive and conscious responds, then the question might be asked if it is at all possible to uphold the ethos a critical culture based on ideas of resistance and negation. And, beyond this, whether the idea of resistance indeed at all makes sense—for, in the name of what should we resist, and what resources could be mobilized if our bodies and cognitive faculties are formed and governed all the way down to the neural substratum by forces that exceed consciousness?

The demand that we must move beyond the critical approach to architecture, and perhaps to cultural production at large—a discussion has mostly occurred within architectural discourse,[37] although the claims, if they are warranted, obviously must have a general applicability—need not base itself in a theory of the noetic and affective, although this connection is probably what gives it its highest persuasive power. In an essay that triggered a lot of the following discussion, "Notes around the Doppler Effect and other Moods of Modernism,"[38] Robert Somol and Sarah Whiting wanted to discern a move from the critical to the projective, claiming that the inherited notions of autonomy as a precondition for engagement has in fact become obsolete, and that what is required, is not so much a critique of reification or a dialectical opposition to society, as an analysis of the conditions of emergence that make possible a more fluid practice. As an example of this different stance, they cite Rem Koolhaas's appropriation of American mass culture, where architecture produces social life, and not a text meant for reflexive reading: its aim is to *seduce* and instigate new events and behaviors. The tools for this are what Somol and Whiting describe in terms of force and affect, and they develop their reading on the basis of the project for the Downtown Athletic Club (included in Koolhaas's book *Delirious New York*). The Club, as Koolhaas proposes, represents the complete conquest, floor by floor, of the Skyscraper by social activity; with the Downtown Athletic Club the American

37. For a general survey of this discussion, see George Baird, "Criticality and Its Discontents," *Harvard Design Magazine*, No. 21, Fall 2004/Winter 2005.
38. Robert Somol and Sarah Whiting, "Notes around the Doppler Effect and other Moods of Modernism," *Perspecta* 33 (2002).

way of life, know-how, and initiative definitively overtake the theoretical lifestyle modifications that the various twentieth-century European avant-gardes have been insistently proposing, without ever managing to impose them. The skyscraper becomes a machine for generating and intensifying desirable forms of human intercourse, which in this case means that the metropolitan bachelor is the ultimate form of life, and the Club the ultimate bachelor machine.[39]

Instead of dialectics and negation, Somol and Whiting see in this what they call a "Doppler effect," where perception depends on the location and speed of the viewer and the source. The disciplinary quality of architecture lies in performance, and here we can note that discipline as analyzed by Foucault (who is cited repeatedly in the essay) is transformed without further ado into an ideal for practice: the diagram and the distribution

39. We should note that Koolhaas's writing as always incorporates massive doses of an almost diabolical irony, where different claims seem to cancel each other out, which is a dimension that gets wholly lost in interpretations such as the above one. This is his superbly tongue-in cheek description of the project: "With its first 12 floors accessible only to men, the Downtown Athletic Club appears to be a *locker room the size of a Skyscraper*, a definitive manifestation of those metaphysics—at once spiritual and carnal—that protect the American male against the corrosion of adulthood. But in fact, the club has reached the point where the notion of a 'peak' condition transcends the physical realm to become cerebral. It is not a locker room but an *incubator for adults*, an instrument that permits the members—too impatient to await the outcome of evolution—to reach new strata of maturity by transforming themselves into new beings, this time according to their individual designs. Bastions of the antinatural, Skyscrapers such as the Club announce the imminent segregation of mankind into two tribes: one of *Metropolitanites*—literally self made—who used the full potential of *the apparatus of Modernity* to reach unique levels of perfection, the second simply the remainder of the human race. The only price its locker-room graduates have to pay for their collective narcissism is that of sterility. Their self-induced mutations are not reproducible in future generations." Koolhaas, *Delirious New York: A Retroactive Manifesto for Manhattan* (New York, Monacelli Press, 1994), 157–158. The theme of a division between non-communicating spaces ("two tribes") can in fact be read as way to reinvent critique not as opposition, but as materializing of contradictions; see chap 5, above.

397

of singularities, particularly as these concepts have been analyzed by Deleuze, are no longer structures of action and reaction whose integration immediately produce deviations and resistances, but have simply become instrumentalized as design tools.[40]

In the projective mood, Somol and Whiting continue, no doubt consciously echoing a retrieval of a postmodernized pop art sensibility (as is indicated by the reference to Jean Baudrillard), we move from hot to cool, architecture ceases to worry about separating itself from everyday in terms of autonomy and resistance, and becomes just as relaxed about reality as television. Curiously enough, they end by ascertaining that such a projective and instrumental practice "does not necessarily entail a capitulation to the market forces, but actually respects or reorganizes multiple economies, ecologies, information systems, and social groups."[41]

That such a conclusion contains an element of wishful thinking was ruthlessly brought forth by Michael Speaks, in a series of essays that unabashedly called for the end of theory as critique, and an adaptation to the forces of the market. Particularly referencing education, he lashed out against architecture school for having failed to develop an intellectual culture in tune with the real world, and instead have been given

40. Deleuze understands the epistemological breaks that Foucault locates in his archeology of knowledge in terms of a divide between the "visible" and the "sayable," which in their conjunction forms and *archive*, whereas the disciplinary dimension belongs to the level of the *diagram* of power and forces, which it what gives a temporary stability to the archive. The concept of diagram has since Deleuze's book been applied in a wide variety of ways to contemporary architecture, first by Greg Lynn in a discussion of the work of Ben van Berkel, in Lynn, "Forms of Expression: The Proto-Functional Potential of Diagrams in Architectural Design," *El Croquis* 72 (1995). For an overview of various uses, see the contributions in *Any* 23, "Diagram Work" (1998). Common to them all is however the symptomatic absence of the dimension of power, struggle, and resistance that was an essential dimension in Deleuze's interpretation.

41. Somol and Whiting "Notes around the Doppler Effect," 77.

over to "Deconstruction and Marxism," creating an "aversion to the marketplace, the very milieu of intervention and shaper of any future architecture."[42] Unlike the comparatively subtle theoretical exercises of Somol and Whiting, Speaks makes no excuses: his essay can be read as call to order, a demand that we should abandon theory in general, and assume a stance that unapologetically opts for the fashionable instead of intellectual reflection. "Theory," Speaks claims, "is not just irrelevant but was and continues to be an impediment to the development of a culture of innovation in architecture."[43]

Such claims could easily be dismissed because of their brutal and summary quality,[44] or because they are merely the echoes of generational conflicts and skirmishes in American academia. And yet they point to a deeper problem, which we noted above: to what extent can the emphasis on the affective, the senses, and the dimension of the noopolitical create concepts that would allow us to gain a distance from the world? Can they all avoid being co-opted by a capitalism that colonizes even the last vestiges of nature and the unconscious?

Jeffrey Kipnis has argued that the strategies of negation must give way to a resistance that instead works by way of *sensations*, suggesting that architecture should work more like a soundtrack in a film, which would allow it to unfold a political power that draws directly on the way it impacts on our nervous system. The analogy with the soundtrack is however not (and is probably not meant to be) unambiguous: on one level, a soundtrack can be taken as a highly specialized service, called upon to support and highlight features in an already set narrative; rarely, if

42. Michael Speaks, "After Theory," *Architectural Record* 06.05, 73.
43. Ibid, 74.
44. A quality that appears even stranger when one reads other essays by Speaks, where "theory" is indeed operative. See for instance the phenomenologically oriented analysis of Olafur Eliasson's *Green River Project*, in Daniel Birnbaum et al, *Olafur Eliasson* (London: Phaidon, 2002).

ever, is it given an agency and critical power of its own. On another level, it contains a whole gamut of possibilities not just for supporting, but also for redirecting or even derailing the narrative, and for establishing unexpected links in an infra-conscious dimension that, as it were, envelops the order of the visible and the spoken.[45] The task of architecture as resistance, Kipnis claims, would be to create new sensations and alliances, and in this he comes close to Lazzarato: the possibility of resistance in the society of control lies in creating connections that resist being appropriated, which is a task that can never be completed; in fact, reversibility might be taken to be their defining feature.

The emergence of something like a control logics on the noetic level seems to demand that the idea of a critical theory be rethought. The various claims that adversary models based on negation, dialectics, and contradiction are obsolete, no matter how exaggerated and one-sided they may be (and some of them are doubtlessly mere ideology in an unsophisticated sense), nonetheless point in the same direction, and cannot be simply dismissed. Here there are of course many avenues that open up, and unlike the theorists of noopower, almost as an inversion of their proposals, some theorists take the step into a full-blown naturalizing of

45. Jeffrey Kipnis, "Is Resistance Futile?" in Log 5 (Spring/Summer 2005). Kipnis draws on Francis Bacon, and his reading of Bacons work in terms of affects and sensations is indebted to Deleuze, *Francis Bacon: Logique de la sensation* (Paris: Éditions de la Différence, 1981). Something of this transpires already in Kipnis's essay on "The Cunning of Cosmetics," in *El Croquis* 84 (1997), which discusses the role of surface, ornament, and the "transformative power of the cosmetic" in Herzog & de Meuron's work, in where he discerns an "urbane, cunning intelligence, and an intoxicating, almost erotic allure" (407). These works function like "sirens," Kipnis says, recalling the famous analysis of Horkheimer and Adorno, although he provides a wholly different reading of the moment of seduction. The discourse of seduction has become widespread in architecture; see for instance the contributions by Sylvia Lavin, Jeffrey Kipnis, and Alejandro Zaera-Polo, in *Quaderns* 245 (April 2005). The various uses of this term, ranging from the "urbane and cunning" to the desire to simply attract clients, testifies to its ideological and theoretical malleability.

consciousness—akin to the various versions of neural materialism that have become widespread in many strands of analytical philosophy—and attempt to ground aesthetic and formal solutions (often reviving classical canons of beauty, as if the whole post-Hegelian tradition of aesthetic philosophy had never existed) to architectural and artistic problems directly in a neuroscience and evolutionary biology. This however seems simply to bypass the question of historical mediation, and moreover renders the question of what a theory could be that understands architecture on the basis of an analysis of contemporary society and power relations vacuous from the start.[46]

But what, then, is this thing that we have referred to in a rather imprecise way as critical theory? What is critical about it, and in what sense is it a theory? These questions cannot be settled by references to the past, or to any particular form of artistic practice that is supposed to hold the key; answering them requires acts of invention. Such acts cannot help but be inextricably bound up with the current state of affairs, and they must draw on the most advanced productive forces while still trying to imagine other possible social relations. In this they always run the risk of becoming indistinguishable from what they attempt to analyze, which is however not something to be deplored; it is in substance the same situation as that of Marx's *Capital* with respect to the world of nineteenth-century capitalism. Critical theory can obviously not congeal into some incessant referencing of the past (the historical avant-garde, the 1960s, or some other moment in time), nor can it leap ahead into a utopian future where it would become sealed in the *purely* imaginary, even though it cannot abandon the imaginary as an outdated relic from the philosophy of consciousness.

46.   This seems to me to be the claim by Harry Francis Mallgrave, in his recent *The Architect's Brain: Neuroscience, Creativity, and Architecture* (London: Blackwell, 2010).

Critical theory must be an immanent practice, moving with its time, always ready to invent new tools. At present, the society of control—which, one must remember, is only one part of a global order that contains many levels of technological refinement, and from which the power regimes of sovereignty and discipline have by no means receded—constitutes our horizon, it generates many images of thought, from the most complex to the most facile, and to extract from them a transformative power of philosophy, art, and politics is a task that always remains to be undertaken anew.

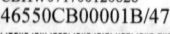